PRAIS

What the Hell

"Donald Lee's new book, *What the Hell is Going On,* defies the mainstream Covid-19 narrative and instead goes for a 'spiritual' journey to see what the whole Covid-19 pandemic narrative means for all of us. Surprise! Covid-19 is not just a struggle against a common cold virus that arose spontaneously, but rather is a calculated attempt by a small group of connected billionaires to control humanity. If you didn't know that before, you should have, as Lee makes very clear in his thorough documentation of the historical/political trends and power plays that have led us to this moment in history.

This work adds to a rapidly growing perspective that we are in a battle for the soul of humanity in which one of two very different futures will occur: That of the World Economic Forum's Klaus Schwab which projects a world in which humans are chattel who 'own nothing, but are happy,' versus one that champions human freedom. In this, Lee demonstrates the nature of the spiritual/cultural war that humanity is embroiled in.

Not sure if he is correct or what's really going on? Read the book and then make up your mind: You will be surprised, maybe horrified, but you won't emerge with the same set of conclusions you went in with."

–Christopher A. Shaw, Ph.D.
Professor, Dept. of Ophthalmology,
University of British Columbia

"As an assertive Covid activist and persecuted pathologist, I can attest that *What the Hell is Going On*? is a well-researched, one-stop Covid resource, from historical correlates to the predicted global catastrophe. It rings the alarm louder than the truckers' honking. So, advice to readers: Do not open before bed!"

–Dr Roger Hodkinson,
the Canadian pathologist with red shoes

"One of the greatest struggles for the average person during the COVID 'plandemic' was discerning truth from lies, real information from disinformation. In this brilliant and well-researched book, Donald Lee connects the dots for us, showing us our collective history and how seemingly separate isolated events are actually connected together in a web of lies and deceit.

What I appreciate most about this book is that its foundation is spiritual, not religious, peaceful, and not enraged. One of my favorite lines from the book: *In this spiritual war, our strategy is love, our tactic is forgiveness, our weapon is non-violent, non-cooperation.* I couldn't agree more."

–Karen Kan, M.D., Doctor of Light Medicine,
Founder of the Academy of Light Medicine™

WHAT THE HELL IS GOING ON?

The Web of Fraud that Is Enslaving Everyone *and* How We Can Escape to Freedom

DONALD LEE

ISBN Paperback: 978-1-990893-00-1
ISBN E-book: 978-1-990893-01-8
ISBN Audiobook: 978-1-990893-02-5

Published by BookLocker.com, Inc., St. Petersburg, Florida.

Library of Congress Cataloging in Publication Data
Lee, Donald

What the Hell Is Going On? – The Web of Fraud That Is Enslaving Everyone and How We Can Escape to Freedom by Donald Lee

BODY, MIND & SPIRIT: General | POLITICAL SCIENCE: General | BUSINESS & ECONOMICS: General

Library of Congress Control Number: 2022916318

Printed on acid-free paper.

Booklocker.com, Inc. 2022

Other Books by Donald Lee

The Band Director's Lessons About Life:
Volume 1 – 50 Parables on Life's Performance Cycle

The Band Director's *Mini* Lessons About Life:
Volume 1 – Five Parables on Life's Performance Cycle

The Band Director's Pocket Guide to Spiritual Growth:
3 Simple Steps to Becoming the Person You Want to Be
(And God Intended You to Be)

Dedication

To all those who retain in their hearts
the courage to fight for liberty and justice,
and to hope for the return of the King,
even in the final battle.

"A day may come when the courage of Men fails,
when we forsake our friends and break all bonds of fellowship,
but it is not this day.
An hour of wolves and shattered shields when
the Age of Men comes crashing down,
but it is not this day!
This day we fight!"

–Aragorn's speech to the Army of Men at the Final Battle
The Return of the King, JRR Tolkien

CONTENTS

Introduction

"I would rather have questions that can't be answered than answers that can't be questioned." –RICHARD FEYNMAN

What's really going on in the world is not what *appears* to be going on. The picture we see on the surface is not the real picture. For many years I tried to make sense of it. After much research, I've put some of the pieces together. I wrote this book to give you a context, a framework, a pattern, so you can understand what's going on around you. I paint a picture for you, a "connect-the-dots" outline. I don't have all the answers, but like the opening quote says, I'm questioning the answers we've been given.

Why do I see patterns others don't? Maybe it's because I'm not an expert in anything. I'm a generalist. I have a degree in economics and an interest in monetary theory, so I see some of the financial and currency fraud. But I'm not so much of an economist that I have the institutional blinders–the "inside-the-box" thinking–of academic economists. I've had enough experience with mathematics, statistics, and mathematical modeling to understand the fundamental deceptions perpetrated by "models." I'm an avid student of history and see the parallels with other dark times. My interest in past wars has helped me see what's happening in this current World War III. Having grown up during the Cold War, I understand something of the disinformation and propaganda once again engulfing our world.

My lifelong spiritual quest gives me a broad view of the nature of this spiritual war and its physical manifestations. I'm not a scientist, but my career has intersected with scientists enough to glimpse how scientific fraud works. I've dabbled enough in philosophy to see how its perversion has distorted the worldview of almost everyone. And perhaps the dichotomy of being both a musician and an athlete, a humanitarian and a hunter, a spiritualist and a strategist, I have achieved enough of a balance between left-brain and right-brain and between my masculine and feminine natures to offer a bit of balance to a world desperately lacking it. Breakthroughs often come when someone connects ideas from disparate fields of study. That's exactly what I've done in this book–connected dots from seemingly unrelated fields to present a picture that very few people perceive amidst the "noise" of too much data and deliberate obfuscation.

I want to help you see more clearly, or to at least perceive events differently. It's not really a question of whether I'm right or wrong. No doubt I am "wrong" about some things. We can perceive things from many sides, many perspectives. Every perspective adds greater understanding. My goal is to help you perceive differently so you can see the "connect-the-dots" picture I see. We are at a turning point and we must choose either right or left, freedom or slavery, life or death.

I'm sure you've noticed the crazy happenings all over our world in recent years. Like me, you've probably asked, *"What the hell is going on?"* No one seems to know. Crazy events seem isolated, spontaneous, unrelated. Lies and fraud seem to be everywhere. Who is telling the truth? Who can you trust? We have trusted our institutions, governments, the free press, and scientists. All that seems to have been a mistake.

How can there be a "climate emergency" when the climate has not changed noticeably during my lifetime? How can the world be on the brink of burning up when it's colder now than at most points during human civilization? How can we fight a war on drugs for fifty years yet both the drug problem and the war apparatus constantly get bigger?

How could there be a worldwide "pandemic" when there were no excess deaths anywhere in 2020? How can it be that "we're all in this together" when American billionaires added 40 percent to their aggregate net worth in less than a year while millions of ordinary people lost their jobs or watched their businesses bankrupted?[1]

Why is it that the answer to every problem seems to be more power and control for governments? Why is it that the real power doesn't seem to be in elected governments at all? Why is it that every government in the Western World seems to be taking its marching orders from the World Economic Forum? The WEF put out a propaganda film about "built back better" and "the Great Reset," and immediately every leader in the world was parroting those terms. *What the hell is going on?*

What's the connection between all these things? Is there a connection? Are they all independent and randomly spontaneous social developments? Is it all just an accident? Or are we the victims of a carefully planned and targeted, multigenerational, totalitarian subversive war? These events seem to be planned, but even if they weren't, it doesn't matter. Like pregnancy, planned or unplanned, the result is the same. Whether by accident or conspiracy, we are on the road to totalitarian slavery.

We are quickly moving toward a one-world totalitarian government—the New World Order—where most people will have been murdered and the rest turned into mechanical/human cyborgs monitored and controlled with artificial intelligence. Most work will be done by robots and most human lives will be slavery. This is what the World Economic Forum and the United Nations have planned. It's not hard to understand. But it's hard to believe. It is *unbelievable*. You have to see the evidence to believe it. That's what this book is about—evidence.

Our "elites" have been using an ever-widening web of fraud to hide their totalitarian control. We are being manipulated with fear to willingly acquiesce to an ever-greater loss of freedom and independence.

But there is hope. We can still escape to freedom. But freedom comes with responsibility. There's a spiritual dimension—and this is key. The war is being waged against us with fear. We must respond with love, the opposite of fear. In this spiritual war, our strategy is love, our tactic is forgiveness, and our weapon is nonviolent noncooperation.

Humans are fundamentally spiritual beings. That's why the transhuman cyborg is *devolution*, not *evolution*—a step down, not a step up. It is not integration with machines that will make us better–it is integration with God. That's where we will find both freedom and the kind of life everyone imagines as *ideal*. Life is never really ideal. An ideal, by definition, is something unattainable. We have an image of an "ideal life," where every person is treated with dignity and respect, where we live in peace and love with each other, where all are free to pursue their own goals and legitimate desires, where we behave as stewards of the world around us, and where we help ever, hurt never. We are far from that ideal. But we could come much closer to it. In fact, I think it is our destiny to do so.

The hour is late. We have been asleep. We have been surrendering in every battle because we didn't even know we were at war. Now is the final battle. I am not exaggerating. It may already be too late. Like the tiny army of men before the Gates of Mordor, we shiver in fear. Many have lost hope in the success of Frodo, the small, Christlike suffering hero struggling against the overwhelming powers of darkness. We feel individually powerless. Yet Frodo dwells within each of us. We have forgotten what power lies within every human heart. Perhaps I am naïve to think we might still win back our freedom and prevent the destruction of the whole world. Let me explain what I see going on and how I think we can still win.

PART 1

The Foundation for Understanding the Frauds

Medical doctors joke about patients who diagnose themselves. I recall such a scene from an old sitcom—a patient is in his doctor's office waxing eloquent with his self-diagnosis. The doctor is half listening and half looking at an X-ray photograph in his hand. When the patient pauses to take a breath, the doctor hands him the x-ray and says, "You're pretty knowledgeable. What do you think of this X-ray?" The patient looks at it for a few seconds.

"That's a compound fracture of the tibia," he declares.

"Really?" the doctor replies. "Actually, it's a perfectly normal set of lungs."

It's funny, but it's also a great illustration of what is going on in our world. The patient was self-confident but ignorant. How could he mistake lungs for legs? We know an X-ray photograph of the lungs appears as a characteristic pattern of light and dark. Clearly, the patient was not familiar with that pattern. If he were taught the pattern of lungs, then he could recognize them. As people in the spy businesses would say, it's all about pattern recognition.

The same thing is going on in our world. There are patterns in the events of the world, but most people are not familiar with those patterns. The events appear random, or they appear to be something else. So, people don't recognize the pattern even though they are looking directly at the events. They look but do not see. In this book, I will teach you the patterns so you can recognize them in world events–communist subversion, psychological warfare, fraud, and the way spiritual laws manifest in our physical lives.

Our adversary is trying to control the whole world and everything in it: money, energy, land, food, governments, corporations, police, military, and even all people by controlling our bodies and our minds. Each chapter in this book shows how each separate fraud works to capture each of these vectors. Each vector is like a noose slowly tightening around the neck of humanity. If we allow these nooses to tighten, there will be no escape.

Our adversary uses fraud to draw power into ever fewer hands. This book exposes many of these frauds. But before we can perceive the frauds, there are fundamental ideas and patterns we must understand. In part 1, we look at how to perceive spiritually, and the basic principles of totalitarian subversion and control. In part 2, we explore earlier frauds. In part 3, we fill in some other important background information about the control system and the role of China. In part 4, we examine recent frauds. Part 5 is devoted to putting the final pieces of the control system in place and explaining how we can escape to freedom. Let's take a look at the patterns so we can recognize them in the frauds. We begin, as we should, with the spirit.

CHAPTER 1

The Spiritual Perspective

"Telling the truth is the secret of all true spirituality, and in order to tell the truth, you must find out what truth is." –NIRMALA

The way we have been taught to see the world is not how the world is. Only by *perceiving differently* can we see the truth. On the surface, this concept may seem strange, but there is always a different way to see the world. Do you see the world the way CNN presents it? Do you see the world the way the president of the United States sees it? Do you see the world the way the Dahlia Lama sees it? You can be sure that you *don't* see the world the way God sees it. As you read this book, please be open to perceiving things differently.

The greatest miracle is to change your perception. Perceive differently, and the world you see changes. If you are willing to accept it, what you perceive is a projection of what you believe. Belief is that powerful. Control of belief is the most powerful control. As we will see in this book, you have given that power to others. Take it back.

Many of the people and institutions we have trusted our whole lives can no longer be trusted. They have methodically lied for years, in some cases for decades, in a way that can only be called fraud. Thus, the title and theme of this book. When we begin to compare the lies to the evidence, we see a pattern and we see the motivation for the lies and fraud.

This is a very difficult change of worldview—of perception. Making even small changes to our worldview is difficult.

Perceiving differently and questioning the official stories challenges us on every level of our being. It is an *intellectual* challenge because we have to sift through evidence to discern what is fact and what is not. It is a *psychological* challenge because part of our identity is tied up with our understanding of our society and the world around us. Changing our understanding of the world means changing our understanding of who we are in that world. It is also a *spiritual* challenge because part of the reason we are here in this material world is to discern truth from illusion.

It's not surprising then, that many people refuse to deal with these challenges and prefer to simply go along with what they are told by "official" sources. But today, so many "official" stories are completely at odds with observable evidence. And so many people who are legitimate experts in their fields are censored and labelled as "conspiracy theorists" that ordinary folks cannot help but ask, "What the hell is going on?" To think that our most trusted institutions are completely corrupt and fraudulent is just too much for many people to accept. They will reject these ideas without seriously considering them. At the outset, please understand that very little in this book is opinion, speculation, or theory. Almost everything is verifiable fact, evidence, and history.

It seems simple, but it's really so complex I had to write a whole book just to scratch the surface of it. I have tried to present evidence to help you perceive things differently without overwhelming you. Let's begin with my central theme: lies and fraud.

The Consequence of Lies

For democracy and a free society to flourish, truth and honesty are required. Lies are destructive on so many levels. We have taken for granted that most people are basically good and honest. This has changed. Honesty used to be one of the most valued virtues in Western civilization. This is no longer true. The consequences are immense.

Totalitarianism, the opposite of democracy, is based on lies and deceit.

If we allow these to flourish, we will end up in communism, fascism, or some other variety of totalitarianism.

When Aleksandr Solzhenitsyn was expelled from the Soviet Union in 1974, he wrote a farewell essay to his countrymen titled "Live Not By Lies."[1] His point was that if you refuse to accept the lies, communism will collapse. Communism is a system built on lies. It is a debilitating and dehumanizing life of lies that destroys the human–body, mind, and spirit. St. John Paul II called it the pulverization of the human person.[2]

Anyone who has lived under communism knows this. The Russian writer Elena Gorokhova said in *A Mountain of Crumbs*, "The rules are simple: they lie to us, we know they're lying, they know we know they're lying, but they keep lying to us, and we keep pretending to believe them."[3]

Here is a basic pattern to learn. Mistakes frequently occur one at a time; lies, never. As most of us discovered in our youth, you can never tell just one lie. The first lie always needs a second lie to cover up the first, and a third to cover up the second, and so on. One lie quickly becomes a web of lies. A web of lies is never the pattern of a mistake. It is always the pattern of fraud. Most people have assumed that our leaders are chronically stupid and have made mistake after mistake. A web of mistakes is nearly as rare as a unicorn. These people are not idiots, but liars. These are not errors, but frauds. It's all about pattern recognition–and never assume you have found the pattern of a unicorn.

As I look around our society today, I am surrounded by lies, many of which will be exposed in this book. Do not acquiesce to the fraud and lies surrounding you. Do not accept lies from your friends, your family, your neighbors, your bosses, your employees, your teachers, your pupils, your politicians, your doctors, your lawyers, your judges–not even from yourself. Accept only truth. Seek the truth. As St. Paul says, "Let your minds be filled with everything that is true" (Phil 4:8).[4] And the Master Teacher said, "Know the truth, and the truth will set you free" (Jn 8:32).[5] Freedom cannot coexist with lies.

I refer to spiritual leaders because our war is fundamentally a spiritual war. It must be, because *everything* is fundamentally spiritual. As Pierre Teilhard de Chardin famously said, "We are not human beings having a spiritual experience, we are spiritual beings having a human experience."[6]

The spiritual dimension of our conflict has many levels. Whatever your spiritual or religious background, you can perceive the truths through the lens of your own understanding. You can even perceive it simply through the lens of psychology and history.

Understanding the Spiritual Reality of Our Conflict

> *"But know that mercy and truth and justice and love are the gift of the divine. And you may only attain the knowledge of such by BEING such, manifesting such, in thy daily walks of life–in thy associations one with another."* –EDGAR CAYCE

To be human is to have a spirit–a soul, created by that benevolent creative energy that I choose to call "God"–fused into a material, animal body. Since some people are put off by the word "God," let me be clear at the outset that it doesn't matter how you name or conceive this idea. Call it "the Universe," "the Source," "Creative Forces," "Infinite Intelligence." It doesn't matter. Nobody fully understands it anyway.

We have both a higher nature–a divine nature–and a lower nature–an animal nature. By focusing on our lower nature, we become more like animals. By focusing on our higher nature, we become more like God, our Father. It is an important spiritual law that whatever we focus our attention on grows. That is the essence of *free will*. We choose. We can raise ourselves higher than angels or drag ourselves lower than animals. The human species has produced almost godlike individuals–individuals who have given us examples of transcendence, in whom we glimpse the divine within ourselves. Yet the human species has also produced individuals more horrible than the worst creature in horror movies. Animals kill only for food or protection. Yet humans can kill each other for dozens of insignificant reasons–even for the simple sadistic joy of killing. Animals don't do this. Only humans can sink to this level. That is the blessing and the curse of free will.

God gives us free will as, perhaps, the greatest spiritual gift. It is an absolutely crucial aspect of our spirit, mind, and body. Take away our free will, and we cease to be truly human. It is impossible to overstate the importance of free will. We will see this again and again.

We can perceive the spiritual aspect of the present conflict in many ways.

1. Lower Human Needs vs. Higher Human Needs
2. Western Tradition: Darkness vs. Light
3. Fear vs. Love
4. Controlling Others vs. Controlling Self
5. Eastern Tradition: Energy Centers
6. A New Great Age

Let's look at each one more carefully.

Lower Human Needs vs. Higher Human Needs

Those who have no religious or spiritual understanding can perceive our present situation in psychological terms. The famous psychologist Abraham Maslow developed his hierarchy of human needs from the obvious idea that some of our needs and desires are more basic and urgent than others. For example, if you are choking, nothing matters except getting air. If you are dying of thirst, nothing matters except getting water. Even though it's presented in various levels, Maslow was clear that life is not so cut-and-dried. Even little children experience the love of beauty (aesthetic needs) and the joy that comes from helping others (self-transcendence). Through the power of your own will, you can transcend lower needs and focus on higher ones, as thousands of heroic stories from POW camps attest. Yet the logic of the hierarchy is self-evident. In a healthy person, all these needs will be understood, acted upon, and some level of fulfillment achieved.[7]

1. Biological Needs: air, water, food, clothing, sleep, shelter, sex.
2. Safety Needs: personal security, employment, health, resources, property.

3. Love and Belonging Needs: friendship, intimacy, family, sense of connection.
4. Esteem Needs: respect, self-esteem, status, recognition, strength, freedom.
5. Cognitive Needs: knowledge, understanding, curiosity, exploration, meaning, predictability.
6. Aesthetic Needs: beauty, form, balance, art, culture.
7. Self-Actualization Needs: desire to become all that one can be, creativity, desire for peak experiences and personal growth.
8. Self-Transcendence Needs: spiritual and psychic experiences, service to others, pursuit of ideals, realization that fulfillment comes only from going beyond the self.

Our present world is mostly focused on the lower two levels of Maslow's hierarchy. We must seek a balance and develop all eight levels of human needs. The next level that requires work is love.

Western Tradition: Darkness vs. Light

The Western religious traditions (Judaism, Christianity, Islam) teach a dualistic spiritual understanding that I summarize as Darkness vs. Light. You can perceive this concept as Satan vs. God, material vs. spiritual, and so on. In a very simplified understanding of the human condition, we can perceive ourselves as animals (our lower/egoic self) with a higher self that is spiritual (our higher/divine self). Pick whichever terms you are familiar with. We are, in a sense, higher or more developed than all other animals. Our higher nature perceives beauty, communicates, creates, modifies its environment, loves, has greater sentience, perceives a divine reality, and seeks meaning to a much greater extent than any other animal.

Many people today, and our present society in general, are mostly focused on our animal nature. But we have come to a point in the development of human civilization that we face the very real risk of destroying ourselves if we don't raise our focus to our higher self. This is the essence of the Great Awakening–awakening to our spiritual nature.

Those who understand the human condition as an amalgam of divine self (or soul, or higher self) and ego (or egoic self, or animal/instinctive nature) will understand that disaster ensues if we allow ourselves to be ruled by the ego. We must focus our attention on our divine self to rise above the fear that characterizes the ego, and live in the consciousness of universal love—our divine nature.

Jesus directed us to turn away from material things—wealth, power, and the desires of the body. He directed us to focus on spiritual things, and the way to do this is through love.

Fear vs. Love

It may seem surprising, but fear is the opposite of love. You might think it is hatred, but if you meditate on this you will realize that hatred is the child of fear. Think about what you hate, and you will find fear behind it. Dispel the fear, and the hatred dissolves. Every true spiritual teaching insists there is nothing to fear. We dispel fear with love. If you can fill yourself with love, all fear melts away like a snowman in July. St. John said, "Perfect love drives out fear" (1 Jn 4:18).[8]

Jesus taught love. The elites of his time—like the elites of all times—were focused on money and power. Jesus taught that love was what they were missing. Love completes the Law of Moses. Love is what helps you transcend power and money, what raises you to a higher level of consciousness—what Jesus called the "Kingdom of God." Every true spiritual tradition teaches love, but only with Jesus was it the main focus. He made it so simple. *We* have complicated it. Jesus summed up all spiritual teaching with "Love God, love everyone." All the rest is commentary. Two thousand years later, we still haven't learned that simple lesson. We have been working on it long enough. The final exam is upon us.

Controlling Others vs. Controlling Self (Free Will)

We can also perceive this dichotomy as controlling others vs. controlling self. The desire to control others ultimately leads to totalitarianism and slavery—great power for a few, great servitude for many, the destruction of free will, and the descent to a lower level of spiritual consciousness and material existence. True spiritual traditions teach their followers to work on *self*-control, not the control of others. Each of us is on our own unique and individual spiritual journey. We cannot live the life of another, nor travel the path of another, nor truly help another by controlling them. In controlling others, you take away their free will and make them dependent upon you. Just as we know when raising our children, you truly help others when you help them to be *independent*—when you help them to exercise their own free will wisely.

You may have heard the ancient Chinese aphorism. *Give* a man a fish and you feed him for a day. *Teach* a man to fish and you feed him for a lifetime. I say, give a man a fish and you make him your slave. (He is dependent upon you for his survival.) Teach him how to fish, and you set him free. Any attempt to control others is ultimately detrimental to them and to us on every level.

On a political level, controlling ourselves rather than others results in democracy and liberty. If you did not notice the creeping social control over the past decades, you must have noticed it during this covid fraud. Everyone in the world has been coerced to do silly, nonsensical, and self-destructive things because of the incredible political, legal, and social control that now exists in our society.

As you read through this book, keep in the back of your mind this question: "Are these people seeking to control themselves or to control others?" It's an illuminating question. Fear and evil seek to control others. Love seeks to control only the self.

Eastern Traditions: Energy Centers

From the perspective of Eastern religious traditions (Hinduism, Buddhism), we can see this conflict in terms of our energy centers, which are called chakras. Here is a quick and superficial explanation.[9]

Chakra	Location	Major Focus	Perspective of One Under This Influence
1	Base of the spine	Security & Survival	Everyone is a potential threat—xenophobia.
2	Genitals	Sex	Constantly on the prowl for new sexual experiences or partners, fantasizing about sex.
3	Solar plexus	Status & Power	Constantly striving to assess and improve power relationships and image in the eyes of others.
4	Center of the chest	Agape Love	Sees every personal interaction as an experience of universal love.
5	Throat	Creativity & Communication	Every personal interaction stimulates creativity—something is produced or planned.
6	Third eye—Mid-forehead	Psychic Awareness	The inner senses are awakened. Personal interactions are perceived on an energetic level, auras may be seen, energy dynamics are perceived in others and in relationships.
7	Top of the head	Transcendence	Sees all things and people as Maya (illusion). Others are perceived as unique manifestations of the Oneness. The person is detached from the world—in the world but not of it—and has compassion for others' suffering but is not perturbed by it.

You may notice the obvious similarity between the chakras and Maslow's human needs. It reflects the unity of our triune nature—spirit, mind, and body. Just as every healthy person expresses all levels of Maslow's needs, everyone perceives and expresses through all seven chakras, though not equally. Each chakra has its own energy, its own power. All are important, as is the balance of these energies. It's not that the lower chakras (security, sex, power) are "bad." It's not an issue of good or bad. It's a question of balancing the energies–controlling our sexual energy and directing it in creative and productive ways, focusing our desire to control others into a desire to control ourselves, transmuting our survival instinct and suspicion of others into a universal love for all people, and transcending the material to perceive our Oneness.

The philosophies and ideologies dominating our world are exclusively focused on the lower three chakras–fear, xenophobia, sex, and power. This is partly because these ideologies are Materialistic, denying the existence of any aesthetic or spiritual reality, as we will see in chapter 2.

Fear, sex, and power are the tools of manipulation and control being used against us. They draw our attention to the lower three chakras and leave us unbalanced. The heart chakra, the sense of universal love, is the pivot between the lower/material and the higher/transcendent chakras. Love is the key. Love is the answer. In the perception of the first chakra, everyone is an enemy to be feared. In the perception of the seventh chakra, everyone is an alternate expression of oneself, to be loved as oneself. We must balance our chakra energies and *perceive differently.*

As individuals and as a society, we must make the transition from the third chakra to the fourth–from a focus on power to a focus on love. This is the transformation the earth is presently going through. Some call it the transition from third density to fourth density. Love and wisdom (found in the higher chakras) must control the lower chakras if we are to ascend spiritually and have material peace on earth. If we remain stuck in the energies of the lower three chakras, humanity will devour itself. There is no end to the lust for power; it must be transcended with love.

A New Great Age

Many esoteric traditions teach that the world, and human consciousness, moves through various great ages with different dominant characteristics. For example, Hindu cosmology describes the Yuga Cycle with four major divisions. We are currently in the Kali Yuga, or Iron Age, in which humanity is so disconnected from spiritual reality that most people can only perceive the material world and not the spiritual world. Even though there is a long time yet in the Kali Yuga, humanity is beginning its spiritual ascent out of this dark age and into a more spiritually enlightened age.

Many will recall the hype around 2012 (really 2011), the end of the Mayan calendar and the supposed end of the world. But it was not the end of the world, but the end of the age. The calendar represents stages of consciousness, and we have now entered the stage of universal consciousness.

In Western Astrology, the ages are divided into the twelve sections of the zodiac and each age lasts about two thousand years. Jesus ushered in the Age of Pisces, which is now ending. We are transitioning into the Age of Aquarius, which, compared to the Age of Pisces, will be dominated by humanitarianism rather than authoritarianism, spirituality rather than religion, natural law rather than man's law, love rather than power.

We can perceive the changes we are presently seeing in the world as the move to a new great age. You can call this shift an enlightenment, an awakening, an apocalypse. The transition will be unsettling, messy, chaotic. Yet every esoteric tradition teaches that we are moving into an age of greater spiritual connectedness and enlightenment–a better world. This perspective should give us great hope. Your choice is to work on your own spiritual ascension or to descend into a darker existence. You will choose either love or fear.

Love and Forgiveness: The Way Out Is the Way Up

The world is going through a spiritual transition. It is a spiritual war–a test like the "refiner's fire" which purifies us. It is a trial we must pass through, like boot camp for the soul. How you perceive the transition is less important than understanding it is happening and recognizing that we have a choice to evolve to a higher level of spiritual development or devolve to a lower level. This choice hinges on our choice of love or fear. Love will cause us to ascend, fear to descend. You can choose only for yourself.

Our adversary wants to keep us mired in fear, hatred, and division, as well as distracted by sex, money, power, and the gratification of material desires. Whatever is done to us in the great frauds of our time, if we respond in kind—with anger, hatred, fear, and violence—we lose. If we respond with the weapons that are used against us, humanity will consume itself. We must respond with God's weapon—love. Our strategy is love, our tactic is forgiveness, and our weapon is nonviolent noncooperation. Only by responding with love will we pass through this time of "trial by fire." We can ascend to a higher consciousness and a world of peace only through love.

Everyone in our world is hurting, is wounded, is in need of healing. Only forgiveness heals. Only forgiveness dissolves the bonds of karma. Only forgiveness opens your heart and allows you to love. People have tried to heal our wounds with revenge, with restitution and retribution, even with fake reconciliation—all to no avail. The freedom we seek—not just political freedom, but emotional freedom, professional freedom, spiritual freedom—can only be found in the healing that comes from forgiveness. Instead of attacking others, criticizing others, and judging others, we must forgive others.

Only by turning to God within will we perceive, with spiritual eyes, this spiritual war and understand our role in transforming ourselves and our world. Only by turning again to God can we regain our freedom. Those of you who know the Bible will remember that every time the people of Israel turned away from God, destruction followed. We've done it again. Western civilization has turned away from God.

You may wonder how and why we turned away from God, and how this can possibly matter. It matters for several reasons. One is that ideas have consequences. The fate of civilizations ultimately rests upon the ideas that motivate the masses. In the next chapter, we turn our attention to the ideas that dominate our thinking and how that came to be.

What You Can Do Now

1. It's all about pattern recognition. Look for patterns–in ideas, behaviors, and events. People lie. Actions reveal motives. Your analysis of patterns will lead you to the truth.
2. Love. Find ways to incorporate more love into your thinking, speaking, and acting. Only through love can we, both individually and collectively, transcend the fear, division, hatred, and addiction that enslaves everyone.
3. Most importantly, turn back to God–especially if you have turned away from God. Recognize that you are an eternal spiritual being on a spiritual journey. Seek your own spiritual development in whatever way seems best to you. In truth, there are no wrong paths to God.
4. Pray and meditate. Both are important to developing your connection to the spirit within you and without you. Prayer is talking to God. Meditation is listening. God is always speaking to us; we are rarely listening. Meditation develops our listening skills. God is the loving Father who will guide us if we allow Him. God is the Force who never forces. Free will is at the root of our "humanness." Join free will to love, and you will become the best you can be.
5. Join a spiritual community that suits you. Meet weekly with other like-minded people to help each other–help on your spiritual journeys, on your understanding of what is really going on in the world, and in meeting your material needs in the difficult times that are upon us.
6. Read this book, read other books, open your eyes, widen your perspective, and see the lies and fraud that surround us. Lies enslave. The truth will set you free.
7. Live not by lies. Do not accept or acquiesce to the lies and fraud. Resist with the strategy of love, the tactic of forgiveness, and the weapon of nonviolent noncooperation.

CHAPTER 2

The Philosophy of Death

"The world had never before known a godlessness as organized, militarized, and tenaciously malevolent as that practiced by Marxism. Within the philosophical system of Marx and Lenin, and at the heart of their psychology, hatred of God is the principal driving force, more fundamental than all their political and economic pretensions. Militant atheism is not merely incidental or marginal to Communist policy; it is not a side effect, but the central pivot." –ALEKSANDR I. SOLZHENITSYN

If we want to understand how totalitarianism has been gradually tightening its noose, we must understand the ideas upon which it rests. Ideas have consequences. And ideas take a long time to become ingrained in a population—about a century, more or less. The Communist Manifesto was published in 1848. The Second World War, a war against Marxist socialism, began almost a century later. We are still struggling with these ideas. The faulty ideas of communism—the philosophy of death, as I call it—are coming to a climax in our day. But let's step back a bit and see how modern philosophy became Marxist through and through and how it has infected your consciousness whether you know it or not.

The Context of Communism

It is helpful to understand the time and place in which communism arose. Later philosophers would say we are "socially constructed," which is silly. But we are definitely *influenced* by the social milieu—the social, political, economic, technological, and cultural conditions in which we come of age.

For Karl Marx, this was mid-nineteenth-century Europe. It was a time of upheaval. Germany, Marx's home, was gradually being unified by Otto von Bismarck through a combination of diplomacy and war. The French Revolution and the Bonaparte dictatorship—which some might say was the first communist revolution—still weighed heavily on the European consciousness. It had destroyed much of the aristocracy and wealth of France, drastically weakened the temporal power of the Catholic Church, and brought about a century of struggle through dictatorship and war (the Jacobins and then Napoleon) in a gradual move toward democracy.

Chastened by France's disaster, other European nations were peacefully moving toward democracy to avoid the bloody destruction of revolution. The rigid class structure of Europe was gradually giving way to a more egalitarian society, mostly due to the increasing wealth and power of the business and professional classes, but also due to the gradual elimination of serfdom and the slow rise of the serfs from abject destitution to simple poverty. The centuries-long process of creating a middle class was slowly and haltingly improving the material well-being of almost everyone. Industrialization provided jobs at a subsistence level of poverty for some of the excess rural population. The emigration of Europeans to the rest of the world also provided some relief for the rural excess.

We must remember that excess rural population in previous centuries simply died quietly of starvation or disease, politely out of sight in the countryside. Now they flocked to the cities and towns looking for wage work amongst the burgeoning factories of newly industrializing Western and Northern Europe.

Yet the process of raising an agricultural economy to an industrial one could not happen quickly enough to prevent a huge concentration of wealth on one hand, and destitute masses of people on the other hand. The transition from a medieval social structure of aristocrats and serfs to an industrial society of democracy and free enterprise takes centuries. What is most amazing is not the slow speed of these changes, but the fact they were accompanied by so *little* violence.

The destitution of the masses was obvious to everyone in the nineteenth century, in stark contrast to the opulent wealth of the industrialists and aristocrats. Charles Dickens famously wrote novels about the poor, but nobody knew how to solve this massive problem—known at the time as "the social question." Karl Marx was one of many who proposed a radical and violent restructuring of society. Forming his ideas mid-century, his understanding of economics was framed not by free enterprise, but by mercantilism—in which economic enterprise is regulated and controlled by governments.[1] Most of the great private fortunes of the nineteenth century were created because of markets restricted by royal monopolies, tariff barriers, or private coercion. Close connection to, and the favor of, governments and kings was at least as important in financial success as independent initiative. In the early nineteenth century, the legal concept of the corporation was more often a creature of government monopoly privilege than of men freely combining their capital for a common enterprise.[2]

Karl Marx invented the derogatory term "capitalism" to describe this. It began as an insult and has never made sense as a descriptive term, especially now. Economics was never merely an issue of "capital" (capital being not just money but all the material means of production including buildings, machinery, technology, etc.). Human life is much more complex than Marx's dangerously simplistic deceit.

It was not capitalism that failed to provide for the miserable masses, and Marx's proposal to destroy capital could never improve anything. By the time he died in 1883, the ideas of classical liberalism were just beginning to bear fruit in freeing markets, allowing resources to be used more efficiently, and freeing people from legal slavery. His philosophy never made sense. As technology progressed, social and legal structures relaxed, and our understanding of human psychology and economics developed, Marx's ideas were seen to be ever more unsound and childish.

Marx turned against the main Enlightenment ideas which were just beginning to flower, a century after they were formulated. The Enlightenment, or Age of Reason, was an eighteenth-century philosophical movement that proposed that the route to all knowledge and understanding lay in the use of reason and the evidence presented to us by our five senses. The Enlightenment philosophers rejected divine revelation as a source of knowledge or truth. This philosophy had huge consequences. The eternal debate of "faith vs. reason" as the path to understanding had swung solidly to the side of "reason."

By the time of Marx, religion had been swept out of the picture. Most people still had some religious faith and practice, but almost no one thought religion provided a route to knowledge and understanding–a route to heaven, perhaps, but not to understanding the world. In fact, the late nineteenth century was a time of intense antireligiousness, partly because of the growing influence of socialist ideas. Socialism countered the Enlightenment principles of individual liberty and religious tolerance with a denial of the individual and violent intolerance of religion.

Because of its intense focus on reason and its rejection of divine revelation, the Enlightenment was also an attack on Christianity in general and the Catholic Church in particular. God had nothing useful to say about the world. He just got in the way and caused trouble for people. Religion came to be seen as the *cause* of human conflict and an impediment to human progress. The philosophers and intelligentsia of Marx's time were typically anti-religion. This is an essential and immutable feature of their philosophies.

Marxist Philosophy

Socialism essentially boils down to the communal ownership of property and the communal organization of the production and distribution of goods and services. This is natural and effective on the scale of the family. It's disaster on the scale of a nation. Once a society progresses to the point of settled agriculture, the private ownership of land, buildings, improvements, tools–in short, property–becomes essential. Without it, no one makes improvements to increase production and a general impoverishment ensues. This pattern has been repeated throughout history. Socialism is an ancient folly. It is not unique to the twentieth century.

Marx believed in the philosophy of materialism, the idea that nothing exists apart from physical reality—matter. He accepted the existence of the body and the mind (assuming the mind to be a "physical" creation of the brain), but rejected the soul. Philosophical materialism presents a mechanistic theory of reality; it sees the whole universe and everything in it as machines. This implies that the "machines" can be understood and controlled by humans and that we can create an ideal world by properly controlling everything.

Marx was also drawn to the dialectic method of Hegel (thesis, antithesis, synthesis), which claims that the basic law of nature is conflict—clearly a narrow view of life. Marx, and his later associate Friedrich Engels, put these together in what they called dialectical materialism. Marx's foundational idea is that human society develops through class conflict. This idea is so incredibly limiting and narrow-minded, such a partial truth, that its inability to yield real insight should be obvious.

Marx and Engels set out their theories in *The Communist Manifesto*[3] (and in Marx's later book, *Das Capital*). All of human history is the story of the eternal struggle between social classes. Individual action, ideas, forms of government, not to mention physical realities such as geography, climate, and natural resources all play no part in history. The eternal conflict is between the bourgeoisie, who control the means of production, and the proletariat, who supply their labor. In general terms, the oppressed majority versus a minority of oppressors. The oppressed masses will ultimately rise up, destroy the bourgeoisie, and create a communistic society where there is no private ownership. Everything will be held in common (by the government) for the benefit of all. Even though this utopia is inevitable and desirable for the majority, communist agitators are needed to stir up antagonism between the social classes. The poor oppressed masses just can't perceive what's good for them. History needs a big push from radical extremists.

Violence and destruction are essential in Marxism. Violence is exactly the point. There is no possibility of incremental improvement. Marxism and its ideological descendants are always about revolution, sowing hatred, destroying existing society, and grabbing power at any cost. It's really all about power, nothing else.

The Communist Manifesto explained that, under communism, the government would own and control everything: all property, all means of production, all money. The government would institute a heavily graduated income tax, abolish inheritance, control all communication and transportation, and abolish all religions and families. Family, religion, and morals would have no place in the communist utopia. The *state* would be the only religion and family. Such is paradise. It's amazing how close we are to achieving it.

Marxism presents an antagonistic social theory which Christianity has opposed with a social theory of cooperation. The fundamental fact of human society is that people cooperate with each other, not that there is constant class conflict. In fact, almost all the conflict in our lives is personal conflict, not class conflict.

The socialists also took up Darwin's ideas of evolution to remove God from their world. Everything is material. There is nothing else. There is no "creation" by God. All life is an accident of nature and human beings are simply the most highly evolved animal. Lacking even the acknowledgment of higher spiritual values, it's not surprising that communism in practice quickly devolves to the level of animals.

With Marx's focus on *groups* as opposed to *individuals*, he theorized that each person is little more than a particle of his social class. This is another idea consistently opposed by religions, which recognize that individuals, not groups, are created by God, have a relationship with God, and experience enlightenment or salvation. To Marx, there is no *individual* action, only *class* action. One's actions conform with one's class and are determined by it. Even a man's thinking patterns conform with his class, so the bourgeoisie cannot even understand the proletariat because their minds work differently.

The great economist Ludwig von Mises clearly and eloquently refuted the nonsensical ideas of Karl Marx. In speaking about Marx's ideas of the class struggle, von Mises said, "As a corrective of these fancies the truism must be stressed that only individuals think and act."[4] That is, man is not simply a corpuscle in the body of his social class. Each person is a unique individual who thinks and acts independently. No group—not a social class, not a race, not any group—is capable of thinking and acting. Only individuals think and act. This malicious misunderstanding will arise again and again. It currently infects our whole world.

Of course, we act as *members* of various groups, as *representatives* of various groups, but it is always individuals who act. No group of any kind thinks or acts. This is a special case of the fact that no *category* of anything has an ontological existence, as philosophers would say. Take, for example, chairs. There are billions of chairs in the world and everyone understands the concept of a chair. Yet the category itself is a mental construct. It exists only in our minds. The *category* of chairs does not have a material existence, only the *individual* chairs in that category do. Mental constructs are extremely important, and we use them all the time. But it's essential to remember what actually has an existence in material reality and what is only a mental construct. Mental constructs cannot think or act—and human groups are mental constructs. This fundamental error of Karl Marx has flowed to his philosophical descendants. Let's look at a few of the key philosophers in his family tree.

Marx's Philosophical Descendants

Friedrich Nietzsche (1844–1900) is best known for his oft-repeated phrase, "God is dead." However, those three words don't really characterize Nietzsche's thought. Here is a fuller quote:

> God is dead. God remains dead. And we have killed him. How shall we comfort ourselves, the murderers of all murderers? What was holiest and mightiest of all that the world has yet owned has bled to death under our knives: who will wipe this blood off us? What water is there for us to clean ourselves? What festivals of atonement, what sacred games shall we have to invent? Is not the greatness of this deed too great for us? Must we ourselves not become gods simply to appear worthy of it?[5]

Amidst his flowery prose, Nietzsche realizes that to kill God is to make ourselves gods. He is saying that humanity (European society at the time) had lost faith in God. The foundation of truth, value, and meaning that had held sway since biblical times was giving way. God had served as the basis of objective moral truth. If there is no God, there is no foundation for the claim that there *is* objective truth and objective moral values. This led Nietzsche to the idea of "perspectivism"—everyone has their own perspective, their own truth, but there is no "Truth." Everything is relative.

Certainly, everyone has their own perspective. But that does not imply an absence of objective Truth—the Truth as God sees it. We might even call this God's perspective. Physical reality, at the very least, remains objective regardless of your perspective. Experience also remains objective. If you murder your brother, he has objectively experienced death regardless of your perspective about it, or his.

Nietzsche came to believe that if there is no objective truth, we should firmly assert our own "truth" in the world by the strength of our own will. In the obvious clash of "wills" and "truths" that ensues, a strong man will emerge—a "superman" who asserts his will over all others and ultimately over reason itself. This has happened repeatedly with totalitarian dictators in our own time.

Jean-Paul Sartre (1905–1980) was strongly influenced by Nietzsche. Sartre saw God as a great threat to his own freedom. Rejecting God was so freeing.[6] "If there is no God," Sartre paraphrased Dostoyevsky, "then everything is permitted." Freedom without responsibility is every teenager's dream of heaven on earth. Pity that it really leads to hell on earth. Beyond freeing himself from social convention, I wonder if Sartre truly understood how horrific is the realization that "everything is permitted."

He founded the philosophy of existentialism, that is, that existence precedes essence. Sartre redefined the meaning of many words that philosophers had used for centuries, such as *essence* and *existence*, thus leading to more confusion of language and ideas—a consistent Marxist tactic. He claimed that existence comes first: that is, there is no real human nature. We "exist" first (are born) and can take any "essence" or nature we choose. Our ideas, values, conduct, truths, and beliefs are all ours to choose—they are subjective, not objective. Thus, we have the culture of self-invention, everything is a social construct, and each person can choose their own identity and truth. This has become the default philosophy of the world, either consciously or unconsciously.

Michel Foucault (1926–1984) was interested mainly in the relationship between power and knowledge, and how they are used as a form of social control through societal institutions—ideas now incorporated into the principles of both Critical Theory and psychological warfare. Those in power will organize language in such a way as to keep themselves in power—and most of this is done unconsciously. The powerful oppressors in society don't even realize what they are doing. Clearly, this pattern suggests that those who "see" (those who are "awake" or "woke") must remove from power those who are "blind," according to the entirely subjective, and constantly changing, evaluation of the "seers." This thinking has overtaken the "woke" world of today.

Postmodernism—Critical Theory

"The majority believes that everything hard to comprehend must be very profound. This is incorrect. What is hard to understand is what is immature, unclear and often false. The highest wisdom is simple and passes through the brain directly into the heart." —VIKTOR SCHAUBERGER

The stream of philosophical nonsense called Postmodernism and/or Critical Theory sprang from a group of Marxists known as the "Frankfurt School" since many of them taught in Frankfurt, Germany during the 1920s and 30s. Being mostly atheist Jews, they left Germany and came to the United States when Hitler's brand of socialism became too uncomfortable. Here, other well-placed socialists inserted them into leading American universities. Thus, Critical Theory started displacing critical thinking amongst the educated classes.

Their fundamentally Marxist ideas have dominated the universities since the 1960s and, therefore, form the philosophical foundation of most university-educated people today. It has conquered not only departments of philosophy, but the humanities, social sciences, languages, and history. It is even attacking the pure sciences.

The Frankfurt School philosophers realized that the Western industrial nations could not be taken over like Russia was. It would be necessary to first change the culture, which is fundamental in society. Change the culture and you change the society. Fail to change the culture and you can't change the society. Hence, they targeted cultural change—now called Cultural Marxism.

Paul Kengor, in his book *The Devil and Karl Marx: Communism's Long March of Death, Deception, and Infiltration*, doesn't mince words in his disdain for these new Marxist philosophers.

> Early in the twentieth century, from the smoldering embers of Marxist-Leninist theory, arose a fiery field of fanatics who came to be known collectively as the Frankfurt School. These Marxists were all about culture and sex. The Frankfurt School protégés were neo-Marxists, a new kind of twentieth-century communist less interested in the economic/class ideas of Marx than a remaking of society through the eradication of traditional norms and institutions. They brought to Marxist theory not a passion for, say, more equitable tax policy or reallocation of private property but rather tenets of psychology, sociology, and Freudian teaching on sexuality.[7]

In their book *Cynical Theories*, Helen Pluckrose and James Lindsay give a nice summary of what Postmodernism believes and what it opposes. This will make your head spin.[8]

Central Themes of Postmodernism

- Doubting that any human truths provide an objective representation of reality.
- Focusing on language and the way societies use it to create their own local realities.
- Denying the universal (things like freedom, honesty, forgiveness,

loyalty, humility, compassion, health, peace, or even a universal human nature).

Enlightenment Ideas Rejected by Postmodernists

- Objective knowledge.
- Universal truth.
- Science, or evidence more broadly, as a method for obtaining objective knowledge.
- The power of reason and the ability to communicate straightforwardly with language.
- A universal human nature.
- Individualism (that is, the moral worth of the individual).
- Also, that the West has experienced significant progress due to the Enlightenment and will continue to do so if it upholds those values.

When these philosophical ideas are laid out simply and clearly, their utter nonsense is clear. Critical Theory has confused many. This is intentional. The philosophers knew exactly what they were doing. They designed their philosophy to spread Marxism in disguise. And they have the fanaticism of ideological zealots. They destroy anyone who stands in their way. As Paul Kengor says,

> And yet, like neo-Marxist pioneer Herbert Marcuse with his notion of "repressive tolerance" (he urged "intolerance against movements from the Right, and toleration of movements from the Left"), they only blast to smithereens the things they don't like. They are willing to tolerate all sorts of novel inventions, from new forms of "marriage" and sexuality to endless gender options.[9]

The Frankfurt School philosophers were supported by the KGB, and they overtly designed a set of philosophical ideas that would subvert Western society along the lines of classic communist subversion. Dr. Ed Prida explained this in his book *Subversion Against America*. As a professor of military intelligence in Cuba, he understands communism from the inside.

Eleven-Point Plan of the Frankfurt School[10]

1. Undermine schools' and teachers' authority.
2. Create racism offenses.
3. Create confusion with constant change.
4. Teach sex and homosexuality to children.
5. Destroy the national identity of the Western nations with massive immigration.
6. Promote excessive drinking and drugs.
7. Empty churches and reduce faith.
8. Create an unreliable legal system with a bias against victims of crime.
9. Create a dependance upon the state and state benefits.
10. Dumb down the media.
11. Encourage the breakdown of the family.

These eleven points are exactly the results of the Frankfurt School philosophy of Critical Theory. Their plan has worked well.

The closely related philosophies spawned by the Frankfurt School—Critical Theory, postmodernism, intersectionality, Grievance Ideology—have such commonalities that they are like individual strands of hair in a horse's tail. Academic philosophers quibble over the individual hairs, but just stand back a bit and they all blend, indistinguishable, into the same horse's tail. Still at the same end of the horse.

Grievance Ideology teaches victimhood. Victimhood makes you a slave because you abdicate your own power to improve your life and achieve your goals. You imagine that power is in the hands of your supposed "oppressors." It is not. This is an ideology of defeat and depression. It is a lie. It is exactly the ideology of power that those who want *power over you* want you to believe. Once you believe that you are powerless and need the autocratic power of a savior to protect you from your fellow humans, you are ready to accept any tyrannical despot who promises to "save" you.

Suffering is not oppression. Problems and troubles and even mistreatment from others are not oppression. These are the grist of life from which we create the wheat of a transcendent soul. Suffering is subjective, not objective. It is our internal response to the difficulties of life. We are not victims because life is difficult for us. Victimhood is something we create ourselves. We choose our response—whether life's difficulties will make us victims or heroes. Be a hero.

There is no escape from the perverse philosophy of Critical Theory, no reconciliation, no justice, and certainly no transcendence. As with all these Marxist philosophies that consider only power relationships, their only resolution is the destruction of society and rebuilding it with the philosophers in power. The end goal of Critical Theorists is a world run by themselves. But even within their philosophy, they don't know how to build. All they do is criticize. When we see these philosophies in action in the modern world, all we see is disaster.

The Inexorable Endgame

"The only real revolution is in the enlightenment of the mind and the improvement of character, the only real emancipation is individual, and the only real revolutionists are philosophers and saints." —WILL DURANT

We have seen the philosophical unity of this stream of thinking from Marx all the way to postmodernism, a materialist philosophy that recognizes only material things. It asserts that spiritual things don't exist. These neo-Marxist philosophers are, to a man, atheists. None of them ever grasped the transcendent nature of humanity, so they leave out the most essential truth—that you are a divine and eternal creation of God. In both theory and practice, we know where this road leads.

When you deny the existence of a transcendent reality, you deny the transcendent qualities of humans. You deny the ability of people to be godlike. You deny the natural human longing for self-transcendence or even for self-improvement. Human beings in this philosophical hell become little more than chemical-mechanical machines. Of course—that's the assumption they began with. Transcendent desires become the stuff of totalitarian propaganda but play no part in real society. Is it any wonder these qualities are entirely absent in nations founded on communist ideas?

Materialist philosophy cannot comprehend humanity. Trying to understand the human condition while denying the existence of the soul is like trying to understand the game of baseball while denying the existence of the bat and the ball. The actions of the people on the field are incomprehensible.

Ideas have consequences because they lead to actions. These philosophers devote all their mental powers to analyzing those things we are most called to turn away from—wealth, power, and the desires of the body—the three great temptations of Christ. This is the lower nature of humanity, the animal nature, the lower chakras. Remember, whatever you focus your attention on grows. Without the balance of the spirit—the higher chakras—the lust for these material desires is insatiable. This is a philosophy of only the dark side of humanity. No wonder they end up in such a dark place. For if you turn away from the light, any road you take leads to darkness. These philosophers are intellectual barbarians, intent on destroying everything they don't understand and bringing about a new Dark Age of the Soul.

Most people of any religion would accept that we are body, mind, and soul and that there is a beneficent creative energy in the universe. God is life. God is the author of life. The denial of God is the denial of life. It is death, the pulverization of the human person, as St. John Paul II said. Ideas have consequences, so the denial of God on a worldwide scale will inevitably bring about the destruction of human life on this planet. We will descend into a global clash of wills between rival tyrants, for never will they have enough power. This is the inexorable endgame of the philosophy of death. I hope the evidence of this book will help you understand why that is so.

Communism aims to make the world a better place by forcing everyone to think and be what the communist tyrants want them to think and be. But you cannot change anyone else; you can only change yourself. So, communism is constant terrorism. It cannot be otherwise. Everyone is terrorized into an ever narrowing and ever-changing straight jacket of political correctness. The only possible way to change the world is to change yourself. *You* are the only person you *can* change. Others, you can only terrorize. This is the message of all religions—spiritual growth, self-transcendence, love, acceptance, and peace—you create it all *within yourself.*

Technocracy

The terms *socialism* and *communism* arose in the nineteenth century. When these ideas were applied in actual governments in the early twentieth century, they initially took on the names of the political parties: Bolshevism in Russia, Fascism in Italy, and Nazism in Germany. As we will see in chapter 4, these were the first great totalitarian takeovers of the century. But socialist ideas seeped into every aspect of Western society, particularly during the 1930s. The Great Depression caused most people to question how the economic system worked and to search for new solutions to economic problems. One of these ideas was a "system" that is almost forgotten today but most closely represents the totalitarianism of the twenty-first century—technocracy.

Technocracy is an idea developed and promoted by a professor at Columbia University during the 1930s. It is a system of totalitarian control that purports to use scientific methods to make all the economic and social decisions in a society.[11] It is a scientific dictatorship. It includes the idea that resources, particularly energy, are so fundamental that the government needs to control all resources, and that all economic decisions should be based on the energy produced or consumed in each activity. Therefore, money will be replaced by energy certificates. Every human activity will be scientifically analyzed, and data will be used to make all economic and social decisions. All life will be controlled by scientists and technocrats. This is the quasi-religion of scientism, and it will replace all other religions and ideologies. Like communism, technocracy tries to bring about societal collapse and then rebuild it according to the designs of those in power—in this case, the technocrats.

We must clarify an important misconception about economic "systems." There really is no "system." The word *system* has so many meanings it makes understanding difficult. We often think of something man-made when we think of a system. For example, an automobile has many systems—the steering system, the braking system, the electrical system, the powertrain system, and so on. These are all designed, built, and operated by people. People can design, build, and operate them differently. No problem.

But an economic "system" is nothing like this. Every single person in the world performs thousands of actions every day to satisfy their own needs and desires as they perceive them, acting in ways that seem most appropriate to them. Each person cooperates with others in hundreds of ways every day. It is all of these trillions of daily motivations and actions, and the quadrillions of interactions, that we call the "economy." It is not possible to plan, predict, or direct this, even to know all the things that happened. Having an AI supercomputer doesn't help. It is impossible to know all the needs and desires and all the factors that go into each person's individual decisions to act in various ways. There is no system in what we call the economy. Nor is there a system in what we might call social development, or society. Capitalism is not an economic system. It is a mental construct composed of various principles. The same goes for everything else that people call an economic system. In truth, there is no such thing.

It almost goes without saying, therefore, that it is not possible to create a "system" that would take the place of every person making decisions and acting for themselves. Yet this is exactly what the various flavors of totalitarianism try to do, because they see all of reality as simply mechanical systems. It makes no more sense than trying to use your conscious mind to control every tiny process and action of every cell and organ in your body. Imagine trying to tell your lungs when to breathe, your heart when to beat, commanding which antibodies to go where in your body and perform which actions. You would be dead within minutes if you had to control everything in your body. The same goes for trying to plan and control the whole world.

Unity of Philosophy—Unity of Ideology

The general term *totalitarianism* encompasses a hundred sub-types. Let's be clear about what it is, because it is different from historical dictatorship. Totalitarianism is not just about political power, it's about *total* power—controlling the very nature of reality. Hannah Arendt, perhaps the foremost expert on totalitarianism, defines it thus:

> A totalitarian society is one in which an ideology seeks to displace all prior traditions and institutions with a goal of bringing all aspects of society under the control of that ideology. A totalitarian state is one that aspires to nothing less than controlling and defining reality. Truth is whatever the rulers decide it is.[12]

This definition describes the essential unity of all the varieties of totalitarian philosophy: technocracy, communism, socialism, anarchism, Fabianism, fascism, Nazism, Marxism-Leninism, progressivism, anarcho-socialism, revolutionary socialism, ethical socialism, liberal socialism, social democracy, state socialism, utopian socialism, Eco-socialism, green socialism, socialist ecology, and so on.

The old term *progressive* is popular today, but it has been used by socialists and communists of all stripes for 150 years. Progressives are totalitarians. Sure, you can be a little bit progressive, just like you can be a little bit totalitarian and a little bit pregnant.

All of these totalitarian terms and doctrines propose various degrees of state control over individual action and property ownership. All of them try to control people and even to control their perception of reality. All of them stem from a denial of God and promote instead faith in the state. They are all selfish, destructive ideologies focused on power and the very worst in human nature. The promise of communism is a dream—the reality is a nightmare. It promises freedom but delivers slavery. It promises peace but delivers constant violence. Its adherents quibble over minor distinctions, but the similarities are what characterize these doctrines. For the purposes of this book, and because it best represents the current totalitarianism, I will most often lump all variants of totalitarianism into the rubric of technocracy.

Transhumanism—The New Eugenics

The philosophy of materialism with its mechanistic conception of the world, and particularly the ideology of technocracy, leads naturally to transhumanism. This is a philosophy promoting the advancement of humanity through technology. It runs the gamut from nanotechnology to AI and even to mind control. It also intends to mold our social, economic, and cultural perceptions—that is, reality itself. The intellectual elites who espouse this idea won't admit it, but transhumanism came out of, and is an extension of, the same eugenics movement that was so popular a century ago and that Hitler so discredited by putting its ideas into action.

If everything in the universe is a machine, and only material things exist, and the mind is produced from matter, then it makes perfect sense that we can improve the body-mind machine with other material things. We can add microchips or wireless nano-bots to our brains to increase our memory storage and retrieval capacity, to connect to the "cloud" and instantly access all the stored knowledge of mankind, to connect with artificial intelligence and with other minds. This connection is two-way. We can give and receive information, messages, instructions, software updates, and so on. Every new thing we learn is instantly added to the "learning" of the whole transhuman race. Through the microchip, we add a mechanical "operating system" to the biological operating system of our bodies. We can add artificial parts to our bodies to overcome the physical deterioration of old age and live for centuries. We can improve ourselves by becoming part human and part machine, taking the best of both. We can create artificial wombs to grow new babies and create superhumans with genetic manipulation. We can be freed from human limitations. This is our new "evolution" as humans—to go beyond human and become transhuman. Our "faith" is in ourselves and in our ability to create ever-improved versions of ourselves as biological-mechanical creatures. We make ourselves "God." This is no longer science fiction; almost all this technology currently exists.

This is the story promoted by Klaus Schwab and the World Economic Forum—their vision for as soon as 2030. The glossy advertising brochure makes it sound so inviting. Reality will be otherwise. As the psychiatrist and author Dr. Peter Breggin observed about transhumanism in his book, *Covid-19 and the Global Predators*, "all physical interventions into the brain to change behavior and conduct eventually have the same effects: blunting the human mind, compromising free will, and dulling spirituality...(these interventions) inevitably render people more docile and easily led."[12]

You may have already sensed other dangers here. Whoever controls this transhumanist agenda can give you access to all the collected knowledge and wisdom of mankind, or carefully censor and restrict your access to information to create in your mind a perception of reality that is pure fantasy. The two-way communication with the "cloud" means you are under constant surveillance. They know your location anywhere in the world 24/7. Your health status, body activity, body chemistry, moods, even thoughts, are constantly monitored. And they can alter any of these. They can remotely improve your health or kill you, make you feel better or worse, and modify any thoughts you might have of independence. This is truly the horrific realization of Sartre's dream—"everything is permitted."

There's more. You lose your identity as an individual. You become simply a part of the species, which is exactly how Marxism sees the individual. It is the "Borg" of Star Trek fame. No more individuals, but simply individual iterations of the "one mind" that sees all, records all, controls all.

This is technology, but it is far more than that. Recall the insightful words of Arthur C. Clarke: "Any sufficiently advanced technology is indistinguishable from magic."[13] In a spiritual sense, black magic perverts what is holy. It does not create. It destroys. It is based on power, not love. Transhumanism is a perversion of the holy human that God created. God creates. The opposite of God destroys. However you choose to perceive the dark side—as evil, as Satan, as black magic, as demons, as lower astral entities—understand that these pervert what is holy. Creation is holy. Destruction is a perversion. Life is holy. Killing is a perversion. Unity is holy. Division is a perversion. Light is holy. Darkness is a perversion.

There are two ways of degrading our souls into something less than the human soul created by God. One is by degrading our consciousness through chronic fear. The second is by degrading our body through transhumanism so that our higher energy body—our soul—is no longer able to connect with our physical body. Both are happening in our world today. Reject these influences. Turn to God. Turn to the Light. In all respects, follow the advice given to Luke Skywalker: "Turn away from the dark side."

This is where the World Economic Forum and our elites are leading us. This is not freedom, but complete slavery. This is not human evolution, but human devolution into quasi-machines, devoid of what makes us truly human–our soul and our connection to God. Understood properly, transhumanism is dehumanism. This is the inexorable endgame of the philosophy of death. It is the devolution to a lower level of evolutionary and spiritual development. It is hell.

On the other hand, if we understand that being "human" means being an amalgam of body, mind, and spirit, then we come to very different conclusions about the future of humanity. If we understand that we are essentially spiritual energy beings, that our bodies are essentially energy "slowed down" into matter, that our minds are the portal between the worlds of matter and energy (materiality and spirituality), then the greater evolution of humanity lies in improving our connection to the world of spirit-energy. All wisdom and intelligence come from God, from spirit-energy, not from any machine. It is not connecting to a machine that will improve us, but connecting to God. Fortunately, this is not difficult, because God is not far away. God is within each one of us. God is *in* creation, is *immanent* in creation. Christians call it the Holy Spirit and it is within us. Those who understand the Eastern traditions understand it as prana or chi within us. Whatever your religious understanding, the energy of God is in us and around us–within us and without us. It is in God "that we live and move and have our being" (Acts 17:28).[14]

The future of humanity lies not in a transhuman existence where everyone is a cyborg slave. Our future lies in a more spiritual existence where each is more independent not dependent, under self-control not outside control, where each is more connected to that *spiritual* source from which we arise and to which we will return. For we are indeed spiritual beings having a human experience. The future of humanity lies in understanding and living the truth that we are here to bring spirit into materiality. Without this understanding, humanity has no future.

Since the socialist ideas of Marx and his philosophical descendants are so clearly wrong and destructive, how have they come to dominate the world? It boils down to tactics. In chapter 3, we turn our attention to the tactics of communist subversion.

What You Can Do Now

1. Avoid postmodernism, Critical Theory, and all their insidious tentacles that reach into every part of our society. It is the philosophical root of our decay. It is a lie. Do not let anyone teach your children this nonsense or infect your business with it. Homeschool your children if that is the only way to avoid this philosophy of death.
2. Avoid universities if you can. Take university courses online and be choosy about your courses and professors. If you must go there, know that they are riddled with Marxist ideology.
3. Stop giving money to schools and universities that teach postmodernist lies and deny honesty and the rights of free speech and free thought. Only by stopping the flow of money can we stop this insanity in education.
4. Beware of transhumanism. You *are* a spirit. You *have* a body. Your body is the temple of God because the Spirit of God dwells within you. Do not defile it. Do not allow anyone to inject anything into your body that could be used to control you, modify you, or monitor you. Do not allow anything into your home that does this. Never step into a vehicle that can be controlled by someone outside that vehicle. Seek self-control. Avoid outside control.

CHAPTER 3

Communist Subversion

"Socialism is a philosophy of failure, the creed of ignorance, and the gospel of envy, its inherent virtue is the equal sharing of misery." –SIR WINSTON CHURCHILL

I came of age during the Cold War. When I started becoming aware of the world, it was in upheaval from the Vietnam War; the Arab-Israeli Wars; hippies (sex, drugs, and rock & roll); Palestinian terrorism; communist terrorists everywhere, including the United States (Black Panthers, Weather Underground, Red Brigades in Italy); communist revolutions in Nicaragua, El Salvador, and Chile; Soviet subversion and the arms race; inflation; the Arab oil embargo; and the rise of Arab wealth. The 70s were heady times. I was well aware of Soviet expansion of their ideology, their military and political power, and their subversive activities in the West. The current generation seems willfully blind to such things.

In this chapter, I explain the tactics of communist subversion. It is a proven method that communists have successfully used again and again to take over dozens of countries. You will recognize these tactics. You have seen all of them. This is based largely on the book *Love Letter to America*[1] by KGB defector Yuri Bezmenov. His book describes the standard operating procedure of the KGB in particular and of totalitarian subversion in general.

These methods form a pattern. They were used by the Bolsheviks, the Fascists, the Nazis, and later by the Soviets to topple dozens of governments. These methods have been constantly used against the Western democracies up to today. It is important to understand that this pattern of communist subversion is *not the pattern of anything else.* Just like the X-ray story, when you see this pattern playing out, you can be certain it is totalitarian subversion at work.

Subversion is an ancient tactic. The Chinese military strategist, Sun Tzu, wrote about it in the fifth century BC. "All warfare is based on deception."[2] That is a good aphorism to remember as we try to understand communist methods in their war against the free world. The strategy in this war is ideological subversion. It is the process of changing the perception of reality in the minds of millions of people all over the world. It's foolhardy to engage in a full-scale military attack against a well-armed and resolute enemy. Far better to subvert your enemy's will to resist–make him believe you are his liberator rather than his new tyrant. That's the goal of the totalitarian war against Western civilization.

We have a romanticized notion of espionage by watching too many James Bond movies. Yuri Bezmenov says the work of communist subversion is much more prosaic, even boring. "The main emphasis of the KGB is not in the area of intelligence at all. Only about 15 percent of time, money, and manpower is spent on espionage and such. The other 85 percent is a slow process which we call either ideological subversion or active measures...or psychological warfare."[3]

As an overview, here are Yuri Bezmenov's "instructions for communists," a summary of active measures.[4]

1. Corrupt the young, get them interested in sex. Take them away from religion. Make them superficial and enfeebled.
2. Divide the people into hostile groups by constantly harping on controversial issues of no importance.
3. Destroy people's faith in their national leaders by holding them up for contempt, ridicule, and disgrace.
4. Undermine the power of elected, legislative bodies by moving power

to the bureaucracy, lobby groups, NGOs, transnational or international organizations or agreements, "citizen's" groups, etc.
5. Always preach democracy but seize power as quickly and ruthlessly as possible.
6. By encouraging government extravagances, destroy its credit, produce years of inflation with rising prices and general discontent.
7. Incite unnecessary strikes in vital industries, encourage civil disorders, and foster a lenient attitude on the part of the government towards such disorders.
8. Cause breakdown of the old moral virtues: honesty, sobriety, self-restraint, faith in the pledged word.

Do you recognize any of this occurring in your lifetime?

The Four Stages of Subversion

Bezmenov describes four stages of communist subversion of a country. It is ongoing, particularly in the big prize—the Western democracies. For the sake of convenience, I will look at its operation within the United States of America.

These are the four stages of subverting a nation and installing a communist totalitarian regime, which overlap in time and occur concurrently up to the completion of the process.

1. Demoralization.
2. Destabilization.
3. Crisis.
4. Normalization.

Most of this is done by Americans to Americans, with the ideological and sometimes financial assistance of communist subverters. Bezmenov says, "Most of the actions are overt, legitimate, and easily identifiable. The only trouble is they are 'stretched in time.' In other words, the process of subversion is such a long-term process that an average individual, due to the short time span of his historical memory, is unable to perceive the process of subversion as a consistent and willful effort."[5]

Those who take part in their own subversion, wittingly or unwittingly, are "useful idiots." This is a technical term, not an insult. Useful idiots fail to see that they are pawns in the game that will destroy them, that they are misled to act in self-destructive ways, and that their perception has been altered so they think they are creating a better world when the opposite is true. Actions have consequences whether you understand the relationships or not. A key part of the subversion process is creating huge armies of useful idiots who do the work of subversion without perceiving it, and without correctly understanding the natural consequences of their actions.

The purpose of active measures is to change your perception of reality to such an extent that, despite ample evidence about the ideological subversion going on around you, you don't see it, and even if you do, you don't realize it's *planned subversion*. Thus, you are unable to come to sensible conclusions in your own interests and in the interests of your nation.

This subversion includes the process that psychologists call mass formation, or mass movement, or mass hypnosis. It has preceded every totalitarian takeover of the twentieth century. As we will see in chapter 4, the people affected act as if they are hypnotized—because they are. The people simply do not perceive what is happening. Just like hypnotized people, they have a different perception of reality; it has been distorted by an ideology. That's why I say you must perceive differently to see what is happening. Let's look at the techniques of subversion.

Stage 1: The Three Levels of Demoralization

The demoralization stage takes at least fifteen to twenty-five years, the time needed to educate one generation of students. The process has now been going on in the West for over fifty years. Our worldview, our understanding of reality, of how the world works, and our basic moral and ideological values, are set during adolescence. Recall that in chapter 2 I explained how our default worldview has become Marxist without our even noticing it.

The goal is to undermine the basic moral values and the foundational ideas of the American republic: limited government, free markets, individual liberty, and faith in God. Demoralization is irrevocable. This is key. Once you form the philosophy—the worldview—of a generation of people, they rarely change their thinking much and will spend the next forty years moving into positions of power and responsibility in their society. From here, their influence becomes ever greater. And they never realize they were manipulated. They think they formed their ideas on their own. This multigenerational demoralized cohort, beginning with the hippie generation of the 1960s known as Baby Boomers, now controls governments, media, entertainment, military, big business, schools, and universities. Even most religious organizations are shot full of Marxist philosophical thinking. It will take at least another generation of properly educated youth to change Western society back toward freedom. But when would such new education begin? And who could be found to teach it?

Bezmenov explains that the process of demoralization proceeds on three levels simultaneously:

- Level 1: The level of *ideas.*
- Level 2: The level of social and political *structures.*
- Level 3: The level of *life.*

Level 1: Ideas Rule the World

True ideas lead to healthy growth in an individual and in society. Untrue ideas are lies that set us on an unhealthy course. Marxist ideas are like a cancer that slowly infects our minds, obscures all healthy ideas, and sets us on a path of self-destruction. Beliefs are incredibly powerful. If you control people's beliefs, you control *them.* Here are some ways Marxists subvert our ideas and beliefs.

Undermine Religious Faith

The United States was founded on the Enlightenment ideas of individual liberty, religious tolerance, and free markets, buttressed by a firm belief in God. The Enlightenment thinkers were men of faith. Whether it's explicit or implicit, the whole idea of natural and inalienable rights and of the equality of people, depends on God. These properties are inherent in humans because we are created by God. Deny God, and we are only animals. Undermine religion, and you can turn people into monsters. It is no wonder that communist subversion aims firstly to subvert faith and morals.

State Education

Bezmenov warns us of the dangers implicit in massive state education: it promotes conformity and dulls individual initiative. The atmosphere of permissiveness and moral relativity in our schools has greatly facilitated Marxist ideological subversion. For several generations, curriculum and pedagogy have both been pushed toward the socialist agenda and philosophy described in chapter 2.

The No Longer "Free" Press

Bezmenov could see that our media was no longer free even in the 1980s. Today the evidence is overwhelming. The mainstream media is unreliable, and social media is censored and full of "bots." The media is the first and most important target of communist subversion.

The Rise of Nonissues

An incredibly important Marxist tactic is to blow a tiny problem into a huge one or create the appearance of a problem where none exists.

> Introduction of nonissues is another powerful method of demoralizing at the level of ideas...An issue, the solution of which creates more and bigger problems for [the] majority of a nation, even though it may benefit a few, is a nonissue... The main purpose of nonissues and the devastating result of their introduction is the side-tracking of public opinion, energy (both mental and physical), money and time from the constructive solutions.[6]

I have watched nonissues explode during my lifetime. Politicians thrive on them, and the mass media depends on them. All of the great frauds I will address in this book are nonissues. They divert attention away from real problems, and from the subversion and power grab that is behind them. They waste huge amounts of money, time, intelligence, and labor and cause massive malinvestment.

Debasing Popular Culture

The idea of debasing popular culture is to quietly assist any artist who is counter-cultural, anti-establishment, or degrades the moral fabric of society. These artists use simpler, increasingly sexual, words and ideas in songs, literature, and movies. Anything artistic that supports the insubordination of teenagers and glorifies their bad behavior, breaks down discipline, or encourages relaxing authority accomplishes the Marxists' goal of producing a generation of people who lack self-discipline, stamina, and high ideals.

> Yes, the KGB encourages the demoralization of America through the "mass culture" by relying upon the help of the "useful idiots" of the entertainment business. No, the Beatles, Punks and Michael Jackson are not on the KGB payroll. They are on your payroll. All the KGB had to do was to slowly and gradually change your attitudes and kill your resistance to the demoralizing addiction your kids call "music," make it acceptable, normal; make it a part of "American culture" where it does not belong and never did.[7]

As a musician, I am disgusted by the pornographic and psychologically deranged garbage that is sold today as "music." It's not simply that I'm old or that I'm a musical snob. Today's music is carefully crafted and subversive mind control exactly as Yuri Bezmenov described it.

What we call "popular culture" is a product of commercial manufacturing. Only a handful of big players decide who the next big pop star will be, what films we will watch next year, what clothes the artists will wear, how much profanity there will be, etc. Popular culture is largely directed by a small cadre of left-wing studio owners who may or may not realize they are following the Marxist script for undermining the very democracy that allows them to flaunt its traditional social mores.

Level 2: Social and Political Structures

Here are some of the ways communist subversion undermines the social and political fabric.

- Break down law and order.
- Treat criminals better than victims.
- Get people to distrust and hate the police and the justice system.
- Allow crime to flourish so people will feel unsafe and demand a stronger "police state."
- Promote rights over responsibilities.
- Encourage people to "get" from society without "giving" to it.
- Encourage licentiousness rather than liberty.
- Publicize every weakness of democracy but don't comment on the atrocities of totalitarian regimes.

Level 3: Demoralizing Life–Unhealthy Body and Mind

Bezmenov's "life" level includes such areas as family life, health, race relations, population control, and labor relations. Communist subverters, both external and internal, have pushed movements that weaken the nuclear family; degrade our health and turn "health" into a controllable industry; foment racial discord; push abortion, euthanasia, and all manner of population reduction schemes; and foster conflict in the workplace. All these things weaken Americans individually and weaken the nation as a whole. Yes, we have done it to ourselves, but it was also the definite plan of communist subversion, and leftists have strategically fostered these social developments.

Racial Inequality

An important part of communist subversion is to exaggerate every flaw in America and encourage self-flagellation while extolling mythic socialist improvements if only the state would bring in stronger laws. A natural target is racial inequality.

Inequality is a constant and natural condition of humanity. The Founding Fathers understood that we are equal as souls—equal in the eyes of God. We are clearly unequal as bodies and minds. When we learn to transcend body and mind and treat each other as souls, then we will come close to realizing equality and respect for all. But communism destroys all understanding of God, spirit, soul. There is far greater racial discrimination and inequality under totalitarianism than under democracy. Race is a nonissue that communists have used to turn us against ourselves. Today, it's called identity politics, but it's an old subversion tactic.

Private Ownership of Land

Private property is the foundation of both liberty and free enterprise. Totalitarianism removes all of these. History tells us that free, independent landowners are the staunchest patriots. People who own nothing have little to lose from revolution, and envy prods them on with the promise of something for nothing. Thus, an important target of subversion is land ownership. Private ownership and control of property are being undermined by sustainable development regulations and by the concentration of control in huge asset managers like BlackRock. Even when people still *own* property, they are losing *control* of that property.

Labor Relations

Union/management problems and strikes were prominent in the twentieth century, but less so now. Yuri Bezmenov and others have documented how communists infiltrated and subverted labor unions all over the world for a century. They even had the "International Trade Union School" in Moscow to which they invited union leaders from every country. It was an indoctrination center for world communism and an incubator for KGB agents who would infiltrate labor unions. The real motivation of the Soviets was subversion. The real motivation of union leaders was not the welfare of their members, but power.

What we see in this century is divisions among all employees. Nonissues, like race and sexual behaviour, and the fact that everything from food to medicine has become politicized, has turned people against each other within every workplace. It's not just union members against managers. Unions no longer even protect the rights of their members but are persecuting their own members instead. Every person is on their own. No more union "brothers and sisters". No more community or solidarity anywhere. It's the isolation of every individual–so the state and its minions (the corporations) can control everyone. That's totalitarianism.

Stage 2: Destabilization

At this stage, the subverter doesn't have to worry about the *ideas* that form people's worldview or the life of the society. These are already corrupted. Now, the goal is to subvert the *power structures* at every level. This includes not only all levels of government, but community organizations, religious organizations, professional associations–any and every "group" within the society.

Step one is to get people to vote into office politicians who promise something for nothing. Get governments to overspend, go into debt, expand "free" services, and make all governments bigger. Promise freedom without responsibility. The government will protect you from all real and imagined "risks": sickness (through better health care), poverty (free money, food, housing, education, daycare, pensions), terrorists (new security and paramilitary agencies), the climate, viruses, and fake news. Life is so risky that only the government can keep you safe; they just need tyrannical powers. But don't worry, they're doing all of it in your best interest. They know how to take care of you better than you do yourself.

Step two is to gradually move power away from elected legislatures and into the hands of unelected bodies–committees, boards, planning agencies, nongovernmental organizations, international and trans-national organizations, political action committees, advisory boards, trade associations, lobby groups, think tanks, and the government bureaucracy itself. The UN "smart cities" and "sustainable development" initiatives bypass the federal and state governments to create unelected regional bodies that are then staffed with carefully selected people who support the one-world government agenda.

The elected government cannot set its own course because its actions are constrained by UN treaties, trade deals, international regulations, and so on. When a real or imaginary crisis arises, Congress has a two-thousand-page bill to pass within days. Where did this come from so quickly? Just like an army has battle plans made up in advance for every conceivable event, the government bureaucracy has draft legislation ready to go at a moment's notice, along with hundreds of pages of unrelated pork-barreling and power-grabbing clauses that have been prepared for just such a crisis. Politicians never have time to even read all this legislation they vote on, much less understand it. Plus, every new law comes with "regulations under the act" that the bureaucracy can change at will. This gives bureaucrats effective law-making power.

Part of step two is to take control of all the "structures" in society: political parties, professional and educational associations, administrative and bureaucratic structures, community groups, religious communities, social clubs, artistic and literary organizations. For example, professional associations are turned away from helping and protecting their members to controlling them. Step out of line, and your license to practice will be taken away. Disagree with the profession's "narrative," and you won't get any contracts. Your books won't be published. You'll be fired from your job.

Controlling these structures is how communist subversion creates a creeping net of tyrannical control over a population. These are the "citizen's committees" of old communism. The names have changed. Their function is the same—implement the totalitarian program. The real power in nations devolves into an alliance of big government (mainly the civil service) with big business and big pressure groups (which have been subverted and controlled by big money). This is how our democracies have died—slowly strangled to death by creeping communist subversion.

Step three is to control information. Politicians and their media allies distort public expectations with the fantasy that the government can solve all their problems. They remove both the obligation and the ability of individuals to direct their own lives. They sap people's will to undertake the slow and tedious work of self-improvement. Your problems are caused by someone or something outside you, and Big Brother will solve your problems by forcing someone else to change. This is the false shortcut to solving social ills—socialism. It never works. It cannot.

Recently, we have also seen the rise of hidden groups of social media trolls (sometimes even secretly paid salaries to do this by "non-profit" front groups), digital "bots" that can instantly create a fire-storm of electronic complaints and pressure on a targeted issue or individual. These groups, both above and below ground, pressure elected politicians and take power away from elected bodies. This method is classic communist subversion. It is the modern version of Yuri Bezmenov secretly financing hundreds of small newspapers in India during the 1960s and 70s to spew communist rhetoric to unwitting readers. China's "fifty-cent army" is an example. Thousands of Chinese people are paid fifty cents for every social media post they make supporting the government or criticizing anyone who disagrees with the government. We have the same thing in the Western world. It appears there is a groundswell of support for the "official" propaganda when much of this is paid shills. Classic communist tactics. This is communist subversion on the level of *structures*—disabling elected politicians, turning organizations into tyrannical control structures, and controlling information.

Defense

The idea here is to weaken an army from within. Sow dissent, disorganization, and sap their will to fight—at every level. The current scandals in many free-world military organizations over such things as sexual abuse and the promotion of homosexuality are almost certainly part of subversion activities to weaken and destabilize Western armies. Communist influence is rampant throughout US business, government, universities, and even armies. It is everywhere. Only a naïve fool could believe this influence is benign.

Foreign Relations

The communist subversion goal here is to weaken the alliances of the target country. Disrupt their relations with friendly nations. Isolate the target country as much as possible. These are exactly the tactics of a schoolyard bully. Choose a target, isolate them from their friends who might stick up for them, and pick on their weaknesses. Everyone has seen this scenario play out in personal relations. The communists do the same thing on the level of nations.

Stage 3: Crisis

The crisis brings about a violent change in the power structure and the economy. It is a crucial part of the strategy of communist takeovers. As we will see in the next chapter, every successful takeover had its crisis. Rarely does a convenient crisis play directly into your hands at exactly the right moment. Usually, a crisis is manufactured, or at least given tremendous help. Everyone who has watched the "covid crisis" unfold since the beginning of 2020 should recognize the steps in this communist subversion "crisis". It is classic–and beautifully done.

"Never let a good crisis go to waste," means always use a crisis to take greater power and control into your own hands–or the hands of a small, unelected group that you control. Make sure you:

- Justify the suspension of citizens' rights.
- Control the media to spread propaganda through both overt and covert means. Silence opposition.
- Take greater control of all aspects of the economy (freedoms to work, travel, trade, buy and sell, etc.)
- Reduce private ownership.
- Make people more dependent upon the government.
- Take greater control of vital industries and increase government regulation everywhere.

- Hamstring everyone with red tape, useless rules, endless forms to fill out, etc.
- Expand the use of police, military, and private militias.
- Reward loyal supporters and redistribute wealth as the government sees fit.
- Never relinquish your emergency powers.

Part of the goal is to get ordinary Americans to welcome a strong leader who takes care of them and protects them from an enemy or threat, real or imagined. People will willingly give up their rights in exchange for the promise of safety and security–even though it is impossible to provide these. Leaders will take "emergency powers" to deal with the crisis, but these powers become permanent.

Stage 4: Normalization

Normalization is the process of making the new rules and laws universally accepted. It cements the new power structure. The "new normal" lasts indefinitely. It provides the quiet period for the government to consolidate its power and remove the most vocal opponents.

During and after the crisis, many people will object to what is happening and resist the changes. Everyone must be made to comply or be eliminated, and the perception of the population must be changed to expect this "new normal."

During this phase of normalization, right-wing "radicals" will be silenced, canceled, or taken out in quiet ways. They will be removed from their jobs, threatened, their businesses destroyed or disallowed, their reputations disgraced through propaganda. The truly incalcitrant can be rounded up by police and coerced or "re-educated" as necessary.

Once the dissenters are eliminated, the population is subdued, and totalitarian control is the new normal, then the removal of the useful idiots begins. All those socialist reformers who aided the destruction of democracy are no longer needed. They know too much. They're no longer useful–they're dangerous. The same "cancel" tactics can be used against them, one at a time. Or now that a police state exists, they can simply be picked up in the night and no one will know what happened to them. State control will be complete, and you will live in a communist paradise–if you're still alive.

This is communist subversion, and it has happened throughout the "free" world. This is the long, slow, almost imperceptible movement from democracy to totalitarianism–from freedom to slavery. We have been quietly led through demoralization, destabilization, crisis, and into normalization with hardly anyone noticing what was happening–in fraud after fraud for my whole life. Those few astute and intrepid souls who tried to awaken the rest of us were ridiculed, derided, ignored, deplatformed, bankrupted, or canceled. Some were murdered. Such is the fate of prophets.

How to Resist Communist Subversion–Parallel Structures

The most important thing is to stay grounded in what is real and what is true. You are a spiritual being having a human experience. Everything you can do to ground yourself in the reality of your spiritual existence, however you conceive that to be, is essential.

The way to defeat a totalitarian government that exercises control over every political, economic, and social structure is to create new "parallel structures." This technique was developed by Vaclav Havel and others in Czechoslovakia to topple the communist regime there.[8] Havel agreed with Solzhenitsyn that the communist system was fundamentally a web of lies. Like him, Havel's underlying advice was to not acquiesce to the lies but to "live within the truth." Speak the truth at your place of work, even if you are censured or fired. Do not allow lies to go unchallenged. Others may attack you, but they will also realize that escape from the official propaganda narrative is possible, and that sane, rational people do this. Even if it frightens them, it will give them hope.

Start to form alternative venues for social and economic discourse. Begin in small ways. Get together with one or two other people and have honest conversations. Share your real culture in any way you want, not the official fake culture. Sing songs, tell stories, share banned books. Join with others in your town or city who desire honest conversation and honest culture. This is culture outside the official channels. It is a parallel structure of society.

Establish channels of communication outside the official channels. With the internet and the explosion of new platforms, this is easy. You can find like-minded people all over the world in a few minutes. It was much harder in the Czechoslovakia of 1970. Start to form groups of like-minded people in your local area and online. As individuals, we are vulnerable. As a community, we are strong.

You can teach your children at home, real education, rather than sending them to government schools where education is often substandard, spiritually perverse, and filled with ideological nonsense. You can even begin to establish post-secondary educational forums outside the official structures. Some former university professors are doing just this.

Seek out suppliers of essential commodities in your local community–farmers if you can, tradesmen, professionals. Buy your food as locally as you can and grow some of your own. Find a doctor or nurse you can turn to for honest medical care outside the official system. Develop relationships with these people. Find people who will accept cash, cryptocurrencies, or barter. In human history, barter has been ubiquitous, and rarely has there been only one type of money. Money is about to change, and we will need flexibility. This is what communities used to be, and can be again.

We may even need a "parallel polis," or separate government structure. As the totalitarian web closes in around us, it will be increasingly difficult to exist outside the official system. Begin building new structures now. Some people will want to escape the cities and form self-sufficient rural communities that are largely self-governing. We will need to completely restructure Western societies if we are to return to democracy. Our former democracies have become functional dictatorships, as we will see more fully in subsequent chapters. We must begin democracy again, and democracy begins in the community. Today, a community may not even need to be geographical.

Instead of the "top-down" governmental structures we have today, we must rebuild democracy from the bottom up. The basic unit of democracy is the sovereign individual. The basic unit of government is the sovereign community or municipality. We can follow the traditional structure of Switzerland where the canton, or municipality, is the main level of government. From there, municipalities may voluntarily join into provinces or states, and these into nations. And they may voluntarily leave these if they wish. The nation must exist at the pleasure of the municipalities, not the other way around. Perhaps such a structure will allow us to avoid the tyranny that springs naturally from the concentration of power.

The time may come when existing municipalities are ready to take this power back and declare themselves semi-autonomous sanctuary cities, free from the tyrannical control of their state or national governments. You cannot wait for this to happen, however. Individual sovereignty means individual responsibility. Take care of yourself and help others in your community. Everything begins there.

The main goal of the parallel structures is not to force the existing structures to change but to build something completely new and outside the existing structures. The existing power structures are likely to both adapt to and suppress the new ideas. The very existence of any community "living within the truth" will pose an existential threat to the totalitarian structure, which must impose a monolithic fantasy of lies and compel everyone to exist within its web.

This is the four-stage pattern of totalitarian subversion. Whenever you see this pattern, it is subversion. It's all about pattern recognition.

What You Can Do Now

1. Communist subversion is real. Totalitarians of every stripe are actively subverting the United States and the whole world. It has been happening for over a century. We are at war. The first step is to realize that.
2. This is fundamentally a spiritual war, and our first defense is a spiritual defense. Remember that communism must destroy God, as Solzhenitsyn said. Ground yourself in the knowledge of spiritual reality in whatever way you perceive it.
3. Understand that if we lose this war with totalitarianism, we will be communist slaves. Be prepared to die on this hill—because it's the *last hill.*
4. Resist this subversion by holding fast to your culture, your religious faith, your family values, your democratic institutions, and most importantly, to truth. Live not by lies.
5. Build parallel structures. Join or build a group of like-minded people to support each other in every way.

CHAPTER 4

Historical Examples of Socialist Revolutions

"The most profound analysts of the totalitarian societies of the twentieth century... come to the same conclusion. The totalitarian states would not have been possible without the moral corruption of the individuals within that society." –JORDAN PETERSON

Jordan Peterson astutely observes the outstanding characteristic and the initiating requirement of totalitarianism–dehumanization. Let's review the major socialist takeovers of the twentieth century with an eye to the pattern of totalitarian subversion. Every society, every time and place, has its own unique qualities, personalities, and social institutions. These affect how the subversion plays out, but the main elements are always the same.

Lenin and the Bolsheviks—1917

"One death is a tragedy. A million deaths is a statistic." –JOSEPH STALIN

As industrialization came later to Russia, its economic and social dislocations peaked in the early twentieth century, a half century later than

Western Europe. Popular discontent, demonstrations, and local revolts were common in the early years of the century. Added to this was the constant agitation and terrorism of socialist groups, who carried out thousands of assassinations, used robbery to raise money, and terrorism to manipulate people.

Russian pride smarted from their loss to the Eastern upstart in the Russo-Japanese War of 1904–05, which added another log to the fire of social unrest. Interestingly, the thousands of Russian prisoners of war received Marxist propaganda literature and instruction during their Japanese captivity, furnished both by the Japanese government eager to undermine their enemy and by American socialists eager to spread their fanciful ideas. They returned to Russia as a radicalized group within the Russian military.

In 1905, a crowd of civilians tried to present a petition to the czar. The army opened fire on them, and hundreds were killed—an event known as Bloody Sunday. A general uprising followed, called the 1905 Revolution. In response, the czar agreed to create a freely elected Duma (parliament) and to cede to it some of his own monarchical rights. It was a first step toward democracy, but in subsequent years, the vacillating czar proved unwilling to give up any real power, and the Duma was wracked by dissenting opinions and parties that could never come to unified action.

Lenin

Vladimir Lenin was a member of the Marxist-inspired Social Democratic Labour Party. But at the 1903 party congress in London, he forced a split in the party. Lenin led a small group, named the Bolsheviks, to form a separate party because he believed they should restrict themselves to professional revolutionaries and violently overthrow the government. Most of the party, the Mensheviks, favored a broad-based membership and gradual change.

Exiled for his part in the 1905 Revolution, Lenin spent much of the years 1905–17 writing propaganda, planning, raising support in the West, and organizing his cadre of "professional revolutionaries." The socialists and communists in Russia had plenty of financial and publicity support from socialist intellectuals in the West, less so from labor groups. The Fabians in England and wealthy individuals in Britain, the USA, Germany, and France contributed huge sums to support leftist organizations.

In the decades leading up to the revolution, propaganda played a pivotal role in the spread of socialist ideas in Russia and the eventual success of the Bolsheviks. The universities were a breeding ground for socialists. The professors, the Russian intelligentsia, and the press were almost exclusively socialist. The Russian state had oppressed the Jews for decades, typical of nineteenth-century Europe. This oppression was supported by public opinion. In the socialist press, the Jews presented themselves as oppressed. It bred a victim consciousness that played into the communist tune.

Bolshevik propaganda was the key to their ultimate victory. Lenin started a national newspaper, but his ideas were not well accepted by the common people. Lenin complained that they preferred to support trade unions because unions actually did things to improve the lives of workers rather than to support the Bolshevik idea of destroying the whole social order.

The Bolsheviks tried to monopolize the conversation, disrupting the production and distribution of other parties' propaganda. They distributed their own paper right at factory gates to get it into the hands of workers before their competitors did. Lenin's writing was simple and direct. He didn't need research or facts because the truth didn't matter. Everything was presented through the lens of Marxist ideology to foment hatred toward the existing government, the aristocracy, and the Bolsheviks' revolutionary competitors. The idea was to overwhelm the largely illiterate population with Marxist ideas. They targeted factory workers, students, peasants, and soldiers, whom Lenin effectively proselytized during WWI.

The two main thrusts of the Bolsheviks' tactics were spreading propaganda and organizing local groups. This "political work" included activities such as organizing peasant revolts and stirring up discontent. An important part of the propaganda, particularly directed at soldiers and sailors, was to undermine their allegiance to the czar and the Russian state. They worked to separate the idea of "Mother Russia" from the existing government.

So far, we have seen steps one and two of communist subversion—demoralization of society and destabilization of social structures. Next comes the crisis.

1917—Events Come to a Head

Almost 85 percent of Russia's population was rural at this time. There were only two large cities—St. Petersburg (renamed Petrograd at the start of WWI) with about 2 million people, and Moscow with about 1.5 million. Most of the key activity occurred in Petrograd.

Events rapidly came to a head during 1917. Russia was losing badly in WWI, and the war was unpopular. The morale of the troops was low, desertions commonplace. Food shortages were everywhere and the government rationed food, which led to panic buying. In January, over a hundred thousand workers went on strike to commemorate the anniversary of Bloody Sunday. The strike continued into February, fueled by socialist agitators, and there were violent clashes between protestors and police. The czar ordered troops to fire on unruly protestors, and dozens were killed. Yet two garrisons of soldiers in Petrograd chose to shoot their officers rather than civilians. The military was divided.

Amid the chaos, and under pressure, the czar abdicated. The Duma then formed a provisional government led by moderates under Alexander Kerensky. The Provisional Government issued a set of liberal principles by which it intended to govern. These principles included improvements to civil rights and freedoms, amnesties for political prisoners, and elections for a constituent assembly. In the spring of 1917, it looked like Russia was headed for democracy.

Kerensky's unpopular decision to continue the war provoked demonstrations. Under pressure from the socialists, he also disbanded the secret police and the Russian Gendarmerie, which was the only national police force. These two security forces were the principal means the government had to control crime and terrorism. With the police forces gutted, the general amnesty proved a disaster. Almost one hundred thousand political prisoners, mostly radical revolutionaries, were released from Russian prisons, and even more returned from exile abroad.

One of these was Lenin, who returned with millions of dollars in Western aid. He rapidly organized local Bolshevik groups in factories and communities, inundated the country with propaganda, and formed a private militia–the Red Guards. There were plenty of former soldiers around who had no love for their government, which had left them to be slaughtered by the far superior German army. Even though the Bolsheviks were a small party in the Duma, they constantly ridiculed the government and worked to undermine its effectiveness–following the "rule or ruin" socialist tactic.

As summer progressed, the political climate heated up. The Russian army offensive suffered massive losses against the Germans, a revolt of workers and soldiers in Petrograd was put down by government troops, strikes escalated, and allegiances within the army were split. In October of 1917, the Bolsheviks staged a coup in Petrograd. They had arranged the support of some sailors and soldiers and convinced most of the army not to interfere. In a matter of hours, the Red Guards had taken control of the key government and administrative centers in Petrograd, and Lenin declared the Bolsheviks in control of the government. Within a week of bitter fighting, the Red Guards had also taken control of Moscow.

Even though the Bolsheviks were a small political party with limited public support and were massively opposed by Russian officials, they managed to grab political power. With a big push from socialist revolutionaries, Russia had progressed through the stages of demoralization, destabilization, to the crisis, and the power grab. Now it was time for "normalization."

I won't dwell on the lengthy process of securing and consolidating that power, which involved a bitter, three-year civil war. But I will note that the Bolsheviks killed almost all the elected members of the Duma, the Mensheviks, and the Social Revolutionaries. Their former socialist allies immediately became enemies. They were the first communist "useful idiots" and died quickly.

Help from the West

In case you thought the Bolshevik Revolution was over by the end of October 1917, it was just beginning. Western governments and businessmen helped them win. Journalist Jean Chen summarized the earlier findings of Dr. Antony C. Sutton.

> They [Lenin and Trotsky] created a revolution with no more than about 10,000 revolutionaries. They needed assistance from the West, and they got assistance from Germany, from Britain, and from the United States...In 1918, the Bolsheviks really only controlled Moscow and what was Petrograd which is now Leningrad. They could not have beaten off the White Russians, the Czechs who were in Russia at that time, the Japanese who entered. They could not have beaten it off without assistance from the United States and from Britain.
>
> After the revolution...they [the Bolsheviks] could not operate the plants. So what do we do? With Averell Harriman and the Chase National Bank and all friends on Wall Street, they go in there...We have these 250–300 concessions with which American companies went into Russia, and they started up the idle plants.... All these top capitalists went in and they got Russia going on behalf of the Bolsheviks, because the Bolsheviks either shot or kicked out all the people out of Russia who would run the plants.[1]

This is a common theme for communist regimes. Left on their own, they collapse rather quickly. But the "free" world usually helps them to stay alive, stay in power, keep murdering their own people, and exporting their evil. We are still doing it.

Mussolini and the Fascists—1922

"Thanks to ideology, the twentieth century was fated to experience evildoing calculated on a scale in the millions." –ALEKSANDR SOLZHENITSYN

Mussolini: Malevolent Opportunist of Chaos

Italy had only become a unified nation in the mid-nineteenth century, similar to Germany, but in this case as a parliamentary monarchy. It was late in industrializing, like Russia. Universal suffrage for men only began in 1912. In the general election of 1913, a coalition of centrist parties called the Liberal Union, under the leadership of Giovanni Giolitti, won a majority of seats in parliament and governed Italy until after WWI.

Benito Mussolini (1883–1945) was the son of a socialist blacksmith. Young Benito followed in his father's footsteps as an atheistic socialist opposed to authority–a common characteristic in revolutionaries. He was a violent youth, being expelled from his boarding school at age ten for stabbing a fellow student in the hand, later stabbing another student and his girlfriend, and leading gangs to raid local farms.[2] This youthful violent behavior is a classic symptom of a psychopath.

He became a journalist and spent the early 1900s traveling around Switzerland, getting involved with its socialist party, and giving speeches praising Marx and preaching violent revolution. He clashed often and violently with the police and was eventually expelled from the country.

He returned to Italy in 1904 and became editor of *Avanti*, the newspaper of the Italian Socialist Party. This gave him both a mouthpiece for self-promotion and the chance to hone his propaganda skills. He helped build the party to prominence as a coalition of left-wing factions.

Always a violent person, Mussolini happily joined the army during WWI. He seemed to relish battle and later bragged about his many scars. When he was wounded in 1917 and discharged from the army, he returned to journalism, again preaching the violent overthrow of the government.

From Propaganda to Power–1919 to 1925

In 1919, Mussolini revived and reformed an earlier party into the *Fasci Italiani di Combattimento*–the fascist party. The *fasces* refers to the bundle of sticks around a battle ax, which was a symbol of power and authority in ancient Rome. The sticks tied together are strong, whereas the individual sticks are weak. The symbol roughly means, "we are strong together." The party appealed to farmers, factory workers, and former soldiers–who made excellent recruits to Mussolini's private militia, the black shirts.

Mussolini worked out his political ideology on the fly, a popularity-seeking mix of nationalist, anti-liberal, anti-Marxist, and anti-democratic rhetoric–a strange and opportunistic collection of totalitarian ideas. Its only real positive value was nationalism, appealing to Italians' national pride and vainglory. Such vague appeals to "national glory" and "duty" were a common feature of the interwar militarism throughout the world. Mussolini was mainly about being "against" things. He was a "Critical Theorist" before Critical Theory.

The Fascists unsuccessfully ran candidates in the 1919 election. This was the first Italian election to use the system of proportional representation, where parties get seats in parliament proportional to their share of the popular vote. This system favors a splintering of parties and ideologies over any need for unity and compromise at the party level, and it encourages the representation of extreme views.

The Liberal Union had held a majority in parliament since the election of 1913, but in 1919, the political landscape was very different. The Liberal Union had largely fallen apart, and new political parties formed. Twelve parties received seats, but the Fascist Party was not among them. With no party having a majority of the seats in parliament, various parties had to join together in a coalition government. This was accomplished, but the ideologically divided and fragile coalition didn't hold together for long, and another election was held less than two years later.

For the 1921 election, the former leader of the Liberal Union, Giovanni Giolitti, tried desperately to cobble together a coalition party that could win a majority. This had been his special political talent in the years before the war when he was able to guide the Liberal Union to successful majority governments. But with proportional voting, this is almost impossible.

In the intervening two years, Mussolini had built the Fascist Party's power and influence through a combination of massive propaganda, local organizing, and brutal violence and intimidation by his black shirts. With his flexible ideology, he managed to win the support of workers in the cities and large landowners in the countryside. His growing political power could not be ignored, particularly since he was the cause of most of the violence in the county. Many political parties had private militias, and they often battled each other. Mussolini declared that only he could restore order and peace—a typical "savior" claim by a tyrant. From 1919 to 1922, the police and army did little to stop the private militias and violence. Fascist squads roamed the country, causing property damage and murdering two thousand political opponents. The people were terrorized.

Giolitti made a calculated maneuver by bringing Mussolini into his new coalition party, the National Blocs, in hopes of stemming the violence and bringing order to the country. In the 1921 election, the National Blocs did well, gaining 105 seats, but still only in third place. Giolitti once again put together a coalition government of six parties holding a total of 363 seats in the 535-seat parliament. Of these, Mussolini's Fascist Party held only 33. But he had the most powerful militia and did everything possible to undermine the effectiveness of his own coalition party leadership and to spread instability everywhere. Rule or ruin.

If at any point the government had used the police or the army to disband the private militias, history would have turned out much differently. But they didn't. Mussolini increased the size and activities of the black shirts, bringing near chaos to the nation. They burned down offices of many competing communist and socialist political parties and violently seized local power in several cities. The majority of moderate politicians were too busy bickering among themselves to offer any unified resistance to the growing violence, terror, and power of the fascists.[3] For twenty years, Mussolini had worked to demoralize Italy. He had largely destabilized the power structures and social structures and created the crisis that he would now exploit.

In October of 1922, Mussolini threatened to march on Rome and seize power if it was not given to him. The government was slow to react. By the time they started to mobilize the army, Mussolini was marching on Rome with thousands of his armed militia, who occupied government offices and communications centers. The king dissolved the government and asked Mussolini to form a new one. With only 6 percent of the seats in parliament, Mussolini had bullied himself into the top political job in the country—excellent manipulation of a "crisis." Now for normalization.

Mussolini's first government was democratic, and he knew his position was weak. He quickly moved to secure his power and to dismantle all democratic institutions—that is, to manipulate the crisis and normalize dictatorship. He demanded special "emergency" powers (always beware emergency powers) that gave him the ability to rig election results, which he used two years later to gain an electoral majority. The Italian parliament made suspicion of being anti-fascist punishable by imprisonment without trial. Naturally, Mussolini moved first against other left-wing organizations. Socialist members of parliament were expelled, and communist members were arrested. The police rounded up socialists and prohibited their publishing activities. Anyone who could not be prosecuted for a crime was detained for five years and placed in internment camps.

Mussolini controlled the media and gradually tightened his control over every profession, trade, and social organization. Even the Boy Scouts were replaced by his fascist youth organization. By 1925, he felt secure enough to announce publicly that he was dictator of Italy.

Mussolini's ideology was never clear during his lifetime nor after it. Today, fascism is universally placed on the right of the political spectrum, which is absurd. Mussolini was a cradle socialist and atheist and never lost that orientation. He knew perfectly well that his ideology was left wing. In 1932 he published *The Political and Social Doctrine of Fascism*.[4] It was mostly ghost-written and mostly rambling nonsense, but a few clear ideas come through. "This will be a century of authority, a century of the Left, a century of Fascism....The century of collectivism, and hence the century of the State."[5]

This is pure Marxism. He even goes beyond Marx in imagining the State as a living being unto itself, the moral and spiritual embodiment of the national character. Here is a taste: "The foundation of Fascism is the conception of the State, its character, its duty, and its aim. Fascism conceives of the State as an absolute, in comparison with which all individuals or groups are relative, only to be conceived of in their relation to the state."[6]

But Mussolini did have at least one lucid moment when he gave a succinct, and likely the most accurate, assessment of his ideology. In October 1922 he said, "Our program is simple: we want to rule Italy."[7] That is, like all totalitarians, it's about power. Nothing else matters much.

Hitler and the Nazis—1932

> *"Nazism conquered Germany because it never encountered any adequate intellectual resistance."* –LUDWIG VON MISES

The Nazi Party started in 1919 as the German Workers Party amidst the chaos after Germany's loss in WWI. The founders had antisemitic and anti-communist beliefs. Hitler joined the party in late 1919. His fiery speeches were popular and motivated people to join, which quickly pushed him into the inner circle of the small party. He was elected leader in July 1921.

From the beginning, the party had a paramilitary wing–that is, a private militia. Many political parties in Europe had these militias. These were both a result of, and an aggravating cause of, the social upheaval of the period. An essential feature of government is the monopoly on violence, but national governments were either unable or unwilling to stop these petty warlords.

Hitler focused on antisemitic and German expansionist policies–scapegoating and glory seeking–which appeals to people's willingness to blame others and aggrandize themselves. In November 1923, they attempted a coup on the government of Bavaria. The idea was to first take this state, then take over all of Germany. The coup failed, and Hitler was jailed for eight months of his five-year sentence. During this time, he wrote *Mein Kampf,* his rambling mixture of autobiography and plan for world domination.

Afterward, Hitler focused on building the party by setting up local organizations throughout Germany and infiltrating the "structures" of society. The Nazis did their best to get party members elected to local and state governments and moved into positions of power and influence throughout German society–professional associations, trade and business groups, and so on. They also took an increasingly visible role in national elections. The militia, the SA called "brown shirts" because of their brown uniforms, were constantly strengthened and used for intimidation, protection at party rallies, and battling other party's militias. Hitler started a second militia, the SS (Schutzstaffel, "Protection Squadron"), as his personal bodyguard, later turned into an elite military unit.

The propaganda, of course, was relentless. Around 1930, Joseph Goebbels was appointed propaganda chief, and he proved to be a master. His efforts to gain public support by blaming everyone else (Jews, communists, the Western Allies, etc.) for Germany's economic problems started to really pay off. In the 1930 elections, the Nazis achieved 18 percent of the popular vote, the second-largest party in the parliament.

Their tools of propaganda were crude by today's standards. Newspapers, leaflets, and posters were quite effective. Public events where Hitler would speak were very successful. His impassioned oratory motivated many, and he perfected his technique of blaming Jews and bankers while praising the noble, hardworking Germans. Goebbels also had great success organizing riotous demonstrations to demand various specific actions by the authorities. Intimidation and carefully targeted violence, even murder, were effective tools for the Nazis in their rise to power.

In 1932 and early 1933, there was a flurry of political activity–including four elections in the space of one year. The communist party supported the Nazis at key moments, a foolish tactic. The Nazi Party never achieved a majority in any election, but they did receive the largest number of votes, leading eventually to Hitler becoming chancellor, the head of the government. Once he had this powerful position, Nazi agents burnt down the parliament building, and Hitler blamed the communists. After accusing several prominent communists, Hitler raided the party offices and arrested its officials, thus incapacitating the party during the next election.

In response to the crisis of the fire, Hitler was able to pass emergency legislation called the "Decree for the Protection of the People and the State," a patriotic-sounding law that relieved the German people of almost all their civil liberties. Sound familiar? It was eerily similar to the *Patriot Act* passed in the United States in 2001–civil rights were denied, greater powers for the government, and a larger police presence. Next, passed due to the "emergency," the *Enabling Act* allowed Hitler's cabinet to pass laws without the parliament. Parliament continued to meet in an opera house, but it was now nothing but theater. Once Hitler could make laws without parliament, he was dictator. Technically, it was the cabinet that made the laws, but since Hitler appointed the members of the cabinet, he had total power.

He had cannily negotiated, intimidated, and duped other politicians and voters. Democracy was over. He then set about to completely destroy his opposition, starting with the communists, who were rounded up and disappeared. He also tightened the noose of state propaganda and control over every aspect of life. "Normalization" began.

Propaganda Perfection

The Nazis are often credited with turning the art of propaganda into a science. Goebbels summarized his techniques in a famous list that was found among his papers after the war. Here I have taken the basic ideas and expressed them in a manner fitting the digital age.[8] These techniques are precisely what came to be called psychological warfare. It is everywhere in our world today.

1. ***Simplification and a Unique Enemy:*** Create a simple, unique brand identity. Do the same for your main enemy. Make it easy to understand–reduce complexities.
2. ***Unified Force:*** Have clearly defined objectives and fight hard against

your single enemy. Collect all enemies into a single identity for easy assault. Label everyone who opposes you as a fascist, racist, homophobe, science denier, anti-vaxxer, etc.

3. ***Deflection:*** Charge your enemies with errors, defects, and faults. Blame someone else. Deflect all attacks on yourself or your narrative onto your enemies. Attack their credibility, replace their facts with your "facts." Truth is irrelevant.
4. ***Exaggeration:*** A big lie is easier to sell than a small lie. Inflate any anecdote or fact to create fear in people so you can manipulate them. Then propose your solution as the only reasonable option.
5. ***Vulgarization:*** Everything must be presented in simple language and ideas, directed to the least intelligent and educated person. Avoid all complexity, nuance, subtlety, and technicality. Appeal to emotion, not intellect. Use slogans, not analysis. Social media helps this tremendously because it is impossible to communicate complex ideas in a tweet.
6. ***Repetition:*** A lie repeated often enough becomes the truth. The same narrative must be repeated over and over on TV, radio, and social media. If people hear it often enough, they will stop questioning it. Be the first to present your narrative and overwhelm all opposition with the volume of your propaganda.
7. ***Reinforcement:*** Your message must be constantly renewed and updated–the same message in a slightly different format. Bombard people with new images and information that reinforce the message. This must be daily–hourly is better.
8. ***Many Voices:*** Transmit your message through many different people and media, from many different perspectives: TV, radio, social media, newspaper, movies, popular music, art, theater, etc. Every message comes to the same conclusion, supporting your narrative. "Everyone is thinking this, so it must be true."
9. ***Silencing:*** Censor all narratives other than your own. If someone cannot be removed, discredit them. Isolate dissenters as idiots, threats to society, conspiracy theorists, Big Oil apologists, climate deniers, racists, etc.

10. ***Association:*** Exploit people by attaching your message to their existing beliefs, biases, and feelings. For example, "All compassionate people will agree with me. Only selfish people (or fascists, racists, etc.) will disagree with me." Associate your message with qualities people associate with themselves so they will identify with your narrative. Use existing terms and movements. Thus, we see terms like social justice, equality, and inclusion taken over and associated with *our* narrative. We tar our opponents by associating them with terms like racist, bigot, sexist, etc.
11. ***Unanimity:*** Create the impression that everyone agrees with your narrative. "95 percent of scientists agree." "The American Medical Association agrees." Therefore, only a fool would disagree.

You must have noticed that all public discussion today follows this pattern of propaganda. That's scary enough. But these tools are as crude as flint arrowheads compared to modern totalitarian tactics. A half century of mind control research by the CIA has developed methods to control you that are so sophisticated they seem impossible, as we will see in chapter 9.

Hitler's path to power followed a similar pattern to Lenin's, Mussolini's, and a hundred others in the twentieth century. That pattern was codified by the KGB and is being used on us today. Once you know the *pattern*, you can understand what's happening. It's all about pattern recognition. The basic ideas of socialism are the same in every case.

Living in Austria, economist and historian Ludwig von Mises had a ringside seat to the rise of the totalitarian regimes in the interwar period. His book *Omnipotent Government: The Rise of Total State and Total War* explains the basic ideas these dictators used to sell their programs:[9]

1. Capitalism is an unfair system of exploitation.
2. It is therefore the foremost duty of popular government to substitute government control of business for the management of capitalists and entrepreneurs.
3. Easy money policy (credit expansion) is a useful method of lightening the burdens imposed by capital upon the masses and making a country more prosperous.

The socialist ideas that Lenin, Mussolini, and Hitler sold to their people are the same ideas that political demagogues are selling us today—someone or something else is a threat to you and you need to give the government greater power to protect you; there are "bad guys" (racists, homophobes, anti-vaxxers, etc.) and we must punish them; the government will make everything better. Most people have already accepted these ideas. All these dictators trash talked capitalism just like Klaus Schwab of the World Economic Forum is doing today. He says capitalism has failed and we need new "metrics," which is sophistry for "new control mechanisms" so the WEF can control all business. If we are to avoid the greatest totalitarian takeover in history, we must come up with, as von Mises says, "adequate intellectual resistance."

Other Aspects of Socialist Revolutions

"The solemn pledge to abstain from telling the truth was called socialist realism." –ALEKSANDR I. SOLZHENITSYN

We cannot look at all aspects of socialism in this book, but there are two crucial ideas you must understand. The first is that our whole concept of the political spectrum is completely skewed, bizarrely meaningless, and is the root of many of the divisions in our society. The second is to realize the importance of the group psychological phenomenon known as mass formation, which is essential to totalitarian takeovers.

The Bizarre Political Spectrum

Something puzzled me my whole life. How did Nazism end up on the right wing of the political spectrum? The whole concept of Left and Right is confusing and corrupted. There are at least a dozen theories about the political spectrum, even complicated multidimensional diagrams. This is nonsense.

We were taught in school that communism is on the extreme left, socialism on the left, liberalism in the middle, then conservatism on the right, and fascism and Nazism on the extreme right. That is to say, craziness on the extremes and reasonableness in the middle. It's a circle. If you go far enough to the extreme left, you come to the extreme right. The only safe and reasonable place is in the middle. Rubbish!

As you know, Nazism is the political movement led by Adolf Hitler. The word "Nazi" is an acronym. Its English translation means the "Nationalist Socialist Worker's Party." Hitler knew perfectly well that he was a socialist. He named his party correctly. In the 1930s, Hitler was known mostly, and particularly in Germany itself, for his economic policies. These were socialist and nationalist, as Ludwig von Mises pointed out.

Fascism is simply Mussolini's Italian version of socialism. I have already shown his ideologically vacuous but essentially socialist beliefs. So, Nazism and fascism, both being socialist ideologies, are left-wing, as is socialism itself. The common reference to "right-wing Nazi extremists" is ridiculous. They are left-wing extremists–no doubt about it.

The political spectrum is simply a continuum of personal freedom, individual responsibility, and private ownership. As you move to the left, you get less of these. As you move to the right, you get more of them. At the extreme left of the spectrum, you have communism. The government owns all the property and tells you everything you must do and cannot do. Everything that isn't prohibited is compulsory. The state determines what will be produced, by whom, at what price, in what quantities, and who will get it. They determine what jobs will be done by every person, what they will be paid for their work, and where they will live. The state even defines reality itself. The state is everything. The individual is nothing. And religion does not exist. All of this is enforced with violence. The more things the government has to control, the more force it uses. History tells us that in a large communist country, you can expect millions or tens of millions of people to be murdered by the government every decade. In China, of course, this is still going on.

The various brands of socialism, including technocracy, come next. They generally allow a large amount of private ownership, mixed in with state ownership of "important" industries, but they control pretty much all economic activity through regulation and a huge army of government employees to check on everything. What's important is power and money–politics and economics. The various brands of socialism mix and match a motley assortment of unrelated policies, philosophies, and fetishes. Socialism is an ideological bonbon of a thousand flavors.

The spectrum gradually drifts through the middle where thousands of economists, philosophers, politicians, and social reformers debate how much government interference in the lives and business of citizens is "optimal." Most of the free world has resided in the middle during my lifetime and constantly drifted to the left–so much so that the "liberal" parties of today are exactly the socialist parties of yesterday.

Conservatives occupy the middle of the political spectrum today. There are basically no far right-wing groups. Neo-Nazis and white supremacists, tiny in number today, are left-wing. They want to restrict personal freedom and liberty and impose their ideas on others. That puts them on the left wing. Neo-Nazi is still Nazi. It is socialist. "Anti-fascist" Antifa is a far-left private militia and indistinguishable from Mussolini's fascist Black Shirts. They even wear the same uniform.

The true extreme right-wing is occupied by libertarians, of which I know only one. Of course, there are more. There are also many confused "libertarians" and many who are really socialists in libertarian's clothes. The very nature of libertarians is to seek extreme individual liberty for themselves and for everyone. They will allow you to do whatever you want as long as you don't use coercion, fraud, or force to restrict the freedom of others. Libertarians do not form organizations to force others to change. Libertarians do not engage in violence. Libertarians don't seek power. They seek to be left alone to live their lives. All the violence and coercion happens on the left wing. It is *exactly* a left-wing idea to use the power of the state or quasi-state to coerce individuals to conform to the state's concept of behavior. The right wing is laissez-faire–live and let live.

The natural antipathy between one left-wing group and all the others leads them to hate other socialists with an even greater passion than they hate conservatives. Since their goal is power, and other leftists seek the same power, they are natural enemies.

Before we leave the chapters on ideology, it's important to notice something about ideology and business. Many Western businessmen supported the Bolsheviks, the Nazis, and the Fascists. At their heart, the ultra-rich are neither left-wing nor right-wing in the traditional sense. They care about power and money—politics is just a means to that end. They get along fine with socialists, fascists, and all manner of dictators. Big business has always happily jumped into bed with dictators if they can get the inside scoop on business deals and government protection for their operations. This is better described as mercantilism—a blending of power and wealth in an aristocracy of rulers and big business owners. This is the ideology of technocracy, whether or not anyone uses that term. Their preferred flavor of capitalism is not free enterprise. It is monopoly enterprise. Widespread freedom and democracy are of no interest and no benefit to them. We shall see this again and again.

Subversion as Mass Hypnosis

How did these totalitarian leaders get people to follow them into insanity? The answer lies in human psychology and in Yuri Bezmenov's core principle of subversion—change people's *perception* of reality so they don't see what is really going on. Totalitarians control reality itself, as Hannah Arendt observed.

These totalitarian takeovers are examples of what psychologists call mass formation, also known as crowd formation and mass hypnosis. Our psychological and social well-being is rooted in the most primitive part of our brains—the amygdala. Logic and rational thinking occur in the prefrontal cortex, a much weaker and more recent evolutionary development. However much you *think* you are a rational being, the instinctive nature of the amygdala is far more powerful and dominates your thoughts and behaviors even when you don't realize it.[10] Psychology dominates intellect. That's exactly why psychological warfare is so effective.

We find mass formation throughout history, but in the nineteenth century these events became stronger, erupting in the totalitarianism of the twentieth century. Totalitarianism is different from a classical dictatorship in which the population is simply scared of a small, powerful group in control of society. Totalitarianism is based on an ideology, not on a group of powerful people. Totalitarianism begins with an ideology and can only be stopped by changing the ideology. These ideologies are always based on some materialistic, mechanistic view of reality—that everything is a machine and humans can control everything. Therefore, more control will improve our lives. Totalitarianism always involves a denial of God, even the destruction of God, because religion presents a completely different view of reality that is opposed to the ideology of control. Religion of any sort is a threat to totalitarianism.

How Mass Formation Works

Mass formation is a specific group dynamic that can take hold in groups and make people incapable of critical reflection and rational thinking. It emerges when four conditions are met in a society.[11]

1. Many people feel socially isolated, and social bonds deteriorate.
2. Life doesn't make sense for many people.
3. Many individuals experience free-floating anxiety that they cannot connect to any solid cause.
4. People generally feel frustrated and angry.

All these conditions existed in Russia, Italy, and Germany prior to their totalitarian takeovers. Industrialization and urbanization led to many socially isolated people who had lost their connection with nature, family, and community. The wars, the social and economic upheavals, and the generations of injustice left many people angry and frustrated. The decline of religious faith during the nineteenth century also disconnected people from their sense of meaning in life and their grounding in spiritual reality. Decades of socialist propaganda had replaced people's spiritual connection with socialist ideology.

If a story is then presented that connects people's anxiety with some clear object and presents a strategy to deal with this object of anxiety, then people will connect their free-floating anxiety to this object and will follow the strategy presented. For example, the object of anxiety could be the Jews (as in Nazi Germany) or the aristocracy (as in Russia). Then, together, the people engage in a heroic battle against the object of anxiety. The heroic battle creates new social bonds and gives meaning to their lives. They can control their anxiety and direct their anger against an identifiable enemy.

What emerges is a very strong social bond as it exists in a mass or crowd. People switch from a very negative mental state to a very positive mental state, *and* they experience a very strong mental intoxication. Psychologists have found that mass formation is not *similar* to hypnosis. It is *exactly the same* as hypnosis. It is mass hypnosis.

This is a psychological phenomenon. It is far more powerful than rational thought. It operates below the level of rational thought, almost on a subconscious level, so people are not aware they are being manipulated. People do not buy into the narrative because it is rational or logical. They buy into it because it leads to this new kind of social bond, which leads to mental intoxication. The story itself, the narrative, can be blatantly wrong, even absurd. People will continue to follow it because it is socially and psychologically satisfying. Those who don't fall for the mass hypnosis are blamed for a lack of citizenship and solidarity. Usually, these narratives are pseudo-scientific in nature. Stalin used historical materialism. Hitler used social Darwinism and eugenic race theory. Today, it is pseudo-scientific theories about the climate and about disease.

The Consequences of Mass Formation

The first consequence of mass formation is that people's attention is focused on the one point indicated by the narrative. All the rest, people *cannot* see. They are not psychologically able to consider things that go against the narrative. Their *perception* of reality has been altered. On a cognitive and an emotional level, they are not aware anymore of what happens outside this small field of attention indicated by the narrative. They are not sensitive anymore to rational argumentation. This is the most striking characteristic of an individual affected by mass formation.

The process of mass formation starts with people's free-floating anxiety, frustration, and anger. These are difficult for people to deal with partly because they do not have an existence in material reality. But when an object of anxiety is presented, that object is something material, like the Jews or the aristocracy—real people. In the great totalitarian takeovers, millions of people were murdered. This is the natural consequence of the heroic battle against something non-material. Hatred needs a real target, or it remains free floating anxiety. But it is impossible to destroy something that does not have a material existence. Ideas cannot be destroyed, neither can categories, labels, mental constructs, theories, nor anything else that only exists in our minds. The attempt to destroy the anxiety (non-material) by destroying the object of anxiety (real people) is doomed to failure. In this heroic battle against the object of anxiety, people believe themselves to be justified, virtuous, even noble as they murder real people. This is how the atrocities of communism are accomplished.

The anxiety itself can never be destroyed by destroying people. Thus, destruction breeds more destruction in a never-ending cycle. In these totalitarian societies, destruction never ends until they completely destroy themselves. This stems from a spiritual truth as expressed in *A Course in Miracles*. "Hate is specific. There must be a thing to be attacked. An enemy must be perceived in such a form he can be touched and seen and heard, and ultimately killed... Fear is insatiable, consuming everything its eyes behold, seeing itself in everything, compelled to turn upon itself and to destroy."[12] Mass formation always leads to mass murder and to mass self-destruction. Amazingly, two centuries before the concept of mass formation was articulated, Voltaire concisely summed up the phenomenon. "Those who can make you believe absurdities can make you commit atrocities."

Once a phenomenon of mass formation starts, it is very hard to stop. It makes people intolerant of alternative ideas. If someone speaks out with a dissonant voice and threatens to wake people up, others respond with fear and anger–products of the amygdala.

The narrative behind mass formation always becomes more wrong and more absurd as time goes by. The narrative typically begins with something that is more or less logical and rational. Over time, it gradually becomes more illogical, absurd, and irrational.

Later, after the new social bond is established, the narrative and the strategy to deal with the object of anxiety become purely ritualistic. A ritual is a behavior with no *practical* meaning–it has a *psychological* function. It is a behavior that shows other people that you belong to the same group, that you connect with them.

The results are amazingly consistent. About 30 percent of the population is hypnotized. I call them the True Believers. About 40 percent think there is something wrong with the narrative and are not hypnotized, but they never go against the narrative. They "go along"–the Fence Sitters. Another 30 percent think there is something wrong with the narrative and they speak up–the Rebels. However, this group is usually very heterogeneous, and they are never able to coalesce as a unified group. If this 30 percent of Rebels could join together and bring the 40 percent of Fence Sitters with them, the whole social dynamic of mass formation would stop. In the socialist revolutions of the twentieth century, this obviously failed to occur.

Who doesn't fall for the hypnosis? Those who have a close connection to nature, to their spiritual source, or to a close social network.

The fact that mass formation has happened so often tells us it is not particularly difficult to achieve. It is merely a matter of reorganizing and manipulating collective feelings in the proper way. It begins by spreading fear–activating the amygdala and silencing the pre-frontal cortex. With today's sophisticated mind control techniques, it's no surprise that it's happening again.

In all the frauds explained in this book, the accompanying psychological warfare has achieved mass formation–mass hypnosis. For a large percentage of people, perhaps the 30 percent True Believers, no amount of scientific evidence or logical reasoning can change their minds. If you have gotten this far into the book, I presume you are part of the other 70 percent who can still perceive the truth.

Like accidents, which are a combination of many factors–remove any one factor and the accident would not have happened–these totalitarian takeovers could have been avoided if people acted differently in a few key ways. Today, the whole world is hurtling toward just such an "accident." Are you willing to *perceive* differently, to question the official narratives, to rethink your ideology? Are you willing to *act* differently, to reject the lies, propaganda, and fraud that we are fed?

In a spiderweb of lies, unravel a few key strands and the whole web collapses. We turn now to the great lies and frauds of our time and how they are manufactured "crises" that serve only to bring about a new totalitarianism.

What You Can Do Now

1. The real political spectrum is a continuum of individual freedom and responsibility. As you move to the right, you get more of these. As you move to the left, you get less of them. Forget all the names that people put on these political movements and philosophies. They have lost all meaning today. If you want personal freedom, you must accept personal responsibility. If you want the government to take care of you, you will be a slave. This is the lesson of history.
2. Mass formation is real. It is mind control. To avoid it (and to be free), keep yourself grounded in reality–in nature, in your close personal friends and family, and in your relationship with your Creator. Avoid everything that is not real–lies and illusion. You must discern the difference using both physical evidence and your intuitive connection with God.
3. If you believe any official narrative, question it publicly and see what response you get. Truth and honesty do not fear questions. If your questions are met with avoidance, blame, or character assassination instead of evidence, you will know you are dealing with a fraud or a mass formation psychosis.

PART 2

The Earlier Frauds

In part 2, we look at the first two great frauds—the war on drugs and the war on the climate. Both are nonissues developed for totalitarian subversion. Both are building toward engineered "crises" which will justify governments grabbing more emergency power that will become permanent in the normalization phase.

But first I need to explain what fraud is and how it works. We also need to understand how our health has been destroyed and how the Philosophy of Death (Marxism) has, not surprisingly, led to the Culture of Death in the Western world. This is a key part of totalitarian subversion on its own, and it's a crucial prerequisite for subsequent frauds.

CHAPTER 5

Prelude to Fraud

"Remember, though, that fraud
is almost inevitably
a collaborative effort." –JACK CASHILL

What is fraud? This chapter shows you the pattern of fraud so you can recognize it the next time you see it. We also introduce the health and nutrition fraud that has debilitated the whole world and made us vulnerable to the covid fraud and the current phase of the climate fraud. But first we touch on how modern totalitarians have expanded the classic communist crisis from a pattern into a replicable process that they use over and over.

Imaginary Crises & Forever Wars

The urge to save humanity is always a false front for the urge to rule it. The whole aim of practical politics is to keep the populace alarmed (and hence clamorous to be led to safety) by menacing it with an endless series of hobgoblins, all of them imaginary." –H.L. MENCKEN

As we saw in chapter 3, to subvert a nation, you need a crisis. Crises are an excuse for governments to grab more "emergency" power that becomes permanent. It's not simply good-willed political leaders doing their best to respond to events. It's a planned and carefully orchestrated tactic. Most elected politicians are ordinary people who don't understand what's really going on. Rarely are they Marxist zealots, but simply the "useful idiots" who are used to carry out the tactics.

The Bolsheviks, Fascists, and Nazis were blessed with real crises. But modern totalitarians have come up with something even better—the imaginary crisis. If a problem isn't real, then it can't really be solved. So, the steps the government takes to solve this "problem" are never enough. The problem gets, or is made to look, constantly worse. Thus, constantly greater government measures are needed, which still don't work, so...You get the idea. A nonissue is blown into a forever war.

The "war" metaphor is psychologically important, as we saw both with communist ideology and with mass formation. For Marxist's, everything is about war, violently achieving and maintaining power. War creates fear in a populace. Fear activates the amygdala and shuts down rational thinking. In mass formation, the great battle is against the object of anxiety, which does not have a material existence and is based on an ideology—a *mis*understanding of reality. The fake unity created by the mass formation psychosis means people cannot perceive reality outside the official narrative. It leads people to violence and to commit atrocities in their vain attempt to destroy the object of anxiety.

War justifies overlooking domestic issues and uniting behind a strong leader to fight a common enemy. War justifies drastic measures—censorship, restricting civil rights, ignoring law and morality, and using fear to control people. War demands action rather than careful thought. Complex issues are simplified: you are a patriot or a traitor. You have to fight, be violent, do audacious things. You can't stop to consider all options or think carefully. Don't think. Panic! The strategic and constant use of fear to control people is an essential feature of totalitarian states and of psychological warfare. It is not a coincidence that these fraudulent "wars" produce an ever-intensifying state of fear and anxiety in society, and ever greater problems. That's the point.

Most of this book is about providing evidence that exposes four major frauds—forever wars. They are not wars in the conventional sense. They have no clear enemy and no conclusion. They fight against something that can never be defeated–something within us or within our environment. Thus, I call them "forever wars." I did not invent this term, but I am expanding its meaning, so I will claim it as my own.

What Is Fraud? The Bre-X Story

I refer to these "forever wars" as frauds. That needs an explanation. A fraud is different from a hoax, which is simply a humorous or malicious deception. With fraud, you cannot just create a grand fantasy out of thin air. People will immediately see through that. Fraud is always a deception based on truth. Fraud always has a purpose–this is crucial–to collect resources (money and power) from many hands into few. And, as Jack Cashill notes in the opening quote, fraud is always a collaborative effort. Few people are aware of the fraud, but many are enlisted to help who don't realize they are being duped. It is surprisingly common. Let me demonstrate the principles with a famous business fraud.

Bre-X (1988–97) was the greatest gold mining fraud of all time.[1] Bre-X was a legally established gold exploration company with experienced senior executives, and its shares traded on the Toronto Stock Exchange. It was exploring for gold in Indonesia, a logical choice since Indonesia is home to one of the world's largest, highest grade, and most profitable gold mines. The geology was favorable. The company was well-capitalized. It had real investors and real money and real drilling going on. As it released its drilling results over a period of several years, it became clear they had discovered one of the world's richest undeveloped gold properties. Stock analysts and mining experts started following the company, commenting on its impressive discoveries, and recommending the stock. All the experts seemed to agree. The story just kept getting better. The preliminary economic assessment looked fantastic. The price of Bre-X shares soared.

These are the facts. So where was the fraud? It was a massive and sophisticated case of the oldest gold mining fraud trick in the books. They "salted" the assays. In mining exploration, you drill into rocks and pull out drill cores–narrow columns of rock going down hundreds of feet. Then you take little sections of those rock cores, grind them into powder, and test them in a lab for their mineral content–the "assays." In "salting" an assay, you simply drop a little gold dust into the ground-up rock sample before you send it to the lab. By meticulously salting the assays, they were able to produce results that reflected a perfectly normal, but unusually spectacular, gold deposit. The results weren't random. They were believable–so believable they fooled the best experts in the business. A few people became fabulously wealthy. Millions of others lost their life savings. That's the purpose of fraud–to gain money and power.

How was this fraud discovered? A major gold mining company, Freeport McMoRan, entered a joint venture with Bre-X to develop the deposit into a mine. The first thing they did was to check the evidence, not just take anybody's word for anything. That's what will reveal a fraud–not *experts*, but *evidence*. Freeport didn't accept any of the previous assays. They drilled their own cores, right beside the Bre-X drill holes, took their own samples, and did their own assays. Newspapers all over the world blazed Freeport's comment in headlines, "What gold?" There was no gold. Almost overnight, the high-flying share price fell to its true value–zero.

Thousands of people either worked for Bre-X, examined their data, or recommended their stock. But it's possible that only one person knew the truth–the chief geologist, Michael de Guzman. Even the company president later claimed to know nothing about it. It doesn't take a lot of people to *conspire* to commit fraud. You just need to *dupe* a lot of people. It helped that the remote jungles of Indonesia are far away. It was difficult for others to check the evidence and easy for de Guzman to control the information. The same is true for the great frauds of our day. This is the pattern of fraud. Once we know the pattern, we will be able to recognize it again–just like the X-ray story.

Here is another dimension to understanding fraud. What everyone came to understand, or believe, about the Bre-X gold deposit was not true. It was, in a sense, an alternate reality that never existed. It only existed in the minds of people. It was a fantasy, and people made decisions based on this fantasy, which obviously turned out poorly. This substitution of fantasy for reality is the same thing that Yuri Bezmenov described in communist subversion–to change your perception of reality so you are unable to make sensible decisions in your own interest. As we will see in chapter 9, this is also the tactic of psychopaths, of mind control, and of psychological warfare. The tactic of distorting your perception of reality is common to all these patterns. To understand what is really going on, you must be open to perceiving differently.

Like Bre-X, the following great frauds are fantasies built on a nucleus of truth. That's why they are deceptive. There really is a problem with drugs and with terrorism. We really do have environmental problems in our world. There really are deadly viruses, bacteria, and other pathogens that can make us sick. These are problems within individuals, within our communities, and within our world. That makes it possible to build an edifice of fraud around them—to create alternate realities that are really fantasies. And you can perpetrate these frauds with very few people knowing the truth.

As we look at the various fraudulent "wars," keep this in mind. The war on drugs, the war on terror, the war on the climate, and the war on the virus are all frauds built around a nucleus of real, but minor, problems which are no cause for fear. The purpose of these frauds is very different from what we have been told. That's why, as we look at some of the details—the evidence—we quickly see that they don't make any sense at all. Instead of believing the "experts," we must look at the *evidence* to see what truth it reveals.

Destroying Health—Promoting Death

"For, the warnings have been given again and again as to how to keep the body fit—as to the foods, the diets, the exercise, the recreation, the rest, the building of the mental body, the time to play and the time to work, the time to recuperate the mental body, the time to make holy and the time to pray... All of these must be observed, if there would be a well-rounded, a well-centered life." —EDGAR CAYCE

Part of stage 1 (demoralization) of the communist subversion process as described by Yuri Bezmenov is to undermine the mental and physical health of the target population. Almost nobody has realized it, but this has been going in the West for over half a century. Let me explain.

Undermining Health

Remember the first point from the "instructions for communists" in chapter 3? "Corrupt the young, get them interested in sex. Take them away from religion. Make them superficial and enfeebled." Part of that corruption and enfeebling has to do with our physical bodies. In the Western world today, we are obsessed with health care, yet we are sicker than ever. In the United States, for the first time in recorded history, life expectancy is falling.[2] The destruction of health and the spread of the culture of death might be partly accidental, but there are many obvious designs as well. And the whole process exactly fits the pattern of communist subversion.

The health status of people in the Western world was gradually improving throughout the industrial age–largely due to better diets, sanitation, and access to clean water–until about the 1960s. When President Eisenhower suffered a heart attack, public attention was suddenly thrust upon the noticeable increase in the rate of heart disease. In retrospect, it's pretty clear this was caused by the increase in smoking.

Ancel Keys was in the right place at the right time to promote his hypothesis that saturated fats (from animal products) were causing heart disease. Despite serious criticism from other nutritional experts, Keys managed to cherry-pick data from his famous "Seven Countries Study," ignore the effects of sugar and intermittent fasting, and turn the whole nutritional world upside down. Those few nutritionists in the 1960s who tried to point out the errors in Ancel Keys's work were "canceled." Yes, even back then. They found themselves professionally disgraced, their research funding canceled, and their careers ended. The corruption of science began long ago. Almost four decades would pass before scientists again, against incredible opposition, started to reveal the scientific truth that was there all along. Animal fats are normal and healthy human food–in moderation, of course.

Governments all over the Western world jumped on the bandwagon and, for the first time in history, started telling their populations what to eat. Things have been going downhill ever since. It is no coincidence that this subterfuge spawned a huge growth in government bureaucracy, advertising, commercial foods, politicized science, and a ballooning medical-industrial complex. A huge multidecade campaign started to encourage people to replace normal meat and dairy products (on which humans have lived for hundreds of thousands of years) with new industrial seed oils (processed canola, corn, safflower, and soybean oils) and sugar (under many names, such as high fructose corn syrup). This is the worst possible advice.

For half a century, bad advice from governments has almost completely destroyed the metabolic health of the whole Western world, particularly in the United States. Was it by coincidence or design that one of the greatest risk factors for covid-19 mortality was poor metabolic health?

Destroying our health with bad nutrition started in the 1970s and constantly worsened once the government started telling us how to live our lives. More than half the US population is overweight. Now (spring 2022), governments are even working to destroy our food systems and replace normal food with lab-grown insects and genetically modified artificial food. And vegetables can now be grown with genetic therapy-mRNA "vaccines" embedded within.[3] The food and nutritional supplements of the whole world are slowly being brought under the control of a few people, led by a little-known group called the Codex Alimentarius Commission (food code).[4] It was created jointly by two branches of the United Nations–the Food and Agriculture Organization and the World Health Organization. It is controlled by a few bureaucrats and the big international food companies. Food is now, more clearly than ever, a vector of warfare and control.

Why is there such a big push to destroy agriculture and get everyone to eat insects, raised in factories and packaged so you don't know what you're eating? It's not because it's healthy, not because it saves the planet, and not because we can't feed everyone with real food. All these are lies. It's for one purpose and one purpose only–to control everyone by controlling all the food. If you will starve without government-supplied food, you're a slave. If you can't control what goes into your body, you're a slave. If you're dependent on the government, you're a slave. That's the point.

The current drive to replace animal products with vegetable oil factory food is no more rooted in good science than was the destructive advice of Ancel Keys. Eliminating meat from human diets will be absolutely catastrophic for human health. That's the objective. The Deep State technocrats (or whoever is behind this) want everyone to eat food made in factories to perpetuate the same chronic diseases that now maintain the massive medical-industrial complex. They want to depopulate the countryside, where farming is done, and move everyone into cities where they can be controlled more easily. This is not theory. It's in their published plans, as we'll see later. Don't fall for it. Eat meat.

Do your own research, as I have, on exercise, diet, and healthy living. But be careful who you listen to. Plenty of excellent books and articles have been published showing the perversity of our government's nutrition advice, such as *Death by Food Pyramid: How Shoddy Science, Sketchy Politics and Shady Special Interests Have Ruined Our Health*, by Denise Minger.[5] She gives a summary of the beginnings of this process and how the work of Ancel Keys was fraudulent. Nina Teicholz, in her book, *The Big Fat Surprise: Why Butter, Meat and Cheese Belong in a Healthy Diet*,[6] thoroughly debunks the falsehoods that painted saturated fat as a problem.

Here are a few basic ideas that seem to be well supported by scientific research but could still be wrong. Humans are omnivores and thrive on a varied diet of plant and animal foods. As much as possible, avoid sugar in its many forms, including alcohol. Eat lots of fruits and vegetables. The standard American diet (SAD) is sadly lacking in these. About three-quarters of what we eat should be fruits and vegetables, and most of that above-ground vegetables. Be careful to keep your grain consumption moderate and avoid excessive starches.

Eat a variety of animal foods—red meats, white meats, fish and shellfish, milk and cheese if you can—and eat as much of the animal as you can stomach. Organ meats, skin, bones, and cartilage all provide much-needed nutrients. And don't worry about the fat. Just be moderate in everything.

Avoid the highly processed seed oils. This means avoiding almost all foods that come in a package. They are rich in all the things we need to avoid. Use fruit oils instead of seed oils for eating and cooking (olive, coconut, avocado oils). I trust Mark Sisson (Mark's Daily Apple[7]) for most eating and exercising advice, but he could be wrong, like everyone. Regarding vegetable oils, he says,

> The reason for my recommendation that people avoid making most oils a large part of their diet also stands: they contain too much linoleic acid, a fragile fatty acid that becomes inflammatory when exposed to heat and creates oxidative stress when incorporated into our cell membranes and lipoproteins. The historic human diet contained very little linoleic acid; the modern industrial diet contains excessive amounts, mostly thanks to our reliance on these oils.[8]

The high carbohydrate, high linoleic acid SAD diet even degrades the functioning of our brains.

Don't eat too much. Most of us do. A calorie-restricted diet is one of the few thoroughly researched methods for living healthy and long. An easy way to start is to eat lots of nutrient-dense foods and avoid calorie-dense foods (and meat is hugely nutrient-dense). Incorporate some form of intermittent fasting into your lifestyle. Keep your weight down—skinny people live longer. Get some fresh air, sunshine, and exercise every day—even if it's only walking a couple of miles. Get plenty of sleep. Most people in the Western world are sleep deprived and don't even know it. This is incredibly destructive on every level—physically, mentally, and spiritually. The Edgar Cayce quote at the beginning of this section really sums it up.

Ancient hunter-gatherers on the verge of starvation had a healthier eating regime than the typical American today. You can thank your government, your food corporations, and your medical-industrial complex. They have created a population of chronically sick people who are addicted to what they sell, believe the propaganda they are fed on TV, need constant medical support, and are incapable of handling any new pathogen in their environment. Combine this with a medical establishment that is dominated by surgery and drugs, is manipulated by insurance and pharmaceutical companies to extract as much money as possible, and almost never gives you good advice on how to stay healthy, and you have an extremely malleable and vulnerable population. That's you.

The Medicine Business Model

I imagine most doctors chose their career out of a genuine and altruistic desire to help people. When a patient walks into their examination room, the doctor's attitude is one of, "How can I help this person?" But take that same doctor and put him on the board of the American Medical Association, and the questions he asks are very different. His position is different. His responsibilities are different. His perspective is different. Now he must ask, "What is good for my profession?" That different question produces some very different answers.

The doctor now becomes an oligopolist businessman, in the business of supplying medical goods and services. Like any good businessman, he must look at the whole market. How do we increase the size of the market? Our market share? Our margins? Our profits? Is our business model as good as it could be? How could we improve it? Can we develop new products and services for this market that increase our profit?

You naturally want to inhibit your competition. Therefore, you do whatever you can to discredit and undermine chiropractors, acupuncturists, herbalists, naturopaths, osteopaths, nutritionists, and so on. Limit any incursions into your profession by related professions such as pharmacists and nurses–hence prevent them from being able to prescribe any medications.

Increase the size of your market. A healthy population would be disaster for the medical business, as would widespread death. The best market is a large number of chronically ill patients who linger for years but never regain optimal health. You want to *treat* illnesses forever, not cure them. Therefore, do not teach medical students anything about human nutrition. Propagate advice that leads to poor health. Develop and prescribe medications that do not cure illness, but treat symptoms, so the treatment can go on forever. Physicians and the pharmaceutical industry have been pumping us full of drugs, particularly psychotic drugs, that don't cure anything and only keep us dependent, sick, and degraded–physically, mentally, and spiritually.

I was absolutely shocked a few years ago when the Canadian Cancer Society announced that half of Canadians would get cancer.[9] We have spent trillions of dollars studying cancer all over the world for decades–yet the problem constantly gets worse. I spent five years of my life working in a research group. If we spent even a tiny fraction of that time and money without coming up with a solution to the problems we were working on, we would have all been fired. Why do we permit this with cancer? I have stopped donating money to cancer research. The whole system stinks. I no longer believe that anyone is actually looking for a cure for cancer. They are only looking for treatments that prolong the business opportunity for everyone, both the medical treatment system and the medical research system. That's the business model.

More and more we are hearing small voices speak up about the corrupt system that connects pharmaceutical companies with doctors and governments and universities–a web of fraud. A glimpse into the medical business model was given by John Abramson of the Harvard Medical School. "The first step is to give up the illusion that the primary purpose of modern medical research is to improve people's health...The primary purpose of commercially-funded clinical research is to maximize financial return on investment, not health."[10]

We don't have a "health care system." We have a "sickness creation and care system." It accounts for a fifth of the entire economy of the Western world.[11] This is a huge misdirection of human productive activity. We spend trillions of dollars on medical research that benefits pharmaceutical companies. But how much do we spend researching longevity? Nobody can profit from healthy living–except you.

We need a new paradigm of health care because the existing paradigm merely keeps everyone sick. It is time to come to a new consciousness about how we live, about health, and about the wisdom of putting our health into the hands of people who only benefit from our sickness. Intended or accidental, it is this subversion of our health and health care that permitted the covid fraud to occur.

The Culture of Death

The right to life is the first and most important "right" in democracy. Yet the "right to death" movement has almost completely undermined it. They played on our natural compassion with stories about a few people's supposedly endless pain and suffering while they slowly died from chronic illnesses. These people want to end their own lives–kill themselves–but they need the help of a doctor. I'm not exactly sure why that is. Thousands of people manage to kill themselves every year without a doctor's help.

Legalize "doctor-assisted suicide," they said, the only compassionate thing to do. Only a heartless bigot would condemn a sick person to a life of endless pain and suffering. Of course, their case has a little truth and a lot of exaggeration. With our current state of medical knowledge, we have very good pain control. No one needs to be in constant, severe pain.

There was no groundswell of popular morality to kill people. But there was a multidecadal, carefully crafted propaganda campaign to soften people's attitudes about the right to life and confuse the morally unsure–which is most of us.

Here in Canada, the long campaign of the "right to death" movement has finally succeeded, with the *courts* (rather than legislatures) demanding that parliament bring in "doctor-assisted suicide" legislation. Now it's legal. These changes are often forced through the courts because you don't need to convince a majority of the people to agree with you, and judges tend to be more socialist than the general public. And you can lose in the courts dozens of times without consequence. You only need to win once to set a precedent. Then you've won forever.

Canadian courts repeatedly ruled against assisted suicide, correctly perceiving that existing laws protected the most vulnerable from abuse, particularly the frail elderly, the disabled, the mentally ill, and the impoverished. But that all changed in 2015 when a supreme court case went the other way. Now assisted suicide is not only legal; it's mandated. It is ironically macabre that the case twisted the idea of our "right to life," arguing that if there is a right to life, there must be a right to death. Ordinary people find it incredible that our supreme court judges agreed with this.

They call it "dying with dignity." It sounds so nice. But what is dignity? Dignity is inside you; it is a quality of character. Dignity is not a situation or condition in which you find yourself, such as a debilitating illness.

In practice, it's not a "right to die" (you are going to die whether or not you have a "right" to); it is a "right to force a doctor to kill you." In most Canadian hospitals, it is still difficult to find a doctor who will kill you. It is the opposite of everything they signed on to do. Most Catholic hospitals and hospices refuse to kill people. But now they are being prosecuted and threatened with having their government funding taken away if they don't kill people who ask for it.[12]

The de facto "right to force a doctor to kill you" law is quickly morphing into a de facto "right to force a doctor to kill your mother" law. This is the opposite of the "right to life." It's just a tiny step more to the "right to kill." The latest revisions to the assisted suicide laws in Canada–they are never finished this forever process–don't even require a fatal or terminal condition.

A good measure of a society's morality is how it treats its most vulnerable, including the very young and the very old. We have been conditioned to accept as "moral" the killing of a quarter of our children in the womb and the murder of our aged parents. As Jordan Petersen noted, moral corruption precedes totalitarianism. This is socially engineered subversion. This moral corruption set the stage, psychologically and spiritually, for the mass extermination of old people that we have experienced with the covid fraud. This was planned. None of it was accidental.

This is part of the culture of death. Human life is not honored for the divine gift that it is. Nor do we honor that divine gift by constantly fulfilling our divine mission of serving others. As soon as we are receiving a pension, we become a liability on the government's balance sheet. We become, in their minds, a "useless eater." Once we cannot be exploited, we are put on a slow conveyor belt to oblivion.

In most Western countries, it is becoming increasingly common for doctors to put DNR (do not resuscitate) on patients' charts in hospitals.[14] This used to be a rare order, only undertaken after consultation with several doctors and the patient's family. The ethics of medicine have gradually shifted away from compassion and toward commerce and the 2030 Agenda ideas.

Fostering a culture of death was necessary to pave the way for the complete control of every human body and mind, and the depopulation agenda that is now unfolding. The Marxist Philosophy of Death has produced our Culture of Death that promotes sickness and tries to solve problems by killing. To create, instead, a Culture of Life, we must promote health and reject killing as a way to solve problems. Fortunately, this is not difficult. You are responsible for the health of your own body, mind, and spirit–not your doctor nor your government. Take back this control. Whatever your health status, you can improve it. This is the first step in taking back control of your life.

Now that governments have adopted social security programs they cannot possibly pay for, there is a huge incentive to eliminate the recipients of social security. The medical business model and the culture of death are intersecting in a way that makes doctors and politicians, for us "old" people in particular, more dangerous than terrorists.

What You Can Do Now

1. Fraud is everywhere in our world today. It only needs a tiny number of conspirators. But millions are nudged or coerced into complicity. Don't be one of these. Be suspicious. Trust no one. Look at the evidence. Do your own research.
2. Beware the medical-industrial complex. Its goal is profit, not your best interests. *You* are responsible for your own health. Act accordingly.
3. Your goal should be good health, not medical care. Adjust your lifestyle to promote your own health so you don't need medical care. Unfortunately, medical doctors cannot be relied upon to give good advice on healthy living.
4. Whatever you think about abortion and euthanasia, both individually and as a society, we must find solutions to our problems that do not involve killing.

CHAPTER 6

Drugs—The First Forever War

"For some time, I have been disturbed by the way the CIA has been diverted from its original assignment. It has become an operational and at times a policy-making arm of the government. This has led to trouble and may have compounded our difficulties in several explosive areas." —HARRY TRUMAN, 1963

A Bit of History

Human beings have used drugs for as long as we can tell. Most primitive cultures have some tradition of intoxicating substances, sometimes used as an aid to spiritual experiences. Typically, it was a mild intoxicant like alcohol, or, if more powerful like ayahuasca, its use was highly restricted and ritualized within the culture. By the dawn of history, we find evidence of wine, beer, or cannabis almost everywhere we find people. Humans are drawn to the various experiences created by drugs, and intoxication seems to be a ubiquitous human problem.[1]

The underlying issue behind the "war on drugs" is a more sincerely moral dilemma than the subsequent fraudulent wars. With drugs (including alcohol and nicotine), it is harder to find the proper balance between allowing people their free will and reasonably protecting ourselves and our brothers from temptation and from the evil depredations of selfish people. For example, to what extent should society restrict the availability of alcohol or leave its use entirely to the free choice of individuals? This is not a simple question to answer. Does the same answer apply to cocaine? To tobacco? To marijuana? To what extent is there a different answer for a five-year-old, a fifteen-year-old, a twenty-five-year-old, or someone with a mental illness? Do the risks, benefits, and social traditions of these substances lead us to find a different balance between legal restrictions and individual free will for each substance? Reasonable people will come to different conclusions. So, it is not surprising that we have struggled with these questions, and with the addictive substances themselves, both individually and collectively.

My purpose here is not to solve the moral questions but to trace the history that brought us to the present fraud we call the "war on drugs." It is a forever war because the temptation to use intoxicants is simply a "forever" part of being human. Every person must face this temptation for themselves. It is as eternal as the struggle of good against evil *within ourselves*. To use this as an excuse for quasi-military repression has no moral justification. It's really about money and power. The "war on drugs" is nothing less than the war on ourselves—the duplicitous cover story behind which the Deep State controls, profits from, and oppresses people.

Deep State is not a good term, but I can't find a better one, so I'll use it and I need to define it. Its current usage comes from a now classic 2014 essay by Mike Lofgren.[2] The Deep State is impossible to define precisely or understand completely. It's the name we put on that idea that our elected representatives don't seem to be the ones really governing us. There seems to be some network of people—in the government bureaucracy, in the administration, in big business, in big media, in the military, in the intelligence agencies, in think tanks like the World Economic Forum and the Council on Foreign Relations, in big banks and old money families—who all know each other and work together to essentially "rule" behind the scenes. Some of this is out in the open and visible; some of it is shrouded behind a curtain of secrecy. The Deep State often works loosely through common principles and philosophies. Yet there might also be a small, hidden group that makes secret long-term plans. Nobody knows for sure. Because the whole idea is so nebulous and ill-definable, it goes by many names—the cabal, Mr. Global, the Global Predators, and others. One way or another, whatever it is, it appears to have a life and power unto itself and to have interests very much at odds with those of ordinary people. We will look more carefully at what the Deep State might be in chapter 15, but it still remains nebulous.

Even though intoxicants have been around forever, events took a more ominous turn in the Industrial Age. We can blame the British for making drugs a strategic tool in the modern era. Britain started trading with China in the early 1700s, buying porcelain, silk, and tea. But the Chinese had little interest in Britain's manufactured goods. They wanted to be paid in money—British pounds sterling. As the volume of trade expanded in the subsequent decades, Britain saw a one-way loss of its silver coins. The prevailing economic understanding at that time is called mercantilism, which we have mentioned previously. In that system of thought, it is believed that wealth accumulates when money flows into your country, and wealth dissipates when money flows out of your country. Britain had a silver standard at that time. Silver was money and money was silver. It couldn't all just disappear into China. This trade was leading to a fall in Britain's money supply with the consequent deflation and depression. So, taking their cue from the Portuguese before them, the East India Company latched onto the idea of trading opium from India in exchange for silk and tea from China.[3]

This brilliantly evil plan worked splendidly. British traders in India became the first drug lords—with the connivance of the British authorities. This is a common pattern, as we will see. Millions of Chinese people became addicted to opium. The demand exploded, the product was cheap and easy to make just next door in India, and Britain got to keep all its silver. This was a great mercantilist setup. With the protection of the crown, the East India Company shipped manufactured goods from England to India, opium from India to China, and silk, tea, and porcelain back to England. They had a royal monopoly on the production and export of opium and made money hand over fist. Of course, it was a disaster for millions of Chinese, causing physical and moral decay and economic destitution.

The Chinese government eventually got mad enough about the situation to fight two "opium wars" with Britain. But by that time (1840–1860), Britain was the most powerful nation in the world and its technology was miles ahead of China's. The outcome was never in doubt.

Britain, and to a lesser extent Russia and the United States, profited from the opium trade that helped to impoverish the Chinese and undermine their social order. It became a matter of state policy—explicitly for Britain, less so for the others. The British opium trade and opium wars may be the first time in history that drugs were used strategically: to cheat customers for monetary gain, to intentionally addict and degrade people, to subvert a society, and to justify war. All of that pretty much characterizes the international drug trade of today.

Other drugs became available in the nineteenth century as well. The coca plant was used by the Native South Americans of the Andes for centuries. Chewing the leaves has a rather mild effect, but once chemists learned how to concentrate the active ingredient, it became a powerful drug—cocaine.

Morphine was isolated from opium in 1805, and by the latter part of the century it was being overused. Wounded soldiers in the American Civil War were often treated with morphine and many became addicts. By the late 1800s, morphine was in most people's medicine cabinets in the form of the common home remedy laudanum.

By the late nineteenth century, alcohol abuse had become a serious problem in many parts of the United States. Even children were alcoholics. Everyone noticed the destruction of lives, the private misery, the social dislocation, and the economic impairment of alcoholism. This is what gradually led to the prohibition movement—it wasn't just prudish housewives. People were motivated by the natural human desire to help others and improve the welfare of their families and communities.

Prohibition: Good Intentions That Paved the Road to Hell

Alcohol was completely prohibited in the United States for thirteen years—well, almost completely. Sacramental wine was still permitted to churches, so at least a few people immediately consecrated themselves as priests and set up bootlegging businesses. You could make your own wine and cider for personal consumption (two hundred gallons per person!), but not beer or hard liquor. Consequently, the sale of grape juice skyrocketed.

Since "medicinal alcohol" was still legal, many physicians and pharmacists profited by writing and filling prescriptions for it, reminiscent of medicinal marijuana during the past decade. The great American drugstore chain, Walgreens, expanded from 20 stores to 525 stores during the 1920s on the profit of selling medicinal alcohol.[4]

Some of the great family fortunes in Canada were made at this time as Canadian whiskey producers earned huge profits on the smuggling trade into the United States. From my standpoint as an economist, it was a great case study in what happens when you outlaw a product for which there is considerable consumer demand–corruption, crime, and smuggling. It wasn't too much different from the old mercantilism. By bribing the police to look the other way, you essentially paid for government protection of your business monopoly. For the monopolist, it's hugely profitable.

The overall results were a mixed bag. The experiment was not quite the disaster it is commonly presented as today. Alcohol consumption definitely went down, as did the rates of alcoholism, cirrhosis of the liver, mental hospital admissions for alcoholism, public drunkenness, and absenteeism.[5] But it also helped to fuel a rise in organized crime.

One result of the experiment is perfectly clear. A government cannot arbitrarily dictate and enforce a code of moral behavior on its citizens. Millions of people wanted to consume beer, wine, and liquor, had a cultural tradition of doing so, and would do it whether or not it was legal. Nations since time immemorial have experienced similar results with other products. Smuggling is the universal solution when governments try to restrict the free flow of goods.

It is also noteworthy that the period began with a general acceptance of, and support for, prohibition.[6] This situation is very similar to the public support for drug laws today. People supported the ideals and goals. But as time went on, the problems of enforcement became insurmountable, the associated crime became unacceptable, and millions of people who just wanted to have a beer with their buddies got fed up. The benefits were small. The disruptions were great.

Once alcohol was prohibited, it was impossible to regulate or tax the trade. Business disputes could not be settled in the courts, so they were settled with guns. Enforcement was an impossible nightmare. Bribing police and government officials was much cheaper than getting caught, so corruption proliferated and, as it always does, gradually infected all parts of society. These same fundamental problems would recur later in the century with other addictive and destructive intoxicants.

Drugs and the CIA

"The war in Southeast Asia ... witnessed a vast explosion in Opium and Heroin trafficking–with the connivance of the CIA." –DAVID GUYATT

Life never follows the neat categories we are taught in history class. But they are an aid to understanding. Thus, the following sections briefly examine the history of our current "war on drugs", how the pattern matches both the old British opium trade and the distinctive pattern of fraud, and what we might be able to do about it.

1940s–The Mafia & French Connection[7]

During World War II, the Office of Strategic Services (OSS), the American wartime intelligence service and precursor to the CIA, worked with the Cosa Nostra Sicilian mafia to gather intelligence on Italy prior to its invasion. In return for intelligence, the OSS/CIA protected the mafia's budding drug business and, after the war, helped the mafia suppress the communists and control Italian politics. The CIA's part in the deal was to protect mafia drug shipments into the United States–for a cut of the action, of course. The CIA also protected the Marseille-based Corsican mafia and helped them import heroin into the United States. In return, the mafia suppressed communists trying to organize port workers in Southern France. This was the French connection.

In the other hemisphere, both during and after the war, OSS/CIA developed contacts with Chinese anti-communist Triads who were involved in the opium, morphine, and heroin trade in Southeast Asia. The OSS/CIA and the US army also worked with the Japanese Yakusa crime and drug organization. In return, the Yakusa helped to suppress communism in Japan. Thanks to the CIA's support of the heroin business, the number of US heroin addicts rose from twenty thousand at the end of the war to over one hundred fifty thousand by 1965.[8]

1950s–The Golden Triangle in Burma

The CIA used an arms-for-opium trade to build up anti-communist guerilla armies in the Burma hills and in the Thai National Police Force. They flew supplies and reinforcements from Taiwan to Burma and returned (through Bangkok and Saigon) with opium, which was distributed throughout Southeast Asia and to the United States. The French Army also operated an opium trafficking network out of French Indochina (later to be Vietnam) to help fund its covert operations, which the CIA inherited when the French left. They even grotesquely shipped heroin back to the US in the bodies and caskets of dead GIs.[9] In *Politics of Heroin in Southeast Asia,* Alfred McCoy writes,

> The State department provided unconditional support for corrupt governments openly engaged in the drug traffic. In late 1969 new heroin laboratories sprang up in the tri-border where Burma, Thailand, and Laos converge, and unprecedented quantities of heroin started flooding the United States. Fueled by these seemingly limitless supplies of heroin, America's total number of addicts skyrocketed.[10]

This was not a demand-led market expansion. It was supply led. The CIA worked just as hard at expanding the drug marketing network in the United States as they did at cornering the supply. The CIA uses drug trafficking profits to help fund its covert activities and support anti-communist guerrillas and terrorists all over the world. At the same time, the CIA's control of the drug trade offers it a powerful tool of covert influence, as explained in exquisite detail in many of the references cited in this chapter. It provides money for bribing governments everywhere, paying for weapons, assassinations, and regime changes, and for exerting de facto control over half the world. For the inscrutable shadow CIA government, it's a win-win situation.

The very public 1980s Iran/Contra/Drugs scandal is one of many such CIA operations. But the whole business continues. It's like a giant game of whack-a-mole. When you expose one CIA operation, five more spring up in its place.

As David Guyatt put it in a 2001 article in SPY Magazine, *The Criminal Cabal of Guns and Drugs*,

> Meanwhile, it is a sad fact that the narcotics industry has been lurking behind almost every major—and most minor—wars over the past five decades...The guns for dope model that developed during the Vietnam war proved effective elsewhere, too. Similar structures were later developed in Afghanistan, El Salvador and even up to and including Kosovo—where the NATO-backed KLA trafficked heroin.[11]

The business model works like this: The CIA, or some private company that operates as a CIA front, buys weapons from the Pentagon inventory at their "book value." They sell the weapons to the Taliban (or any other group or country) for the current black-market price, making a good profit. The Pentagon then replaces these weapons with new ones from the US supplier at the current price. The US taxpayer covers the cost, and the defense contractor makes a good profit. Next, the CIA takes the Taliban's heroin as payment for the guns. It ships the drugs safely to markets in the United States and Europe—no worry about local police forces—and puts them into the retail market, again making a huge profit. The CIA then funds its secret covert operations with the profits, pays bribes to everyone involved, and launders money through "legitimate" businesses and cooperative banks. Huge profits are made by everyone involved in these criminal operations, and a huge price is paid by taxpayers and ordinary people everywhere. People's lives are destroyed by addiction, families are impoverished, productive agriculture is undermined, and both the producers and consumers are trapped in a net of control.

Has anything changed in recent years? Not likely. Recently, the so-called "Fast and Furious" operation to sell guns to Mexican drug cartels through legitimate guns shops in Arizona (supposedly to follow the trail back to the cartels and arrest them, but no arrests were ever made) was a CIA-supported plan to arm the Sinaloa cartel against the Los Zetas.[12]

Sex, Drugs, and Rock & Roll– The Flower Children as Naïve Stooges

The "Hippie Era" has been extensively documented. It was a time of awakening, of rebellion against authority, sexual permissiveness, and a general degradation of individual and social behavior. Yes, there were many genuine causes within Western society, but the results were precisely the goals of communist subversion, and they occurred just as the Soviets and Chinese were ramping up their subversion efforts in the West. For example, *How the Specter of Communism is Ruling Our World* gives an overview.

> The accounts of many Soviet spies and intelligence officials and declassified documents from the Cold War suggest that infiltration and subversion tactics were the driving forces behind the counterculture movement of the 1960s.
>
> From the mid-1960s to mid-70s, the mostly young participants of the counterculture movement were motivated by various pursuits. Some opposed the Vietnam War; some fought for civil rights; some advocated for feminism and denounced patriarchy; some strove for homosexual rights. Topping this off was a dazzling spectacle of movements against tradition and authority that advocated sexual freedom, hedonism, narcotics, and rock 'n' roll music.

> The goal of this Western Cultural Revolution was to destroy the upright Christian civilization and its traditional culture. While apparently disordered and chaotic, this international cultural shift stemmed from communism. Youthful participants of the movement revered "the Three M's"–Marx, Marcuse, and Mao.[13]

Sexual liberation resulted from communist subversion and the Cultural Marxist philosophy of the Frankfurt School. It wasn't just horny teenagers. These have always been. The rapid destruction of sexual morals is a rare event in the history of civilization.

> Combining Marxism with Freudian pansexualism, Marcuse's theories catalyzed the sexual liberation movement. Marcuse believed that repression of one's nature in capitalist society hindered liberation and freedom. Therefore, it was necessary to oppose all traditional religions, morality, order, and authority in order to transform society into a utopia of limitless and effortless pleasure.
>
> Marcuse's famous 1955 work *Eros and Civilization: A Philosophical Inquiry into Freud* occupies an important place among the vast number of works by Frankfurt scholars for two specific reasons: First, the book combines the thought of Marx and Freud, turning Marx's critiques on politics and economy into a critique on culture and psychology. Second, the book builds bridges between Frankfurt theorists and young readers, which enabled the cultural rebellion of the 1960s.[14]

Herbert Marcuse even coined the famous phrase "make love, not war."[15] This dissolute philosophy was perfectly tailored to corrupt and enfeeble a whole generation. Adolescents and university students are an easy mark for a message of rebellion against authority and sexual licentiousness. Millions of "hippies" jumped onboard this bandwagon. I was one. Why not? Our motto was "If it feels good–do it!" As a teenager, I didn't yet know "why not," and the parents and teachers of our day were not able to formulate a coherent answer to that eternal question of youth.

The rebellious hippie generation gradually took their places in society where they became the driving force behind the hard left turn in politics later in the century. That was the plan. This is subversion step 1—demoralization (see chapter 3). The hippie era was a watershed period in the subversion of Western civilization. It tore society apart in ways not seen again until the late 2010s. Most of us who had long hair, wore tie-dyed shirts and bell-bottomed pants, and even smoked the odd joint had no idea we were naïve stooges assisting the demise of the very society that gave us the liberty to do all those things.

The War Declared: 70s & 80s

The term "war on drugs" officially started with President Richard Nixon in 1971, but as we have seen, the fighting began long before that. The "war" was a great excuse to ramp up the military-industrial-intelligence complex—a wonderful new "war" to replace the Vietnam conflict that was then winding down. The Western governments (especially the USA) would use one hand to make the drug problem worse (the CIA and other covert agencies) and another hand to "fight" against the problem they created (the DEA, FBI, etc.). Ordinary people all over the world were caught in the middle and paid the price in myriad ways. This is the scam. This is the fraud.

Throughout the 1970s and 1980s, the CIA and the whole apparatus of the US government supported South American dictators in Chile, Bolivia, Panama, and elsewhere who worked hand-in-glove with the CIA cocaine operations. The human rights abuses of all these dictators were well known to the US government. Human rights were irrelevant to both Democrats and Republicans. All that mattered was that a dictator cooperated with the CIA.

Most of the cocaine was grown in Bolivia, shipped through the cartels in Columbia, transited Panama, and was delivered to the United States under the protection of the CIA.[16] Production exploded, and street prices dropped from $1,500/gram in 1975 to $200/gram in 1986.[17] The CIA helped to fuel the spread of crack, which was much more addictive, and the business boomed. Really a marketing innovation, low-priced crack was targeted to poor inner-city neighborhoods. You'd almost think it was designed to destroy black communities.[18]

For a short time during the late 1970s, the US government took a public health approach to the drug problem. But the bureaucracy and the Deep State didn't want to solve the problem. Peter Bourne was Special Assistant for Health Issues (in charge of the federal drug program) to President Jimmy Carter. In a PBS *Frontline* interview in 2000, Bourne said,

> I only came to realize later the extent to which bureaucratic wars in Washington often transcend the pursuit of policy, and that one of the objectives in DEA always was to increase the budget and its influence in Washington. One way to do that was to always say the drug problem is getting worse... If you're winning the war against heroin, and the person in the White House says we have reduced overdose deaths to the lowest level in thirty years, everybody in the DEA says, "They're going to cut our budget. They're going to reduce our agents. Some of us are going to be laid off."[19]

When President Reagan took office in 1981, the public health approach was thrown out and the criminal approach took over. If you didn't "Just Say No" to drugs, you were a criminal. Combined with the cheap crack to addict the poor, the war on drugs became a sort of ethnic cleansing of young African American men from the inner cities of America. Overdose deaths went up again. The drug problem got worse. The Deep State grew bigger.

In 1987, Thai drug lord Khun Sa offered to stop 900 tons of his heroin going annually to the United States if the US government would help him eradicate the drug business in Southeast Asia and convert his people to other agricultural crops. The administration responded, "We have no interest in doing that."[20]

So much information has been published and provided to Congress showing the US government itself is behind the drug problem, that it's obvious either the government is powerless to stop drugs or has no interest in it.

Why Afghanistan? Opium

The US had several reasons to create a long war in Afghanistan. It had the benefit of disrupting China's ambition to expand its influence through Central Asia to Europe—as does the current US proxy war against Russia in Ukraine. But the issue of China was minor at the time. As we have seen, the opium/heroin trade has been important for two hundred years, since the days of the East India Company. Opium has often been cultivated in war zones to provide quick and easy profits to pay for arms. We saw this in Southeast Asia and also in the Bekaa Valley in Lebanon during the long civil war there (1975–1990), as has been attested to by numerous authors such as Carol Marshall in *The Last Circle.*[21]

The CIA was involved in this trade, supervising the drug shipments into the United States and, through connections to European police and intelligence agencies, into Europe as well. But the Bekaa Valley is a small place compared to Afghanistan. Perhaps as peace gradually returned to Lebanon after 1990, agriculture may have slowly returned to growing food, and the CIA needed a new source. The heroin trade the CIA had developed in Afghanistan during its war with the Soviets also declined and fell into the control of the Taliban during the 1990s. As we shall see in chapter 10, plans were developing that would put Afghan heroin back into the CIA's hands in the next decade. Afghanistan's war against the Soviets in the 1980s had been a huge source of CIA covert funds. It's hard to replace the kind of money mentioned by Loretta Napoleoni in her book *Modern Jihad.*

> William Casey, Reagan's CIA chief, used Pakistan and its BCCI bank as fronts to train Afghan rebels against the Soviets. Covert operations required a 'black network' within the bank and its state equivalent, the notorious ISI. The bank financed and brokered covert arms deals, complete with full laundry service. The short and logical step from there was a

> BCCI/ISI/CIA move into drug smuggling to feed the needy, and leaky, money pipeline to the Mujahedin. The Pakistani-Afghan connection became the biggest single supplier of heroin to the US, meeting 60 percent of demand, with annual profits a stratospheric $100–200 billion.[22]

The new war with Afghanistan "coincidentally" came in very handy. When the United States went to war with Afghanistan in 2001, the country produced about 100 tonnes of opium. In 2017, through many ups and downs, opium production was 9,000 tonnes. Mission accomplished.[23]

Most of the money laundering in the world is done by, or protected by, the CIA and national governments. The rest of us get hassled with paperwork and suspicion if we try to buy a mobile home in Phoenix, where we can pass a quiet winter without snow. But the CIA drug lords move billions around the world with impunity and maintain a private criminal army. We dutifully comply because we think the invasion of our banking privacy is somehow reducing the "criminals" money laundering. Nothing could be further from the truth.

The CIA's drug business is a system to both generate vast amounts of money off the books, and to enslave whole countries—just like the East India Company did. As Catherine Austin Fitts says,

> The drug business is the leveraged buyout of a place using the money from the place itself. I sell them something that makes them weaker and makes it easier for me to take them over cheaper...If the drugs were legal, the whole business model would collapse. Those who control the drug business control it (and the whole country) from the bottom up, from the level of counties...The drug business gives you control over every community, every person, everything. It is a control model.[24]

The "war on drugs" is a complete fraud. There is not, and never was, any intention to stop the drug trade—only to use it to increase the size and scope of the Deep State and to extend its control everywhere in the world. We must stop it—*and stop all of it!*

The drug trade is part of the Deep State game of geopolitics. The endless wars in Afghanistan have driven farmers there, as in many war-torn nations before, to grow opium poppies instead of wheat in order to survive. Warlords and terrorists use drugs to finance their operations. The millions of lives lost and destroyed are just collateral damage in a country that's been a pawn in proxy wars of the great game. I wonder what the country would be like today if, instead of the United States spending a trillion dollars to fight Afghans, they had spent that money in a Marshall Plan effort to educate and rehabilitate Afghans? Just a thought.

Fentanyl–China's Revenge for the Opium Wars

China too has turned the tables on the Western nations and launched its own drug war against the democracies. Almost all the fentanyl that makes its way into the American and Canadian markets comes from China.[25] The Chinese authorities just can't seem to find the labs and shut down this trade. For a totalitarian communist country, the world leader in mass surveillance of its citizens, the creators of "social credit" scores, such a claim is unbelievable. Nothing gets exported from China without the approval of the Chinese Communist Party. More likely, the "new opium trade"–Chinese fentanyl–is used to weaken and addict Western democracies. It seems to be an explicit strategy of the Chinese communists. China expert Gordon Chang says it bluntly: "China is intentionally killing tens of thousands of Americans every year with fentanyl."[26]

Fentanyl is a wonderful synthetic opioid. Used in a hospital setting, it is powerful, fast-acting, relatively free of side effects, and doesn't last long. It's great for surgery. As a recreational drug–it's disaster. It is so powerful that only a tiny amount will get you high, a wee bit more will kill you–and frequently does. Fentanyl is one hundred times stronger than morphine, fifty times stronger than heroin. And now it's being added to other street drugs.

To make matters worse, it's pretty easy to make. In fact, the malleable chemical structure of opioid drugs makes it fairly easy to modify the structure a bit and come up with slightly different chemical compounds that are still deadly opioids. The cumbersome legal work needed to put a new compound on the list of restricted drugs makes it easy for drug dealers to simply change their chemical structure and produce an opioid that isn't regulated.

This is the ploy that drug pushers and the Chinese Communist Party have used to simply mail fentanyl and other synthetic opioids through the postal service. In the past decade, the fentanyl problem has become so big, it has eclipsed all other drugs combined. US drug overdose deaths started this century under twenty thousand, rose slowly for a decade or so, then took off once fentanyl entered the market about 2014. In 2021, deaths were over one hundred thousand, mostly due to fentanyl.[27] More Americans now die of drug overdoses than car accidents.

The variability in the concentration of fentanyl, and its inclusion in other drugs, makes it impossible for users to know what they are taking.[28] A drug dealer assures them it's "good," and they end up dead. Much of the fentanyl in the US is now being shipped in bulk from China to Mexico, where it is processed and moved across America's intentionally porous southern border. Drug seizures at the Mexico-US border increased dramatically in early 2021, with fentanyl in the lead.[29] And guess where it's coming from.

> It turns out that Wuhan is the global center of fentanyl production. The city's chemical and pharmaceutical manufacturers hide fentanyl production within their otherwise legitimate operations and then ship the drug abroad by devious means. Aren't the Chinese clever? And to make the situation more galling, ABC News reports that "huge amounts of these mail-order [fentanyl] components can be traced to a single state subsidized company in Wuhan."[30]

Wuhan. Now, where have you heard that name before? An American journalist was able to figure this out but for some reason the Chinese authorities can't. The biggest drug crisis yet in North America, all coming from the largest communist country in the world, intent on destabilizing and overpowering the Western democracies, and our governments do almost nothing. It all strikes me as too much of a coincidence to be a coincidence.

It's not just China. As Yuri Bezmenov says, we do it to ourselves. The opioid crisis of the past decade was really started by American companies and doctors fraudulently distributing highly addictive OxyContin, which the FDA fraudulently approved in 1995 as a "nonaddictive" pain killer.[31] As with all the frauds, enemy subverters are both foreign and domestic.

We have two major issues to deal with–how to end this fraud, and how to heal our people. The documentary film, *Facing Fentanyl: How Americans Are Facing the Facts, Overcoming Stigma, and Saving Lives Today,*[32] explains the problem and shows its human dimension. These addicts are broken. They need our help to heal. That is our mission here on this earth–forgiveness, love, and healing. Every day, 227 people are dying from fentanyl in the United States. Our brothers and sisters are in pain. They are crying out to us for help. All of us are being lied to and manipulated and killed by a fraud perpetrated by the very people we thought were protecting us. It is time for radical change.

The War Apparatus

The Drug Enforcement Agency (DEA) has the main responsibility for enforcing drug laws. But drug enforcement still involves the FBI, the US Customs Service, the Department of Homeland Security, and every police force in the country. Their main enemy in the "war on drugs" is the CIA. But that enemy is too powerful to attack head-on, and whenever they do put a case together, the courts and the Department of Justice (DOJ) dismantle it if the CIA is involved. But don't take anyone's word for it, not even mine. Do your own research. Start with Captain Rodney Stich's book, *Drugging America.*[32] The DEA mainly catches small-time operators, addicts, and ordinary drug users. The business carries on as usual.

The DEA has a budget of over $2 billion–huge, but still far less than the CIA profits from the drug business. How can a "war" go on continuously for half a century with constantly greater "fighting" and constantly less "success"? You guessed it. It's not a "war." It's a business. We will never "win." Only the Deep State wins.

For the past quarter century, the mainstream media and politicians of all parties have been complicit in this fraud. The truth has been out at least since the 1993 "60 Minutes" TV program where several DEA agents complained about the CIA drug smuggling operations that were protected by the DOJ.[33] Also in 1993, former DEA agent Michael Levine published his book, *The Big White Lie*,[34] which exposed CIA involvement in cocaine trafficking. The facts have been in the public domain for a quarter of a century. Ignorance is not an excuse. Willful ignorance *is* complicity.

Since then, more and more published evidence has accrued, showing exactly what I have outlined in this chapter: the United States government and other national and state governments—through their intelligence agencies and militaries and courts and politicians and bureaucrats and wars and proxy wars and deceits—have caused the spread of illegal drugs all over the world. There have been affidavits and testimonies before Congress and articles and books published. All to no avail. The whole "war on drugs" is a deadly fraud that furthers the interests of the Deep State and destroys everyone else.

Remember that behind the fraudulent war on drugs is psychological warfare. The purpose of psychological warfare (active measures) is to change your perception of reality to such an extent that you don't see the ideological subversion going on around and within you, despite ample evidence. Thus, you are unable to make sensible decisions in your own interests and those of your nation. As I said at the beginning of this book, you must *perceive differently* if you are to understand what is really going on.

What to Do About Drugs

The solutions to the drug problem have almost nothing to do with the problem as it is usually framed. The first step in problem-solving is always to define the problem. If you don't understand the problem, you cannot solve it. That's exactly what has happened with the "drug problem." We have never understood it properly—by design—so everything we have done cannot possibly solve the problem—again by design. This is exactly the pattern of a communist nonissue crisis.

As we learned in the section on mass formation psychosis, we can never battle something that does not have a material existence. There can never really be a "war on drugs." "Drugs" is a category. It is impossible to punish "drugs" or to defeat "drugs" or to imprison "drugs." The "drug problem" is an immaterial characteristic of human nature. So, in the "war on drugs" we imprison real people, destroy the lives of real people, murder real people. This fraudulent "war on drugs" bears all the hallmarks of a mass formation psychosis endless cycle of destruction.

Neither have we learned the lessons of prohibition. Banning popular consumer goods leads to smuggling. Smuggling leads to the corruption of government officials and police, and corruption spreads everywhere in society. Trade in illegal goods creates criminals. More criminals create a need for more police—but it's not effective because they are corrupt. Profit from crime creates the need for money laundering and corrupts bankers. Corrupt police and government officials can be blackmailed, leading to even greater control of government by criminals. It is a vicious cycle that is destroying Western civilization. We have to stop it.

At the same time, drugs are a scourge on humanity. Outside of medical use, they have no redeeming qualities. They do not provide a practical path to spiritual enlightenment. Spiritual enlightenment comes through greater self-control, not through losing control to drugs, regardless of what esoteric experiences you might have while intoxicated. Spiritual growth involves developing greater acuity of sensation, perception, and intuition. Dulling these senses with drugs cannot lead to spiritual growth. Drugs destroy individual lives, impoverishing and traumatizing whole families. Trillions of dollars are wasted on destructive pleasure-seeking and are used to draw economic resources into criminal and destructive activities instead of healthy, life-giving, productive activities. Every one of us has seen this, either in our own lives or in the lives of those around us.

And yes, for the past half century, drugs have been a tactic for foreign and domestic communists to destabilize Western society and for the CIA and other elements of the Deep State to manipulate individuals and governments to gain power.

As long as we treat drug abuse and addiction as a crime, it will further only the interests of the military-industrial-intelligence complex. We must deal with drug abuse and addiction as what they really are—health problems. Partly physical health, partly mental health, partly spiritual health. Addicts need help, not prison. As unpalatable as it is for many people, we must decriminalize all drugs. The use of drugs may increase, but I doubt it. What *will* happen is the collapse of the evil and fraudulent business model of crime, corruption, manipulation, and psychological warfare.

We have to legalize drugs, destroy the drug cartels, disband the CIA, stop the wars, stop the crime, stop the corruption. Each of us has to take responsibility for our own behavior, our own sobriety. Only in responsibility is there freedom.

We must reject killing as a means of solving problems. We must oppose communism, but not by killing people because of their ideas. We become what we fight against. Almost all the wars, drugs, destruction, and murders have been "justified" in the name of fighting communism, yet in the process, we have done exactly what we hate the communists for doing. We have seen the enemy–and it is us.

Drug abuse is a personal temptation that each one of us must face and master. This is an aspect of personal development and spiritual growth that no one can do for us. But we can help each other. We must. Teach your children to avoid drugs. Show them how. That might mean *you* have to learn how. That's part of the maturity process that parenthood forces on us.

The government is not capable of protecting you from the risks and temptations of life. Only a dictator pretends to do this–in order to make you his slave. Every one of us needs to raise our consciousness to the level where we realize that we must face and overcome the temptations and risks of life ourselves. Just as a child grows by meeting and overcoming challenges, just as a muscle is strengthened by ever greater stress, we also mature and raise our consciousness in meeting and overcoming the physical, mental, and moral challenges of life. In this is freedom. In this is responsibility. If we abdicate this freedom and this responsibility, we allow ourselves to be enslaved.

Do not ask the government to protect you from the temptation of drugs, or from terrorism, or from the climate, or from a virus. All of these are normal challenges of human life. You must deal with them yourself. Fortunately, you can. God does not give us problems we are unable to handle. God will help you. *Together*, with God you face your problems. Regardless of how lonely you feel, you are never alone. God is with you. God is within you.

What You Can Do Now

1. The drug business is a control business. The CIA is behind it, for money and power. But almost every "intelligence" agency and government is part of this fraud. It's time to shut down the whole game. We are people, not pawns. Reject this. Live free. Drugs are a personal temptation that every one of us must master. Self-control, not "others" control.
2. Help someone you know who suffers from addiction. Users and addicts have lost their free will and are controlled by others. They are disconnected from their souls. Start by being a friend. We must help each other. Teach your children to avoid all drugs.
3. Explain this fraud to everyone who will listen. It must be exposed.
4. Pressure your elected officials to come clean about this drug fraud (or to learn the truth if they really don't know). Do not accept the lies any longer.
5. Pressure your elected officials to disband the CIA, DEA, FBI, and other intelligence agencies.
6. Pressure your elected officials to decriminalize all drugs and start treating addiction as an illness rather than a crime. We need to help our brothers, not condemn them.

CHAPTER 7

Global Warming—The Second Forever War

"Empirical evidence is the truth that theory must mimic, not the other way around." —DR. JUDY WOOD

Global warming is a perfect forever war. It's a nonissue that can never be solved. This fraud is based on the truth that the earth's climate changes, and these changes affect humans. The fraud then develops lies around the idea that atmospheric carbon dioxide is a "control knob" for the climate. The fraud is also built around the technocratic idea that humans can control everything, including the climate. Most people don't understand much about science, particularly journalists and politicians. These can be hoodwinked. Those who do understand science can be bribed, coerced, or canceled. As usual, only a few people need to know the truth, but millions collaborate as "useful idiots."

The whole global warming program is riddled with obvious lies, propaganda, questionable assumptions, political motives, profiteering, scientific malpractice, statistical deception, and tampered data. This isn't how science is done. But something else is done this way—fraud. Remember, the purpose of active measures is to change your perception of reality to such an extent that, despite ample *evidence*, you don't realize what's really going on around you. Your perception of reality has been intentionally distorted.

I'll review a bit of the basics, touch on models–on which I feel a tiny bit qualified to comment–and try to show how the Climate Forever War fits into the whole scheme of global control.

The Basic Facts

"Another way to cover up the truth is to begin with a theory, and then omit evidence that doesn't fit your theory." –DR. JUDY WOOD

The Carbon Dioxide Correlation

The global warming fraud started off by claiming there is a correlation between rising atmospheric CO_2 concentrations (measured at the Mona Loa research station in Hawaii) and rising average temperatures–mostly measured at weather stations around the United States and Western Europe and very much distorted by the urban heat island effect in the late twentieth century. Even a cursory examination of the data shows there is no such correlation. Global temperatures exhibit long-term, intermediate-term, and short-term cycles, none of which correlate with atmospheric carbon dioxide levels.[1] The sun controls temperatures on earth. Solar irradiance, the energy we receive from the sun, *is* clearly correlated with global temperature changes. Dr. Willie Soon is one of the world's most respected climate scientists. In a very clear and simple paper that destroys the whole climate crisis fraud he says, "Seven independent records–solar irradiance; Arctic, Northern Hemisphere, global, and US annual average surface air temperatures; sea level; and glacier length–all exhibit these three intermediate trends...These trends confirm one another. Solar irradiance correlates with them. Hydrocarbon use does not."[2]

This planet has been around for about four billion years. If the global warming hypothesis was correct, the earth would have burned up long ago. Carbon dioxide levels have been orders of magnitude higher in the past, and the planet didn't burn up then. In fact, the great age of plants, two hundred million to six hundred million years ago, took almost all the carbon dioxide out of the atmosphere and "sequestered" it in rocks.[3] Plants use CO_2 from the air, energy from sunlight, and water and nutrients from the soil to build their leaves, branches, and roots. When the plants die, all their material falls back into the soil (or the seabed), is then covered with more material for billions of years, and the carbon is lost from the biosphere. It eventually becomes carbonaceous rock or hydrocarbon deposits. Today, over 90 percent of all the carbon on this planet is tied up in sedimentary rocks.

Even if human CO_2 production did affect the climate, the "human production of 8 Gt per year is negligible compared with the 40,000 Gt per year residing in the oceans and biosphere."[4]

Every child learns about the carbon cycle in junior high school. All life on this planet is carbon based. On earth, carbon is life. It is not possible for carbon to be a pollutant. By definition, pollution is something that destroys life or is detrimental to life. Carbon *is* life. The term "carbon pollution" is oxymoronic nonsense. Carbon dioxide is an essential part of the carbon cycle. A little more carbon dioxide is unambiguously good for plants and for all life on this planet.[5] With higher atmospheric CO_2 levels, plants all over the earth are growing more and faster and are much more drought tolerant. We can clearly see the difference in satellite photos, particularly in semi-arid parts of the planet. The earth is greening due to higher CO_2 levels and secondarily to improvements in land management by humans.[6]

Historical Temperature Changes

We are still coming out of the Little Ice Age. Global temperatures dropped for five hundred years, from about AD 1200 to about AD 1700. Temperatures have been slowly rising for the past three hundred years. We likely have another two hundred years of warming to go, in spite of any effects from rising carbon dioxide. The planet still isn't as warm as it was one thousand years ago during the Medieval Warm Period, nor as warm as it was during the Roman Warm Period, two thousand years ago. Nobody knows why.

It's also obvious that warming periods correspond with the flowering of civilizations. Warm periods are good. Cool periods are bad. Crops fail, rainfall patterns change, people starve and become desperate. The Minoan Warming corresponds with the height of Bronze Age Culture—the subsequent cooling with the collapse of the Bronze Age civilization about 1200 BC (due to a cooler climate resulting from a massive volcanic eruption in Iceland—so the latest theory goes).[7] The Roman Warm Period peaked a bit before the time of Jesus and corresponds to the growth and prosperity of the Roman Empire. The empire later weakened when temperatures cooled and eventually collapsed and was destroyed in the 5th-century—particularly in Europe, or the Western Roman Empire. The Eastern Roman Empire, or the Byzantine Empire, occupying warmer geography, survived for another thousand years. The colder period of roughly AD 500–900 is what we call the Dark Ages and the collapse of European civilization. Thereafter, the climate warmed in what we now call the Medieval Warm Period. Europe finally dragged itself out of the Dark Ages with the flowering of medieval culture and the building of the great cathedrals around AD 1000–1200. Then cooling set in again—the period we call the Little Ice Age. The promise of the medieval rebirth came to a disastrous end in the thirteenth century with wars, crop failures, plague, and starvation. Only the Renaissance, wealth from the New World, and technological development pulled Europe out of this malaise before the climate warmed up. We are still coming out of it. We need about another 1°C of warming just to get back to the climate of AD 1000. Should we worry about global warming? Not likely.

We are in the Pleistocene Ice Age. You read that correctly. We are in an interglacial warm period within an ice age. We can see this repeating pattern very clearly in the ice core data from Greenland and Antarctica. The glacial periods tend to last about one hundred thousand years, and the interglacial periods about twenty thousand to forty thousand years. This present interglacial period started about fifteen thousand years ago. So, the glaciers could return any millennium now. As you can see from the graph below, we are nowhere near the warmest temperatures during this interglacial period.[8]

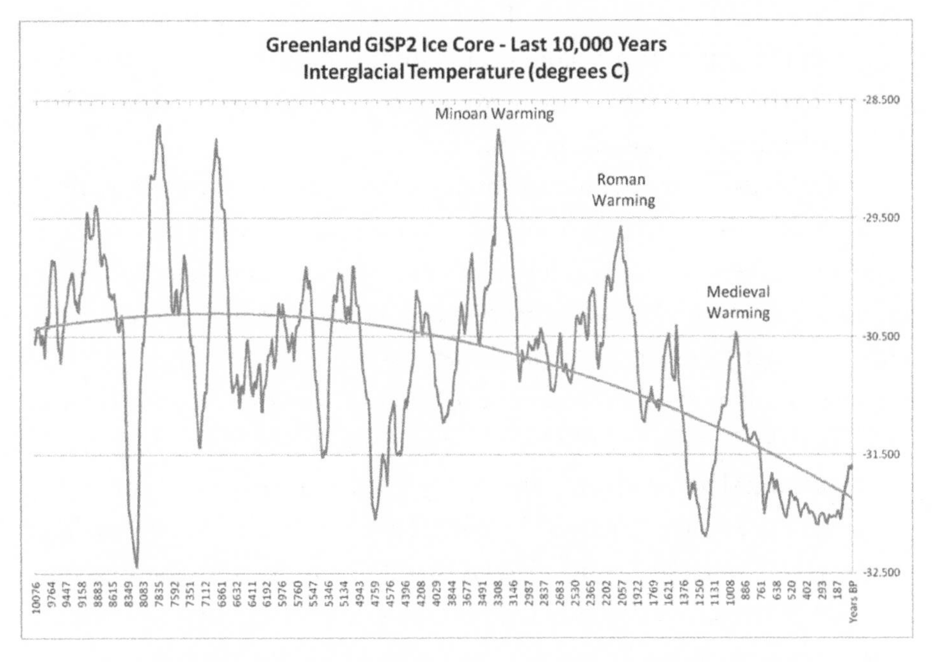

What? Me worry about global warming? This is the evidence that theory must mimic. It has nothing to do with carbon dioxide.

All these well-known climatic changes over the millennia still baffle our best scientists. No one has come up with a widely accepted theory to explain them. We do not have a general theory of climate. We know some things about the climate, but we don't know enough to explain the evidence we see. It stands to reason that if we cannot even explain the climate changes of the recent past, we certainly cannot predict what's going to happen in the future.

Lies, Damn Lies, and Models

"The 'human-caused global warming' hypothesis depends entirely upon computer model-generated scenarios of the future. There are no empirical records that verify either these models or their flawed predictions." –ARTHUR B. ROBINSON

"Climate model" is a misnomer. They are not "models" in any meaningful sense of the word. As an economist, I studied models and worked with them. I'm no expert, but I have a wee bit more insight into mathematical modeling than the average person.

Working with mathematical models of the economy is the daily chore of an economist. Mathematical models are such useful tools that they are applied in every branch of science. But as with every tool, you must know what the tool is good for and what it's not good for, its properties and capabilities, when to use it, and when to set it aside. Despite your proficiency with a hammer, you must resist the temptation to see every problem as a nail. Let's look at the basics of mathematical models. A basic understanding is essential because these are the tools used to hoodwink humanity.

What are called "models" in science are systems of equations. You may recall from high school algebra that if you have two equations and two unknowns, you can find a unique solution for the two unknowns. For example,

$$2x + 3y = 13$$
$$3x + 4y = 18$$

Clearly, $x=2$ and $y=3$. This is the only solution to this simple system of equations. You may even recall the common quadratic equations in the form of

$$y = ax^2 + bx + c.$$

To prepare you for what's coming next, just keep in mind that x and y are the variables and a, b, c are called the parameters (or coefficients) of the equation. This equation describes the relationship between x and y. They could represent, say, the interest rate and gross domestic product, or imports and consumer spending, or any two variables (things that change) in the economy that are somehow related to each other.

We can create large systems of equations. As long as we have as many equations as we have unknowns, we can solve the system. However, as the number of equations increases, the number of calculations required to find the answers increases exponentially. After about four equations, they become unsolvable with pencil and paper because you won't live long enough to complete all the calculations. So mathematical modeling wasn't used much until the 1970s, when computers were developed.

Computers were designed to crunch numbers. It's their strong suit. With the proliferation of desktop computers in the 1980s, mathematical models of everything became all the rage. Now we could use our carefully developed quantitative theories about how the economy worked to create big, multi-equation mathematical models of the economy. If the Bank of Canada raises interest rates by 1%, what will the effect be on Gross Domestic Product? Plug that 1% into your mathematical model and see what number the computer spits out for GDP. Voila! So scientific. So beautifully quantitative. But wait a month and see if the model output matches real life. That didn't work so well. But they're getting better.

In fact, economic models have become accurate enough to be useful. We can never predict the future, which is, by definition, unknowable. But economic models are helpful. However, let's be clear about what they do.

Mathematical models essentially project the past into the future, quantitatively. As long as the future is pretty much like the past, this works pretty well. To be more specific, as long as the relationships (equations and parameters) between all the variables stay the same in the future as they were in the recent past, then the model projections will be fairly accurate. In economics, these relationships are all about how people behave. For example, if many people change the way they respond to an increase in interest rates, then our projections will become useless. In economics at least, it turns out that the immediate future usually *is* pretty much like the immediate past because human behavior usually changes little and slowly.

In economics, we use a class of models called time series models. We are always projecting next month, or next quarter, or next year. If you have an accurate model, your projections for the next time period can be quite accurate, maybe plus or minus ten percent or so. Two time periods into the future and your projections become weak, maybe plus or minus thirty percent or so. Try to go three time periods into the future and your accuracy drops to that of a coin toss. And if something fundamentally changes in human behavior, you're sunk. These are *mathematical* properties of time series models. It doesn't even matter whether your model is good or bad.

Economic modeling is far from perfect. It's not an exact science. It's not science at all, really. It's mathematical speculation. But the results are good enough to be useful because we have a good general theory of the economy and good data. The economy is a *human* system. Being humans ourselves, we can understand human behavior. We can describe our general theory of the economy in words and in mathematics.

When it comes to climate "models," we have two unsolvable problems. We don't have a general theory of climate, and we don't have enough data. If you can't even explain the climate system in words, there's no way you can write mathematical equations to explain it.

It is impossible to create a system of mathematical equations that accurately mimics the behavior of a complex, dynamic, natural system that you do not understand. Period.

The second reason we don't have a "climate model" is the problem of parameterization. You need to be able to estimate values for those *a*, *b*, *c* parameters. In economic models, we use the data from previous years on how these factors changed together. As long as humans keep reacting the same way, the parameters based on past behavior will work pretty well.

With the earth's climate, we are impossibly short of the data necessary to parameterize a mathematical model. As Dr. Tim Ball (a real climate scientist) wrote in his book *Human Caused Global Warming: The Biggest Deception in History*,

> There is virtually no weather data for some 85 percent of the world's surface. Virtually none for the 70 percent that is oceans, and of the remaining 30 percent land, there are very few stations for the approximately 19 percent mountains, 20 percent desert, 20 percent boreal forest, the 20 percent grasslands, and 6 percent tropical rain forest. The horizontal and vertical global coverage is inadequate, but it also lacks

> the length of record for adequate model construction. There are only 1000 stations with 100 years of records and they are almost all in the Eastern US and Western Europe.[9]

If that wasn't enough, according to Dr. Ball, "To get the results the political masters wanted, official data agencies, such as NASA, GISS, altered all the records."[10]

In short, we do not have any climate model. **What we call "climate models" are complicated quantitative methods of projecting assumptions into fantasies.**

What people sloppily call "climate models" are general circulation models based on a complex set of equations dealing with fluid dynamics. They do not describe or mimic the earth's climate, and they are not predictive of future climate conditions. The output of so-called "climate models" is not science. It is not prediction. It is not even estimation. It is not scientifically responsible. It is irresponsible fantasy. It can only be called fraud.

The climate fear that has gripped the world is not based on evidence. Remember, *"evidence is the truth that theory must mimic."* The fear is based solely on the "models" that produce fantasy. As with all the frauds, climate hysteria is not science, but a quasi-scientific ideology that has been used to create mass formation psychosis and is leading to totalitarianism. People are not able to perceive the obvious evidence of their own senses. They cannot perceive reality but can only perceive the fantasy of the official narrative. The truth is that the earth's climate has not changed noticeably during my lifetime. There is nothing to fear.

The Solutions Cannot Work

"There is no energy crisis, only a crisis of ignorance." –R. BUCKMINSTER FULLER

Even if you think that anthropogenic carbon dioxide is destroying our planet and we need to reduce our consumption of fossil fuels, it's clear that all the programs undertaken to do so are completely ineffective.

Remember, this is exactly the pattern of a subversive nonissue–the solutions don't solve any problems. They just create bigger problems. It's all about pattern recognition.

For example, so-called "carbon taxes" are simply another fuel tax. We've had fuel taxes for a century, and they haven't changed the climate. I assure you, as an economist, *you cannot change the weather with taxes*. That's not what taxes do. Taxes raise money for governments. Period. Carbon taxes are meant to take money and power away from people and corporations and put them into the hands of governments. But taxing any commodity does one other important thing–it raises the price of that commodity. Carbon taxes make energy more expensive. These are clearly the goals–make energy expensive and collect money and power into governments.

Electric cars are not a solution to the mythical fossil fuel problem. In most Western nations today, there are laws to replace all internal combustion engine vehicles with electric vehicles by 2035. This would require a doubling of electrical generation and distribution capacity. Yet there are no plans to do this! Every power plant (most of them burning fossil fuels) would need to be twinned with another. Every power line and transformer would have to be twinned. The electricity generation and distribution systems that have taken over a century to build would all have to be duplicated in a decade–with no plans to do so. This is pure fantasy. It is impossible, not just cost-prohibitive. Electric cars are not a solution to any problem. They just create bigger problems. Obviously, something else is planned.

I live in Canada, the coldest country in the world. We need to travel in cars and trucks, and we need to heat and light our homes and workplaces. It doesn't matter how expensive it is, we will still turn on the heat and the lights. A carbon tax is utterly incapable of changing this. It will only make it more expensive. Therefore, it cannot change fossil fuel use in Canada to any meaningful extent. Everyone has known this for at least half a century. The oil crisis of the 1970s demonstrated how inelastic the energy demand is.

And what is a meaningful extent, anyway? If everyone in Canada was to suddenly vaporize and all human activity in Canada stopped, there would be no measurable change in the global climate, or in global anthropogenic CO_2 production, or even in the output of "climate models." Anything we do is completely meaningless.

Solar panels and wind turbines are expensive, intermittent, and unreliable. And they are definitely *not* environmentally benign. Windfarms kill hundreds of thousands of birds and bats. They are an eyesore—a blight on the landscape. With their low-frequency vibrations, it's not safe to live near them.

As we saw in chapter 4, it is typical for mass formation to be quasi-scientific and for behaviors to become purely ritualistic, with no practical meaning. So, it is with the global warming fraud. Many people are impervious to reason and truly believe this is science (it's not), and truly believe their efforts to reduce their imaginary "carbon footprint" will actually change the climate (it won't).

All the "solutions" our governments have tried do absolutely nothing to change the earth's climate. They just make energy more expensive, make our whole economy less efficient, waste resources, increase animosity, frustration, divisions in society... which is exactly the intention.

Alternative Energy

I am a great supporter of alternative energy. Energy is the foundation of our modern society—our wealth, prosperity, and technological growth. The more energy the better—and the more options for energy sources the better. Without the harnessing of fossil fuels, beginning about two hundred years ago, modern civilization could never have occurred. We would still be mostly living in villages with 90 percent of people working in agriculture, using horses to pull plows, and with a world population about 10 percent of what it is today. Without fossil fuels, 2022 would look a lot like 1822. Two hundred years from now, we will most certainly have developed better, cheaper, more productive, and more efficient means of generating energy. And we will likely be using vastly more energy per person than we do today. In a sense, energy is everything. It is difficult to overstate its importance. This is exactly why energy production and use are being targeted. Those who want to control the world must control energy. The blackouts and brownouts the Western world are facing today are completely man-made. It's easy to produce electricity. I was a power engineer, and I'm familiar with how it's done. Generating and distributing electricity is so easy, most people shouldn't even have to think about it—and most people didn't think about it before the global warming fraud.

Up until the turn of this century, nearly everyone understood that the two most important factors in energy production and distribution are cost and reliability. That's why, in most places, fossil fuel-fired, steam turbine-driven electrical generators formed the main baseload power generation of electrical grids. In a few places, hydro-powered water turbines or nuclear-powered boilers were cheaper. Despite the remarkable advances in various technologies, this remains true today.

Wind and solar are not capable of replacing fossil fuels for baseload electrical generation.[11] Nuclear energy is the only technology presently available that could replace fossil fuels. It could produce all the electricity we need and even be used on all ocean-going ships. This would dramatically reduce the burning of fossil fuels.

Why don't we do it? The answer has nothing to do with safety or the environment. Why is the only real solution ignored while trillions of dollars are wasted on stupid ideas that cannot possibly work? Cheap and reliable energy is obviously not the goal. Reducing anthropogenic carbon dioxide is obviously not the goal. When you step back and look at where all these "green" policies are leading, they lead to just one endpoint—governments controlling all people by controlling all energy. That's the goal.

Far more powerful and efficient energy technology already exists. It has been intentionally suppressed. (More about this in chapter 11.) The truth about energy technology will set us free from fossil fuels. The next energy revolution is already upon us. This is not the silly "fourth industrial revolution" that Klaus Schwab talks about. The new energy technologies will usher in the next great step in prosperity and human development on a similar scale to the revolution wrought by fossil fuels. It will involve directed energy, plasma energy, "free" electricity, and possibly nuclear fission or fusion. Low energy nuclear reactions (LENR), also known as cold fusion, look like they offer a solution to household or neighborhood energy independence.

I learned long ago that when politicians propose solutions that cannot possibly work, they are not stupid. They are deceitful. The predictable outcomes of their "solutions" are the real goals. The real goals are to collect money and power into the hands of national governments and transnational power structures such as the United Nations, and to control everyone in the world by controlling all the energy in the world. This is technocracy. We can tell that's the goal, because that's what's happening. Look at the evidence. That's how you expose a fraud.

Why the Fraud?

"We know that no one ever seizes power with the intention of relinquishing it. Power is not a means; it is an end." –GEORGE ORWELL

I have long realized the climate change story is a pack of lies, but I couldn't figure out why it persists. Clearly, a few people were getting rich from it. That's an obvious reason. Al Gore has made a fortune by selling both the disease and the snake oil to cure it. But there's lots more. Just about every major company in the world has jumped on the gravy train. With trillions of dollars up for grabs, who wouldn't?

As one tiny example, the global carbon trading market is worth almost $1 trillion as of 2021.[12] Wow! No wonder banks and greedy people are interested. That's a lot of money for trading an invisible substance where nothing is delivered to no one. That's right. No physical product of any kind changes hands–just money. Nobody reduces their production of "greenhouse gases." Nobody changes anything. They just create an imaginary product that is delivered to no one and paid for with tax dollars. It's purely a money game. And banks make a fortune by selling the emperor his new clothes. But even the trillion-dollar number understates the money involved. By using derivatives and various fraudulent schemes, the elites have produced a business out of "thin air" that creates literally trillions of dollars of wealth for them.

Big banks and big businesses have been co-opted and corrupted into this fraud with our tax money. Very few people have such strong scruples as to be incorruptible. Almost everyone has a price, or a weakness to exploit, or a sin to conceal.

I see four main purposes of the climate change fraud. The main one is to control every country, company, and person in the world by controlling their use of energy through carbon budgets.

A second is to suppress all *real* new energy technology because this would cause the Deep State to lose control of energy. The next two purposes I didn't realize previously, but both are appearing in early 2022.

The third purpose is to restrict the use of fossil fuels so productive businesses will have to shut down. This will add to the other factors that are now bringing about economic collapse in the world. There will be shortages of everything. This is an old communist trick to make everyone dependent on the government. "Do what we say, or you won't get the essentials of life."

A fourth purpose is the destruction of agriculture and the control of food. In 2022, they are pushing the ridiculous idea that now nitrogen (another inert gas that comprises 80% of the atmosphere) is destroying the climate and must be controlled. Farms have to shut down and fertilizer use restricted. This is more "scientific" insanity. There is no basis to this idea in science or scientific evidence. Restricting food production will add to the economic and societal collapse which is leading to starvation, impoverishment, and social disruption–which will cause people to call for a strong "savior" who will bring in greater tyranny under the banner of "safety and security." Energy is everything. Control everyone's energy, and you control everyone.

How It Started

The origins are a bit murky, but it looks like the climate fraud started in the 1970s with the Club of Rome–when "global cooling" was the scare of the day. The Club of Rome is a European think tank composed of politicians, scientists, diplomats, and economists. As a teenager in the mid-70s, I read their first publication, *Limits to Growth.*[13] It may be the first attempt to use a "computer model" to predict disastrous environmental outcomes. It scared the crap out of me. That was its intention. It said the world's population was growing faster than food production and the world didn't have enough resources to support all the people. We had to take drastic measures to lower the world's population before we all starved to death. *Limits to Growth* was not even up to date when it was published in 1972. It ignored the "green revolution" that had been going on for a decade. By improving seed varieties, farming practices, and adding fertilizers, food production easily kept pace with population growth in the free world. We even produced enough extra food to save China and the USSR from starvation several times. Food production has always kept pace with population growth in the modern world because it's easy to produce food. Starvation basically isn't a problem anymore. Poverty still is, but that's a different problem.

Decades would pass while none of these dire predictions came to fruition before I realized what utter nonsense the Club of Rome was peddling. Even more decades would pass before I began to understand what they were really trying to do. The Club of Rome is anti-population, anti-development, anti-free enterprise, and wants to bring about a world government headed by—guess who?—them. These ideas started to become popular again in the 1960s. The famous neo-Malthusian Paul Ehrlich published his bestselling 1968 book *The Population Bomb*[14] with the startling claim, "The battle to feed all of humanity is already lost." He was already wrong then and he still is.

The truth is that the world has plenty of resources to meet everyone's needs. The price system directs resources to their best and most efficient use. We can easily feed, clothe, house, and educate far more people than we will ever have on this planet. It is simply a matter of allowing each individual to make the best decisions they can about their own lives, about how to use their own skills and aptitudes, and about how they can create the best life for themselves and their families. That's precisely the opposite of what the Club of Rome wants. These elites want to control everyone and everything in the whole world, plan and direct all activity with their computers, and make themselves into kings. I'm not kidding. More on this in chapter 13.

One more thing about the Club of Rome. Right from the outset, their policy was to create a world government. Therefore, no nation should ever be too powerful. They want to eliminate all nations, so all of them must be weakened, especially the strong ones. Hence, use the climate fraud to "deindustrialize" the Western democracies, particularly the United States. This is exactly what the climate fraud has accomplished. Don't listen to what they say. Watch the outcomes of their policies. Actions reveal motives. Results reveal intentions.

The Conspiracy of Science-Psychological Warfare

"A dictatorship means muzzles all round and consequently stultification. Science can flourish only in an atmosphere of free speech." –ALBERT EINSTEIN

Science has been weaponized. It was a brilliantly evil move. Scientists and doctors are the most trusted professionals. Turn science and medicine into weapons, and no one will suspect it. Few understand it. Anyone who claims to can be easily discredited–the perfect setup for psychological warfare. Propaganda is an essential part of psychological warfare. As you read the next section, remember that science asks questions. Propaganda prohibits questions. Which pattern do you see?

Global Warming as Psychological Warfare

The global warming fraud can be best understood as part of a psychological warfare operation. Over the past forty years, the Club of Rome has gradually perfected its techniques and tightened its control. They saw in global warming a platform to push their ideology on the world. In their 1991 publication, *The First Global Revolution,*[15] they state, "In searching for a common enemy against whom we can unite, we came up with the idea that pollution, the threat of global warming, water shortages, famine, and the like, would fit the bill...The real enemy then is humanity itself."[16]

Since the "problem" was global in nature and transcended national boundaries, it could be used to overcome national independence to form a one-world totalitarian government. So, they manufactured a crisis and used power, money, and deception to corrupt everyone in positions of influence. So far, it's working beautifully.

Step 1: Corrupting the Environmental Groups

The anti-pollution movement was just getting started in the 1970s, and the Club of Rome set out to subvert it. This was the first step—corrupting the environmental movement. Greenpeace is a good example of what happened. Dr. Patrick Moore was a cofounder of Greenpeace. He has a PhD in biology and served as president of Greenpeace during the late 70s and early 80s. But he left the organization in 1986 because it abandoned science and environmentalism and turned to politics and scaremongering.[17] (Read the whole story in his book *Confessions of a Greenpeace Dropout.*) This is stage 2 of the communist subversion program—take control of organizations and turn them to your cause (See chapter 3). The pattern of subversion is clear and has been repeated throughout the movement—rule or ruin. Environmental nongovernmental organizations (ENGOs) were subverted by the Club of Rome and its related organizations during the 1980s and 1990s. They were given prominence and power in the UN, and they received money and the support of billionaires—as long as they supported the Club of Rome agenda. Since then, they have been almost exclusively focused, not on real environmental problems, but on pushing the "green agenda."

Step 2: Corrupting the Scientists

Using the subversion tactic of "division and confusion," the Club of Rome either co-opted scientists or separated them, demoralized them, demonized them, and destroyed their credibility and careers. One of the first was Dr. Tim Ball. Our paths crossed several times during the 1990s when I was working in the Western Canadian fertilizer industry. Dr. Ball was highly respected as the "go-to" climatologist at agricultural meetings. But he didn't go along with the global warming agenda, so he was canceled before that decade was out. He describes how the whole fraud started.

> The few people involved in climatology before 1990 knew what the IPCC was doing from the start. There were so few actually studying climatology that they were easily marginalized by personal attacks and lawsuits. Marginalization

> involved creating a group, so it was a fringe. First, it was Global Warming Skeptics, knowing the public view of skeptics is different and that all scientists must be skeptics. When the facts changed, the concern switched; Skeptics became Climate Change Deniers, with the Jewish holocaust connection.[18]

Dr. Ball spent over a half million dollars to defend himself against lawsuits intended to shut him up. Very few people have the resources and courage to do that. Scientists bought into the global warming program because the government pays their salaries, either directly or through supporting their universities and/or providing research grants. If your research doesn't support the global warming agenda, it doesn't get funded. If your research challenges the political agenda, you get disgraced and canceled. Scientists have been corrupted by the promise of power and money and the threat of poverty and disgrace. The carrot and stick technique has worked splendidly.

Dr. Judith Curry from the University of Florida, another one of the world's most respected climatologists, couldn't work in academia anymore because of the pressure and abuse. Dr. Peter Ridd in Australia[19] is the world's leading authority on the Great Barrier Reef, but his university fired him because his research clearly shows that the reef, and all the world's reefs, are doing just fine. Dr. Susan Crockford is the world's leading polar bear expert, but her "funding was cut" and she was laid off at the University of Victoria because her research consistently showed that polar bears are thriving. That doesn't fit the narrative. The list goes on.

The global warming cabal completely controls the world of science. If you want to have a job, you "go along" with them. It's just like Nazi Germany in the 1930s. It's like Soviet science. Your results have to fit the ideology. Once again, this isn't how science is done. This is how fraud is done. The only scientists who have the courage to speak the truth are either retired or close to retirement.

Here's another example. Dr. Rex Fleming used to work for the National Oceanic and Atmospheric Administration (NOAA) until he decided to tell the truth. Most honest people have known for years that the NOAA is "propaganda central" for this fraud. A recent article says the following:

> "Censoring evidence, 'fiddling' with data and silencing skeptics were part of life at the National Oceanic and Atmospheric Administration," WND reported. "Rex Fleming admitted that while he worked for NOAA, he attributed global warming to carbon dioxide despite 'having doubts.'"
>
> Now, Fleming has completely disavowed the argument that carbon dioxide from emissions is causing so-called catastrophic climate change on a global scale....
>
> "The 'deniers' have so much evidence, [while the global-warming believers] bring nothing to the table of scientific proof"... "All they have is hearsay. All they have is media coverage. All they have is government people saying it's true."[20]

There are hundreds, maybe thousands, of such personal stories. But not nearly enough. Many scientists are reluctant to say *anything* in public. The risk is too great. Perhaps that's why the media had to ignore the world's leading climate scientists and turn to a teenager for a hero—Greta Thunberg. We are allowing emotional and intellectual children to run our world.

The Intergovernmental Panel on Climate Change (IPCC) is a UN agency set up in 1988 to be the world's clearinghouse for information on man-made climate change. It is a political organization that poses as a scientific one and is the main UN vehicle for controlling people by controlling energy.

The media has convinced the world that the IPCC is the most expert, knowledgeable, and reliable source of climate science. A great con job. The truth is that the IPCC is an ideologically motived and closed shop of handpicked, appointed, politically connected, agreeable people, many of whom are not even scientists. Thousands of the world's leading scientists from all relevant fields are excluded because they don't toe the party line. It is not a scientific body. It is a political body using scientific fraud to push the technocracy agenda. It should be disbanded. *Never* trust it.

Step 3: Corrupting the Data

Those scientists and universities who support the political agenda see their careers flourish and their research budgets balloon. The Climate Research Unit (CRU) at the University of East Anglia in the UK is one of these. Many of us thought the Climategate scandal of 2009 would show up the fraud and finally end it. This is when scientists at the CRU were exposed for perverting the data and the scientific process—acting not as scientists, but as conspirators to push the fraud.

> Then somebody leaked 1000 emails from the CRU, who disclosed a series of wrongdoings, all designed to achieve the climate results they wanted, namely that human-created CO_2 was the cause. They controlled peer reviews by reviewing each other's work; they attacked editors including getting one fired; and created a website to attack and create propaganda. One person, William Connolley, controlled 500 Wikipedia items, until he was exposed. A year later, another 5000 emails were released, detailing the degree of manipulation, corruption, and control.[21]

It was in the news for a while, then the media papered over the whole thing and ruled that nothing was wrong. In truth, everything was wrong.

Let's look at just one instance of the data tampering fraud. Compare these two graphs below. They should be exactly the same. The first one is the US annual mean temperatures from 1880 until 1998, clearly showing that the warmest decade of modern times was the 1930s. It also clearly shows the well-documented cooling trend from the early 1940s to the early 1970s. The graph was published by NASA in 1999. Next, we have the "same" graph published by NASA in 2019. What happened in those twenty years? They changed the data. History ain't what it used to be. How are we to know what to trust? What is the real "science"?

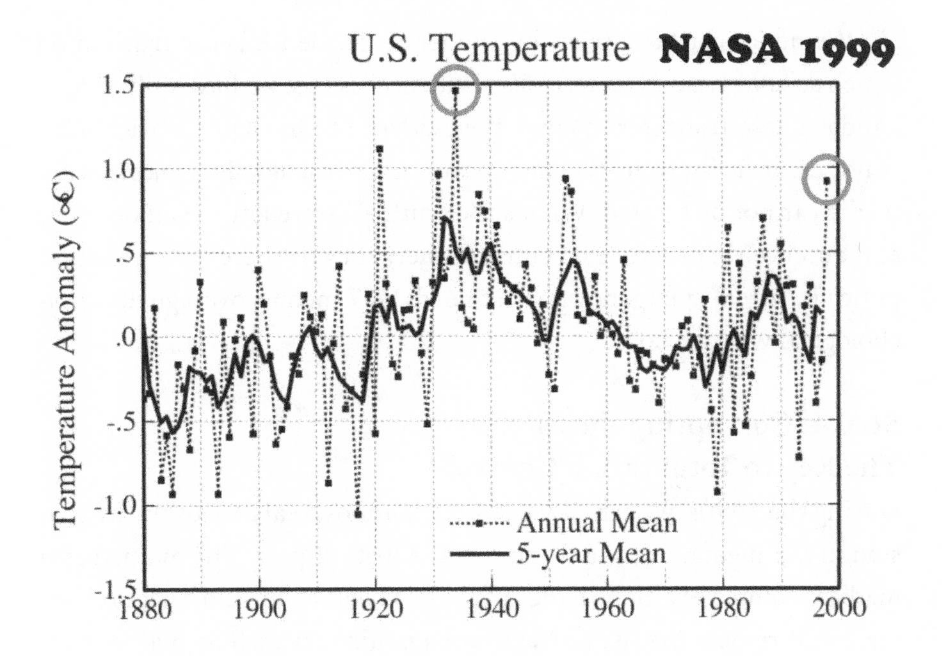

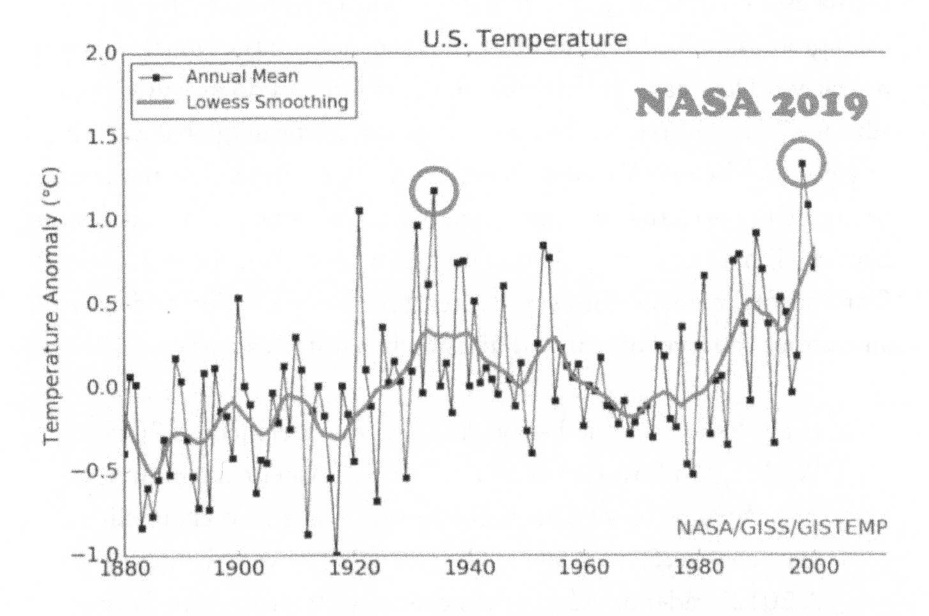

US Historical Temperatures. How Can Historical Data Change?[22, 23]

We no longer have scientific evidence. Evidence is the truth upon which science rests. Now that the "evidence" is lies, we have only propaganda. These fraudsters change the evidence to fit their theories. This is not error. It is crime. Scientists cannot be trusted. The mainstream media cannot be trusted. What's the truth? We are left to walk outside and observe that there is no climate emergency. If there was, we would notice it. A real emergency doesn't need 24/7 media coverage. But psychological warfare does.

Step 4: Corrupting the Media– The Key to Totalitarian Control

During the 1990s, we actually had a bit of almost real debate and discussion in the media. But that is now in the distant past. The mainstream media is completely in the hands of the propagandists. Flip back to chapter 4 and review the list of Nazi propaganda tactics. The mainstream media uses all of them in the climate fraud. Their own editorial guidelines prohibit publishing anything that goes against the global warming narrative. They constantly promote the fraud and do everything possible to silence the truth. They don't even use the term "global warming" anymore. It's been replaced with more hysterical terms. Global warming became climate change became climate chaos became climate disruption became climate emergency. The mainstream media's purpose is to spread fear and fuel demand for ever greater government action and control. Just notice the level of fear and division in Western society.

> If adults are worried silly, children are terrified. A 2019 Washington Post survey showed that of American children ages thirteen to seventeen, 57 percent feel afraid about climate change, 52 percent feel angry, and 42 percent feel guilty. A 2012 academic study of children ages ten to twelve from three schools in Denver found that 82 percent expressed fear, sadness, and anger when discussing their feelings about the environment, and a majority of the children shared apocalyptic views about the future of the planet. It is telling that

> for 70 percent of the children, television, news, and movies were central to forming their terrified views.[24]

This is exactly the pattern of using nonissues in the process of subversion—use fear to turn tiny problems into big ones. That's what is happening. That's what the evidence shows.

Naturally, the global billionaires and elites behind this fraud don't use their own money to pay for their campaigns. They use yours. All the money comes from the pockets of taxpayers, homeowners, and car owners all over the world. You pay for all the phony research and for the UN, IPCC, NOAA, and all the other "science" organizations through your taxes. You pay for the "green energy" through higher utility costs to heat and light your home and run your car. You pay for the psychological warfare every time you turn on your TV, or radio, or pay your monthly cable bill. As far as money goes, the whole fraud is a scheme to take money out of the pockets of ordinary people and put it into the pockets of the rich and powerful.

Step 5: Corrupting the Politicians

Corrupting and hoodwinking the politicians wasn't terribly difficult. Most politicians are not scientists; in fact, they are not experts in anything. If they've been successful in politics, they have typically learned to respond to political pressure and sail where the political winds blow. You don't build a career in politics by speaking truth to power. That's the role of a prophet and usually gets you killed. Politicians bought into the global warming fraud because they were hoodwinked by fraudulent science and scientists. If that didn't work, then pressure groups forced them with propaganda and slander—the same pressure groups that are funded by the rich left-wing elites. These same elite billionaires, often through their self-funded NGOs and think tanks, fund the political campaigns and line the pockets of malleable politicians. This isn't democracy. It is technocracy.

Climate Change? No—Weather Control? Yes

Humans do not have any significant effect on the earth's *climate*, but we can and do affect the *weather*. For example, we know for sure that forests cause cooling. Trees shade the ground and absorb energy from sunlight. They cause the air above the forest to cool, moisture to condense, and rain to fall. We have repeatedly observed that when you cut down a whole forest, the area warms up and dries up. This has often caused the decline and fall of ancient cultures when they deforested their country.

More importantly, the United States military has been experimenting with weather modification and control for almost a century.[25] For decades, HAARP (High-Frequency Active Auroral Research Program) has been researching the atmosphere and developing weapons that, among other capabilities, can affect and even control weather events. It is highly secret, but researchers have gleaned nuggets of information about their capabilities from HAARP patents. The military has publicly stated that, from their phased array radar site in Alaska, they bounce directed energy beams off the ionosphere and cause parts of it to warm up.[26] Maybe blaming carbon dioxide is partly a cover for the intentional atmospheric heating the US government is causing with HAARP. They are using various types of directed energy weapons. We will see these again.

The US government received some bad publicity about the project a decade ago, claimed to have shut it down, and transferred the facility to the University of Alaska. But this has long been a subterfuge tactic of the military–contract the work to universities so it disappears from the military but continues to be run by military "contracts." The facility is still in operation. That tells me the weather weapons are still in operation, although it seems likely they have developed newer techniques for controlling the weather. A US military spokesman said, *"We're moving on to other ways of managing the ionosphere."*[27] Weather weapons and weather manipulation are real. The climate crisis is not.

The Communists Are Laughing

More and more people are gradually realizing this climate hysteria is a fraud. The insiders have known it for decades. Occasionally, the truth accidentally slips out. Dr. Ottmar Edenhofer, one of the UN's top climate officials, effectively admitted that the organization's public position on climate change is a lie. In a November 14, 2010, interview with the

Swiss newspaper *Neue Zürcher Zeitung*, Edenhofer, co-chair of the IPCC's Working Group III, made this shocking admission, "But one must say clearly that we redistribute de facto the world's wealth by climate policy... One has to free oneself from the illusion that international climate policy is environmental policy. This has almost nothing to do with environmental policy anymore."[28] Exactly my point.

China, Russia, India, and many other countries are laughing at this nonsense in the West. All three of these countries are building more coal-fired and nuclear power plants—two of the cheapest and most reliable sources of electricity. That's what matters: cost and reliability. The countries that have most moved away from this principle have the highest cost and least reliable electricity. Should that surprise anyone?

In earlier chapters, we learned to recognize the patterns we see in global warming—the pattern of fraud, the pattern of communist subversion, the pattern of psychological warfare, even the pattern of mass formation psychosis. "Climate change" is an idea, a mental construct, a theory. It can be used to create fear and anxiety, but you cannot fight against it. You can only fight against something that exists in material reality. So, climate change anxiety needs an object of anxiety that can be attacked. Real people can be attacked, manipulated, and controlled. That's the goal. As with all mass formation, real people will eventually be murdered, and the murderers will think themselves noble for doing it. Just look at how the climate change zealots already think themselves noble for coercing, manipulating, robbing, and terrorizing other people. Murder is only a short step away.

It's all about pattern recognition. It is not a mistake, not an accident, not a misunderstanding. These have different patterns. Climate change is a carefully constructed and managed fraud that has been slowly steamrolling its way over all logic, common sense, and scientific evidence. Many people have been taken in by this quasi-scientific hypothesis. They are "true believers". It's not a religion, as a few people claim. It's an ideology that has no basis in scientific evidence. These people are honestly hypnotized. You cannot talk reason or facts to them. They cannot hear it. And when we see mass formation, we know we are looking at totalitarianism.

Stop believing these lies. Start exposing the fraud at every opportunity. Stop giving money to "green" organizations. Stop attending their rallies and demonstrations. Stop allowing your local governments to spend money wastefully on expensive "green" projects. You are not saving the planet. You are destroying yourself. Encourage your politicians to get out of the IPCC and to cancel your climate change departments in government.

You scientists who are "going along" with this global warming fraud, understand that the day will come when you are held to account. You are responsible. Even if you honestly don't understand that you are engaged in fraud–maybe the climate is not your specialty–you have a fiduciary duty. It's your *job* to know. Because of your expert knowledge, the rest of us trust you to tell us the truth about the earth's climate. That's what a fiduciary duty is–a duty you hold because others trust in your specialized knowledge.

You "journalists" who are complicit in this fraud–beware. The public will have no mercy for you. Once the public realizes what you have done for the past three decades, there will be hell to pay. Your fiduciary duty is to tell the truth. Start now.

What You Can Do Now

1. There are hundreds of books and websites that have truthful scientific information that exposes the climate fraud. Educate yourself. Do your own research. That's your responsibility.
2. Demand that your politicians accept the truth that the global warming scare is a fraud designed to control the whole planet. Only vote for candidates who understand this and promise to stop the fraud.
3. Explain this fraud to everyone who will listen. Direct them to this book and to other books that explain the truth.
4. Scientists and scientific journals cannot be trusted. I take no pleasure in this realization. This does *not* mean that everything scientists say is wrong. But we cannot simply accept things at face value anymore without careful examination. Like most people, I don't know enough

about science to be able to read scientific papers, understand them thoroughly, and detect errors. I need other scientists to do that for me and explain the issues in layman's terms. That's exactly why free discourse is essential in science and in society. Muzzling free discourse is exactly how the censorship we now experience has corrupted science and public policy. "Do your own research" means that you have to seek out divergent voices. Look at the evidence yourself. Use your own mind. However feeble you think it is, it's your only defense.

5. The mainstream media is lying to you. They are all active participants in this fraud: TV, radio, movies, newspapers, magazines. Ignore all of them. Shut it all off.
6. All "climate" research and promotion organizations, ENGOs, and government departments must be shut down completely. This includes the IPCC, NOAA, NASA, and all related organizations. Pressure your elected representatives to do this. Stop donating money to "environmental" groups. They are, in fact, political groups taking part in environmental fraud in return for money and power.
7. Our "official" scientific organizations are corrupted and cannot be trusted. We must build alternate, parallel scientific organizations.
8. The totalitarian elites are trying to control you by controlling your energy use. Resist this. There is no such thing as a "carbon footprint." Learn about small-scale energy generation. Strive for some level of energy independence, either personal or with your small community.

PART 3

An Interlude for More Background

We need to pause our analysis of the frauds to fill in more background information about the role of China and the whole issue of mind control and media control. We saw in chapters 6 and 7 how the media has been instrumental in perpetrating the frauds. We saw in chapter 4 how control of the media is essential in totalitarian takeovers, and we learned about the group psychological process of mass formation. We now need to understand more about the methods of mind control, particularly with mass communication. Unless we understand this, the frauds of Part 4 will seem too unbelievable.

Also, we looked at the Bolsheviks, the Fascists, and the Nazis. But today those are all gone. What remains is China. We must look at how China has changed in recent decades and taken leadership of world communism. Other than the supranational Deep State (which we examine in chapter 17), China is the only entity that has both the ability and the intention to control the whole world. That's scary. China's idea of warfare is even scarier. It has infected our whole world. Let's take a look.

CHAPTER 8

China Ascendant

"Don't make a fuss about a world war. At most, people die...Half the population wiped out–this happened quite a few times in Chinese history...It's best if half the population is left, next best one-third." –MAO ZEDONG

Why a chapter on China? What role does it play in these frauds to take over the world? China has a quarter of the world's people and the second largest economy. Any plan to control the world must include China. Yet China has its own plans for world control. Let's try to connect some dots in the complex and enigmatic relationship between the Western elites and China's elites. We pick up the story in the mid-1970s when Deng Xiaoping took over from Mao Zedong and China pivoted to the West.

For two decades after its founding in 1949, the Chinese communists cooperated with the USSR and China sucked all the technological and financial aid it could out of the Soviet Union. Gradually, the Soviets realized that the Chinese had no intention of being vassals in a future communist world ruled from Moscow. They saw the future world ruled from Beijing. Tensions between them rose, cooperation declined, and military clashes erupted on their border. By about 1970, China started looking westward and began to gently court their avowed enemy, the United States of America.

About the same time, a few Western elites began to envision ways to include China in their own plans for world domination. Beginning in the early 1970s with President Nixon and his national security advisor, Henry Kissinger (a Council on Foreign Relations member), and continuing with President Carter and his national security advisor, Zbigniew Brzezinski (a founding Trilateral Commission member), China-US relations thawed and gradually blossomed into massive cooperation.

As usual, all parties were trying to strategically play everyone against everyone else. The Americans were trying to drive a wedge into the communist China-Russia axis, weaken their enemies' alliance, and use the threat of China-US cooperation against the Soviets. The United States was also overjoyed with the possibility of wooing China away from communism altogether and guiding it onto the path of capitalism and democracy.

The Chinese used this hope, and their propaganda that it was being realized, to manipulate the West for strategic and economic advantage. They also used the "Western cooperation" card to forestall Soviet aggression against them. China's pivot to the West brought it unimaginable gains in its hundred-year marathon and put them in a perfect position to pick up the mantle of world communist leadership two decades later when the Soviet empire disintegrated.

The US policy of cooperation with China has remained consistent since it began with Nixon. (At least until Donald Trump, who wasn't part of the Deep State elites.) It's no surprise. The China policy never came from the US government. It came from the Trilateral Commission and has remained so.[1] Democratic and Republican presidents and Congresses came and went, but the US-China relationship continued to be constantly more "cooperative." As we will see more fully in chapter 17, government policy is made above the level of governments.

As part of the new policy of cooperation, China was allowed into international organizations such as the United Nations. However, their intention was never to *contribute* to international cooperation, but to *control* world affairs by controlling these international organizations. That's how communists work–rule or ruin.

Chinese Subversion

Chinese communist subversion of the West also took on a different character beginning in the 1970s. Rather than following the Soviet subversion model, they adopted a softer approach. Almost all their subversion efforts went into "peaceful" cooperation and subtle manipulation of the West. They sent their brightest students to Western universities. The Chinese Communist Party (CCP) "partnered" with many universities and cities to "share" information and research. They started working with Western corporations, first to license foreign technology, then for joint projects where they could quietly steal Western technology and use Western money to develop China's industries. Since the CCP controlled the economy, they could easily ensure that Western businessmen earned generous returns on their investments. They courted Western leaders and diplomats, gradually extending their influence into every country in the world. Western business and political elites gradually became enmeshed in China. Their success was tied to China's success. They were, in a sense, "captured."

For example, Joe Biden's family business connections with the Chinese have compromised him. They did not enter into business deals with the Biden family because it was "good business." They did it to "capture" him. The CCP is not in business. Their only "business" is power. These relationships were cultivated by the Chinese to gain political influence. The Chinese Communist Party views Joe Biden as an "asset." He will do nothing to stand in the way of China's plans. The same is true for thousands of politicians and business leaders around the world. China has accomplished this control for less than the cost of an aircraft carrier–and it gives them far more power.

The CCP considers this influence and infiltration of the West to be a "weapon."

> The Chinese regime has found particular success in its "United Front" operations aimed at influencing America's elite to get them to act in ways approved by Beijing...Dubbed by CCP leaders as a "magic weapon," "United Front work"

> involves the efforts of thousands of overseas groups that carry out political influence operations, suppress dissident movements, gather intelligence, and facilitate the transfer of technology to China. Many of the groups are coordinated by the Party agency the United Front Work Department (UFWD). An investigation last year by Newsweek found about 600 such groups in the United States...."United Front organizations have been allowed to operate with near impunity in the United States for many, many years."[2]

It's almost funny. "United Front" is even the same name the communists used in the 1930s when they were working for the USSR. This is precisely what the Comintern did for most of the twentieth century. Now China is doing it everywhere in the world. China simply picked up the reins of world communist leadership from a weakened Russia. This is part of China's "three warfares" strategy against the United States.[3] These are psychological warfare, public opinion warfare, and legal warfare. As with all subversion, China is playing a long game.

One part of the United Front is China's "1000 Talents" program, which entices outstanding scientists to work with the Chinese—to get the latest scientific knowledge and technology, either legally or not. For example, Harvard Professor Charles Lieber was convicted in December 2021[4] of felony charges related to his work with the program and sharing his cutting-edge technology of welding transistors onto nanoparticles and turning them into nanobots. Lieber is just one of hundreds of known or suspected US participants in this Chinese program.

China ingratiated itself to the West, scrubbed its public image, and used everyone it could to further China's interests. Their strategy was to suck everything useful out of the West, apply it in China, exceed all the West's accomplishments, then dominate and control the whole world. It is China's *Hundred-Year Marathon*, the title of a book by China expert Michael Pillsbury.[5] China intends to supplant the United States as the world's superpower and control the whole world by 2049, the hundredth anniversary of the People's Republic of China.

The Chinese "Miracle" Unmasked

China does not have capitalism, or free enterprise. They have communism, really technocracy. We could also call it mercantilism. Some property ownership is allowed, but the communist party still decides the main production goals, political goals, social goals, and religious goals (which is, the state is God). If you want to start a business, the communist party has to agree. If you want to do business outside China, the communist party is your controlling partner. Even though China is more economically successful today because of its "market-based" reforms, don't mistake this for capitalism. Freedom exists in general or not at all; it cannot be allocated to business only. Free enterprise cannot exist without democracy.

The Chinese "miracle" was never a miracle but merely better planning and a slight lifting of the destructive insanity of state control—allowing ordinary people the freedom to begin solving their own problems. Hungry peasants were permitted to plant gardens and eat the food they grew, perhaps to even sell some in the local market. Small businessmen were permitted to serve their customers with the goods and services those customers asked for. Industrial enterprises were permitted to actually use prices to calculate what to produce and how to produce it. Human progress isn't rocket science. The main ingredient is freedom. A free economy and free people will always outperform a planned economy and a controlled people.

The rapid improvement in the Chinese standard of living, their rapid urbanization, and their consistent double-digit increases in GDP can largely be explained by these changes.

1. Ending the ridiculous social and economic disruptions of the Cultural Revolution and giving people at least enough economic freedom to solve their own problems.
2. Central planning based on well-established business principles that are best described as mercantilism or technocracy. These include:
   a. A focus on "export-led" growth—that is, producing simple products for an export market with simple technology and cheap labor costs to undercut the production costs of competitors. This is a

classic business entry strategy. Japan did it after the Second World War, as have countless other countries and businesses.

b. A focus on controlling resources (a key mercantilist principle) and developing a manufacturing industry that a large population can then support.
c. Weakening the currency to gain a competitive advantage for their exports.

3. A decades-long modernization to replace their ancient technology, either licensed or stolen from the West. This simple step improves productivity in a generation with technology that took the world centuries to discover.
4. A massive and sustained credit expansion. This is usually forgotten. Between 1980 and 2020, China experienced the largest and most sustained credit expansion in the history of the world. However, as in the West, they are now buried under a mountain of debt.[6]
5. A decent and universal education system along with a relative suppression of corruption. These are the top two factors long identified as the greatest impediments to third-world economic growth—corruption and poor education.

Other factors were involved, of course, but these are enough to produce the "China miracle." It is not the supposed "hybridization" of capitalism and communism. The state controls the whole economy and everyone's personal life. They simply stopped some of the obvious stupidity, adopted reasonable business strategies and management practices, employed modern technology, had good education, and consistently printed money. Their economic growth is slowing because the easy successes have already occurred, and organic growth is much slower. Massive debts eventually bring to an end the benefits of credit expansion and expose the waste and malinvestment.[7] Technological growth slows when you have to actually invent things on your own—and innovation stagnates under the oppressive control of communism.

China's days of rapid economic growth are behind them. It is unlikely they can keep up this game much longer. Also, they are facing a demographic crisis in the coming decades because of their former one-child policy. It is extremely difficult to achieve economic growth with a declining and aging population.

The New Imperialist

China has taken a page from the book of American imperialism to exert power and control over almost half the world. Just like in the stories of the economic hitman John Perkins (as we will see in chapter 11), China loans money to third-world countries to pay Chinese firms to build infrastructure in their countries. Then, when the small countries cannot pay back the loans, China steps in and takes control of their natural resources and infrastructure. It's an old imperialist ploy, and it works really well. Even little Malta[8] and Montenegro[9] are suffering under the crime, corruption, and economic manipulation of this imperialism. This tactic is exactly what China has been doing in Central Asia as part of its One Belt program and throughout Africa to get its hands on natural resources. Our mainstream media doesn't report it, but China has become the hidden ruler of Africa and the new imperialist power in the world.

Another example of how China uses business as a weapon of war is the case of the rare earth metals market. I learned about this during the 1990s when I worked in new products research for a large Canadian fertilizer manufacturer. We could have refined some rare earth elements from the byproducts of our phosphate fertilizer production. I did a preliminary study of the production and marketing economics of the idea. The production economics were favorable, but China presented a marketing problem.

The rare-earth elements are fifteen elements that range in atomic number from 57 to 71. The "rare" in rare earths is a misnomer. They are not rare. They are found everywhere in the earth's crust. It's just that they usually occur in such tiny concentrations that recovering them is not economic. There are only a handful of places in the world where they have been found in high enough concentrations to make mining and refining them worthwhile.[10]

Only small amounts of these elements are used—they are sold by the pound, not by the ton. But they are increasingly important in many applications such as specialty glass (think solar panels), magnets, batteries, and industrial and automotive catalysts. Because they have important military applications, rare earths are considered to be strategic metals. Since the rare earth metals market is tiny, highly specialized, and has strategic importance, it was the first international market that China set out to control in the 1980s.

China has reasonable rare earth deposits, but economics are not the overriding concern to a communist government with strategic goals. During the 1980s, China developed these deposits and started producing rare earth elements in large enough quantities to swamp the world market. Prices collapsed for key elements, which forced almost all other producers out of business. Once other companies were bankrupted, China could then control the supply and gradually raise prices. Since then, China has produced about 90% of all the rare earth elements in the world, giving them near monopoly power. They have excess production capacity so they can overproduce, drop the world prices, and drive out any new entrant. This is known as a predatory business practice. For our company, this business risk made the whole idea unfeasible. When such tactics are employed by a nation-state, it's not predatory business. It's warfare. For China, this is all about control. They don't have to make money in this business. The whole world is dependent upon China for its rare earth elements. This is business used as a weapon of war.

China's strategic control of the rare earth metals market is a template for how they operate in other markets as well. It's not about business. It's not about economics. It's about control and power.

The New Warfare

"War is everything. Everything is war." –DONALD LEE

Since the beginning of this book, I've said we are in a war. To make sense of that statement, we need to understand something about what war has become. Like everything else, you have to learn to perceive differently if you are to understand what is really going on.

Unrestricted Warfare

China has become militarily aggressive, threatening countries on all its borders. China has colonized atolls in international waters and in Philippine waters in the South China Sea—dredging them to make artificial islands and build military bases on them.[11] This, despite warnings from the United States and their own promises not to do so. They have disputed with Japan over islands in the East China Sea. They have encroached on India's territory in the Himalaya Mountains and engaged in border skirmishes—killing more than twenty Indian soldiers in 2020. They continue to threaten Taiwan and are increasing their deliberate incursions into Taiwanese airspace.

China is expanding its nuclear arsenal to match the level of America. They have publicly stated they are willing to sustain massive nuclear casualties (hundreds of millions) in order to win a war. But most of China's military build-up is focused on asymmetric warfare. They intentionally keep their military spending low to avoid rousing suspicion. This is an ancient Chinese strategy of weakening your enemy by enticing *him* to spend huge amounts on *his* military.

For example, rather than spending trillions to build a blue water navy to challenge America's eleven carrier groups, they have focused on weapons to neutralize American dominance. American aircraft carriers have no defense against Chinese hypersonic missiles. Sink the carrier, and the supporting vessels are sitting ducks. They can be sunk by Chinese aircraft and high-speed shkval torpedoes launched from China's many submarines. A few million dollars' worth of weapons can take out trillions of dollars' worth of surface ships and completely disable America's ability to project power.[12]

China is also trying to dominate space.[13] Russia and China have both placed weapons on satellites and are developing directed energy weapons that target US systems. China is also building a huge power plant in space 35,000 kilometers above the earth.[14] It will be up to megawatt capacity by 2030 and gigawatt capacity by 2050. Allegedly, it will beam energy down to earth. There is no chance this is economic as a power plant. What's more likely is it will serve as the power source for directed energy weapons so China can destroy American satellites, control space, and control the whole planet.

China is trying to overthrow America. This is an existential challenge to the whole world. In May 2019, China declared a "people's war" on the United States.[15] It is no secret—except our mainstream media is not reporting it at all. The hawks in China want to wipe out the Americans and settle America with Chinese people. The "secret speech" of China's defense minister laid it all out in 2003.

> Only by using nondestructive weapons that can kill many people will we be able to reserve America for ourselves. There has been rapid development of modern biological technology, and new bio-weapons have been invented one after another. Of course, we have not been idle, in the past years we have seized the opportunity to master weapons of this kind. We are capable of achieving our purpose of "cleaning up" America all of a sudden.[16]

China's strategy to subvert and then control the world was encapsulated in a now famous book written by a pair of People's Liberation Army (PLA) officers and published (in English) in 1999—*Unrestricted Warfare*.[17] In short, everything is war and war is everything. The book focuses on the United States as a distinct enemy, but the principles really apply to the whole world. After all, if China controls the United States, no one will be able to stand against them. The book argues that US military strategy neglects the wider field of engagement. That leaves America vulnerable to other types of warfare. This thinking is straight from Sun Tzu's *The Art of War* over two thousand years ago.

Here are some examples of China's "unrestricted warfare." International laws or regulations that weaken your opponent but not you are an excellent form of warfare. (Keep this in mind when you think about climate change.) Social disruptions in your opponent's country that cause it to war against itself are perfect. (Keep this in mind when you think about China's encouragement of American riots in 2020.) Something like a deadly virus that would paralyze your opponent and shut down his economy would be an absolute godsend. Does this sound familiar? A cyberattack on your opponent's industry, infrastructure, or any part of the economy is now run-of-the-mill unrestricted warfare. China conducts cyber warfare constantly, both to steal technological and military secrets and to disrupt Western economies. And if you could hack your opponent's election and get people elected who will further China's interests and foolishly work against their own country's interest? Who would even need guns when you have that much power? Are you starting to recognize a pattern? This is exactly what China is doing. This is not theory. This is history. They even published their strategy.

China has what they call "civil-military fusion." It means there is no boundary between the military and civil society. Business is war. Culture is war. Politics is war. China turned around the famous dictum of Clausewitz, who said that war is politics by other means. For China, politics is war by other means. In fact, *everything* is war by other means. When you interact with any Chinese citizen, you must understand that you are dealing with the CCP and the PLA. War is everything. Everything is war.

Fifth-Generation Warfare

The Chinese concept of unrestricted warfare is very similar to what American military strategists call fifth-generation warfare. They consider the various technological and tactical changes in warfare as "generations." First-generation warfare was basically everything up to the use of rifles in the mid-nineteenth century.[18] It used line and column tactics and an orderly battlefield.

Second-generation warfare (2GW) was rifles, automatic firing weapons, and artillery up to the First World War. The battlefield became increasing disordered and chaotic, yet generals tried to impose order on it. The tactics relied heavily on massive artillery to destroy the adversary's equipment, defenses, and personnel.

Third-generation warfare (3GW) is the use of highly mobile and fast-moving weapons such as aircraft, missiles, tanks, motorized infantry, and the associated tactics of quickly breaking enemy lines, outflanking, precisely targeted artillery, and attacking areas in the enemy's rear. Rather than attempting to impose order on a chaotic battlefield, 3GW tactics rely heavily on rapid maneuvers to adapt to the chaos and take advantage of it. This warfare characterized World War II.

Fourth-generation warfare (4GW) is insurgency of all types—blurring the lines between war and politics, combatants and civilians. It uses guerrilla warfare tactics—small, independent units operating on initiative rather than commands, decentralized rather than centralized forces, self-discipline rather than external discipline, objectives rather than orders, and forces making themselves untargetable rather than impregnable. Nation states lose the monopoly on organized violence and even on social organization itself. Irregular, nonstate entities become factors in warfare. This was the Vietnam War where US soldiers never knew who was friend or foe. Village children might be planting landmines on the jungle trails. Vietcong units would ambush US patrols and then melt into the jungle. It is extremely difficult to defeat a fourth-generation insurgency. Up until now, these are the only types of wars the United States has lost.

In some ways, the advantage of 3GW over 2GW can be seen in its decentralization, fluidity, and quick reactions. The centralized decision-making, rigid command structure, and process-ridden operations of 2GW are simply overwhelmed. This is exactly how the German army overwhelmed the French in 1940. A similar comparison is valid between 4GW and 3GW. Next, fifth generation warfare becomes unbelievably chaotic.

Fifth-generation warfare (5GW) almost doesn't seem like war. Many people will not even notice it's going on—nor will it be clear *who* is waging the war. That's part of the idea. It is conducted primarily through non-kinetic means, such as social engineering, disinformation, mind war, cyberattacks, terrorism, bioweapons, directed energy weapons, artificial intelligence, political manipulation, and so on. When you don't even know war is going on, you can't defend yourself. "Attacks" could come from anywhere—your neighbor, employer, doctor, news anchor, internet service provider, banker, police, soldiers, judges, and politicians. Most likely, they won't understand what's going on either. The strategic goal is control. You don't have to destroy buildings or shed blood.

Former psychological warfare and intelligence officer Jeffrey Prather describes 5GW this way.[19] 5GW has two main weapons systems. The first is the information influence operations to "prepare the ground" for the main battle. The "ground" in this case is the minds of the participants, most of whom don't know that warfare is being conducted against them. In the "old days," this was simple propaganda, even including dropping printed leaflets on the enemy forces telling them they have no hope of victory and will be treated well if they surrender. Now it involves sophisticated social media campaigns with micro-targeting and pattern analysis using artificial intelligence, as the United States used in the Arab Spring wars. Information influence operations also include controlling the traditional media channels to manipulate the thinking and beliefs of the target population in ways that suit the attacker's purpose. This is part of psychological warfare, and it is incredibly effective. Modern militaries have mastered it. It is a "force multiplier" because it makes your kinetic forces vastly more effective—to the point that you might not even need to use them.

Once the ground has been prepared with the information influence operation, the second weapons system is deployed. This can be any combination of non-kinetic weapons—biological, mitochondrial, genetic, electromagnetic, directed energy, cyber, digital, financial, legal, regulatory, political, economic, and more. The combinations and permutations are almost endless. If any one of the weapons proves ineffective, then others will pick up the slack. The population won't even know these are weapons and that they are being subjected to a carefully executed, multipronged assault in a fifth-generation war. Whether you call it unrestricted warfare or fifth-generation warfare, war is everything and everything is war. China is doing this—but so are governments all over the world.

Everyone in the world is being attacked by their own governments in a fifth-generation war. A few people have realized this and are responding with a fourth-generation insurgency war—the resistance. Yet the governments have a centralized structure that is appropriate to second generation warfare, and the one world government they are trying to establish will only make this worse for them. Insurgencies are extremely difficult to defeat. They are impossible to defeat with 2GW. The greater the oppressive actions of our governments, the greater will be the insurgency reaction. The more people begin to understand what's going on, the more the eventual defeat of governments is assured.

As more people learn that our illnesses are an attack with biological and other weapons, the more they will avoid becoming victims. As more people learn that our governments themselves are the enemy, the more these state institutions will be marginalized and become ineffective. As people build alternative structures to replace the corrupt and weaponized existing structures, all that exists today will crumble to dust and the new structures will be all that's left standing. Our nation states are self-destructing. But in their place will not be a one world totalitarian dictatorship as they intend, but a decentralized network of sovereign individuals and communities. More on this later.

From a spiritual perspective, all attack (and even defense) springs from fear. Yet it can never abolish fear, which lives only in hearts. Fear is non-material. It cannot be destroyed by any attack. Only material things can be destroyed–like people. Fear is never destroyed; it is simply replaced with love–one state of consciousness to replace the other.

American military strategists seek "full spectrum dominance," which means dominating every nation, every person, and every force in the world and above it. This is insanity. This is uncontrolled fear and the lust for power. No more is ever needed than a credible defense as a deterrent against foreign attack. As both spiritual and material advice, turn from fear to love, and your lust for "full spectrum dominance" over your brothers will fade away.

The Solution: Shun China

We must understand how thoroughly the Chinese Communist Party (CCP) controls the people and the country and how the civil-military fusion affects all life in China. Nothing leaves or enters China without the knowledge and permission of the CCP. If you think cell phone videos are "leaked" out of China, it's not likely. These are targeted propaganda of the CCP. If you do business with a Chinese company, CCP agents are controlling every part of the deal. Any Chinese company engaged in business outside China must be understood as an arm of the communist party. Everything is war. Their business activities outside of China are completely to achieve Chinese political objectives—to gain control of raw materials, markets, and foreign companies; influence foreign elites; strengthen China; weaken everyone else; and ultimately control the whole world. Everything you do with China furthers *its* goals.

If you are involved in a cultural exchange with China, you must understand that this is an exercise in communist subversion as far as they are concerned. If you are involved in a university or research effort with the Chinese, you must understand that this is an intelligence operation for them.

China is a giant international bully. Everything China does is war. We must shun China—have nothing to do with them. This will be painful for us, but it will be disaster for China. Stop buying things from China. Stop selling things to China. Stop allowing Chinese students to attend our schools. Stop allowing Chinese companies to buy Western companies or invest in our stock markets. Stop Western investment in Chinese stock markets. Stop all exchanges with China—cultural, scientific, educational, technical—everything. Stop allowing them to participate in international organizations. Cut China off from the rest of the world completely.

This is not hatred. It is simply protecting ourselves nonviolently. Remember, our strategy is love, our tactic is forgiveness, and our weapon is nonviolent noncooperation. Do not cooperate with those who are attacking us. That includes China. Will anyone be willing to do this? I don't know. But I'm not alone in my recommendation. China expert Gordon Chang says exactly the same thing. People are very slowly waking up to this threat and the need to completely separate ourselves from our enemy—China.

What You Can Do Now

1. Look at everything around you in terms of fifth-generation warfare. You will begin to see it if you perceive differently. Question everything.
2. Shun China. Stop buying anything made in China. This will be difficult. Before you buy a product, check where it was made and try to find products made elsewhere.
3. Don't buy shares in Chinese companies, or in companies that are involved with China, or in mutual funds that invest in China.
4. Do not allow Chinese companies to buy shares in Western companies, nor vice-versa. Delist Chinese companies from Western stock exchanges.
5. Shun and dismantle every organization that is part of the United Front.
6. Do not engage in any educational, cultural, or athletic exchanges with China.
7. Encourage your alma mater to sever all ties with Chinese institutions.

CHAPTER 9

Mind and Media Control

"The most dangerous of all sciences is that of molding mass opinion, because it would enable anyone to govern the whole world." –TALBOT MUNDY

As former intelligence officer Jeffrey Prather said, the first weapons system in fifth-generation warfare (5GW) is information influence operations. That's a fancy way of saying "mind control." It is "preparing the battlefield" because in 5GW, the battlefield is inside each person. Psychological warfare, biological warfare, genetic warfare, and electromagnetic warfare are all conducted *within you*. Fifth-generation warfare is not kinetic. Nobody shoots you with a gun. They control or kill you with the means just listed or with legal, financial, economic, or political weapons. Step one is to control your mind, but if you realized someone was doing this, you would stop it. It's that way with all subversion. Remember, the purpose of active measures (psychological warfare) is to change your perception of reality to such an extent that, despite ample evidence about the subversion going on around you (or within you), you don't see it. Even if you do, you don't realize it's *planned subversion*. Thus, you are unable to come to sensible conclusions in your own interests and in the interests of your nation.

If you perceive differently, you will see that mind control been happening for years and you didn't even realize it. What you think are "your thoughts" have been placed into your mind for decades. You didn't really choose them. This chapter outlines the basics of these techniques and technologies and shows how the mainstream media has become a key vector for mind control. As always, once you learn the patterns, you will recognize what's going on.

Mind Control Basics

"The ultimate tyranny in a society is not control by martial law. It is control by the psychological manipulation of consciousness through which reality is defined, so that those who exist within it do not even realize that they are in prison." –BARBARA MARCINIAK

Domestic abuse is pretty much the same as dictator abuse.[1] Both spring from the same narcissistic need to control others and both use the same techniques. Psychopaths seem to come by this knowledge naturally. The CIA turned it into a science. Starting in the 1950s with the MK Ultra project, the CIA set out to learn how they could control people's minds.[2] No stone was left unturned. They experimented with drugs like LSD, radioactivity, abuse (including torture and sexual abuse, even of children), hypnosis, electroshock therapy, and more. They found methods of using abuse to "split" personalities and create dissociative identity disorder. This produces multiple personalities (alternate personalities or "alters") that can be independently programmed. The "handler" can use specific "triggers" that have been programmed into the victim's mind to get the victim to switch between these alters, like a hypnotist snaps his fingers to either induce the hypnotic state or end it.

To successfully manipulate another human being, or masses of humans, a controller has to:[3]

1. Conceal his aggressive intentions.
2. Know the psychological vulnerabilities of the victim and modify the tactics accordingly.

3. Be ruthless enough to not care if the victim is harmed.
4. Use covert aggression in the form of relational or passive-aggressive tactics.

Thousands of American lives continue to be wracked by the trauma of these MK programs, but most people don't know anything about it. Here are a few other mind-control techniques that are used both on an individual and a mass scale.

Traumatic Bonding

One method of covert aggression is the calculated use of positive, negative, and intermittent reinforcement. The controller starts with massive positive reinforcement. This is called "love-bombing"–used in the early stages of a relationship to create a false sense of closeness and bonding. It sets the victim up to crave more positive reinforcement, which is then taken away intermittently, to create confusion and anxiety. The victim begins to accept increasing amounts of negative reinforcement sprinkled with positive. Eventually, the controller can torture the victim, who will become so desperate for the love and attention he once got, that he will accept more and more periods of abuse. The victim is now under complete control emotionally and physically.

This process is called "traumatic bonding." It changes not only the victim's behavior but his thoughts and perceptions–his actual reality–and gradually removes his individual will and personal power. It is dehumanizing. Being victimized has nothing to do with intelligence. This is a psychological phenomenon, not a cognitive one, and when used on a mass scale it is psychological warfare. Actually, the more caring, open, and trusting someone is, the easier they are to manipulate.[4] You may have seen this happen to a battered wife or in other personal relationships. But the same thing happens with a totalitarian tyrant and a whole population.

Coercive Persuasion

Another technique is called "coercive persuasion."[5] Information is controlled and selectively given to the victim to alter his perceptions of reality.

(Think propaganda and censorship.) Fear, shame, and guilt are used to shape a person's mind, especially the fear of physical harm or death. (Did you notice this with covid?) Coercive persuasion causes the victim to adopt the desired ideology, beliefs, ideas, attitudes, or behaviors. Here are the tactics. [6] They are common in religious cults, and they work on both individuals and groups. They have been used on our whole society in recent years.

- Increase suggestibility using audio, visual, and verbal stimuli.
- Establish control over the social environment, using social isolation to build dependence on the controller.
- Prohibit disconfirming information. That is, censor anything contrary to the controller's agenda.
- Force re-evaluation of a person's perception of self. Undermine the victim's awareness of reality, their worldview, and emotional control. Instill in them a new reality.
- Create powerlessness by subjecting victims to frequent actions that undermine their confidence and judgment.
- Create negative emotions through punishments such as shaming, guilting, and social isolation.
- Intimidate the person with threats of punishment if the victim doesn't go along with the controller's attitudes, beliefs, ideology, etc.

These techniques are particularly devasting to children, who have not yet developed a strong perception of reality or worldview, and who are emotionally and psychologically vulnerable. We are being manipulated by tyrants, just like an abused wife is manipulated by her psychopathic husband. We cannot comply our way or love our way into a healthy relationship. We must just leave this relationship, regain our own health (spiritually, mentally, physically), and build new relationships and new parallel structures.

Coercive persuasion is about controlling information. This is the simplest form of mind control. Others are controlling the information you receive. Take back that control. You must be the watchful gatekeeper of your mind. Feed your consciousness with what is real and true. Avoid what is illusion and lies.

Language and Belief

"The basic tool for the manipulation of reality is the manipulation of words. If you can control the meaning of words, you can control the people who must use the words." –PHILIP K. DICK

That opening quote completely sums up this section. Controlling people by controlling words, thoughts, and beliefs is a complex and powerful phenomenon. There are more layers here than in an onion. Let's start peeling back some of those layers and see what we find.

The Degradation of Language

Few people write about this. Almost no one understands it. But the people who run our media industry are trained in it. Our language has been degraded, partly to fit the medium of communication and partly as a tactic of totalitarian subversion. Back in the 1960s, Marshall McLuhan said the *content* of any mass media is less important than how it *operates*–how it changes us, neurologically and temperamentally. He famously realized that "the medium *is* the message." By its very nature, any medium of communication lends itself better to communicating some types of messages than others, and the medium even affects people's minds, consciousness, and brain functioning.

For example, a novel allows for a great expansion of the reader's imagination. Scenes and characters are described, which leads readers to *create* their own images in their own minds–with their *imag*ination. Your image of Bilbo Baggins, the unlikely hero from *The Hobbit*[7] by J.R.R. Tolkien, is somewhat different than mine. Each of us "created" an image of the character in our minds as we read the book. But if we see the character in a film, our imagination isn't needed because he is presented visually.

The novel can devote many pages to description and background information. But a film requires nearly constant action, so description is left out and action is elaborated. The same story, in two different media, are two quite different realities. Most of us have read a book and later seen the movie—then said, "The book is better."

There is more to it than this, but you get the idea. This is why McLuhan said that the medium of communication so constrains what is actually communicated *and* how the message is perceived in the receiver's mind, that the medium itself controls the message, not the other way around. As various media of communication have been invented over the past century, people have gone from getting their information mainly in print (1900–1930s), to radio (1930s–1950s), to television (1950s–2000s), to mobile devices and social media (after 2010).

In the 1860s, Abraham Lincoln's speeches were mostly read. Very few people were in attendance. Newspapers printed the entire speeches, which were later read by people all over the country. Thus, Lincoln wrote his speeches for this medium. He could develop complex ideas, use complex sentence structures, and write at length. Read his two inaugural addresses and you will see what I mean.

Winston Churchill's speeches were mostly heard on the radio. He wrote specifically for this medium—shorter speeches, pithy phrases, simpler ideas, emotional impact.

With the advent of television, the visual impact exceeded the verbal. Image dominated substance. The evening news programs wanted "sound bites," not ideas. Speeches were built around a collection of trigger phrases and emotion-generating nonsense terms. Think about Barrack Obama's 2008 campaign slogan, "Change we can believe in." What on earth does that really mean? It can mean anything you want it to mean. Perfect.

Television communicates images instantly, but the viewer's attention cannot be held long enough to present complex ideas. A single carefully selected image can convey more in one second than a lengthy reasoned argument. Ideas are out. Images are in. Perfect. Images are so much easier to manipulate.

Our language has been degraded to a simple and coarse level. Our perception of reality has been flattened and turned monochromatic. In truth, reality is complex, nuanced, colorful, and multidimensional. And imagination, which is constricted by television, is an essential faculty of the mind that enables us to perceive multiple layers of reality and to connect to our spiritual essence. If your communication is entirely tweets and Facebook posts, then you have condemned yourself to forever be a prisoner of slogans, because that is the only level on which your mind operates. To perceive truth, you must perceive differently. To comprehend complex ideas, you have to actually read a book.

Newspeak: The Perversion of Language

We've seen a *degradation* of language. But the totalitarian subverters have also achieved the *perversion* of language. Those who truly understand communism realize the importance of language in controlling people, as the opening quote to this section affirms. The Frankfurt School philosophers understood this, as did George Orwell, as he showed in *1984*.[8] He created the term *newspeak* to describe how language is manipulated to control thought.

We use language to describe the world around us and what meanings we put on the world. At the same time, however, the very words we use constrain our understanding of the world. We cannot even imagine something we have no word for. That's why we instantly make up new words for new things and new ideas. There was no such thing as "white privilege" until somebody made up the term. Suddenly, it existed. We create our reality with our words. Words really are that powerful. And if there are certain words you cannot say or think, those things cease to exist.

I say "perverted" rather than "corrupted" because our language has been turned against its own purpose. This is the sense I mean by the word "perverted": against purpose. Language is the only means humans have to communicate ideas. Yet by changing the meaning of so many key words, communicating ideas has become impossible. This is newspeak. The Marxists do not want people to communicate ideas. They want language to elicit an immediate emotional response that bypasses critical thinking–activates the amygdala not the prefrontal cortex. "White privilege" is an obvious racial slur. But it has become an emotional plea for justice and freedom by denying exactly those things to some people on the basis of their skin color. So "white privilege" is no longer a racist slur but a call for justice. That's newspeak. The words no longer mean what the words mean. It has made communication impossible and has destroyed freedom of speech.

Here are a few other examples of "newspeak" in our society.

- "Social Justice" has become the injustice of destroying those who disagree with you.
- "Science denier" is someone who insists on consulting the scientific evidence and following the scientific process.
- "Racism" has nothing to do with skin color or ethnicity and everything to do with adherence to an ideology.

None of these are exaggerations. These are used in perfect seriousness by people who should know better. Constantly disrupting the language and the meaning of words is part of the whole strategy of subversion and mind control. Those who control the meaning of words, control you.

The media programmers are masters in the use of language to persuade you to their point of view without you even noticing. It works on the subconscious level. Using specific words and phrases can literally shape a society's direction and create a desired mentality–one submissive to authority, or one roused to violent anger and war–as we saw when the covid submissiveness instantly gave way to agitated hatred over the Russia-Ukraine War. They are adept at the science of neuro-linguistic programming (NLP)–the study of the connection between language and behavior. A skilled practitioner can motivate people to do and believe things they would not do or believe on a conscious level.[9] As more research is done on how the brain works, the more knowledge a few people have about how to manipulate the rest of us. Asymmetrical knowledge equals asymmetrical power.

Be careful how you use language and be alert to how it is used against you. If you are willing to accept it, we create our reality with our words. Speak the truth. Avoid parroting the words that others feed you. We can, once again, return language to its rightful place as the means of *communication*, not *manipulation*.

Political Correctness–The New Thought Police

Totalitarian countries always exercise strict control over speech and thought. "Political correctness" is a communist term. In the 1980s, it came to the "free" West. Today's "thought police" use political correctness to control thought and speech just like the Soviets did. Few have grasped its ideological origins and subversive goals. The surface meaning is to avoid using language that is discriminatory or insulting. However, the hidden goal is mind control.

What is politically correct is intentionally ill-defined. That way, it can constantly change so we are never stable, constantly second-guessing ourselves, never sure what is safe to say or how to say it. We self-censor, usually choosing to say nothing for fear of backlash from others. That's exactly the goal of totalitarian destabilization. When no one speaks up, a tiny minority can control a whole nation. Even if you still think, you don't speak or act. You are controlled. This is planned subversion but hardly anyone realizes it.

Political correctness has not brought about a more civil society. Just the opposite. It is tearing us apart. That's its purpose. Political correctness is an ideological weapon of subversion, behavior control, and mind control. Do not succumb to this tyranny. The only way we can bring back free speech is for everyone to speak freely. Say what you mean and mean what you say. Speak the truth as you understand the truth. But in humility, remember that you might be wrong. So, speak your truth with love, kindness, and forgiveness, and remain open to the truth as others perceive it. Their perception has something to add to your own.

Cancel Culture as Mind Control

Cancel culture is the name given to the current practice of disgracing, defaming, and slandering, someone and forcing their employer to fire them, their customers to boycott them, and their professions to disbar them. It's an old communist tactic that works beautifully, particularly in the present climate of political correctness as de facto law. Marxist stooges and useful idiots are ravaging our society by "canceling" everyone who stands in their way and expresses a conservative or Christian viewpoint. It instills fear into everyone and forces "voluntary" compliance and self-censorship, so it's a technique of terrorism.

This tactic has been around forever. Sun Tzu refers to it in *The Art of War*. The Pharisees did it to Jesus. Kings and royal courtesans have used it forever to eliminate rivals. It doesn't need social media. But social media works so beautifully, who can resist it? You don't need proof of anything. An accusation and an orchestrated Twitter storm are all that are required. And now, you hardly need any people. Most of this can be arranged with digital bots.

The target person can be disgraced, reputation destroyed, fired, or have their professional certification removed and their livelihood destroyed. These are exactly the tactics used by the Bolsheviks, Fascists, and Nazis to control their populations and murder millions. The Canadian philosopher Stefan Molyneux recently said, "Cancel culture is a dress rehearsal for mass murder...if people can be disappeared from social media, and if people accept people being disappeared from social media, then they will accept people being disappeared from the world."[10]

Cancel culture is a tactic promoted by the communist Saul Alinsky in his famous book *Rules for Radicals*.

> One of Alinsky's most infamous rules is to isolate the target and vilify it. This was the thrust of Alinsky's final and most egregious rule for radicals (no. 13): "Pick the target, freeze it, personalize it, and polarize it." He advised cutting off the support network of the person and isolating the person from sympathy. He cruelly urged going after people rather than institutions because people hurt faster than institutions.[11]

The psychology of this process, called "mobbing," is described by Dr. Daniel Amen.

> The process of mobbing can include overt and/or covert psychological harassment, non-violent hostility, gossiping, undermining, making false accusations about the person—and related hurtful behavior. It's a systematic effort by a group of people to diminish the value, contributions, or credibility of someone with the primary objective of driving that person away....
>
> In 2019, a study on the psychological trauma caused by mobbing was published in the Archives of Neuropsychiatry. The researchers found that of those who had been subjected to workplace mobbing, 71% developed symptoms of PTSD and 78% had major depression.[12]

In short, it's psychologically devastating. Naturally, it's psychological warfare. This is not kindness. This is an intentional tactic of totalitarian subversion. Not surprisingly, it is also an example of mass formation psychosis. Once again, an ideology (political correctness) attempts to fight something that does not exist in material reality—racism, sexism, homophobia, and similar *ideas*. But the object of anxiety must be material. Hatred must focus on something having a physical existence—a real person. So, a person is attacked, injured, perhaps destroyed. As we have learned previously about mass formation, and as Stefan Molyneux observed, this will lead to mass murder. The millions of people who are caught up in this Critical Theory ideology we call "wokeness" do not realize they are victims of mass formation psychosis.

On the other hand, whoever has planned this mass formation violence doesn't care about real racism, sexism, or even about real people. It's just a tool of power. It is "strategic racism" used as a weapon to eliminate ideological opponents. It's a way to manipulate language, manipulate people, and manipulate minds.

Social justice warriors attack phantoms—a racism here, a sexism there, here a homophobe, there an Islamophobe. Like Don Quixote charging windmill sails with his lance, they attack what exists only in their own hearts and minds. Yes, in the hearts and minds of others as well, but to kill it there you end up killing real people. In truth, the evil you wish to banish you can only banish from *your own heart.* You can never destroy it in the heart of another. Trying to do so only leads to mass murder. To "cancel" another person is exactly the opposite of the spiritual quality of acceptance. Love accepts. Fear and hatred cancel. Our path out of this mess is through love, forgiveness, and acceptance of everyone.

Cancel culture springs from imagined victimhood and imagined micro-offenses and blames everyone outside oneself. Victimhood and offense-taking are irresponsible behaviors. They put responsibility for how you feel on other people. It gives away all your personal power and responsibility. This is psychologically and spiritually childish and opens the door to oppression. If your feelings are so sensitive that you need a "protector" in society, you are a slave. This is not how God created you.

Spiritual maturity takes responsibility, even responsibility for your feelings. *Feel* your feelings—don't deny them—but don't identify with them either. You are *not* your feelings. You are a divine and eternal being of light and love. Your feelings are internal to you. Nobody *makes* you feel a certain way. Your feelings are always *your reaction* to others, and thus, are always your choice.

While feelings come without our bidding, we chose to invite them to stay or leave. More importantly, we choose our responses—either from love or from fear. We have that mental and spiritual power. Our spiritual challenge is to transmute our negative feelings into something divine by responding with love. Cancel culture denies both your power to do this and your divine existence. Turn away from cancel culture and turn toward love. If *you* do not control your mind, someone else will. Cancel culture wants to control your mind. Do not allow it.

Cancel Culture Conquers the Media

Cancel culture has taken control of the whole media industry. Journalists either conformed to the wave of totalitarian ideology, censorship, and control, or they were pushed out. At the beginning of the second decade of this century, the practical life of a journalist started to really go downhill as cancel culture and censorship replaced honesty, integrity, and free speech. Below are a few brave journalists who have spoken out about how their industry has become little more than a totalitarian propaganda business.

Sharyl Attkisson, a well-known investigative reporter for CBS News, eventually left the TV business altogether and wrote about the industry's corruption in *Slanted: How the News Media Taught Us to Love Censorship and Hate Journalism*.[13] She describes how the "narrative" was increasingly controlled by shadowy people who knew how to manipulate public opinion, how to exploit social media, and how to use a network of NGOs, websites, and quasi-journalists to push their narrative–exactly the combination of factors and forces that are controlling our world (as we will see in chapter 17). There seemed to be a coordinated campaign to pressure the media companies to pursue certain narratives and avoid others. Journalists were powerless to push back against it.

In 2020, Bari Weiss published her letter of resignation from the New York Times, which has become a den of ideology and totalitarian coercion far worse than ever in its long leftist history.[14] The abusive harassment she suffered is not just unprofessional: it's illegal. Kari Lake, a respected and successful TV news anchor in Phoenix, quit in March 2021 because she couldn't work in this stultifying atmosphere.[15]

What is true in the United States is equally true, often more so, in other countries. German journalist Udo Ulfkotte worked for Germany's leading paper, the *Frankfurter Allgemeine Zeitung*. In 2013 he published a blistering exposé of how the journalism business in Germany really worked.[16] It was also a *mea culpa* in which he admitted that he had been a willing dupe for years, used by the CIA and the BND (German intelligence) to promote the frauds that the intelligence community wanted to pass off as "news."

The CIA in particular, and the military-industrial-intelligence complex in general, control the media in many visible and invisible ways. Catherine Austin Fitts reports a comment from a CNN employee regarding the military's influence. "The US military controls our satellite feeds. CNN will do whatever they say."[17]

As Dick Russell said in a 2021 article, "CIA's Extraordinary Role Influencing Liberal Media Outlets,"

> It is also well-documented, though often forgotten, that since its inception more than 70 years ago, the CIA has orchestrated news and editorial coverage in America's most influential liberal national news organs...These outlets continue to hew faithfully to CIA theology on globalism, biosecurity, coerced vaccinations, Russiagate, a militarized foreign policy, censorship, lockdowns, vaccine passports, digitized currencies and other issues.[18]

Cancel culture is just one, but an important one, of many techniques for controlling the whole media industry and turning it from the defender of democracy into the apologist of tyranny. The whole industry has become such a propaganda machine that honest journalists aren't welcome and can't work there. It has become the mind control arm of the Deep State. Shut it off. Live free.

Media and Social Programming

"The mind is everything.
What you think, you become." –BUDDHA

Every day, we unwittingly allow our thoughts and behaviors—yes, our minds—to be manipulated. Of course, there is misinformation, things *mistakenly* called fact, and disinformation, lies planted *on purpose* to further someone's agenda. Both of these words are really psychological warfare terms. Disinformation almost always comes from governments or quasi-state organizations for the purpose of subverting the target population.

During the Cold War the Soviets had a whole Ministry of Disinformation. But social programming and mind control is much more than this.[19] Our whole concept of reality–our worldview–is being created for us.

Most people in the Western world spend more time looking at a screen than they do working.[20] The screens present images and ideas about reality that we accept uncritically. Mostly, this isn't our fault. It's the nature of the technology, and it's intentionally programmed to do so. This is social programming–techniques to manipulate, coerce, and influence whole populations without them even realizing it's happening. Not surprisingly, it also goes by the name of mass mind control programming.[21] In the book *Mind Wars: A History of Mind Control, Surveillance, and Social Engineering by the Government, Media, and Secret Societies*, the authors say,

> Because most of society watches television, it's an ideal delivery mechanism to induce the mind into an hypnotic state. Anything being projected onto a screen, such as a movie, or from a computer monitor, would also produce the same emotional response. Over a sustained period of time, it can create an artificial reality and thus have a profound impact upon society's ability to objectively rationalize.[22]

As a teenager, I came across a massive tome that tweaked my interest–*Four Arguments for the Elimination of Television.*[23] The author, Jerry Mander, worked in advertising, cut his teeth on the insights of Marshall McLuhan, and realized that not only is "the medium...the message," but that the medium is also inherently autocratic, perhaps even inherently evil.

Here are his four arguments for the elimination of television:

1. Television promotes autocratic control.
2. It is inevitable that the present powers that be (or controllers) use and expand using television so that no other controllers are permitted.
3. Television affects individual human bodies and minds in a manner that fits the purposes of the people who control the medium.
4. Television has no democratic potential.

All of this happens on a subconscious level, and the subconscious mind cannot distinguish between what is real and what is imagined. Television shifts the brain into right-brain activity, which shuts off critical thinking (a left-brain activity), accepts what it receives without question, and responds emotionally.[24] We believe what's on TV partly because our right brain accepts as true whatever news, facts, science, or "expert" opinion it sees on TV.

Television also shuts down the neo-cortex–higher-order cognitive thinking–and activates the limbic system–the more primitive part of the brain that works with emotional and psychological responses. Negative emotions work much better on TV than positive emotions. Fear and anger keep you glued to the tube. Love and peace don't. That's exactly why TV news became famous for its programming slogan "If it bleeds, it leads." The lead story will be about today's murder with images of the blood-splattered sidewalk. That will get viewers. These strong emotions create strong neural pathways in your brain, so your thinking quickly follows these pathways in the future.

TV also acts like an opiate, releasing endorphins that make us excited and addicted to the television. The same is true for all screens, and it doesn't matter what the program is. Video games, movies, sitcoms, documentaries–everything we see on a screen affects our brains in this way.

The media programmers have many specific techniques they use to get you to react the way they want. "Framing" creates for you a context or worldview through which to perceive new information. The information is not simply given to you; you don't get to put it into your own worldview. The programmers give you the "frame," or worldview, or perspective, they want you to have. Then you naturally agree with the meaning they put on that information. Have you noticed that no alternative worldviews are ever presented? Whether it's a movie or a documentary or the "news," the information and worldview are all downloaded into your mind together. It has all been given to you. Your mind has been programmed.

Paradigm-building is similar but more comprehensive. Paradigms are patterns of thought, behavior, and worldview. Through repeated framing and other techniques, the programmers create in your mind paradigms about almost everything. Then, when new information is presented, it doesn't need much new framing. After you have heard daily for weeks on end that Vladimir Putin is a monster who invaded a sovereign, democratic nation without provocation, today's news doesn't need much framing. You have already accepted the media's paradigm of the situation. And the constant repetition of the message creates and strengthens those neural pathways in your brain that the media programmers intend.

There is also "predictive programming." Ideas and events are presented as fiction, so your mind accepts them as possible realities. Those "controllers" who make long-term plans for society use the mass media to inject these ideas into your mind to prepare you to accept them when they really happen. Movies like *Contagion* (2011),[25] where a new virus from bats creates a pandemic and kills millions of people, are not just prescient. They are intentional predictive programming.

Through techniques such as these, all forms of media work together to create and reinforce in your mind a misunderstanding of reality. Lenon Honor, author of *Media Mind Control: A Brief Introduction*, put it this way. "While in the midst of the media mind control global apparatus an individual will not realize that they are being subconsciously influenced nor will they realize the sometimes overt, but mainly covert, means of subconscious manipulation present within the media mind control global apparatus."[26]

Television, and everything we call "screen time," is a medium of communication that is beautifully suited for mind control—so sophisticated that you don't have the slightest idea that it's happening to you. Our entire perception of reality has been carefully manipulated. That's why I say you must perceive differently to understand what's really going on. As well, you must shut off your TV.

Some people talk about the media "narrative," but they are not simply selling you an ideological narrative. It is a "prescribed reality." They are constructing your whole worldview—your understanding of reality—in a way that allows them to manipulate you.

The only safe conclusion we can come to is that everything we receive through communications media—news, TV, radio, films, newspapers, magazines, advertising, popular music, social media, documentaries–is a psychological warfare operation. It is MindWar, part of the fifth-generation World War III. *You* must be the discerning gatekeeper of your own consciousness. You must constantly be on guard and ask yourself, "What is true? Who is trying to manipulate me? How? Why?" And, as always, look for *evidence.*

The mainstream media is the principal avenue of this mind control. It has lost all credibility. It is overwhelmingly a force for disunity, subversion, and evil. Shut off your TV and radio. There is no longer enough of value there to waste time looking for it. Spend your time with real people, not imaginary, flickering images on a screen. Read a book. Take a walk. Play with your kids, your friends. Help your neighbors. Visit your extended family. Learn something valuable and useful. This is real life. What you see on the screen is not real. It is illusion. It is mind control.

From PSYOP to MindWar

This is the title of a US military discussion paper from 1980. It lays out ideas for making military psychological operations more effective in the post-Vietnam War era. History shows that these ideas have been put into action. Although it doesn't use these words, the paper presents the idea of going beyond simple propaganda and psychological operations to creating a reality in the minds of people that fits US military objectives. That is, MindWar is mind control. It is exactly what the earlier quote from Barbara Marciniak describes, a manipulation of consciousness so that people don't even realize their perception of reality and "their" decisions are being created for them. The paper says, "You seize control of everything by which his government and populace process information to make up their minds, and you adjust it so that those minds are made up as you desire."[27]

As I said earlier, if you knew your mind was being controlled, you would take steps to stop it. So, the control must be hidden from you. Also from the paper, "For the mind to believe its own decisions, it must believe it made those decisions without coercion. Coercive measures used by the operative, consequently, must not be detectable by ordinary means."[28]

The discussion paper briefly mentions a few ways this could be accomplished. Even in 1980, these techniques were known. Now, forty years later, the military has perfected them. "There are some purely natural conditions under which minds may become more or less receptive to certain ideas, and MindWar should take full advantage of such phenomenon as: atmospheric electromagnetic activity, air ionization, and extremely low frequency waves."[29]

This sounds futuristic. Now, the future is here.

Mind Control of the Future Is Here Today

Unbeknownst to you, the CIA and the Defense Advanced Research Projects Agency (DARPA) have been working on all manner of technologies to control your thoughts and actions from afar using sound, heat, light, pulsed high-frequency microwaves, and electrical transmissions. It's been going on for decades.[30] Here are a few examples.

Voice to Skull (V2K) technology is old hat. Dr. Joseph Sharp of the Walter Reed Army Institute of Research first demonstrated it in 1973. V2K wirelessly sends voice commands right into your head. This quickly developed into a whole field of research on pulsed microwave radiation as a method of controlling people.[31]

There is a whole range of Directed Energy Weapons (DEW). DEW can include any kind of direct energy–light, sound, heat, electrical, microwave, or kinetic–and can target a specific person or object or cover a general area. Some of these weapons have been in use since the 1970s.[32] DEW include area denial weapons that use microwaves or sound waves (used on covid protestors by the Australian police in 2022) to cause burns and intense discomfort so people run away. The largest category of DEW is lasers, several types of which are deployed by the US military. Some type of DEW has been used against "targeted individuals" for decades. Many people have written about their experiences, such as Gloria Naylor in her autobiographical book *1996*[33] and John Hall in his books *Guinea Pigs*[34] and *A New Breed.*[35]

Russian author and mind control expert N.I. Anisimov in his 1999 book[36] *Psychotronic Golgotha* says existing weapons can do the following:

- Kill at a distance, imitating or causing any chronic illness.
- Turn a person to irresponsible or criminal behavior.
- Create aviation, railroad, or automobile accidents in a matter of seconds.
- Destroy fundamental structures.
- Destroy, create, or provoke any climatic cataclysm.
- Control the most complex instrument or mechanism.
- Control the behavior of people and any biological object.
- Change the worldview of the population.

All this was possible a quarter century ago. It's not science fiction. It's part of fifth-generation warfare. What I have written here only scratches the surface of the mind control technology that is being used against us. It seems prudent to hold your beliefs lightly. They might not be true, and they might not be *yours.*

Media Consolidation and Control

"The media's the most powerful entity on earth. They have the power to make the innocent guilty and to make the guilty innocent, and that's power. Because they control the minds of the masses." –MALCOLM X

Business consolidation is a natural phenomenon in mature industries. It brings economic efficiencies but also market control as industries slowly move from nearly perfect competition with many sellers to oligopoly with few sellers. In a monopoly, one seller controls the entire market–not only price but every aspect of the product such as quality, quantity, packaging, delivery, and so on.

When the product is information, society faces an obvious risk when the control of information–which can be easily manipulated to control society itself–falls into the hands of only a few people. And there is great incentive for collusion and control in oligopolistic industries. This control is what despots want and democracies want to avoid. For this reason, the United States (and most countries) passed laws to restrict consolidation in media industries. In the United States, these restrictions were gradually relaxed during the latter part of the twentieth century. Together with natural market forces, this led to consolidation–fewer companies controlling not just newspapers and magazines but also radio, film, and telecommunications, as well as advertising on all these platforms.

As the internet grew in the 1990s, and social media a decade later, fewer people were tuning in to the traditional media outlets. Advertisers followed the consumer "eyes" to the internet and social media. Since the media business model depends on advertising, this spelled death. What followed was a typical phenomenon in a declining industry–consolidation. As newspapers ran into financial trouble, many went bankrupt or were merged or sold to larger and better-financed companies. By 2012, a mere six companies controlled the majority of American media. It was only to be expected that media consolidation coincided with a massive increase in censorship.

A list of the world's largest media companies (ranked by revenue in billions of dollars) was presented in an October 2020 article in Investopedia. All of these are American except for the Japanese company, Sony. But that obscures the fact that Chinese companies have significant ownership interest in many of the US firms, seats on their boards of directors, and influence in company policies.[37]

1. Netflix–$234
2. Walt Disney–$220
3. Comcast–$209
4. AT&T–$203
5. Charter Communications–$130
6. Sony–$95
7. Thompson Reuters–$40
8. Viacom/CBS–$18
9. Fox–$15
10. Dish Networks–$14

Notice that the largest six companies account for over 90 percent of the revenue—massive dominance. The vast majority of the world's media is controlled by a very small number of companies and people—perfect for controlling information.

The internet has now also come under the control of political operatives. As Wikipedia cofounder Larry Sanger describes in his book *Essays on Free Knowledge: The Origins of Wikipedia and the New Politics of Knowledge*, Wikipedia specifically (and the whole internet in general) is now the field of propaganda, indoctrination, and control. It is not free—and neither are you. Sanger says, "The digital revolution has been corrupted. What began as a celebration of freedom has become a machine for monitoring and control. What began as history's greatest dream of enlightenment has been twisted into an anti-intellectual nightmare of indoctrination."[38]

As we will see more fully in chapter 17, it's even worse than this. Media is just one of many industries, and the interlocking network of ownership and control through the financial world means that almost everything is controlled by a very small number of people and companies. The top of the pyramid of money and power is tiny. Remember that very few people need to conspire in a fraud.

As always, much is hidden, much is unclear. But this much *is* clear: mind control power is in the hands of the mass media and the military-intelligence agencies. It is controlled by a very small number of people. They are using their media and mind control power to achieve their goals in this fifth-generation World War III—a one-world tyrannical technocracy. We will see all this play out in the next two great frauds.

What You Can Do Now

1. There really are people trying to control your mind—and they've been pretty successful so far. Now that you understand this, take steps to avoid it.
2. Avoid screen time as much as possible. Shut off your TV and radio, cancel your Netflix and cable subscriptions. Pay no more attention to the mainstream media in any form. Very little of what you see on a screen is real. It is mostly illusion, intentionally constructed for you. These devices are tools that can be used for good *and* evil. If you do not control them, somebody else will use them to control you.
3. Spend your time with real people. Read a book. Take a walk. Play with your kids, your friends. Help your neighbors. Visit your extended family. Learn something valuable and useful. This is real life. These are real people. Stay grounded in reality and avoid illusion.
4. Do not let anyone you know be canceled by cancel culture. Stand up for them. There is strength in unity. We need each other. In every situation, there is a mechanism for legitimate complaints to be aired and addressed. Keep it off social media. Have compassion. Forgive. All of us are human. All of us make mistakes and say things in anger or thoughtlessness. None of these are crimes; they are universal human failings. Have mercy.
5. Political correctness is thought control. Don't participate in it. Being truly human means having free will; defend yours and others'. That requires freedom of speech, which means tolerating idiots saying the most outlandish, rude, and foolish things. Get over it.

CHAPTER 10

Surveillance or Sovereignty

"The rise of the internet has given these companies unprecedented power to control public policy, to swing elections, to brainwash our children, to censor content, to track our every move, to tear societies apart, to alter the human mind, and even to reengineer humanity." –DR. ROBERT EPSTEIN

The Surveillance State—Big Brother Is Here

"The NSA has built an infrastructure that allows it to intercept almost everything." –EDWARD SNOWDEN

Edward Snowden opened the eyes of the whole world in 2013 when he revealed that the US government was spying on absolutely everyone. The military and intelligence agencies had the capability to capture and surveil all digital communications, and that's exactly what they were doing. Many people still haven't caught on.[1] The vastness of this endeavor shocked everyone in 2013. Rightly so.

The National Security Agency (NSA) started the PRISM project in 2007 after the passage of the *Protect America Act.* It became the biggest source of raw intelligence data for the US government. Even encryption didn't stop them, as Yasha Levine explains in his book *Surveillance Valley: The Secret Military History of the Internet.*[2]

> [PRISM uses] a sophisticated on-demand data tap housed within the datacenters of the biggest and most respected names in Silicon Valley: Google, Apple, Facebook, Yahoo!, and Microsoft. These devices allow the NSA to siphon off whatever the agency requires, including emails, attachments, chats, address books, files, photographs, audio files, search activity, and mobile phone location history. According to the Washington Post, these companies knew about PRISM and helped the NSA build the special access to their network systems that PRISM requires, all without raising public alarm or notifying their users.[3]

The NSA has also found ways to infect any computer in the world with malware that allows them to see everything on it.[4] Since 2014, all this personal and private information is likely being stored at the Utah Data Center, concisely named the Intelligence Community Comprehensive National Cybersecurity Initiative Data Center. Your digital footprint gives massive amounts of information about you to whoever buys that information–and you don't even know who has it. Asymmetrical information equals asymmetrical power.

The Internet

The internet is the most powerful surveillance weapon ever invented. The US military developed it as a tool for electronic and psychological counter-insurgency warfare–not only for military command, surveillance, and control, but for the control of human individuals and groups. The internet is dual use, as the military calls it, civilian and military. It was a DARPA project called ARPANET. The military wanted to organize the massive amount of information it had collected about hundreds of cultures and tribes around the world to find out what caused people to turn to communist revolt. This information was of no use stuck in thousands of filing cabinets. They wanted to be able to organize, sort, and analyze it to predict when and where the next communist revolution would start. Then they could head it off before it happened. Today, that's called predictive policing.

The first ARPANET node went live in 1969 and linked Stanford University and UCLA.[5] That same year, university students rioted to stop this invasive and tyrannical technology. Immediately, the military and intelligence wonks abused it. By 1975 a scandal erupted when the public found out the military was already using the ARPANET to spy on Americans—at a time when hardly anyone even knew what a computer was.[6] It's much worse today. As John Hall says in his book *Guinea Pigs: Technologies of Control*, "The NSA has a multibillion-dollar budget and unrivaled technological sophistication which allows them carte blanche access to every form of communication."[7]

DARPA soon spun the internet off to private industry—essentially, the same six massive companies that control the media industry today.[8] DARPA has always maintained a technological lead over anything that's in the public domain, and they have kept a "back door" into all this technology. Even the Tor network that everyone thought was secure and private was developed by the US Navy, funded by the government, and constantly monitored by intelligence agencies.[9] That's how the infamous Silk Road online "drug" store got shut down after about a year of operations. The government knew everything that was going on there.[10]

Edward Snowden alerted us that almost nothing happens on the internet without passing through some kind of US government bug. The entire internet is one big de facto intelligence gathering apparatus.

Google—The Surveillance Business Model

Dr. Robert Epstein is a research psychologist with the American Institute for Behavioral Research and Technology. In his recent paper, *Google's Triple Threat—To Democracy, Our Children, and Our Minds*,[11] he lays out the results of research he has done for many years on how Google and other IT companies affect us, manipulate us, surveil us, and control us. It's scary. He says that Google is the biggest and most dangerous online manipulation platform, partly because it is run by utopians. Whether they know it or not, this is a classic communist ploy. They think they can make the world better by making everyone think and act the way they want. That's the behavior of a psychopathic despot. It creates a *dystopia*.

Dr. Epstein explains the surveillance business model that Google uses, and others have copied. The user *is* the product. Google captures information about you and sells it to anyone who wants to buy it.

> Google is, by far, the most dangerous member of the Gang. It is the most aggressive in its surveillance, censorship, and manipulation activities. It also invented the "surveillance business model." ...Here is how it works:
>
> 1) You attract people to online surveillance platforms where you extract as much personal information about them as you can multiple times a day.
>
> 2) You motivate them to visit these platforms by offering them trivial services "free of charge." These services–like Gmail, the Google search engine, and Google Docs–truly are trivial. If you had to pay for them–all of them–they would cost you about $10 per month.
>
> 3) You monetize the personal information you are collecting, a process that is now bringing Google nearly $150 billion per year in revenue. Even though you continue to provide the same trickle of trivial services to your users every day, over time, the profile you have compiled about each and every one of them–including the children–has become enormous. If you have been using the internet for a decade or more, Google has collected the equivalent of about 3 million pages of information about you. They are currently monitoring you and your kids over more than 200 platforms, most of which you are completely unaware of.

4) Google uses this profile to create a digital model of you that they use both to predict your behavior and needs and to influence your attitudes, beliefs, opinions, purchases, and votes. The surveillance business model is brilliant from a profit perspective, but it is also fundamentally deceptive, and I and many others believe it should be made illegal. Google services are not free. We pay for them with our freedom.[12]

The surveillance business model manipulates and controls you. It overrides your free will with central control. You lose your individual sovereignty. Without free will, you lose your spirituality and your humanity. You stop being human. This is the perfect segue into transhumanism. Surveillance and mind control, like all the frauds, are essentially business models that fit together like separate divisions of a giant business conglomerate to run the world.

Social Media for Surveillance and Subversion

Most of our information technology came from the military and has a military purpose. For example, DARPA had a project to create an AI Personal Assistant That Learns (PAL). It was later spun off to Apple as Siri. Another project was called "LifeLog," and it worked to create a permanent, searchable electronic diary of a person's entire life–movements, conversations, connections, everything they watched, listened to, read, or bought. This project was shut down just as Facebook started up. Facebook's first big investor was Peter Theil, a Bilderberg Group member with close ties to the intelligence industry. Another early executive was former DARPA manager Regina Dugan, hired to run Facebook's secretive "Building 8" research division, which is involved in everything from artificial intelligence to drone-based wireless internet networks. You need a very strong belief in coincidences to think it was just a coincidence that Facebook looked so much like LifeLog.[13]

Facebook tracks your location, what apps are on your phone, when you use them and for what, accesses your webcam and microphone, your contacts, emails, calendar, call history, text messages, files you download, games you play, and sees your music, photos, and videos. What if there was a technology to connect all this Facebook information with the AI capabilities of Siri and your coming digital ID? The government would know everything about you 24/7 and be able to predict your next moves, maybe even your thoughts. That's exactly what the US Information Awareness Office was working on in 2003 using DARPA technology.

> The stated aim of the IAO (Information Awareness Office) is to gather and store the personal information of every US citizen, including their personal emails, social networks, lifestyles, credit card records, phone calls, medical records, without, of course, the need for a search warrant. This information would funnel back to intelligence agencies, under the guise of predicting and preventing terrorist incidents before they happened.[14]

This raised alarm bells in 2003 and the IAO was defunded by Congress. But its key project, Total Information Awareness (TIA), was moved over to the NSA. Two decades have passed, and we can be pretty sure the NSA has accomplished these old goals. TIA is really a principle, not just a program, that fits perfectly with the whole transhumanism–global control agenda.

By about 2010 or so, the military-intelligence community had developed both the internet and social media as surveillance systems. They had also developed the dark web, and Tor in particular, for at least three distinct purposes. It was a means to use the public internet for secret spy and military communication without being detected. It was a means to organize subversive groups all over the world without their own governments being able to see it (but the CIA saw everything). And it was a honey pot to collect thousands of people whom the CIA could watch doing illegal things. This system enabled great control over populations, but it needed a good beta test. Enter the Arab Spring. As we will see in chapter 11, the Arab Spring was just the cover story for the military's "7 Countries in 5 Years" plan. Using the dark web and social media, the

CIA could make this massive and evil plan look spontaneous.

The CIA had been broadcasting American propaganda and psychological warfare campaigns into "hostile" countries since the end of WWII. In the 1970s, these programs were taken over by Congress and put under the control of a department called the Broadcasting Board of Governors (BBG).[15] Their stated goal was to promote democracy, which includes freedom movements—but that also means insurrections. How convenient. They promoted internet freedom and anti-censorship in countries the United States targeted for regime change. That's where the dark web and the Tor network came in. Tor was a military-intelligence surveillance and subversion network masquerading as an anti-government "internet freedom" network. The CIA—with the help of the State Department, the BBG, Facebook, and Google—trained "activists" all over the world in how to use these internet and social media tools to organize and communicate without their governments knowing about it.[16] These tools worked brilliantly to topple one government after another.

> The Arab Spring provided the US government with the confirmation it was looking for. Social media, combined with technologies like Tor, could be tapped to bring huge masses of people onto the streets and could even trigger revolutions. Diplomats in Washington called it "democracy promotion." Critics called it regime change. But it didn't matter what you called it. The US government saw that it could leverage the Internet to sow discord and inflame political instability in countries it considered hostile to US interests. Good or bad, it could weaponize social media and use it for insurgency. And it wanted more.[17]

Later in that decade, the CIA and other intelligence agencies turned precisely these tools against the American people. If we want to understand what the hell is going on, we have to realize that "the biggest hoax ever perpetuated on the public was fostering their dependence on Google and Facebook, two of the most powerful data mining tools ever conceived by the Government and passed off as completely private sector entities."[18]

Brain-Computer Interface

DARPA has been working on the brain-computer interface (BCI) since the 1960s. The little tricks that Elon Musk recently showed off with monkeys[19] are not very different from demonstrations by Jose Delgado in the 1970s.[20] This was a diversion by Musk. The real technology is miles ahead of that. In 2018, DARPA started a project with five hundred human volunteers. They all received chips implanted in their brains, and they are linked together into a hive mind–just like the Borg on Star Trek. DARPA had great success doing this with rats and needed some human beta testers before they launched this product on the whole world.[21] But even implanted computer chips aren't needed anymore. For decades, DARPA has been surveilling, attacking, and controlling people remotely.

Advances in brain stimulation technology took a huge step forward in the late 1960s and early 1970s. It turns out, the human brain is very responsive to externally applied electromagnetic fields, which can be used just like brain implants. In his 2015 book *Guinea Pigs,* John Hall writes, "At least since 1991 and the lawsuit of John Akewei against the NSA, it was revealed that the NSA/DoD had advanced proprietary equipment that could remotely analyze all objects, either man-made or organic, that have electrical activity."[22]

Let that sink in.

Starting in the 1970s, DARPA pursued the idea that since thought precedes speech, the brain must produce specific electrical activity that corresponds to specific words, even before the mouth speaks those words. By measuring the brain's activity, one should be able to put together a "dictionary" of brainwaves. This idea turned out to work, and you don't need to connect electrodes to the person's head. It can be done remotely. This process is called remote neural *monitoring.* First, you direct wireless transmissions at a person. "Essentially, the two incoming signals would entrain with the brain's inherent electrical frequency and an interference waveform would be returned to a receiver."[23]

Then they learned how to reverse the process. Once DARPA has your "dictionary" of brainwaves, they can beam thoughts and feelings back into your mind. This is called remote neural *control*—what we would call mind control.

> More modern research has focused on converting the received electromagnetic waveforms back into audible thought that can be monitored and recorded. Essentially, mind reading has come of age and has been in use among intelligence agencies for a number of years now...Once a dictionary of EEG waveforms corresponding to various emotional states was created, it became relatively easy to cause a normal subject's brain to entrain the desired waveform to produce a desired emotional state.[24]

This is how they will make you "happy" even though you own nothing. Our military and intelligence agencies have been testing such weapons on people for decades. They are called "targeted individuals," and it's not a pleasant experience. Other people think they're crazy. They hear voices in their heads and suffer all kinds of debilitating pains and illnesses.

It turns out these EEG waveforms can also be broadcast over TV, radio, and 5G microwave systems, unnoticed by the listeners, and produce the desired emotional state in everyone watching, listening, or within the range of the 5G transmissions. This is mass mind control. This is existing technology. It would be naïve to think it is not being used.

This summary gives you a glimpse into the government surveillance that is known publicly. You can be sure the military-intelligence agencies have even better surveillance technology that we don't know about. We live in a surveillance state. The same tools used for surveillance are also used for manipulation and control. Surveillance "de facto" steals all your freedom—your personal sovereignty. To be a sovereign individual, you must avoid surveillance.

There is hope. You can de-Google your life and drastically reduce all types of surveillance. You can largely resist external entrainment of your thoughts and emotions by intensely focusing your attention on the thoughts and emotions you want. This is exactly the self-control that is the foundation of spiritual growth. Let your thoughts constantly be on love, peace, and forgiveness. Do not let anyone or anything draw you into fear, hatred, or violence. Daily prayer and meditation on the consciousness you want to develop is a great help. The road to freedom and personal sovereignty remains, as it always was, through *self-control.*

What You Can Do Now

1. Surveillance equals slavery. Even if this idea is hard to grasp, it is true. Whether or not you have something to hide is not the point. Personal sovereignty and freedom *are* the point. Personal sovereignty requires personal privacy. Protect your privacy as if your life depends on it. It does.
2. Seek out computer operating systems, social media platforms, and internet programs that do not facilitate surveillance and data collection and are not controlled by the big corporate controllers. "De-Google" your life.
3. Avoid all "smart" devices. Their main function is to track you and watch everything you do. The risk they pose is not worth the slight convenience they offer.
4. Never get into a self-driving car. Someone else is controlling it. You need to control your life. Do not give any of that control away. If you do, sooner or later, it will be used against you.
5. Avoid 5G as much as possible. Get these transmitters out of your schools and neighborhoods. Learn more about personal protection from EMF, because we cannot escape it completely.

PART 4

The Later Frauds

Part 2 explained the first great frauds as totalitarian nonissues that were blown into crises to gain emergency powers that became permanent. Only by perceiving the frauds in this way do they make sense. The same is true of the bigger frauds explained in part 4.

All these frauds are leading us inexorably to a totalitarian one-world government. It seems clear to me that these are planned. The obvious presence of an intelligent design implies an intelligent designer. It's highly unlikely that society would evolve this way on its own—even though simple human nature plays a role in the increasing authoritarianism and the increasing acquiescence to that authoritarianism. But as I have said before, like pregnancy, planned or unplanned, the result is the same. Whether by accident or design, we are on a road to totalitarianism. We know this because we've seen it all before. We know the pattern. It's all about pattern recognition and evidence.

We look now at the evidence of the war-on-terror fraud and the war-on-the-virus fraud. To control the world, one must control food, energy, governments, health, police and military, and ultimately, all bodies and minds. This is the essence of totalitarianism, which is always accompanied by mass formation psychosis. It seems unbelievable, but we are watching it all unfold. Believe the evidence of your own eyes.

There is still hope. We can still get on a different road, both individually and collectively. You can still choose. You still have free will—if you choose to exercise it. This war is still fundamentally a spiritual war. Turn to God, however you conceive Him to be. It is by connecting with God, with our own soul, and by radical self-control that we will avoid the tyrannical control of despots.

CHAPTER 11

What's Behind Terrorism?

"Most terrorists are false flag terrorists, or are created by our own security services. In the United States, every single terrorist incident we have had has been a false flag, or has been an informant pushed on by the FBI." –DAVID STEELE, MARINE INTELLIGENCE OFFICER AND FORMER CIA OFFICER

Most of the terrorism in the world is perpetrated by the Central Intelligence Agency (CIA), either directly or through the myriad groups it starts, fronts, organizes, funds, supports, or controls. The CIA was supposed to be under the direct control of the president of the United States. That illusion ended long ago. It is a loose cannon, not controlled by the president, nor by Congress–seemingly, not by anyone. It is a power, a government, and an army unto itself. We could consider it the military-intelligence arm of the world's shadow government.

The CIA's efforts to destabilize the whole world and build its own American Empire started in 1947, so one might consider terrorism to be the first forever war. But terrorism was raised to a whole new level on September 11, 2001. It was then that an American president first used the term "War on Terror," which is why I date this forever war from 9/11. The purpose of this chapter is to provide evidence to support the claim made in the opening quote. But let's back up a bit and try to understand how this developed.

The Rise of the CIA Shadow Government

"We will know our disinformation program is complete when everything the American public believes is false." –WILLIAM CASEY, CIA DIRECTOR, 1981

The Military-Industrial Complex

Upon leaving office in 1961, President Dwight D. Eisenhower warned Americans to beware the military-industrial complex. Thus, the term entered our lexicon. His whole speech is even more insightful today than it was sixty years ago. It could be given today. It is prescient–even prophetic.

> We yet realize that America's leadership and prestige depend, not merely upon our unmatched material progress, riches and military strength, but on how we use our power in the interests of world peace and human betterment.
>
> Throughout America's adventure in free government, our basic purposes have been to keep the peace; to foster progress in human achievement, and to enhance liberty, dignity and integrity among people and among nations. To strive for less would be unworthy of a free and religious people. Any failure traceable to arrogance, or our lack of comprehension or readiness to sacrifice would inflict upon us grievous hurt both at home and abroad....
>
> Our military organization today bears little relation to that known by any of my predecessors in peacetime, or indeed by the fighting men of World War II or Korea...This conjunction of an immense military establishment and a large arms industry is new in the American experience. The total influence–economic, political, even spiritual–is felt in every city, every State house, every office of the Federal government...In the councils of government, we must guard against the acquisition of unwarranted influence, whether sought or unsought, by the military-industrial complex. The potential for the

> disastrous rise of misplaced power exists and will persist. We must never let the weight of this combination endanger our liberties or democratic processes. We should take nothing for granted. Only an alert and knowledgeable citizenry can compel the proper meshing of the huge industrial and military machinery of defense with our peaceful methods and goals, so that security and liberty may prosper together....
>
> The prospect of domination of the nation's scholars by Federal employment, project allocations, and the power of money is ever present and is gravely to be regarded. Yet, in holding scientific research and discovery in respect, as we should, we must also be alert to the equal and opposite danger that public policy could itself become the captive of a scientific-technological elite. It is the task of statesmanship to mold, to balance, and to integrate these and other forces, new and old, within the principles of our democratic system—ever aiming toward the supreme goals of our free society.
>
> Down the long lane of the history yet to be written America knows that this world of ours, ever growing smaller, must avoid becoming a community of dreadful fear and hate, and be instead, a proud confederation of mutual trust and respect...Together we must learn how to compose differences, not with arms, but with intellect and decent purpose...As one who knows that another war could utterly destroy this civilization which has been so slowly and painfully built over thousands of years—I wish I could say tonight that a lasting peace is in sight.[1]

In the America of the twenty-first century, Eisenhower's fears have been realized—his hopes have not. As he feared, through deceit and obfuscation, America was drawn into an undeclared war in Vietnam that killed millions of people, the sole beneficiary of which was exactly the military-industrial complex that Eisenhower warned about in 1961. Since US forces left Vietnam in 1973, we have watched reruns of the same film again and again. In August 2021, US forces desperately evacuated Afghanistan as those of us old enough to remember flashed back to images of US helicopters on the roof of the Saigon embassy. Once again, hundreds of thousands of people killed, trillions of dollars wasted, and the only beneficiaries were the military-industrial-intelligence complex. Follow the money to find the real reasons for war.

President John F. Kennedy tried to bring the "complex" under control–withdraw the American military "advisors" in Vietnam, disband the CIA, and bring the government back under the control of elected politicians. He was killed. His nephew, Robert F. Kennedy Jr., described his family's seventy-five-year running battle with the CIA in his book *American Values*[2] and explains why he believes the CIA murdered both his father and his uncle. As Eisenhower feared, we have been captured by "a scientific-intellectual elite," and the military-industrial complex does have "unwarranted influence." The United States is no longer ruled by its elected politicians. It is ruled by the military-industrial-intelligence complex or some other entity that is sometimes called the shadow government, or the Deep State. They create the very problems–terrorism, in this case–they pretend to fight against. Then they provide the solution, which is always more money and power for the Deep State. Ordinary people everywhere are continually the victims. Let's look at just a bit of the evidence.

American Imperialism & Economic Hit Men

American imperialism began around the turn of the twentieth century. It is exactly the opposite of what the Founding Fathers intended for the country, which was to have freedom at home and to leave other nations alone to pursue their own freedom. The "American Empire" really took off after the Second World War when a small group of rich and powerful people conspired to gain ever wider and deeper control of the world's wealth and resources.

John Perkins was an economic hit man. He explains how it works in his books, such as *The Secret History of the American Empire.*[3] The system cycles money from taxpayers in the Western world, through the World

Bank and the International Monetary Fund (IMF), to third-world countries who agree to development projects that are pushed on them, and back to Western multinational companies who do the work. This leaves the third-world countries with massive debts that are paid by their own poor taxpayers, the money going back to the international banks. Then the whole process repeats. Their debts keep the third world countries hostage to international bankers, businessmen, and politicians.

If the target country doesn't agree to the "business deal," then the economic hit men depart and the "jackals" are sent in. The CIA is behind this game and uses assassination, destabilization, and regime change to put in place malleable political leaders who will accept the "business deal."

> This [American] empire is ruled by a group of people who collectively act very much like a king. They run our largest corporations and, through them, our government. They cycle through the "revolving door" back and forth between business and government. Because they fund political campaigns and the media, they control elected officials and the information we receive. These men and women (the corporatocracy) are in charge regardless of whether Republicans or Democrats control the White House or Congress. They are not subject to the people's will and their terms and not limited by law.[4]

This nebulous collective of elites has come to be known by many names. As I mentioned in chapter 4, I'll use "Deep State." It's a poor term for a lot of reasons, but I have to pick something. Perkins says it's ruled by a sort of "king." It's more like a technocratic dictator and the CIA acts like his army.

The CIA system of economic hit men and jackals is part of a strategy of controlling the third world by keeping every country politically weak, divided, poor, undeveloped, lacking its own technology and industries, dependent upon Western aid, and in debt to the West (and therefore under the control of the West)—in short, keeping them as vassal states in the American Empire. If you can control every other country as a vassal state and control the United States behind the scenes, you can control the whole world. That's the idea. It's evil. It's time to just stop it.

How The CIA Created Terrorism

The obfuscation, shifting alliances, and political duplicity in this sordid tale would make Byzantium look like a sorority house. But you need to glimpse the truth about the rise of Muslim terrorism, the CIA, and how it set the stage for 9/11.

The CIA has been behind the vast majority of violent regime changes all over the world since it was created from the wartime Office of Strategic Services (OSS) in 1947. These regime changes have nothing to do with fostering democracy. They are completely about extending American (read CIA/Deep State) power and profit at the expense of the whole world. Just to name a tiny few (in case you don't know), the CIA arranged to topple the governments of Iran (1952), Guatemala (1954), Belgian Congo (1960), Brazil (1961), Iraq (1963 and again in 2003), the Dominican Republic (1965), Indonesia (1965), Chile (1970), Bolivia (1971), Angola (1975), Zaire (1976), Grenada (1983), and Panama (1989). And that's just the tip of the iceberg. "Former CIA station chief John Stockwell, who ran the CIA secret war in Angola, estimated the CIA had mounted approximately 3,000 major operations and 10,000 minor operations of this nature, which killed over six million people."[6]

This matches the scale of Hitler's genocide. These operations have greatly increased in size, scope, and audacity during the past thirty years and now often involve regular American military troops and billions or trillions of American taxpayers' dollars.

Things took a turn for the worse in the 1980s when the CIA created a monster in their proxy war against the USSR in Afghanistan, which was essentially a Soviet client state until problems arose in 1978. The country is a motley assortment of half a dozen distinct tribes, each with their own ethnicity and language, that nobody can rule. It's been called "the graveyard of empires" because no empire since Genghis Khan has been able to subdue it. In 1978, the religion of Islam and the enduring influence of the Persian Empire were the most unifying aspects of the nation. Afghanistan was one of those few remaining backwaters of the world where the twentieth century was still a stranger.

Then the local Afghan communist party staged a coup, deposed the king, and took over the government. They set about the usual communist reforms and control that are universally hated. The rural people resisted, and the communist government repressed them. The locals picked up their guns and started fighting–something Afghan tribesmen have loved to do for centuries. The country descended into civil war. When the second-in-command in the communist party killed the first-in-command, the Soviets got concerned he would court the United States of America. Unwilling to have either a foe or a disruption on its southern border and at the request of the Afghan communist government, the Soviets sent in an army. Their tanks quickly rolled down the highway to Kabul and they put their local favorite in power.

But the tribes, now agitated, would have none of that and kept fighting. The Soviets soon found themselves bogged down in their own "Vietnam" in the mountainous and primitive country. The CIA, smelling blood better than a shark, saw an opportunity. The Western nations decried Soviet "aggression" in Afghanistan but weren't stupid enough to enter a land war in Central Asia against the world's second strongest army to defend a wild bunch of garrulous and half barbarous tribesmen. The CIA held no such qualms.

The movie *Charlie Wilson's War*[7] (2007) gives the Hollywood version of what happened next. Presenting Tom Hanks as a loveable patriot, they show *part* of how the CIA provided the local militias, collectively known as the Mujahedeen, with arms. These included, significantly, shoulder-launched surface-to-air missiles that could knock out the helicopters and ground attack aircraft that the Soviets used to harass the countryside. Of course, the Western media played their part by publishing all sorts of damning evidence of Soviet atrocities. I have no way of knowing how much of this was true. In the 1980s, I still trusted the media and believed what I saw on TV and read in the newspapers. Silly me. Along with the rest of the public, I thought the Americans should help those poor, abused, democracy-seeking tribesmen against the big bad wolf of Soviet oppression. I have no idea what the truth really was. I only know what happened next.

The Origins of Jihadism

Jihad, or "holy war," is an ancient idea dating to the beginning of Islam in the seventh century. To the extent that it is ever "holy" and not just a means to manipulate the gullible, it is an internal "war", exactly the way I describe a spiritual war. In truth, jihad is everyone's struggle against the evil within themselves. But modern Jihadism was essentially started by the United States. After WWII, The CIA and MI6 (British Intelligence) created the Muslim Brotherhood, mainly to undermine the Moslem parts of the Soviet Union. It was not a religious organization. It only used religion as a cover and as a means of manipulating its members. It was a political and terrorist organization sponsored by the CIA and MI6, as explained by the French journalist Thierry Meyssan in his book *Before Our Very Eyes, Fake Wars and Big Lies: From 9/11 to Donald Trump*.[8] It is fascinating to imagine how history might have unfolded if the CIA had never tried to subvert the USSR by starting the Muslim Brotherhood.

> This brainwashing enabled the CIA and MI6 to use adepts to control the nationalist Arab governments, then to destabilise the Muslim regions of the Soviet Union. The Brotherhood became an inexhaustible reservoir of terrorists under the slogan–'Allah is our goal. The Prophet is our leader. The Qu'ran is our law. The jihad is our way. Martyrdom is our vow'.[9]

The CIA used the Muslim Brotherhood, particularly its paramilitary wing, to battle communists in the Arab countries, to control those Arab countries, and to destabilize the Soviet Union. But it proved to be such a great tool that it was eventually used to bring about regime change whenever it suited the CIA to dispose of an uncooperative head of state. Meyssan writes,

> In 1977...Brzeziński decided to use Islamism against the Soviets. He gave the Saudis the go-ahead to increase their payments to the Islamic World League, organised regime changes in Pakistan, Iran and Syria, destabilised Afghanistan, and made US access to oil from the "Greater Middle East" a national security objective. Finally, he entrusted the Brotherhood with military equipment.
>
> This strategy was clearly explained by Bernard Lewis during the meeting of the Bilderberg Group, organised by NATO in Austria, April 1979. Lewis, an Anglo-Israeli-US Islamologist, assured that the Muslim Brotherhood could not only play a major role against the Soviets and provoke internal trouble in Central Asia, but also balkanise the Near East in favour of Israel. [10]

That is, the CIA used the Muslim Brotherhood to control all the countries of the Greater Middle East, prevent their normal development as nations, and keep them as vassal states of the US. Of an even more enduring significance, the CIA basically started Al Qaeda. Former state department official Michael Springmann describes this in his book *Visas for Al Qaeda*.[11] The CIA collected not only Afghan tribesmen but violent and sadistic young men of the Muslim Brotherhood from all over the world. They illegally brought them to the United States, illegally gave them military training, and illegally inserted them into a foreign country to illegally mount a civil war. The CIA is a law unto itself.

One of the major players was Osama Bin Laden. From Saudi Arabia, the son of a wealthy family with a successful construction business, Osama had excellent contacts throughout the Arab world. He raised millions of dollars from wealthy Arabs, Muslim charities, and from the CIA. He arranged for weapons and ammunition and was essentially Saudi Arabia's point man in the US proxy war against the Soviets. Bin Laden molded this disparate group of Islamist fanatics into the unified army that became known as Al Qaeda. Meyssan gives more detail. "Brzeziński set up 'Operation Cyclone' in Afghanistan. Between 17,000 and 35,000 Muslim Brothers from about 40 countries came to fight the USSR, which had come to the defence of the Democratic Republic of Afghanistan, at its request. There had never been a 'Soviet invasion', as US propaganda pretended."[12]

The operation worked well. American taxpayers paid for much of the proxy war. The CIA-backed Mujahedeen emerged victorious in 1989, but the various mujahideen factions fought amongst themselves for three more years. Osama, with Saudi backing, now turned his private multinational army of Al Qaeda against the next infidel target–the United States. But he was playing both sides. The CIA supported bin Laden in his efforts to destabilize the Arab world. At the same time, he worked to undermine the United States.

Bin Laden moved the Al Qaeda headquarters to Sudan in 1989, which had been enmeshed in civil war since 1983. Al Qaeda quickly involved itself in the violence of the whole region, claiming responsibility for the attack on two American Black Hawk helicopters during the 1993 Battle of Mogadishu in Somalia.

The CIA continued to make use of Bin Laden's Al Qaeda army for decades, later rebranding the same group as ISIS even after they had been declared "enemies" of the United States. The CIA moved Al Qaeda into Bosnia in 1992 to bolster the Moslem forces in that civil war. Yugoslavia had not been cooperative with Washington. Now they paid the price. Meyssan hits the important points.

> The war in Bosnia-Herzegovina began in 1992. On instructions from Washington, the Pakistani secret services (ISI), still supported financially by Saudi Arabia, sent 90,000 men to participate in the fight against the Serbs, who were supported by Moscow. Osama Bin Laden received a Bosnian diplomatic passport and became the military advisor to President Alija Izetbegović (for whom US citizen Richard Perle was diplomatic advisor, and the Frenchman Bernard-Henri Levy was Press advisor). Bin Laden formed an Arab Legion with

> ex-combatants from Afghanistan and supplied financing from the Muslim World League. Either by a sense of confessional solidarity or in competition with Saudi Arabia, the Islamic Republic of Iran also came to the help of the Bosnian Muslims. With the Pentagon's blessing, it sent several hundred Guardians of the Revolution and a unit of the Lebanese Hezbollah. Above all, it delivered the main weapons used by the Bosnian army. The Russian secret services, who penetrated Bin Laden's camp, found out that the Arab Legion's entire bureaucracy was written in English, and that the Legion was taking its orders directly from NATO. After the war, a special International Tribunal was created. It launched criminal proceedings against a number of combatants for war crimes, but not one was a member of the Arab Legion.[13]

Former State Department official Michael Springmann confirms this.

> NATO, the CIA, and European Union all supported the Bosnians in their war against rump Yugoslavia, which consisted of Serbia and Montenegro. This fact made Osama Bin Laden and his Al Qaeda army field allies of the United States in Bosnia and Kosovo. During his trial for "war crimes" in The Hague, Serbian president Slobobdan Milosevic tried to inform the world about the Al Qaeda presence in Muslim-dominated regions of the former Yugoslavia but his words fell on deaf ears. Milosevic died under suspicious circumstances in his prison cell in The Hague.[14]

As the decade progressed, cooperation between Islamists, including bin Laden and his Al Qaeda army, and the CIA and the Pentagon increased. The Americans ramped up "terrorism" while they made plans to take over Afghanistan, Iraq, Syria, Lebanon, Somalia, Sudan, Libya, Cuba, and Iran. This later turned into the "7 Countries in 5 Years" plan. These plans were being developed in the 1990s, but it was only known at the very highest levels. It started to make its way down the chain of command right after 9/11, as General Wesley Clark (retired) reported in a 2007 interview. He was a four-star general and former Supreme Allied Commander of NATO during the war against Yugoslavia.

> I had been through the Pentagon right after 9/11. About ten days after 9/11, I went through the Pentagon and I saw Secretary Rumsfeld and Deputy Secretary Wolfowitz. I went downstairs just to say hello to some of the people on the Joint Staff who used to work for me, and one of the generals called me in. He said,
>
> "Sir, you've got to come in and talk to me a second."
>
> I said, "Well, you're too busy."
>
> He said, "No, no." He says, "We've made the decision we're going to war with Iraq."
>
> This was on or about the 20th of September. I said, "We're going to war with Iraq? Why?"
>
> He said, "I don't know." He said, "I guess they don't know what else to do."
>
> So, I said, "Well, did they find some information connecting Saddam to al-Qaeda?"
>
> He said, "No, no." He says, "There's nothing new that way. They just made the decision to go to war with Iraq." He said, "I guess it's like we don't know what to do about terrorists, but we've got a good military and we can take down governments." And he said, "I guess if the only tool you have is a hammer, every problem has to look like a nail."
>
> So, I came back to see him a few weeks later, and by that time we were bombing in Afghanistan. I said, "Are we still going to war with Iraq?" And he said,
>
> "Oh, it's worse than that." He reached over on his desk. He picked up a piece of paper. And he said, "I just got this down from upstairs"—meaning the Secretary of Defense's office—"today." And he said, "This is a memo that describes how we're going to take out seven countries in five years, starting

> with Iraq, and then Syria, Lebanon, Libya, Somalia, Sudan and, finishing off, Iran."
>
> I said, "Is it classified?"
>
> He said, "Yes, sir."
>
> I said, "Well, don't show it to me." And I saw him a year or so ago, and I said, "You remember that?"
>
> He said, "Sir, I didn't show you that memo! I didn't show it to you!"[15]

The 1990s brought important developments. Notably, the Pentagon got involved, motivated by concerns about oil and power. As the decade progressed, there was an ever-greater concern about "peak oil," the idea that the world's total oil production would peak shortly after the turn of the century, but demand would continue to rise. Cheap energy is the foundation of our industrial world. And to control the world, you must control energy, so the Deep State wanted to control the world's oil supply. This made it even more important to keep the whole Middle East destabilized. In fact, they wanted to break up most of the countries into smaller ones and have them run by radical Islamists of the Muslim Brotherhood whom, so they thought, could be controlled from Washington. This was a basic strategy that Israel had been pushing for over a decade. Christopher Bollyn says in his book *Solving 9-11: The Deception That Changed the World*,[16]

> An Israeli official named Oded Yinon revealed the Zionist strategy to Balkanize the entire Middle East into ethnic mini-states in the early 1980s. The plan for a global "War on Terror" to accomplish this goal has been articulated since the mid-1980s ad nauseam by Benjamin Netanyahu, the former Israeli prime minister of the extreme right-wing Likud party.[17]

By at least the mid-1990s, this was the plan: use terrorism, war, and regime change to destabilize and balkanize the Greater Middle East to keep these countries weak, divided, and controlled by Washington. This would also allow Washington to control the international oil business and, thus, energy. Before we turn the calendar over to the twenty-first century, we need to consider the FBI.

The FBI

Starting in 1995, former FBI agent Ted Gunderson started spilling the beans about some of the dirty business going on in America.[18] He said even the FBI has an overt branch and a covert branch, which had been involved in the assassination of JFK because he planned to clean out the shadow government. Gunderson reported that in the 1980s, Congress proposed anti-terrorism legislation, but it violated constitutional rights. A DOJ (Department of Justice) attorney publicly stated that "Before this passes, people will have to be killed." Ted thinks that was the reason for the 1993 World Trade Center bombing, which was carried out by the FBI but must have had CIA acquiescence.[19] Unfortunately, only six people died. It wasn't enough. Two years later, they did it again–the Oklahoma City bombing where 168 people were killed. Congress passed the anti-terrorism bill one year later. The evidence now shows that both of these bombings were FBI operations.

Incidentally, both of these bombs were created using the fertilizer ammonium nitrate. I spent two decades in the fertilizer industry, and I'm quite familiar with ammonium nitrate. It's not a great explosive and not a great choice to destroy a building. You need lots of it to make a big bang (but if you have thousands of tons, you can make a *really* big bang). In fact, on its own, it's not an explosive at all. It's an oxidizing agent. But it's readily available from fertilizer dealers, so you can make it appear that an angry citizen-terrorist is the culprit. Remember David Steele's quote from the beginning of this chapter. "In the United States, every single terrorist incident we have had has been a false flag, or has been an informant pushed on by the FBI."

Of course, the FBI monkey business hasn't abated in recent years. For example, the plot to kidnap Michigan Governor Gretchen Whitmer in 2020 was an FBI operation. Half the "plotters" were FBI operatives. They instigated the plot so the FBI could "come to the rescue" and claim the country is full of right-wing domestic terrorists. The men accused were acquitted by the court when the jurors realized it was all an FBI setup.[20] Evidence is also coming out that the completely overblown January 6, 2021 "insurrection" at the US capitol Building was another FBI operation.[21] These are just a few examples of FBI criminality. Plenty more examples are easy to find if you care to look for the evidence.

In August 2022, the FBI raided the home of former president Donald Trump and it seems likely the DOJ will indict him on criminal charges. This has never happened before in American history.[22] Even the obvious crimes of Richard Nixon and Bill Clinton were pardoned by their successors. This breaks the long tradition of never attacking a past president. This is the use of law as a weapon against political opponents. It doesn't happen in democracy. It happens in dictatorship. This is "rule *by* law," instead of the rule *of* law. Sad to say, but the FBI and the DOJ have completely lost their way and need to be disbanded.

The CIA (and other intelligence agencies) had spent decades developing a worldwide network of terrorist organizations and spreading the fear of terrorism in the West. The main goal was to expand the American Empire by controlling most governments through bribery, regime change, debt slavery, and so on. A second goal was to use "terrorism" as an excuse to build a de facto police state everywhere in the world. By the end of the twentieth century it was going well, but they needed a big leap in public fear to take the next major steps—particularly the "7 Countries in 5 Years" plan. A great spectacle was already being planned. It would shock the world.

What You Can Do Now

1. Understand that you are being manipulated with the fear of terrorism. It is all coming from our own governments. It is a fraud. Act accordingly. Do not fear. Love.
2. The apparatus of international money corruption must be disbanded. The World Bank, the Bank for International Settlements, and the International Monetary Fund must all be dissolved. The international banks are a key link in the chain of corruption and control, as explained by John Perkins. Encourage your elected leaders to withdraw their support from these institutions.
3. Intelligence agencies all over the world need to be pruned or shut down. It's time to retire the "cloak and dagger" business. The arch-evil entity is the CIA. It must be disbanded completely, so must every other non-military intelligence agency–MI6, NSA, DEA, NCO, DHS, and even the entire FBI. They are all out of control.

CHAPTER 12

Terrorism—The Third Forever War

"Let us not forget that violence does not and cannot exist by itself; it is invariably intertwined with the lie. They are linked in the most intimate, most organic and profound fashion: violence cannot conceal itself behind anything except lies, and lies have nothing to maintain them save violence. Anyone who has once proclaimed violence as his method must inexorably choose the lie as his principle." –ALEKSANDR SOLZHENITSYN

Just as the opening quote proclaims, lies and violence are inextricably linked. We have seen this with mass formation, with the earlier frauds, with Marxism–the Philosophy of Death, and with every totalitarian regime. In the last chapter, we have seen it with the whole operation of the CIA and the American Empire. This chapter looks at 9/11 and its consequences–a great lie and the greatest terrorist act of all time. The event is so covered with multiple layers of lies and deception that we may never know the whole truth. But some things are incontrovertible. The evidence is clear. As always, we mostly consider evidence, not experts, to see what truth it may reveal.

9/11: Fraud for the New Millennium

"Another way to cover up the truth is to begin with a theory and then omit evidence that doesn't fit your theory." –DR. JUDY WOOD

Prelude to 9/11

During the 1990s, the CIA, like Osama Bin Laden, was also playing both sides–privately working with Al Qaeda and publicly blaming them for terrorism. Bin Laden continued to play a key role in the CIA and Pentagon plans despite his declining health. French journalist Meyssan writes, "Seriously ill with kidney disease, Bin Laden was hospitalised, in August 2001, at the American Hospital in Dubai. A head of one of the Gulf states assured me that he had visited him in his room, where security was provided by the CIA."[1]

Meanwhile, the United States military and its NATO partners had been practicing the 9/11 attack for years. Military planners not only expected a terrorist attack by flying airplanes into buildings, but they also developed the plans for it.

- In 1999, NORAD conducted hijacking exercises where planes were flown into the Pentagon and the World Trade Center.
- The US military held an exercise rehearsing a response to an airliner crash at the Pentagon on October 24–26, 2000. Emergency responders from the Pentagon and Arlington County assembled in a conference room in the office of the Secretary of Defense for a mass casualty exercise that involved a commercial airliner crashing into the Pentagon and killing 341 people.
- Department of Defense medical personnel trained for the scenario of a "guided missile in the form of a hijacked 757 airliner" being flown into the Pentagon in May 2001.[2]

A new defense policy had also been laid out. After the fall of the Soviet Union in 1989, the United States had to rethink its post-Cold War defense policy. Again, from Meyssan:

> The Gulf War had hardly ended when Republican George H. Bush Sr. asked Paul Wolfowitz to write the Defense Policy Guidance (a classified document, but extracts were published by the New York Times and the Washington Post). Wolfowitz, a militant Trotskyist and at that time the future Assistant Secretary for Defense, presented his theory concerning US supremacy.[3]

The "Wolfowitz Doctrine," as it came to be known, was the basis of the coming wars. It proposed to prevent the emergence of a new global rival. Part of this doctrine involved taking control of all the hydrocarbon reserves in the Greater Middle East through the wars and insurrections already mentioned. It was the old empire-building strategy—"divide and conquer" rebranded as "destabilize and control." As we have seen, it is also a communist strategy. The lust for power, under every ideology, destroys humanity.

This would involve great political will. The Deep State thought the younger George W. Bush would be the man for the job, and they managed to get him elected. But George W. Bush balked at these massive illegal wars, as Meyssan writes. "However, the new President was not particularly obedient, which forced his backers to organise a shock for public opinion, which they compared to a "New Pearl Harbor", on 11 September 2001."[4]

The stage was set. The public had been led to believe that radical Islamist terrorism was on the rise. The military strategy for destabilizing and taking control of the Arab world was in place. Initial planning for the "7 Countries in 5 Years" wars had begun. Detailed planning and practice for the 9/11 attacks had taken place in several military exercises. Invasion plans for Afghanistan were prepared. The British fleet was deployed to the Gulf of Oman, and NATO had transported forty thousand men to Egypt—all before 9/11. Everything was in place.

As well, there was a drill going on that very morning in Washington, as Bollyn reports.

> On 9-11, an agency of the Department of Defense and the

> CIA was conducting a terror scenario in which an imaginary airplane from Washington's Dulles International Airport was to crash into one of the four towers of the suburban campus of the National Reconnaissance Office (NRO) in Chantilly, Virginia, just a few miles from the Pentagon. The plane that allegedly crashed into the Pentagon, American Airlines Flight 77, departed from the same airport at 8:20 a.m. on 9-11.
>
> When the terror scenario became real in New York and at the Pentagon, the NRO exercise was cancelled and nearly all its three thousand employees, the people who operate the nation's "eye in the sky," were sent home.
>
> The government said it was a "bizarre coincidence" that the NRO...had planned a simulated exercise with a mock "plane-into-building" crash on the morning of 9-11. "It was just an incredible coincidence that this happened to involve an aircraft crashing into our facility," spokesman Art Haubold told the Associated Press in August 2002. "As soon as the real world events began, we canceled the exercise."
>
> As the agency that operates many of the nation's spy satellites, the NRO personnel come from the military and the CIA. When the attacks occurred, however, most of the three thousand people who work at the agency were sent home. Why would they do that?[5]

Good question. As a former US Army intelligence officer has said, "The easiest way to carry out a false flag attack is by setting up a military exercise that simulates the very attack you want to carry out."[6]

Also at the same time, NORAD was running a war game exercise, ironically codenamed "Vigilant Guardian" with the Northeast Air Defense Sector. When they got calls about hijacked airplanes, they first thought it was part of their war game. The United States Airforce was not at all vigilant that day. The most evil, treacherous, and treasonous military attack in history was about to unfold.

The Official Story

It was the defining event of this generation. Like a generation earlier when JFK was assassinated, everyone remembers where they were and what they were doing that day. 2001 was my first year as a schoolteacher, and I was so overwhelmed by my new job that I couldn't figure out why the TV was playing all morning in the staff room. Everyone in the school knew what was going on in New York while I was just focused on teaching band. When I finally caught on, I was stunned–like everyone else. I was stunned again when I began to understand that the official story was all lies.

You know the official story. Those nasty Al Qaeda terrorists trained some of their guys from Afghanistan to fly 767 commercial jetliners. They boarded four planes in New York, Washington, and Boston early on the morning of September 11, 2001. They used plastic box cutters to kill a few people on the planes, threaten the others, break into the cockpits, and kill the pilots. Then they turned the planes around and flew them back to New York and Washington (we don't know the planned destination of the fourth plane), flying low to avoid being detected by radar, at 500 miles per hour, landing exactly on their target of the two World Trade Center towers (not much wider than the planes themselves) and the Pentagon. In Washington, the pilot had to make a hairpin 330^0 turn (which would have torn the wings off the plane at that speed and altitude), conduct an extremely difficult navigation over a hill, then descend quickly to strike the ground exactly at the base of the low Pentagon building, thereby destroying the accounting office. It's funny they didn't attack the other side of the building where the senior general staff had their offices, which would have allowed a much simpler approach up the Potomac River. In New York, the planes entered the buildings (virtually nothing bounced off and fell to the ground), exploded, and started fires. The fires spread, weakening the steel structures, which then collapsed to the ground, killing almost three thousand people in the process. It was the greatest *terrorist* attack ever on American soil and the deadliest *military* attack on American soil since Pearl Harbor.

The whole world was in shock. All the senior government and military officials professed bewilderment.

- President George Bush said, "They [al-Qaeda] struck in a way that was unimaginable."
- Secretary of Defense Donald Rumsfeld said, "Never would have crossed anyone's mind."
- General Richard Myers, Deputy Commander of the Joint Chiefs of Staff, said, "You hate to admit it, but we hadn't thought about this."
- White House Press Secretary Ari Fleischer said, "Never did we imagine what would take place on September 11th, where people used those airplanes as missiles and weapons."
- National Security Advisor Condoleezza Rice said, "I don't think anybody could have predicted that these people would take an airplane and slam it into the World Trade Center, take another one and slam it into the Pentagon; that they would try to use an airplane as a missile, a hijacked airplane as a missile."
- Air Force Lt. Col. Vic Warzinski, a Pentagon spokesman, said: "The Pentagon was simply not aware that this aircraft was coming our way, and I doubt prior to Tuesday's event, anyone would have expected anything like that here. There was no foreshadowing, no particular warning that would have led anyone with any reasonable view of the world to think this was a threat we faced."[7]

These are unbelievable comments from people who knew about the previous plans and exercises. Only a few people had their wits about them enough that day to realize it didn't make sense. Meyssan reports,

> Thus, on the evening of 11 September, on Channel 9 in New York, Donald Trump contested what was already becoming the official version. After having reminded his listeners that the engineers who built the Twin Towers had since joined his company, he observed that it was impossible for Boeings to break through the steel frames of the towers, and that it was impossible for such an accident to provoke their collapse. He

> concluded that there had to be other factors involved which were as yet unknown.[8]

Other intelligence professionals knew right away this massive operation could not have been the work of Al Qaeda. Bollyn states,

> Eckehardt Werthebach, the former president of Germany's domestic intelligence service, Verfassungsschutz, told me in 2001 that "the deathly precision" and "the magnitude of planning" of the 9-11 attacks would have required "years of planning." Such a sophisticated operation, Werthebach said, would require the "fixed frame" of a state intelligence organization... It was carefully planned years in advance and carried out for one strategic purpose: to kick-start the Zionist-planned "War on Terror."[9]

How could all this have happened without even a simple response from the US military? Intercepting errant commercial aircraft is routine.

> Between Sept. 2000 and June 2001 [10 months], the FAA [Federal Aviation Administration] scrambled fighter jets to intercept errant aircraft 67 times. Interceptions are routine and usually occur within 10 minutes of a sign of trouble, such as permanently loosing radio contact or flying off course. Yet on Sept. 11, 2001, four commercial airliners were off course and out of radio contact and not one of them would be intercepted.[10]

This is too unbelievable to be accidental.

It is safe to assume that the intelligence agencies and leaders of the world's major countries all knew this official story was an impossible lie. I'd guess that the largest countries would say to themselves, "If Bin Laden couldn't do it, and we couldn't do it, only the United States itself could do it." It was a "shock and awe" demonstration of power, also intended as a warning to America's enemies *and* allies.

By the next day, we no longer heard questions like, "Where did the buildings go?" Two of the world's largest buildings seemed to just disappear. Nobody on TV asked why the whole US Airforce could not get a plane in the air. No one mentioned the military exercises that were going on that very morning off the coast of New York. People stopped asking about the BBC news report that announced the collapse of Building 7 a half hour before it happened. Viewers could see Building 7 still standing out the window behind the reporter. To anyone with a critical mind, this was clearly a psychological warfare operation. Remember that the purpose of psychological warfare is to change your perception of reality to such an extent that, despite ample evidence about what is going on around you, you don't see it. Even if you do, you don't realize it's *planned*. Thus, you are unable to come to sensible conclusions in your own interests and in the interests of your nation.

The media censorship clamped down right away. As of September 12, the world only heard what the Deep State wanted us to hear. Anyone who brought up difficult questions or had contrary evidence was declared an idiot, a liar, or a conspiracy theorist. It's pretty ironic being sloughed off as a conspiracy theorist when the official Deep State story is about a conspiracy by a bunch of terrorists living in caves in the mountains of Afghanistan conducting a military-style operation on the continental United States on the same scale as the Imperial Japanese Navy, with four aircraft carriers and a thousand airplanes, pulled off at Pearl Harbor. There's a sketchy conspiracy theory.

The cleanup, and the coverup, started immediately. Despite the fact that the World Trade Center should have been considered a crime scene, all the evidence was quickly carted off and sold to a steel mill in Asia where the scrap steel was melted down within a few months. Within hours, our intelligence agencies (which, apparently, knew nothing about this huge operation beforehand) had figured out that a hitherto unknown Arab terrorist in Afghanistan was behind the whole thing.

While the official story satisfied most people and all of the media, it started unraveling almost immediately. The official investigations into the disaster were hamstrung in a hundred ways, learned nothing that contradicted the official story, and were widely seen as a whitewash.

With mercurial swiftness, Osama bin Laden and "his" terrorist organization, Al Qaeda, were declared the enemy, a new "War on Terror" decreed, and the army landed in Afghanistan less than a month later. Truly an incredible feat of military planning and operational efficiency from the same military that on September 11 could not put a single armed fighter plane in the air during the whole unfolding tragedy.

What Really Happened—Where Did the Towers Go?

Whole books have been written about 9/11, and I won't even ask all the questions, much less propose answers. My purpose here is twofold: to briefly present the only scientifically coherent explanation of the evidence, and to show how the reaction to the events changed our world. That's already a big task. Remember, what uncovers fraud is *evidence*. I'll just hit the high points. And I'll only consider the World Trade Center.

There has been only one proper forensic engineering study ever done on the World Trade Center tragedy, the one performed by Dr. Judy Wood. Her book, *Where Did the Towers Go?*,[11] presents the results of her many years of scientific work. Dr. Wood is a professor of engineering, and her specialty is forensic engineering. She was shocked to see the photos and explanations of 9/11 that defied the laws of physics—for example, massive steel and concrete office towers "collapsing" at faster than freefall speed. The official explanation was simply not possible. She devoted years to doing a proper forensic engineering investigation of what happened—not based on what anyone said, but on the physical evidence alone. She had no ax to grind, no politics to justify, just the burning desire to use her knowledge and skills to investigate the (then) greatest fraud in history.

Dr. Wood points out that a crime was committed on 9/11, a crime that should be solved by a forensic study of the *evidence*. As she says, "Evidence is the truth that theory must mimic, not the other way around." Dr. Wood presents not a theory, not a speculation, but a description of what happened based on the physical evidence. Her forensic study of the evidence revealed that the government's "investigation" and its NIST report are frauds.

The most fundamental fact is that the towers *did not fall.* They disappeared. They just went away. This is so impossible to believe, so outside our experience of the world, that we watched it happen right in front of our own eyes and didn't see it. There was almost nothing left of those towers. They were each 110 stories of offices. Yet not a single piece of office furniture was found. Out of tens of thousands of filing cabinets, only one was found–from the Ben and Jerry's ice cream shop. It was melted and twisted almost beyond recognition, yet inside were still some paper files and crisp $20 bills, untouched by heat. How can this happen?

From an article titled "What Happened to the Bodies?"

> The biggest piece of office furniture recovered from Ground Zero was a tiny fragment of a telephone keypad...Of the 2,800 people killed in the attack, only about 300 bodies were found intact. Of the 20,000 pieces of bodies found, 6,000 were small enough to fit into a test tube. The attack presented investigators with a case unlike any seen before. In all building collapses prior to the World Trade Center towers, bodies were recovered intact. Falling buildings crush victims – they don't shred them or cause them to vanish altogether. In the Twin Towers attack, more than 1,100 victims simply disappeared – not one shred of skin or piece of bone could be found despite meticulous sifting efforts to recover the remains.[12]

It wasn't just the twin towers. Every single building with a "WTC" prefix disappeared. World Trade Center Buildings 1, 2, 3, 4, 5, 6, and 7 were all destroyed, yet only two were struck by "airplanes." Building 7 didn't even suffer any damage by the time the twin towers had both disappeared. Of the thousands of tons of concrete, glass windows, steel beams–almost everything simply turned to dust and blew away. What does this?

To summarize her conclusions, Dr. Wood found:

1. The towers did not slam to the ground. They turned to dust in midair.
2. If they had slammed to the ground, there would be over a million

tons of debris left in a pile. That didn't happen. Less than 5% of these building's materials remained on the ground.

3. Manhattan would have been flooded. That didn't happen. The towers were built on bedrock 70 feet below the level of the Hudson River, inside a dike known as "the bathtub." If the towers had crashed to the ground, they would have ruptured the bathtub and flooded all of lower Manhattan.
4. The seismic record would have detected the "thud." That didn't happen. The "thud" would have been analogous to dropping a barbell on a waterbed. What did happen was analogous to lifting a barbell *off* a waterbed.

In short:

- The buildings were not destroyed through kinetic energy.
- The buildings were not destroyed through thermal energy.

The book's foreword provides a great summary.

Let us make a list of the things that Dr. Wood proves in *Where Did the Towers Go?*—proves not just beyond reasonable doubt, but beyond any doubt whatsoever:

1. That the "official" or "government" explanation for the destruction of the World Trade Center on 9/11 is, scientifically, false through and through.
2. That the WTC buildings were not destroyed by heat generated from burning jet fuel or from the conventional "burning" of any other substance or substances.
3. That the WTC buildings were not destroyed by mini-nuclear weaponry.
4. That the WTC buildings were not destroyed by conventional explosives of any kind, be they TNT, C4 or RDX, nor were they destroyed by welding materials such as thermite, thermate, or "nano-thermite."
5. That there was in fact no high heat at all involved either in bringing about the destruction of the buildings or generated by the destruction of them.

And now let us turn to what Dr. Wood proves beyond any reasonable doubt.

She proves that the kinds of evidence left behind after the destruction–including "fires" that emit no high heat and have no apparent source ("Weird Fires"); glowing steel beams and molten metal, neither of them emitting high heat; the levitation and flipping of extremely heavy objects, including automobiles and other vehicles; patterns of scorching that cannot have been caused by conventional "fire" ("Toasted Cars"); the sudden exploding of objects, people, vehicles, and steel tanks; the near complete absence of rubble after the towers' destruction, but instead the presence of entire buildings'-worth of dust, both airborne and heavier-than-air ("Dustification"), Dr. Wood proves that these and other kinds of evidence cannot have been created by conventional oxygen-fed fire, by conventional explosives, or by nuclear fission. At the same time, however, she shows *that all of them are in keeping with the patterns and traits of directed-energy power*, of force-fields directed into interference with one another in ways following the scientific logic of Nikola Tesla's thought and experimentation–*and* in ways also paralleling the work of contemporary Canadian scientist and experimenter John Hutchison, who, following Tesla's lead, has for many years produced again and again and again "the Hutchison Effect," creating results that include weird fires (having no apparent fuel); the bending, splintering, or fissuring of bars and rods of heavy metal; the coring-out, from inside, of thick metal rods; and the repeated *levitation* of objects.[13]

Where Did the Towers Go?

Two 110-story office towers "went away" and didn't even leave enough material to fill the lobby. Every single piece of office furniture, every computer, telephone, toilet, desk, chair, filing cabinet (except one), and over 1100 human beings simply disappeared into a cloud of dust and blew away. What power, force, or weapon can do this? Certainly not a handful of terrorists living in a cave in Afghanistan.

Dr. Wood ends her book on a positive note, and echoes the same dichotomous choice I see.

> He who controls the energy, controls the people. Control of energy, depending on what that energy is, can either destroy or sustain the planet.
>
> We have a choice. And the choice is real. We can live happily and fruitfully and productively, or we can destroy the planet and die, every last one of us, along with every living being on this planet.[14]

The official story is a lie and people at the highest level of the United States Government and armed forces have always known it's a lie. For a whole host of reasons, neither Osama Bin Laden nor Al Qaeda nor any other terrorist organization nor any other intelligence agency nor military organization could possibly have carried out this attack. This attack could only have been carried out by the armed forces of the United States of America.

Andrew Johnson drew the obvious conclusions in a 2017 article.

> If one is to accept these truths, then one must also accept there is a separate "power elite" group that both possesses such advanced directed free energy technology and the means to deploy it. Not only that, as I have been documenting for over 10 years, it can cover up these things to the point that almost no one recognises this massive deception for what it is....
>
> It had become clear how well the 9/11 cover up had been planned. It had also become clear how vitally important it was to keep the connection between 9/11 and energy covered up.[15]

This is a huge fraud, as is the entire war on terror. This fraud was perpetrated on the whole world to make us go along with a series of wars and insurrections intended to destabilize dozens of countries, control them as vassal states, control the world's energy, solidify the "shadow government" control over all the developed nations, and turn the whole world into a police state controlled by the military-industrial-intelligence complex. They have killed millions of people and displaced tens of millions. This fraud was perpetrated by godless people whose only desire is for power. They will kill *any number of people*. God help us.

Democracy is Over—The Consequences of 9/11

"When people who are honestly mistaken learn the truth, they will either cease being mistaken, or cease being honest." –ANONYMOUS

As I have mentioned previously, when government actions make no sense, don't listen to what the government says. Watch what it does. Actions reveal motives. What are the real outcomes of its actions? Those are the real objectives. With 9/11, the outcome was an incredible increase in the police state, in pointless wars and destruction, and in the military-industrial-intelligence complex. All over the world.

I don't know the people behind this operation. Thierry Meyssan calls them the "11 September men." It's a fitting name. With a flexible definition of "terrorism," the stage was set to suspend the Bill of Rights whenever it suited the state. "Emergency" terrorist legislation (such as *The Patriot Act* in the USA) was passed in every country and has essentially become permanent. As always, once a government takes more power, it never willingly gives it up. And immediately, a huge manhunt began to find Osama Bin Laden. It was a fraud. He was never the culprit of 9/11, and he soon died of natural causes anyway. Thierry Meyssan learned what really happened.

> Although Osama Bin Laden suffered from chronic kidney disease, he died on 15 December 2001 from the consequences of Marfan Syndrome. A representative of MI6 was present at his funeral in Afghanistan. For a while, several more or less life-like body doubles kept his image alive, one of whom was himself assassinated in 2005 by Omar Sheikh, according to Pakistani Prime Minister Benazir Bhutto.[16]

By the time US forces started looking for Osama Bin Laden, the CIA already knew he was dead. But they needed to keep the fantasy going to justify their wars and official terrorism. When Seal Team 6 "captured Osama Bin Laden" on May 2, 2011—ten years later—whoever they captured wasn't the right man. So, they had to dump the body in the ocean. No one could know about the fraud. But then, Seal Team 6 also had to be eliminated. This was done a few months later on August 6, 2011, in Afghanistan. Once again, the Muslims got blamed. The helicopter carrying the whole team–and then some, thirty-eight men plus a dog–was shot down by an "insurgent" missile (or maybe a rocket-propelled grenade, or maybe something else). This mass assassination was codenamed "Operation Extortion 17." According to Captain Field McConnell, it was approved right from the top.[17] The chain of command for this operation started with Barrack Obama. The official story claimed the black box from the helicopter was not recovered because it was washed away in a flash flood. But it doesn't rain in Afghanistan in August. Check the weather records. Only evidence uncovers fraud. A 2021 documentary about this tragic event, *FALLEN ANGEL Call Sign: Extortion 17*,[18] discusses the military's coverup of the "accident" and presents evidence that it appears to have been planned.

7 Countries in 5 Years–
Destabilizing the Arab World (and Europe)

The 9/11 event was actually a coup d'état. The "alternate government," AKA the Deep State, had orchestrated a false flag attack on the United States, blamed it on far-off terrorists, usurped the elected government, and used the whole fabricated crisis to justify their planned wars of aggression that would embroil the US for the next two decades and justify ever greater power and control for themselves. Democracy ceased to exist.

Anyone who spoke up against this treason was labeled a conspiracy theorist or a fool or was "suicided." People at the top echelons of power faced a choice–either shut up and go along, or speak up and be eliminated. Meyssan describes how the insiders are also caught in the web of fraud.

> Everyone was therefore faced with a question of conscience. By ignoring the coup d'état of 11 September, one could avoid being ridiculed as a conspiracy theorist, but one also lost the

> only effective means of silencing the war drums, and was thus obliged to allow the next crime, which was the invasion of Iraq.[19]

American soldiers were still tied down in Afghanistan but, no problem, the Deep State geniuses were completely prepared to start a second land war in Asia. The standard CIA "regime change playbook" would be used in every situation, with local modifications as needed. The script goes something like this: start an argument over anything, blame the country's leader for some really bad stuff, instigate "protests" and even an "uprising" so the leader will brutally repress the dissidents, use your media allies and impassioned speeches to whip up public demand at home for a military intervention to "save democracy," send in the marines to topple the government, and put your predetermined, compliant, "local" president in charge. With all these Arab countries, the plan was to put the Muslim Brotherhood in charge, which the CIA could control.

The "7 Countries in 5 Years" plan was immediately thrown into action after 9/11. Cuba and Iran were dropped from the older list of Afghanistan, Iraq, Syria, Lebanon, Somalia, Sudan, Libya, Cuba, and Iran. How modest.

Afghanistan was invaded less than a month after 9/11. Twenty years later, trillions of dollars spent, and hundreds of thousands of lives lost, the Taliban emerged victorious in August 2021. The US and its allies beat a hasty retreat and an embarrassingly incompetent evacuation. It's so unbelievable it must have been planned that way. They left $100 billion worth of military equipment, including Humvees and Black Hawk helicopters.[20] All this war material may have been left to ensure a strong "terrorist" presence that will justify another war. As well, the war suppliers will now have to replace all those weapons, at taxpayers' expense. Qui bono? Unsurprisingly, China immediately moved into the political/military vacuum left by the Americans and is now operating Bagram Airforce Base.

I still wonder, "Why Afghanistan?" It sure wasn't for access to pomegranates. Maybe it was a great chance to double-cross Osama bin Laden in a big way and use him as a scapegoat to justify their endless wars in the Greater Middle East. It certainly played into the CIA/Deep State use of the international drug business for profit and subversion. We have already seen in chapter 6 how the US war managed to balloon Afghanistan's opium and heroin production. It provides most of the world's supply and it flowed through the hands and the bank accounts of the CIA, who have likely profited to the tune of trillions over these two decades.[21]

The next Arab country up was Iraq. Meyssan explains, in exquisite detail, the almost unbelievable corruption, deceit, murder, and mayhem as the US and its NATO allies tried to execute the "7 Countries in 5 Years" plan. Iraq was blamed for having weapons of mass destruction—as if that justifies a war. At least a dozen other countries *definitely* have weapons of mass destruction—including the United States, by the way. None were ever found in Iraq. It didn't matter. It was just a rouse anyway. Conquering Iraq was the cover for (mostly) Americans to rape it for their own wealth, leave it in ruins, and use it as a base of chaos to infect the neighboring nations. The CIA has modified the old communist dictum to "rule *and* ruin."

The plan next moved to Tunisia. The lead actors in Washington and London performed beautifully as they feigned surprise at the "Jasmine Revolution," planned and executed by the CIA. Even though the Tunisian leader, Zine el-Abidine Ben Ali, had been a faithful CIA agent, his usefulness had come to an end. In 2010, the CIA brought in their "protest organizer," Gene Sharp, and his men to stage "spontaneous demonstrations." The Tunisian Chief of Staff, General Rachid Ammar, persuaded the president to take a leave of absence abroad, just long enough to restore order—the same trick the CIA used on the Shah of Iran years before. It worked. The president left the country. The Western press ran stories of his corruption. MI6 brought in the West's hand-picked successor from exile in London—Muslim Brother Rached Ghannouchi—and he was placed in power. The Muslim Brotherhood now ruled Tunisia, which was under London's influence rather than Paris's. And he knew that he owed his position and his life to the Western intelligence agencies. Mission accomplished.[22]

As Meyssan explains,

> Now it was Egypt's turn. Gene Sharp's men and the supposedly "non-governmental" NED [National Endowment for Democracy, a CIA front group] took over Tahrir Square. It was the "Lotus Revolution". This time it was ambassador Frank Wisner (Nicolas Sarkozy's father-in-law) who came to inform President Hosni Mubarak that he was fired. Mubarak had no more to be ashamed of than did Ben Ali...but he also had no part to play in the British plan. The international Press once again ran amuck, exposing the dictator's hidden fortune. Except that this time it was all a lie, because Hosni Mubarak was not a thief. But no matter, MI6 organised the return of the Muslim Brotherhood anyway.[23]

Then came Libya. "In Libya, the African immigrant workers were the only ones who understood what was happening. They witnessed the mass arrival of Western special forces in Benghazi, and expected that the Westerners were about to overthrow the régime, as they had in the Ivory Coast."[24]

Libya took more manpower. The United States had to get NATO involved in an actual war to overthrow the country. There was never an "uprising." The whole operation was a foreign war of aggression to completely destabilize the most prosperous nation in Africa and a major oil producer. It remains a quagmire of political instability to this day.

As with all these CIA operations, the carefully orchestrated propaganda was essential. The psyops were more important than the actual political and military operations. In Libya, MI6 was in charge of propaganda. They started preparing for the "Arab Spring" propaganda as early as 2005. Meyssan explains some of their deceptions.

> At the beginning of the Arab Spring, MI6 set up a coordination center for the Atlantist and Western-oriented TV channels in Doha, Qatar. Al-Arabiya, al-Jazeera, BBC, CNN, France 24, and Sky joined up, along with small, CIA-created

> Arab-language stations. Together, they produced images of the revolutionaries pouring onto Green Square in Tripoli, which were broadcast for the first time by Sky, on the second day of the battle for the control of the Libyan capital. Careful examination of these images reveal that they were filmed in an open-air studio.
>
> Certain of the Square's buildings are not rendered in detail. Above all, the scaffolding that the Gaddafists had erected the week before the battle, in order to hang a huge portrait of the Guide, was absent. This was perhaps the first time in history that fiction film was broadcast and presented as live footage of combat operations. The effect on the Libyans was catastrophic. Persuaded that they had been invaded and had lost the war, many of them gave up resisting.[25]

"Seeing" is no longer "believing." What the media feeds us is pure fiction. In Syria, the CIA war was such a mess of nonsense and lies and double-crossing that it would take many books to catalog all of it. "For example, in the suburbs of Damascus, they filmed a parade of the Islamic Army, with four tanks and a few hundred extras who marched past the camera, then turned around and went by the camera again, several times."[26]

Syria and Lebanon went badly wrong for the Pentagon and the CIA. These countries didn't play along with the script. Plus, the Russians saw plainly what was going on and refused to let their ally be completely overrun. The Syrian debacle is too long and Byzantine to even begin explaining here. Read Thierry Meyssan's book for all the details, *Before Our Very Eyes: Fake Wars and Big Lies from 9/11 to Donald Trump.*[1]

Seven countries were marked for American invasion, destabilization, destruction, and control. The Pentagon and CIA achieved varying degrees of success in each country but now, two decades after the 9/11 fraud, every one of these countries remains an unstable mess. Millions of people have been killed, economies destroyed, cultures decimated, and tens of millions of refugees and migrants set to wandering around the world to scar both the countries they leave and the countries they enter. Even the casual observer of these wars must conclude that nothing good has come from them. The main result has been ever more power and control for the Deep State. The outcome shows the goal. Actions reveal motives.

Some might say that it's not possible to get so many people to conspire in the military-industrial-intelligence complex. But recall that only a handful need to conspire. Thousands of others are drawn into either reluctant or unwitting collaboration by the carrot and the stick. Shut up and see your career flourish and your wealth balloon. Speak up and have your job, wealth, reputation, family, and even life threatened. As we have seen, these people will kill anyone who stands in their way.

Others might say it's not possible for corruption to be as deep and wide as this implies. Oh, yes it is. During prohibition, virtually every segment of society was corrupted. And that only lasted a decade. The CIA frauds have been going on for a lifetime. They have created a massive web of fraud that can only be stopped by shutting down the whole CIA and most of the intelligence industry. It stopped being intelligence long ago. It is simply a vector for controlling citizens.

The time has come to end this web of lies and deception. Our media companies are propaganda outlets. Our governments take our money and play war games with the lives of millions of people. All of us ordinary people are utterly disgusted with it. We are constantly being lied to. The "War on Terror" is a giant fraud. Stop it.

Organized Migrations as Weapons of War

The "7 Countries in 5 Years" plan turned millions of people into migrants. Yet it's not just here. The whole Western world has been overrun by migrations in recent years. Why wasn't this a huge problem in years past? Because now it is a deliberate policy of destabilization.

Some Americans say the Democratic Party's support of unrestricted immigration is a ploy to register more Democratic voters. There may be a bit of truth in that, but the real reason is much more treacherous. It's a key part of the overarching goal of communist/technocratic subversion—to destroy loyalty to the nation-state and provoke societal collapse so people will cry out for a "savior" to restore order. The "New Order" will be a one-world government without nations or borders or freedom.

The plan to destabilize the Middle East sent millions of migrants to Europe from all over the Greater Middle East. The collapse of Libya opened up a route for sub-Saharan Africans to migrate to Europe. Everybody had their own selfish goals in trying to manipulate migrants–playing with them as if these human beings were little plastic game pieces on their giant *Risk* board. It is inhuman.

Meyssan explains some of the complex reasons for displacing human populations–to justify war, to remove unwanted ethnic populations, to provide cheap labor and lower domestic labor costs, to strip the Arab nations of the very skills and knowledge they need to rebuild, and to destroy national identities. It's all explained in an essay by Kelly Greenhill, *Strategic Engineered Migration as a Weapon of War.*[27] These migrations are planned and orchestrated as part of the subversive, fifth-generation World War III.

Turkey took advantage of the CIA war in Syria because it wanted to boot out the Turkish Kurds and move in Syrian Sunni Muslims. The European industrialists wanted to bring in cheap immigrant labor to lower wage rates.[28] Incidentally, George Soros has been paying for thousands of Central American migrants to be bussed to the US border. Soros has been a disaster speculator and socialist ideologue his whole life. If he is paying to create a disaster, you can be sure he has a plan to profit from it.

When millions of migrants settle in our modern welfare states, they create a massive drain on government treasuries. They receive welfare, free medical care, free education, often free housing–yet they don't have jobs. They don't contribute economically or socially. Every community will have people who won't assimilate, thereby dividing society. Every classroom will have students who can't speak English and lack the prerequisite knowledge to be there. Everyone's learning suffers. All of this is part of the plan–societal collapse.

Communities and nations are disrupted by the loss of people, the gain of people, financial pressures on families when their income is lost, and financial pressures on governments supporting migrants with tax money. Think back. Can you remember why all this happened? Was there any good reason for the United States, along with the other Western Allies, to attack almost every country in the Greater Middle East? I forgot the reason too.

The social situation in Europe is almost to the point the great planners—the "11 September men," the Deep State, or whoever is behind all this—are shooting for. The social disintegration is leading to an ideal communist crisis that will enable the next phase of Deep State control. This is mass migration as a tool of totalitarian subversion. It is working wonderfully.

The Growth of the Police State

As planned, the 9/11 attacks led to the stripping away of civil liberties, not only in the United States but all over the world. It caused a massive increase in military-industrial-intelligence-police spending, again, all over the world. It led to a massive increase in wars, killing, destruction, drugs, population displacement, and human misery—again, all over the world. Simple policemen have been militarized. Particularly after 2020, you have seen them in your streets and on news reports, armed and armored for war, arrayed in battle formations, supported by military vehicles. For what war? You have seen them attack unarmed civilians and beat up grandmothers who have done nothing wrong. Along with most Canadians, I was outraged to see exactly this in peaceful, polite Canada in February 2021. Are you beginning to see that WWIII is being fought between the Deep State controllers and ordinary people everywhere?

This massive military-industrial-intelligence-police structure is out of control. Not only is it costing us trillions of dollars, but it is enslaving us. We don't need all this "protection." Other people and nations are not out to kill us. All of us human beings must let go of this destructive fear of each other and realize we only have our own governments to fear. A physicist, Dr. Katherine Horton (a "targeted individual") points out, "The only real threats to national security in the world are the military and the intelligence agencies."[29]

My American friends, you may not know that you are paying for and suffering under at least seventeen separate intelligence agencies. In case you don't believe me, here is the list.

1. CIA–Central Intelligence Agency
2. NSA–National Security Agency
3. DHS–Department of Homeland Security
4. DIA–Defense Intelligence Agency
5. INR–State Department Bureau of Intelligence and Research
6. ISR–Air Force Intelligence
7. NSB–FBI National Security Branch
8. ISC–Army Intelligence and Security Command
9. CGI–Coast Guard Intelligence
10. OIC–Department of Energy Office of Intelligence and Counterintelligence
11. OIA–Treasury Department Office of Intelligence and Analysis
12. DEA–Drug Enforcement Administration
13. NGA–National Geospatial Intelligence Agency
14. US Marine Corps–Marine Corps Intelligence Activity
15. US Navy–Office of Naval Intelligence
16. ODNI–Office of the Director of National Intelligence
17. NCO–National Reconnaissance Office

In addition, the granddaddy of them all is the ODNI (Office of the Director of National Intelligence).[30] These are all self-policing, secretive agencies. There is no effective oversight in Congress or anywhere. They have created a war economy and a war psychology without any need for a war.

The Path to Peace

The "War on Terror" is a giant fraud. It promises to fight against terror, yet it delivers terror–just like communism. It is another case of mass formation psychosis. "Terrorism" is an idea and a tactic. Like anything non-material, it cannot be attacked or destroyed. But you *can* control and destroy people. That's what the "War on Terror" does. It is a fraud perpetrated by a small group of rich and powerful people whom I can only identify as the "Deep State." This reality is so bizarre, so different from your understanding of the world, so unbelievable, that you are reluctant to believe it. My friends, look at the evidence. Experts do not expose a fraud—only evidence does.

You must take away their toys. Shut down the CIA and fund your local police. Keep your own neighborhoods safe and stop destroying everybody else's neighborhood. Just like you want to be left alone to live your life in peace, let everyone else in the world live their lives in peace. You will find that the rest of the world *doesn't* want to destroy you.

Nobody needs to be the world's policeman. People and nations can solve their own problems if other people and nations would just leave them alone. Find a way to elect political leaders who are not part of the Deep State, people who are outsiders. Rein in the power of NGOs, lobbyists, and bureaucrats. Put power back into the hands of elected representatives—who can be thrown out at the next election. Democracy depends upon leaders who are beholden to the people who elected them, not to the big companies who paid for their political campaigns, nor the big media companies, nor the CIA, nor whoever is running the Twitter mobs, nor whoever is blackmailing people into obedience because they were entrapped in compromising actions, nor whoever else might be behind the curtains of power.

Empire is the enemy of democracy. History teaches us that you cannot have an empire abroad and a democracy at home. Throw out the empire builders and dismantle the American Empire. Only then can you recreate the American republic you pine for.

You must understand that you have been lied to. Understand that you are surrounded by fraud. You are being manipulated. As Eisenhower said, "Only an alert and knowledgeable citizenry can compel the proper meshing of the huge industrial and military machinery of defense with our peaceful methods and goals, so that security and liberty may prosper together." Since you are reading this book, you are now alert and knowledgeable. You must act. You must stop living by lies. You must stop cooperating with lies. You must demand the truth from your elected leaders, your police, your judges, your teachers, your friends, your neighbors.

If you are a judge, it is time to do your duty. The people responsible for the 9/11 attack must be brought to justice. The truth must be told to the American people and to the world. The military-industrial-intelligence cabal must be torn apart if America is to ever regain Eisenhower's vision of a nation "to keep the peace; to foster progress in human achievement, and to enhance liberty, dignity and integrity among people and among nations." We are living in exactly the "disastrous rise of misplaced power" he foresaw. The weight of this combination has, indeed, robbed us of our liberties and our democratic processes. Public policy has been "captured" by the scientific-technological elite, just as he feared.

The CIA must be disbanded. All security and intelligence services need to be trimmed back and placed clearly under the control of their respective national legislatures. An intelligence agency must be the servant of democracy, not the master.

The incredible power of directed energy that was demonstrated on 9/11 must be de-classified and released to the world. The essence of democracy is that all power is distributed to the people, not collected into the hands of the rulers. This power cannot reside in the hands of people who have demonstrated they will use it only for destruction and murder. This is the abundant and cheap energy that will fuel a new industrial revolution throughout the world. If you still think fossil fuels are bad, then free directed energy is what will make fossil fuels obsolete. The Deep State fears this because a key part of their plan to control everyone is to control all energy. Free energy will destroy their plan and their cabal. That's the most important reason *everyone* must have it. Free energy will free us all!

But directed energy is not the only secret the CIA and Pentagon need to release. *All* their dark secrets need to see the light of day—the secret space program, the secret mind control, the secret weather manipulation, and a thousand other secrets must be told. It's time for truth to replace lies.

My friends, there is a path to peace. But we are not on that path. We are on a path to destruction. There is hope, but not yet. The latest, greatest, and most evil fraud of all time is upon us now.

What You Can Do Now

1. The "revolving door" between industries and the government agencies that regulate them (as explained by John Perkins[31]) must be closed. People will have to choose either a career in government or a career in industry–not both. The revolving door gives both the hens and the foxes the key to the hen house. Guess who loses.
2. The energy that destroyed the World Trade Center is owned by the US military. It must be shared with the world. Great power cannot be held in the hands of a few. That is tyranny. Democracy, freedom, and peace demand that power be in the hands of everyone.
3. Work to defund the "intelligence" control apparatus and fund your local police.
4. Support politicians and judges who will investigate the 9/11 fraud and prosecute those responsible for the murders.

CHAPTER 13

Pandemic—The Gathering Storm

"In times of universal deceit, telling the truth is a revolutionary act." –WRONGLY ATTRIBUTED TO GEORGE ORWELL, SOURCE UNKNOWN

I have intentionally borrowed the title of Winston Churchill's first book about World War II. In it, he describes the events leading up to the outbreak of the war. Germany, Italy, and Japan spent years preparing for war while their future enemies blithely ignored the evidence and failed to respond appropriately.

That's also what happened in the decades leading up to 2020. The Chinese and the Deep State constantly worked toward their goal of world domination–subverting their enemies, developing their weapons, building their arsenals, establishing their command and control systems, and drilling their troops. Just as Hitler scored many victories before ever firing a shot–annexing Alsace-Lorraine, Austria, and the Sudetenland–the Deep State scored victory after victory without anyone realizing it was war.

But the attack on Poland required kinetic warfare. It couldn't be hidden. It had to be sudden, massive, and overwhelming because Hitler knew that France and Britain would react. In a similar way, when China and the Deep State launched the most massive biological warfare attack in history, it had to be sudden, massive, and overwhelming. It was. This chapter illuminates the prelude to 2020. Chapters 14 and 15 look at the covid campaign.

As always, it doesn't matter what anyone *says*; only *evidence* exposes a fraud. In this case, the evidence clearly points to both the SARS-CoV-2 virus and the "vaccines" as being biological weapons. The world is under attack from a massive assault of fifth-generation warfare–biological and psychological. But let's back up and take it one step at a time.

Setting the Stage

"Never do anything against conscience even if the state demands it." –ALBERT EINSTEIN

We might consider this beginning phase of the assault to be the information influence operation as described in chapter 8. Everyone's mind had to be prepared, as did all the structures in society–part of the subversion tactics as described by Yuri Bezmenov.

A Crisis in Science

There is a crisis in science, and medicine in particular, of which the public has largely been kept ignorant. We have seen how nutritional science was corrupted starting in the 1960s (chapter 5) and how climate science was corrupted starting in the 1980s (chapter 7). Today, science is corrupted everywhere. Most scientific research is worthless, wrong, or both. I will give just a little evidence to substantiate my claim. You can research it for yourself.

The two most reputable medical journals in the world are *The Lancet* and *The New England Journal of Medicine*. Dr. Marcia Angell summed up the state of medical research.

> It is simply no longer possible to believe much of the clinical research that is published, or to rely on the judgement of trusted physicians or authoritative medical guidelines. I take no pleasure in this conclusion, which I reached slowly

> and reluctantly over my two decades as an editor of *The New England Journal of Medicine*.[1]

An editor of *The Lancet* has made similar remarks, to the effect that at least half of all scientific literature may be simply untrue, and that science has taken a turn toward darkness.[2]

It is also ironically insightful that both *The Lancet* and *The New England Journal of Medicine* were caught publishing clearly fraudulent papers in June 2020. *The Lancet* paper purported to show that hydroxychloroquine (HCQ) was ineffective in treating covid-19. Yet the data upon which this conclusion was based was found to be completely fabricated.[3] The authors of the papers retracted them because, faced with criticism from other scientists, they could not ascertain the accuracy of the data–which, of course, they should have done beforehand, as should have the peer reviewers. The fact that the authors didn't seem to know where the data came from suggests these papers may have been ghostwritten by someone in the pharmaceutical business–an alarmingly common and corrupt practice in the world of medical journals. The whole mess stinks of fraud.

Yet the mainstream media continued to report the fraudulent conclusion for months as if it were real "science." This is not simply an unfortunate error. It's a familiar tactic of psychological warfare. Immediately, the FDA used the fraudulent HCQ study to revoke its emergency-use authorization (for off-label use against covid-19) because of the alleged risks, even though HCQ has been scientifically proven to be one of the safest medicines in the world. The next week, Remdesivir was *given* emergency-use authorization, even though it has well-documented and huge side effects–heart arrhythmias, liver and kidney damage–and had *never* been shown to be effective against *any* disease.

These FDA decisions were intentional fraud. They were planned and tactical moves in a biological war and evidence that these organizations have been subverted and cannot be trusted. That's the thing about trust–once you lose it, you don't get it back. Science in general, and medical science in particular, is broken and corrupt and cannot be trusted. It has become nothing more than a tool of totalitarian control. We have been taught to regard science and medicine as unassailable bastions of truth. But a prudent person would say "Show me the evidence" rather than "Trust the science."

Predictive Programming and Dress Rehearsals

We reviewed predictive programming in chapter 9. It's a common mind control technique, and Operation Covid-19 is full of it. For the past twenty years, we have had no end of "experts" telling us the world is overdue for a pandemic. Anthony Fauci did this. Bill Gates did this. The World Economic Forum did this. It was predictive programming. They were planning it. If you understand this, you realize the Deep State is announcing its plans.

Just like with 9/11, the covid operation was such a huge event that they had to plan, prepare, and practice for years. Likely, SARS-CoV-1 and MERS were practice runs for SARS-CoV-2. But they also rehearsed the psychological warfare—controlling the public response to the biological warfare. There were several rehearsals, maybe more. I will tell you about two of them. You will notice how frighteningly similar they are to what actually happened with the covid fraud in 2020. This was not coincidence. It reveals a plan. The first big rehearsal was Operation Lockstep in 2010. Yes, the pandemic has been planned for over a decade.

Operation Lockstep

British medical doctor and author Dr. Vernon Coleman explains the operation.

> In 2010, the Rockefeller Foundation...organised a scenario planning exercise. It wasn't secret but it wasn't terribly public either....
>
> It dealt with a zoonotic viral pandemic that killed millions of people around the world. The Lockstep described "a world of tighter top-down government control and more authoritarian leadership, with limited innovation and growing citizen pushback."

> In what was effectively a war game, the new virus killed 20% of the population and had a deadly effect on industry, tourism, economies and supply chains. Shops were closed and empty for many months. China imposed mandatory quarantines and sealed its border and these policies saved many lives. Western countries were too lax and there were many more deaths. Around the world, political leaders ordered their citizens to have their body temperature taken at public places such as railway stations and shops. At the end of the pandemic the control measures which had been introduced were kept and intensified to prevent a future outbreak. Citizens around the world gave up their privacy and accepted mandatory biometric IDs—all in order to be safer and to regain some of their lost stability. States became more controlling and political leaders were free to introduce new laws as they felt appropriate. Millions were imprisoned in their homes and mandatory health screenings became commonplace.[4]

Event 201

In the fall of 2019, Bill Gates and the WEF conducted a big, expensive planning exercise just as covid-19 was launching in Wuhan, China. It's reminiscent of the "terror" exercises going on the morning of 9/11. Dr. Mercola describes it well in a March 2021 article titled "How Bill Gates Premeditated COVID Vaccine Injury Censorship."

> Many high-ranking men and women with governmental authority participated in Event 201, which coincidentally simulated a worldwide pandemic triggered by a novel coronavirus, just months before SARS-CoV-2. . . .
>
> They included representatives from the World Economic Forum, the Centers for Disease Control and Prevention, Johns Hopkins University Population Center, the World Bank, the Chinese government and vaccine maker Johnson & Johnson. During the event, the group developed strategies to control

> a pandemic, the population and the narrative surrounding the event.
>
> At no time did they investigate using current therapeutic drugs and vitamins or communicating information about building immune systems. Instead, the aim was to develop and distribute patentable antiviral medications and a new wave of vaccines....
>
> Gates spoke to the BBC April 12, 2020, and claimed these types of simulations had not occurred, saying, "Now here we are. You know we didn't simulate this; we didn't practice, so both the health policies and economic policies...we find ourselves in uncharted territories."
>
> Yet, videos of the event are available and Johns Hopkins Center for Health Security released a statement naming the Gates Foundation as a partner in sponsoring the pandemic simulation. It seems strange and alarming that a man with the responsibility of running the Gates Foundation and the powerful influence he has over global public policy decisions had forgotten an exercise he organized only six months before the interview. Or was it deception?[5]

Bill Gates and the WEF left nothing to chance. They planned the virus, planned the psychological operation, planned the response of ignoring treatment and prevention, planned the censorship and propaganda, and planned the imposition of a vaccine. That's why the whole operation was soon dubbed the "plandemic." It is no wonder that every country in the world followed the same script. The script had been written years in advance, distributed to all the actors, and professionally rehearsed. They even had a good director–Bill Gates.

A Short History of Biological Weapons

"No enterprise is more likely to succeed than one concealed from the enemy until it is ripe for execution." –NICCOLO MACHIAVELLI

Both the Russians and the Japanese were developing biological weapons by the 1920s and deployed them during the Second World War. The Americans got into the game when they realized what their enemies were up to. They built Fort Detrick in North Carolina and the Plum Island facility in New York (just off the northeast tip of Long Island) specifically for biological warfare research. After the war, the US Army grabbed the German and Japanese bioweapon secrets and scientists to further their own program, as part of the well-documented Operation Paperclip.[6] But as Murphy's Law attests, accidents happen.

Bioweapon Accidents

The consequences of biological weapon accidents can be horrendous. In 1979, anthrax powder escaped from a Russian production plant in Sverdlovsk, and over one hundred people died. In a comical and prophetic twist, officials blamed the deaths on tainted meat from a "black market" and warned people to stay away from outdoor meat markets.

In the United States, the Plum Island facility was given to the Department of Agriculture after a few years of army ownership, making it look like simply agricultural research. The government denied it, but the facility continued to work very closely with Fort Detrick on projects for the army, including offensive biological weapons. They used hundreds of thousands of ticks as biological "vectors," as they're called, which are great carriers of viruses and bacteria. You infect the ticks with a virus, release the ticks, and they find animals and birds to bore into and infect with the virus.

Despite official denials, plenty of circumstantial evidence points to the bioweapons station on Plum Island as the source of Lyme Disease. It was named because the first recorded occurrence (of this particularly destructive strain) occurred suddenly in 1975 in the little town of Old Lyme, right across the water from Plum Island. From there it spread in concentric circles to gradually cover all of North America.

The same situation occurred in 1967 when the Dutch Duck virus, hitherto unknown in North America, suddenly wiped out all the famous duck farms on Long Island, just downwind from Plum Island. At one time, these duck farms raised six million ducks per year. After 1967, the industry ceased to exist. Again, it can't be proven–but nobody knows where the virus suddenly came from.

Bad luck (if you can call it luck) struck again in 1999 with the West Nile Virus. Cases suddenly started popping up on the mainland right across from Plum Island. Author Michael C. Carroll has documented the history of Plum Island in his book *Lab 257: The Disturbing Story of the Government's Secret Germ Laboratory.*[7]

Biological weapons research was supposed to be stopped in 1972 when the United States and the USSR signed the Biological and Toxic Weapons Convention. They both lied. In the United States, the work was hidden offshore or outsourced to private companies and universities. In the Soviet Union, things were just getting started. Ken Alibek was the number two man in charge of the Soviet bioweapons program until his defection in the early 1990s. As he explained in his 1999 book, *Biohazard: The Chilling True Story of the Largest Covert Biological Weapons Program in the World–Told from the Inside By the Man Who Ran It:*

> Over a twenty-year period that began, ironically, with Moscow's endorsement of the Biological Weapons Convention in 1972, the Soviet Union built the largest and most advanced biological warfare establishment in the world...Through our covert program, we stockpiled hundreds of tons of anthrax and dozens of tons of plague and smallpox near Moscow and other Russian cities for use against the United States and its Western allies. What went on in Biopreparat's labs was one of the most closely guarded secrets of the Cold War.[8]

Weapons aside, trafficking germs and viruses is quite legal, and the Russian bioweapons program purchased many lethal viruses: Machupo from the United States, Marburg from Germany, and so on. By 1990, the Soviets weaponized both Marburg and Monkeypox and had worked on such diseases as anthrax, smallpox, Bolivian hemorrhagic fever, Argentinean hemorrhagic fever, Lassa fever, Ebola—all the standard biological weapons.[9]

One important lesson we can learn from these bioweapon accidents is that those responsible act quickly to contain the pathogen, limit the outbreak, and use censorship to downplay the incident. In 2020, they did exactly the opposite, which indicates it was not an accident. It was planned.

Viruses as Weapons

Viruses are difficult to weaponize, so the West discarded this idea early on. The Soviets plodded along for many years without a major breakthrough, but still managed to weaponize smallpox. The invention of gene splicing technology in the 1980s opened up new possibilities. By the 1990s, they had developed several genetically altered strains of smallpox that were far more deadly than the original. Other countries caught on as well, and bioweapon research on viruses picked up everywhere, as Dr. David Martin—who has been following these developments for over two decades—soon discovered.

Ken Abilek explains that the Soviets worked mostly with a nasty family of viruses called filoviruses.[10] From these, they had weaponized both Marburg and Ebola during the 1990s. They also developed stealth bioweapons, which slowly incapacitate people instead of killing them quickly. They developed what are called chimera viruses. A chimera is a mythical monster with the head of a lion, the body of a goat, and the tail of a snake. Biologists use the word to describe something made of diverse genetic material—that is, inserting genes from some other pathogens into an already deadly virus to make a truly monster virus. Similar work was going on in the West, but the Americans chose a different strategy and a different virus family—coronaviruses.

During the first bioweapons inspections between Russia and the United States in 1991, both sides were able to effectively hide their bioweapons work from the other. The Russians did this by showing only a few of their several dozen sites and by altering labs, moving equipment, and carefully rehearsing staff on the elaborate lies to explain suspicious-looking equipment. The Americans had already moved almost all their bioweapons research to other institutions. The United States was "officially" not doing any. Unofficially, it was contracted out. They call this "dual use." They claim to be doing vaccine research, but it's bioweapon research at the same time. That's why you see DARPA and the DoD funding it.

This outsourcing of sensitive activities was part of the great privatization push of the 1980s and 1990s. Bioweapons research was called vaccine or medical or agricultural research. The US Army had contracted it to NATO, foreign companies, universities, the CDC, and the NIH, among others, and moved various parts of the program to US bases in foreign countries. To any but the most knowledgeable insider, it disappeared. There was no budget for it anywhere, no expenses, no money, no paper trail. But the bioweapons research and development kept going–everywhere.

Viral infections usually do not respond to antibacterial medicines. There are a few antiviral medicines, but they are often ineffective, have serious side effects, and impair the human immune system. The most common way to deal with a viral bioweapon is vaccination.[11] As a result, vaccine research *is* virus research. Any lab doing vaccine research is, de facto, doing virus research. Whenever this involves gain of function (that is, making a virus more deadly), the real purpose is bioweapons development. That's not the reason anyone will give you, but that's the truth. They work at making a super virus with the particular characteristics they desire for a particular kind of "mission." Then they make a vaccine for it so they can protect their own "troops." That's why the best place to find a vaccine against a new virus is in the lab that created that virus. Check out the labs that have been doing gain of function research on coronaviruses, and you'll find the vaccine. How did we "find" a vaccine so quickly for a "novel" coronavirus? As we're about to see, they've been developing the vaccines for decades, right along with the bioweapons research on coronaviruses.

But the Americans came up with an evil twist to the standard bioweapons strategy—one more suited to the "battlefield" it seems they had in mind. They put the virus-vaccine combo together differently—the *vaccine* would be the real bioweapon. The *virus*, simply the bait to lure the enemy into the trap.

Patents—Coronavirus Bioweapon Evidence in the Public Record

Dr. David Martin is one of the world's leading experts on intellectual property (IP), and his business is tracking new IP developments. Dr. Martin has been following coronavirus research for over two decades, noticing massive violations of the bioweapons treaty. Early in 2021, he published a report on the patent trail and the many crimes committed—*The Fauci/COVID-19 Dossier*.[12] Patents are not expert opinion. They are physical evidence. Only *evidence* reveals a fraud. There are over five thousand patents dealing with coronaviruses. They have been the subject of extensive research, manipulation, and development as biological weapons for over two decades. The kingpin of all this research is none other than Dr. Anthony Fauci, for forty years the director of the National Institute for Allergies and Infectious Diseases (NIAID).

Dr. Martin started drawing attention to the bioweapons work in 2003.

> In our 2003-2004 Global Technology Assessment: Vector Weaponization, M·CAM highlighted China's growing involvement in Polymerase Chain Reaction (PCR) technology with respect to joining the world stage in chimeric construction of viral vectors. Since that time, on a weekly basis, we have monitored the development of research and commercial efforts in this field, including, but not limited to, the research synergies forming between the United States Centers for Disease Control and Prevention (CDC), the National Institutes for Allergies and Infectious Diseases (NIAID),

> the University of North Carolina at Chapel Hill (UNC), Harvard University, Emory University, Vanderbilt University, Tsinghua University, University of Pennsylvania, many other research institutions, and their commercial affiliations.[13]

Dr. Ralph Baric at the University of North Carolina–Chapel Hill (UNC) started working with beta coronaviruses in the early 1990s. In 1999, Anthony Fauci gave Baric a NIAID grant to figure out how to amplify certain pathogenicities of coronaviruses–that is, gain of function research.[14] Dr. Baric was already an expert on coronaviruses and cardiomyopathy in rabbits. The work he did, starting in 1999 and published in 2002–03, suggested there were parts of the coronavirus that could be modified, specifically the ACE-2 receptor (angiotensin-converting enzyme) and the S-1 spike protein, to make coronaviruses more deadly to humans. Let that sink in. Anthony Fauci and Ralph Baric started weaponizing coronaviruses in 1999. And coronavirus vaccines are not new. Pfizer submitted its first patent application for a coronavirus vaccine for dogs in 1990,[15] which specifically dealt with the S-1 spike protein.

In April 2002, Dr. Baric applied to patent the severe acute respiratory syndrome (SARS) coronavirus, the method to produce it, and the use of the PCR test to detect it. In the dossier, Dr. Martin summarizes how this patent was illegal and the extreme measures that Anthony Fauci took to finally get the patent approved in 2007.[16] The NIH tried to patent all the coronaviruses, methods of testing for them, and the vaccines. No one else would be able to research these without express permission from Fauci. The most logical reason for doing this is because you don't want anyone else to follow, work on, or develop treatments for your biological weapons.

It was only *after* the patent application for a SARS virus that we had the outbreak of SARS-CoV-1. It appeared in Southeast Asia in late 2002, causing great public concern but only a small outbreak of disease. This was clearly a leak from a bioweapons lab, either accidental or intentional. It is not a natural progression in the evolution of coronaviruses. No SARS-CoV virus has ever been found in nature. It could only have been created in a lab. It is a man-made biological weapon. This outbreak was followed by the Middle East Respiratory Syndrome (MERS) outbreak in 2012, also a coronavirus with a spike protein attached. Again, not many people became infected or died.

China was also working on coronaviruses and Fauci often contracted research to them, beginning at least by 2004 when he was funding coronavirus vaccine trials in animals. Military organizations got involved—a sure sign this was a weapon. Money from DARPA and other branches of the US military started pouring in at least by 2005. Also in 2005, Fauci was publicly acknowledging the association of SARS with bioterror potential and that he was developing vaccines focused on the SARS-CoV spike protein.[17] Work continued on coronaviruses up to the present, but Dr. Martin says coronavirus was completely weaponized by 2002.[18]

There are no novel coronaviruses. Every minor variation has been patented. This is exactly what you do when developing a biological weapon. You create multiple strains and test their properties, develop vaccines, and experiment with how to deliver them. The "variants" we hear about are likely other strains of the SARS-CoV bioweapon that have been developed and prepared in advance. Since coronaviruses mutate so easily, they likely have dozens of variants ready to be released sequentially over a period of years so they can keep the fear and the fraudulent pandemic going. Any natural mutations that happen to occur are just icing on the cake. As Dr. Martin explains, in seventy-three patents issued between 2008 and 2019, every single feature that was supposedly novel in the SARS-CoV-2 virus is covered under one or more patents. You cannot patent anything in nature; the patents, therefore, prove these "novel" features are all man-made.

The SARS-CoV-2 virus seems preadapted to human cells.[19] It does not bind well to most other species, including bats. In fact, the Wuhan lab even bred a variety of mice with the human ACE-2 receptor so they could better test the bioweapon. And SARS-CoV-2 has never been found in the wild—not in any animals at the Wuhan market nor any other animal (except where the virus was transmitted *to* animals *from* humans). In other words, SARS-CoV-2 is a virus engineered for humans. It is a biological weapon. This is not because anyone said so. It is because the physical evidence in the form of patents says so. Only evidence reveals a fraud.

Dr. Judy Mikovits (and other scientists) claims the SARS-CoV-2 virus has parts of the HIV and the XMRV viruses spliced into it.[20] She should know. Dr. Mikovits spent decades researching both these viruses and likely understands them as well as anyone. SARS-CoV-2 is designed to destroy your immune system, just like HIV and XMRV do—and just like the "vaccines" do.

Dr. Francis Boyle, who drafted the US Bioweapons Act, constantly monitors disease outbreaks all over the world to see if they are intentional or natural. Almost always they are naturally occurring. The Wuhan virus, however, appears to have almost certainly come from the Wuhan research facility. He says this is an offensive, dual-use, biological warfare weapon. First, attack with the virus, then attack with the vaccine.[21]

Scientist Dr. James Lyons-Weiler reports evidence of CRISPR, the gene splicing technique, all over this virus.[22] Chinese virologist Li-Meng Yan, who defected to the United States in April 2020, has written several papers on the SARS-CoV-2 virus. Her research shows it is definitely a biological weapon.

> We use in-depth analyses of the available data and literature to prove that these novel animal coronaviruses do not exist in nature and their sequences have been fabricated.
>
> The scale and the coordinated nature of this scientific fraud signifies the degree of corruption in the fields of academic research and public health. As a result of such corruption, damages have been made both to the reputation of the scientific community and to the well-being of the global community.
>
> Importantly, while SARS-CoV-2 meets the criteria of a bioweapon specified by the PLA, its impact is well beyond what is conceived for a typical bioweapon. In addition, records indicate that the unleashing of this weaponized pathogen

> should have been intentional rather than accidental. We therefore define SARS-CoV-2 as an *Unrestricted Bioweapon* and the current pandemic a result of *Unrestricted Biowarfare*.[23]

We are at war.

The Wuhan Institute of Virology

The Wuhan Institute of Virology (WIV) is China's premier site for research into viruses and vaccines. Although it is officially under the umbrella of the Chinese Academy of Sciences, many of the researchers are military staff, and it is closely supervised by the People's Liberation Army (PLA). Of course, there is military-civil fusion. It is impossible to separate military from civilian institutions in China. The military is embedded everywhere. Everything is war and war is everything. The WIV has been under direct military command since January 26, 2020, when Major General Chen Wei, China's top biowarfare expert, took over.[24] They have been researching coronaviruses for years and bat viruses for a quarter century.[25]

The WIV was doing research for Dr. Anthony Fauci for well over a decade, particularly after the US Congress suspended gain-of-function research. In just one example, the NIH gave a large grant to Eco Health Alliance, led by Peter Dazak, who turned around and contracted gain-of-function research on coronaviruses at the Wuhan Institute of Virology.[26] We also know China was weaponizing coronaviruses on its own. A Chinese document from 2015 outlined their plans.

> Titled "The Unnatural Origin of SARS and New Species of Man-Made Viruses as Genetic Bioweapons", the paper predicted that World War Three would be fought with biological weapons.
>
> Released five years before the start of the COVID-19 pandemic, it describes SARS coronaviruses as a "new era of genetic weapons" that can be "artificially manipulated into an emerging human disease virus, then weaponised and unleashed in a way never seen before."[27]

The WIV is also known to be a "leaky" lab and has poor safety standards.[28] In the fall of 2019, some staff members at WIV became sick with covid-like symptoms.[29] Then there is the evidence, ignored by the media, that covid-19 was in Wuhan October 18–27, 2019, during the military world games (International Military Sports Council, or CISM). Many of the nine thousand athletes became ill during or immediately after the games, taking the virus back home to their 110 different countries.[30] In March 2020, China angrily accused the United States of releasing covid-19 at the CISM games as a bioweapon. They said the US athletes were infected just before they came to Wuhan and then spread their infection to the other international athletes.

In the late fall of 2019, there were news reports of an early and nasty "flu" season in America. On a personal level, several friends and family members of mine came down with a terrible "flu" in December 2019 and early 2020, all before talk of covid-19 became common. Dr. Larry Romanoff produced a paper with excellent evidence that raised lots of questions in December 2020. The pattern of illnesses around the world could not possibly have been produced by a naturally occurring virus. That's just not how viruses spread. And there is plenty of evidence that this virus was all over the world by about mid-2019.

> *As I noted above, there is no such thing as a natural 'second wave' for an epidemic, much less of this next kind: No one has yet addressed the fact that virtually all countries in the world were hit with COVID-19 virtually at the same time, in two blasts. There were two waves—the first hit 25 countries on all continents, where medical practitioners confirmed their first domestic infection all within three days of each other. In the second wave, almost exactly one month later, 85 countries confirmed their first domestic infection, again almost all within three days of each other, and all in multiple locations. It shouldn't be necessary to point out that no natural epidemic can manifest itself this way without human assistance.*[31]

Of course, you can never believe what the Chinese Communist Party says, but that doesn't mean they're *always* lying. Maybe the covid-19 release *did* come from the US military. It's clear that both China and the United States have been developing coronaviruses as bioweapons for two decades. SARS-CoV-2 came from one of them or both of them. One way or another, covid-19 was clearly in Wuhan by October 2019 at the latest. Its sudden appearance points to a lab leak—maybe accidental, maybe intentional. That question was answered by the response it got.

Fauci & Company came up with a brilliantly evil mix of ideas. Instead of starting with a deadly virus, they started with a common and innocuous cold virus and turned it into a chimera virus. But no virus makes everybody sick. So, they made a vaccine that itself is a stealth bioweapon. They planned to use fear and coercion (psychological warfare) to make everyone in the world take the "vaccine." But the "vaccine" is even more than a dual-use weapon, as Dr. Boyle claims. It is a stealth bioweapon with multiple functionalities, and we may not even know all of them yet.

Coronaviruses may have been completely weaponized by 2002, as Dr. David Martin claims, but a few more pieces still needed to fall into place—the control of the propaganda systems, the control of the power structures within society, the 5G communications systems, the quantum computers and AI, and the self-assembling nanobot operating system. The pieces were finally coming together in 2019. Keep in mind, if this was an accidental release, we would see a medically logical and effective response. If this was deliberate, we would see psychological warfare.

Prelude to Crisis—Controlling the Power Structures

We saw in chapters 3 and 4 how essential it is to control what Yuri Bezmenov calls the "structures" in society prior to launching the crisis. We saw in chapter 9 that the mainstream media is completely controlled through ownership by a handful of billionaire elites. The media is financially dependent on a few industries, notably the pharmaceutical industry, for advertising revenue. And once the covid assault started, governments became the largest advertisers all over the world. Media content is constrained by billionaire-controlled think tanks, NGOs, and pressure groups (such as the censorship group "Trusted News Initiative"[32]) to comply with the Deep State narrative. Most people still believe what the mainstream media tells them, so the public is "captured" in its web of propaganda.

China also has a huge propaganda influence all over the world through many channels. It cultivated relationships with virtually every media outlet in every country and provides them with easy-to-use "news" articles through content-sharing agreements.[33] These daily inputs of news content are really a sophisticated system of fantasy creation by the masters of mind control. It is not reality. It is psychological warfare.

Once Operation Covid-19 started, social media, controlled by a handful of Deep State–Global Elite billionaires, clamped down with a level of censorship never before seen.

Every government in the Western world, to varying degrees, has been stripped of its power. Policy decisions have long been made at some level higher than national and state legislatures. These faithfully followed their instructions from the World Health Organization, the World Economic Forum, the UN, or whatever other "above government" authority they salute to (More on this in chapter 17). As we saw in chapter 12, most of the world had become a de facto police state, and militarized police would be used everywhere to enforce whatever illegal decrees various governments chose to create.

Professions had become largely controlled by a top-down structure that gave the power of economic life or death, and social dignity or disgrace, to the very few people at the top. These were under the strong influence of Deep State operatives in one way or another. We saw in chapter 7 how scientists are controlled. If they step out of line, the government will remove their funding, their own professional associations will turn against them, and journals will refuse to publish their papers. Additionally, everyone has seen how the universities have become woke, totalitarian bullies and despots. Once again, money and ideology are behind this. Universities depend on government grants and will do whatever the government tells them. They have become intellectually castrated by Critical Theory and the power of communist sniping. They eagerly fire professors for nothing more than professing common sense.

The same is true in other professions. The American Medical Association, and other mainstream medical associations, have a stranglehold on everything to do with health. Professional associations for teachers, engineers, accountants, and you-name-it have developed a similar control over their members. Step out of line, and you will be destroyed. This is not what professional associations were meant to be. But this is exactly how professional associations are controlled by totalitarians. Of course, unions have been manipulated by communists for a century.

The totalitarian control of all these "structures" in society had reached a peak hitherto unknown in the modern world—and almost no one even noticed what had happened. Perfect subversion. The biological and psychological weapons systems were built and tested. The command-and-control systems were in place. The world was ready for the greatest biological and psychological warfare attack in human history.

What You Can Do Now

1. Understand that science and scientists have been corrupted and cannot be trusted. But it's not all lies. You have to use your own intelligence, look for evidence, listen to a variety of experts, and make up your own mind. You are being intentionally manipulated. Use your own free will to disrupt that manipulation. You will often be wrong, so keep your mind open.
2. Even a cursory understanding of the history and practice of biological warfare leads one to see that SARS-CoV-2 is a bioweapon. Now that you know, act accordingly.
3. Remember that all the "structures" in our society have been subverted. Do not allow your boss or your professional association to control you. Insist on returning to your original relationships. Your professional judgement and bodily autonomy are legitimate and legal parts of your free will.

CHAPTER 14

Operation Covid-19—World War Three Goes Public

"Truth is the first casualty of war. With the covid war, truth was dead before the first shot was even fired." –DONALD LEE

Until 2020, only a tiny number of people realized we were at war. I didn't. Like almost everyone, I was busy living my life. I knew there was something wrong with the climate nonsense and the fake terrorism panic, but I figured these things would eventually work themselves out and cooler heads would prevail.

But when the covid fraud hit, I knew this was a whole new ball game. Not only did nothing make sense, but it immediately affected everyone's life. I was in the midst of planning a cross-Canada book tour when the whole world shut down, leaving me with a thousand copies of my new book in the basement and a ten-thousand-dollar VISA bill I couldn't pay.

The Deep State had to know that the covid assault would blow their cover. I wouldn't be the only one to realize this was a fraud. They had successfully remained hidden through the earlier stages of communist subversion–destabilization and demoralization. But the covid crisis was so massive that an overwhelming psychological warfare operation would be needed to accomplish their strategic objectives and suppress any resistance. In this chapter, we review the key events and facts of the initial assault of Operation Covid-19.

Biological Assault with Psychological Warfare "Air Cover"

"We therefore define SARS-CoV-2 as an Unrestricted Bioweapon and the current pandemic a result of Unrestricted Biowarfare." –LI-MENG YAN

The Official Story Is All Lies

Reminiscent of 9/11, the official story is all lies, developed years in advance, and sprung on an unsuspecting world as a massive fifth-generation warfare attack. Remember, mistakes typically happen sporadically. A web of mistakes is extremely rare. On the other hand, lies are never isolated. One lie quickly leads to a web of lies. When the web of lies appears all at once, it had to be planned. It's all about pattern recognition. Covid-19 exactly fits the pattern of fraud, of biological warfare, and of psychological warfare.

Some of us saw this quickly. But we usually believe what we are told by people in authority, and it takes time to assemble evidence. So, perhaps we can forgive our "leaders" who took the bait and swallowed the whole story–hook, line, and sinker. But within six months, there was ample physical evidence to see the truth. After that, these people were willfully ignorant, morally culpable, and legally guilty of malfeasance, if not worse. Let's expose the key lies in the official psychological warfare narrative.

The Virus Came from Nature

As we saw in the last chapter, the SARS-CoV-2 virus is the result of a quarter century of biological weapons development. Virtually every step and variation has been patented. It did not come from nature and has never been found in nature. All the public fuss over the origins of this virus is theater. It is a distraction as part of the psychological warfare.

It's a Novel Virus

We also learned in the last chapter that every allegedly novel feature of SARS-CoV-2 has been patented. It is not novel in any way, and it does not present a difficult challenge to the human immune system. The world's best immunologists suggested this at the very beginning. They were ignored and canceled.

People Have No Immunity

Humans have dealt with coronaviruses for millennia. We have what are called cross-reactive antibodies–antibodies developed against similar coronaviruses.[1] A study in Vancouver found that up to 90 percent of people have these.[2] This natural immunity is both strong and long-lasting. In April 2020, a group of thirty German scientists published a paper showing that 34 percent of people in Berlin who had never been in contact with the Sars-CoV-2 virus showed T-cell immunity against it.[3] Now that the virus has circulated for over two years, the vast majority of people test positive for SARS-CoV-2 antibodies.[4]

The Virus Is Deadly

By early summer 2020, it was clear the coronavirus would be a typical flu, slightly more serious than most flu strains, but nothing out of the ordinary. By then we knew the initial estimates of the case fatality rate (CFR)[5] were twenty to fifty times too large, that the numbers of dead and sick were perfectly normal, and that none of the extreme restrictions (lockdowns, social distancing, masks, etc.) had any measurable impact on the progression of the disease. Some people have died of covid-19, but mostly the death numbers have been intentionally and fraudulently inflated. Death rates overall, and from the flu/covid, were not unusual in 2020.

There Are No Treatments

There are effective treatments for covid-19, and doctors discovered these very early in the saga. Yet all the efforts of the WHO, CDC, NIH, and other medical authorities were directed to showing there is no treatment. This only makes sense when you understand the real strategic objective was to inject everyone in the world with a "vaccine" bioweapon.[6] The FDA cannot issue an emergency approval for a vaccine if there is an approved treatment. Thus, it was essential the FDA never approve a treatment. That explains the massive propaganda campaign against all possible treatments and anyone who proposed them. This part of the psychological war was prepared well ahead of launching Operation Covid-19, and was a key part of the "war games" such as Event 201.

Hydroxychloroquine (HCQ) is an anti-parasite medication that has been used effectively against malaria for over sixty years and was shown in 2005 to be effective against SARS-CoV-1.[7] Doctors around the world, particularly the famous French doctor, professor, and infectious disease expert Dr. Didier Raoult, quickly reported their success with HCQ. As noted earlier, the pharmaceutical industry immediately got a fraudulent study published in *The Lancet* in June 2020. The FDA used this study as the pretense to revoke HCQ's emergency-use authorization for covid.

The WHO quickly arranged the Solidarity study,[8] but their intent was obviously sinister. The Solidarity study used extremely high dosages of HCQ that were well known to be toxic. It was designed to fail—and to kill lots of people. Dr. Meryl Nass, a physician from Maine, wrote, "The high dose regimen being used in the SOLIDARITY trials has no medical justification. The trial design, with its limited collection of safety data, may make it more difficult to identify toxic drug effects, compared to standard drug trials. This is entirely unethical."[9]

The trials ended in disaster due to overdosing with HCQ. Other countries copied the same basic study. Italy had the DISCOVERY trial, Britain had the RECOVERY trial, and France did the same. All used the same toxically high doses of HCQ. In Britain, where the study was supported by the Gates Foundation, the HCQ component of the trial was soon halted after a quarter of these patients died. When questioned about it afterward, the head of the UK study appeared not to know what the lethal dose of HCQ was[10] even though the WHO had determined in 1979 that 2.5 to 3.3 grams is lethal and that the drug stays in the body for a long time, having a half-life of several months.[11] Patients in these studies were given almost 10 grams over 10 days with 2.4 grams on the first day alone.[12] The UK's maximum recommended dosage for HCQ is 6.5 mg/kg of body weight, or about 500 mg per day. It is unbelievable that a medical doctor conducting an experiment with medicines would not know the lethal dose of those medicines. These doctors knew they were committing fraud and murder—at least they had a fiduciary duty to know.

In July 2020, Dr. Joseph Mercola wrote an article that beautifully summarized the HCQ issues.[13] In short, at normal dosages of about 200–500 mg a day, it worked extremely well. He explains that what really happened was a propaganda war against its use and in favor of Remdesivir, which has not been approved for anything. That's not science. That's fraud.

Ivermectin is also an anti-parasite medication that has been used for three decades all over the world. The experience of doctors during the past two years has shown it to be even more effective than HCQ, and it's now an approved treatment for covid in many countries. Notably, both Japan[14] and India used ivermectin to completely end their covid outbreaks. Hundreds of scientific studies show its efficacy. Doctors knew about this treatment at least by the summer of 2020. After that, the official position was obvious lies. A 2021 review of ivermectin by Dr. Tess Lawrie of the Evidence-Based Consultancy Group in the UK clearly demonstrates this fact. In summary,[15]

- Ivermectin is an excellent prophylactic, reducing infections by about 90 percent.
- Ivermectin reduces the length and severity of a covid-19 infection; that is, it is an effective treatment.
- Ivermectin reduces the risk of death from covid-19 by over 60 percent.
- There is little or no risk of side effects from ivermectin.

There Is Nothing You Can Do to Stay Healthy

Incredibly, the official narrative did not say anything about how to stay healthy or what to do if you get sick. Instead, they ridiculed and canceled anyone who did. They denied the scientifically proven and well-documented beneficial effects of vitamin D, vitamin C, and zinc on the immune system. The official recommendation was to stay home, do nothing until you are almost dead, then go to the hospital where they will finish you off with Remdesivir and ventilators. This goes beyond malpractice. This is not medicine. The only explanation is that whoever is behind this wanted to kill as many people as possible.

The Only Solution Is a Vaccine

Vaccines take years to develop. Treatments are needed immediately. Dr. Peter McCullough repeatedly laid out the normal four pillars of dealing with a disease outbreak.[16]

1. Try to control the spread of the disease.
2. Treat patients early to avoid the illness becoming worse.
3. Provide hospital treatment for severe cases.
4. Vaccination.

Yet treatment was intentionally neglected and even vilified. This is not a medical response. A medical response would involve steps 1, 2, and 3–preventatives and treatments. This is fraud. It is psychological warfare in support of a biological warfare attack.

Modeling Tells Us What Will Happen

Recall my earlier comments about "models" in chapter 7. To create a system of mathematical equations that accurately mimics the behavior of any real-world system, you need an accurate theory that describes the system, and you must understand all the main relationships between the important factors within that system. You must have all the variables right, all the equations right, and all the parameters right. In the spring of 2020, the data needed to create a real model was still unknown. There were no "models." There were only quantitative methods of turning assumptions into fantasies. This is not science. This is fraud. The "modeling" was not a failure. It worked perfectly–for its *real* intended purpose, to create fear and justify unleashing the rest of the weapons.

Some of the reported weaknesses of the initial "model" include the following:[17]

1. It was riddled with computer programming errors.
2. It used its own outputs as inputs.
3. It assumed humans had zero immunity.
4. It assumed all the beneficial impacts from mitigation practices. There was never *any* evidence that *any* of these practices would have *any* effect.
5. Both equations and parameters were assumed.

Who did the world turn to for a scary computer model? None other than the College of Disrepute, Imperial College in London. In a real epidemic, one might turn to the world's leading virologists and epidemiologists for advice, such as Dr. John Ioannidis at Stanford University. But instead, the WHO turned to the modeler-of-a-thousand-failures, Neil Ferguson. In a February 2021 article, Thierry Meyssan described him with candor and humor. "Neil Ferguson is one of those scientists who demonstrate what is asked of them, not those who seek to understand unexplained phenomena. His curriculum vitae is just a long succession of errors commissioned by politicians and denied by the facts."[18]

Dr. Vernon Coleman is not so charitable.

> Ferguson, of course, has an appalling track record. In 2002, he predicted that up to 50,000 people would die from mad cow disease. He said that could rise to 150,000 if sheep were involved. In the UK, the death total was 177. In 2005, he said that up to 200 million people could be killed by bird flu. The total number of deaths was 282 worldwide. In 2009, he advised the Government which, relying on that advice, said that swine flu would kill 65,000 people in the UK. In the end, swine flu killed 457 people in the UK.[19]

With the Swine Flu, he was off by a factor of a thousand. With the Bird Flu, he was off by a factor of a million–six orders of magnitude. That's not incompetence. That's fraud. So why ignore the world's experts and turn to serial fraudster Neil Fergusson for a covid-19 "model"? I'm guessing it's because he has been so useful in the past pandemic dress rehearsals.

He is a reliable modeler of doom. His work has been supported by the Bill and Melinda Gates Foundation for years. Why? Why would you support a serial failure? The only reason that fits a pattern is that his wild predictions were useful for the plan. They needed an apocalyptic model to terrify people into going along with both their mad power grab and the upcoming "vaccine" bioweapon.

You Can Have the Disease and Transmit It to Others Even if You Have No Symptoms

This is called this *asymptomatic transmission*. Yet the real evidence soon showed this simply didn't occur.[20] If you have no symptoms of illness, even if you are infected with the virus, your viral load is so low that it is essentially impossible for you to infect others. And there is no transmission at all outside.[21] Almost all transmission appears to happen in close quarters inside residences. In fact, a Canadian study showed that almost all transmission occurred inside government-run or -regulated institutions: hospitals, prisons, and nursing homes.[22]

The PCR Test Can Identify Disease Cases

We are using a polymerase chain reaction (PCR) test to diagnose covid-19. Yet the inventor of this process, Kary Mullis (who won the 1993 Nobel Prize in Chemistry for it), said definitely and repeatedly that this process cannot diagnose any illness.[23] He says that PCR is not a test. It is a process. It takes tiny amounts of DNA material and makes lots of it. It takes a piece of DNA material and doubles it, then doubles it again, and again, in as many "cycles" as you want to run.

By adjusting the number of cycles you run, you can produce positive or negative results at will. Run ten cycles, and you will always get a negative result. Run sixty, and you will always get a positive result. Kary Mullis said you can find anything you look for if you run enough cycles. Most people who test "positive" for covid-19 are not sick. Doing the PCR "test" on a healthy person means nothing. By long-standing medical understanding, if you have no symptoms of illness, you are not sick. You are not a "case" of anything. The fearmongering about "cases" is not science. It is propaganda. It has never been done before in the history of medicine. But millions of fake "cases" were essential to the psychological warfare campaign because there simply weren't enough sick people and deaths to scare everyone.

A paper published in September 2020 presented some interesting information about the PCR results.[24] If you are truly sick with covid, then you have viruses actively living and reproducing inside your body. We can take a sample (usually mucus) from you and culture real viruses from it. The question is, "How many of these PCR positive 'cases' are really sick with the disease, and how many are just finding tiny bits of DNA that don't mean anything?" These researchers compared the test results run at different numbers of cycles to whether or not they could culture live viruses from these people. They found that if they ran the PCR test to twenty-five cycles, 30 percent of the "positives" were false. At thirty cycles, they got 80 percent false positives. At thirty-five cycles, they got 97 percent false positives.

Most jurisdictions won't say how many cycles they are running. British Columbia has been doing thirty-five cycles, sometimes more.[25] The chief microbiologist for Manitoba, under oath in court, admitted that Manitoba uses forty (and even forty-five) cycles in its PCR "tests."[26] This practice is typical for jurisdictions all over the world. They may also be changing the cycles and manipulating the number of "cases" at will to manipulate the level of public fear. Even Pepsi, milk, and mango chutney have tested positive for covid-19.[27] The truth is, this "data" means nothing. There were no more sick people in 2020 than there are every year. The simple truth is there was no real epidemic of anything anywhere in the world.

The Virus Is Spread on Surfaces, So Disinfect Everything

The scientific evidence shows that this virus is transmitted mostly in aerosols–tiny, microscopic particles that you breathe out, right through your useless mask. The virus does not survive long on surfaces, so their incessant disinfecting has almost no effect on the transmission of the virus.

Nonmedical Interventions Are Necessary to Stop the Spread of the Disease

Lockdowns, social distancing, masks, plexiglass screens in businesses, one-way aisles in grocery stores, incessant hand sanitizing, and dozens of other measures have no historical precedent. Until recently, none of these measures were recommended in the medical literature or disease protocols. They have been adopted only recently and without evidentiary support.

Dr. Paul Alexander published an excellent article in December 2021, *More Than 400 Studies on the Failure of Compulsory Covid Interventions.* He lists and provides hotlinks to these studies that debunk every single nonmedical intervention. In summary, "The great body of evidence... shows that COVID-19 lockdowns, shelter-in-place policies, masks, school closures, and mask mandates have failed in their purpose of curbing transmission or reducing deaths. These restrictive policies were ineffective and devastating failures, causing immense harm especially to the poorer and vulnerable within societies."[28]

Where did this idea of lockdowns come from? Not from medicine, as the insightful journalist Thierry Meyssan explained in a recent article. It came from the World Economic Forum. Another piece of the puzzle falls into place. "The source behind the lockdown is CEPI (Coalition for Epidemic Preparedness Innovations). This association was created in Davos on the occasion of the 2015 World Economic Forum."[29]

We are already beginning to see almost everyone in power try to escape responsibility for these disastrous nonmedical interventions. It's hard to know who is really responsible. Who *really* ordered lockdowns, masks, and everything else? It seems to have come from Bill Gates, to GAVI, to Tedros, to the WHO, to individual countries through their contracts with the WHO. That's not democracy. But it gives us a peek into the technocratic dictatorship that we have fallen into.

These measures have never been included in pandemic planning until 2020. In fact, only one country in the world followed the WHO's 2019 pandemic planning guidelines—Sweden. The media condemned Sweden, but they suffered less than any other developed nation and emerged from the pandemic sooner.[30]

As we saw in chapter 4, the group psychology of mass formation psychosis uses such actions that lack any physical purpose and are purely symbolic. They are rituals. Their function is psychological. They identify you as a member of the "right" group. You belong. You are engaged in a noble struggle against the evil virus. You are one of the *good* guys. You are on *our* side in this noble battle against the *bad*, unvaccinated guys. Have you not felt this sentiment in society and in the propaganda? This psychological warfare is meant to turn us against each other, to fill us with fear and hatred so we tear ourselves and our society apart, and to justify atrocities against whoever the government chooses to target. This also distracts your attention onto a million meaningless details so you don't perceive what's really going on. The Nazis did exactly the same thing. It's a common tactic. These rituals are utterly meaningless in any medical sense, but they are essential to the psychological warfare.

You Should Be Afraid of Everyone and Everything

This message of fear was constantly hammered into everyone's consciousness. It had no basis in fact, but it was essential for psychological control. Remember, when someone is trying to make you fearful, they are trying to control you. Reject fear and embrace love. Reject slavery and embrace freedom.

Children Can Infect Old People

This might be the evilest of the lies. Children experience very mild symptoms from covid-19 and rarely transmit it to others.[31] This seems to be because children have few ACE-2 receptors in their respiratory tracts, which is the main way the virus attacks the human body. This lie is also behind the propaganda to vaccinate children, for which there is no medical justification.

Medical Doctors Are Spreading Lies and Need to Be Silenced; Trust Only Your Politicians and the Mainstream Media

When it is expressed this clearly, almost everyone can see it for the lie it is. We were told to take our medical advice from politicians, bureaucrats, news anchors, and celebrities while ignoring the world's leading epidemiologists (like Dr. John Ioannidis of Stanford University), Nobel laureates in infectious diseases (like Dr. Luc Montagnier), and vaccinologists (like the former Pfizer vice president and chief scientist, Dr. Michael Yeadon). We were also told to ignore the Great Barrington Declaration, signed by tens of thousands of the world's leading medical doctors and medical scientists. Nothing spells "fraud" better than this.

Remember the psychological warfare principles from chapter 3? Constantly hammer the public with your narrative. Remove every other narrative. Discredit anyone you can't remove. That is exactly what happened. Thousands of highly qualified doctors and scientists have been discredited. Hundreds of thousands of people have been deplatformed. The mainstream media has been completely controlled, and covid news has overwhelmed the airwaves twenty-four hours a day for two years. Once you know what to look for, it's easy to see. It's all about pattern recognition. We have seen the unmistakable pattern of propaganda and psychological warfare.

Millions of People Have Died from Covid-19

How many people have actually died *from* covid-19, not from cancer or diabetes or a heart attack with a positive PCR test? Nearly everyone knows people like this. Even traffic deaths and gunshot victims were claimed as covid deaths.[32] We will never know the truth about these deaths because the data is completely corrupted.

Neither do we really know who dies from influenza or pneumonia. Such respiratory infections are often the last straw that pushes an old person out of his mortal coil. When a ninety-year-old, chronically ill patient is admitted to a hospital and dies a week later, what really was the cause of death? Was it the coronary artery disease that had afflicted him for the past twenty years? Was it the colorectal cancer he'd been fighting for five years? Was it the liver failure that showed up in his laboratory results? Or was it the pneumonia he developed in the last two weeks of his life? Take your pick. Who is to say for sure? The proximate cause might seem to have been the pneumonia, and maybe that's what the physician will put on the death certificate. That's part of the reason why we never really know how many people die of the flu each year. These numbers are estimated by a "model."

So, when the Centers for Disease Control and Prevention announced in August 2020 that for only 6 percent of the covid-19 deaths was covid-19 the *only* cause of death listed on the death certificate, knowledgeable people were not surprised.[33] Italy, the first Western nation to experience the "pandemic," later quietly admitted that 97 percent of the reported covid deaths were not due to covid at all.[34] The truth is that *real* covid-19 deaths have been relatively small and will never be known for sure. What we *do* know for sure is that there was no statistically significant increase in mortality anywhere in the world in 2020. That had to wait for the "vaccine" bioweapon.

The evidence clearly shows that every single point in the official story is a lie. And our leaders stuck with the lies even in the face of the evidence. What is this the pattern of? This is not the pattern of errors, not even the errors of fools and idiots. This is not the pattern of good-willed people making honest mistakes dealing with a novel situation. This is the pattern of only one thing—fraud.

The Initial Biological Warfare Attack—Releasing the Virus

Despite its twenty years of development and trillion-dollar price tag, the biological warfare operation was much smaller than the psychological warfare operation. All they had to do was release the virus and make sure it spread around the world, or maybe release it all over the world. There is so much evidence that the release was planned, I can only scratch the surface. Financial people knew it was coming. Economic forecaster Martin Armstrong started picking up signals in August 2019.

> I have stated that our computer began to pick up capital flow distortions in August 2019. Bill Gates bought into the BioTech vaccine in September 2019. Gates began to liquidate some stock positions in December 2019. There were rumors floating around at that time that "a virus was coming" and I know

> that by January 2020 Schwab was telling people a virus was coming and stepping out of the market. I believe Schwab sold all stocks and bond investments of the WEF in January 2020 ahead of the covid crash.[35]

The virus was released in late 2019, unnoticed at first. As people became sick, they naturally assumed it was the flu, since it has flu-like symptoms. But back in Wuhan, a few people started raising the alarm. They were silenced. The first doctors to mention a new and serious influenza were "canceled" in all the usual ways. Finally, on December 31, 2019, the Chinese Communist Party admitted there was a viral outbreak, and the WHO made the announcement. On January 11, China reported the first death. There had certainly been deaths from covid before that date. They lied. On January 21, the first covid case was confirmed in the US. On January 23, China locked down the city of Wuhan.

For at least two months, China did nothing to stop the spread of the virus and intentionally denied there even was one. Then they quickly locked down the whole city and the surrounding province, just like the rehearsals, all the while insisting that it was no big deal. They shut down domestic air travel to and from Hubei Province while promoting international flights, saying they posed no risk, and it was only because of anti-Asian prejudice that other countries were trying to shut down air travel. China did its best to cover up the origins of the virus, its knowledge of the virus, its research on the virus–in short, everything about it. All their actions seem designed to make the virus spread all over the world as quickly as possible. In this, China was abetted by the World Health Organization every step of the way. When your enemy makes an obvious blunder, assume deception.

Some may argue that this reaction is typical for communist countries, or even typical for Chinese culture. That may be so, but it is also completely consistent with a planned release of a biological weapon. Stage one was to release the virus and get it to spread all over the world as quickly as possible. Stage two was to fire up the psychological warfare and spread fear and panic.

Elsewhere in the world, the virus appeared in northern Italy, England (especially London), and the United States (especially New York City). Although cases appeared everywhere, the massive deaths were strangely localized. In all these places, evidence later emerged that other factors were decisive in these deaths, not covid-19. Most Americans know about the ridiculous actions of the Governor of New York. He removed infected seniors from hospitals and sent them back to their nursing homes, where the disease spread in the closely confined living spaces. All the while, a US Navy hospital ship sat empty in New York harbor. Instead of quarantining the sick in a hospital ship, he spread the sick all over the city and quarantined the healthy.

Lesser known is how hospitals and nursing homes in England used massive amounts of the sedative Midazolam (also used for lethal injection executions in the United States) to kill thousands of seniors in care homes and hospitals.[36] These deaths were all blamed on the evil virus and used by the psychological warfare machine to whip up fear and justify illegal actions against billions of people all over the world.

What Does Affect Covid-19 Mortality?

Based on information available at this time, here are some factors that are correlated with covid-19 mortality.

1. Severity of the previous year's flu season.
2. Average age of the population.
3. Metabolic health status of the older population segment.
4. Obesity rates.
5. Covid-19 treatments used.
6. The number of people exposed to the SARS-CoV-1 virus in 2002–03 (in East Asian countries).[37]

Many other commentators have noticed this, but the mainstream media is not telling you about it. Obesity is a huge risk factor in covid-19. The World Obesity Federation has found, taking data from over 160 countries, a linear correlation between covid-19 mortality and obesity rates.[38] Obesity is a sign of poor metabolic health, that same metabolic health that our government nutrition advice and medical ignorance have destroyed. Interestingly, covid-19 mortality is also highly correlated with distance from the equator. All countries within 35^0 north or south had very low mortality rates. Vitamin D deficiency is rare in these latitudes while it is at epidemic levels in the temperate regions.[39]

Government health departments have been giving you the worst possible nutrition advice for two generations. The food industry is serving you food that destroys your health, makes you fat, cripples your metabolism, and gives you chronic diseases. Then the pharmaceutical industry sells you handfuls of pills that don't solve any of your problems but keep you coming back for more. And now, someone has produced a biological weapon to selectively kill off most of the sick people the other industries have helped to create. I have a hard time seeing coincidence in all of this.

There Never Was a Pandemic

A pandemic is an epidemic that occurs everywhere, but the WHO has watered down the official definition of "pandemic" so much that it can declare a pandemic whenever it wants to. For ordinary people, an epidemic is a widespread disease that causes many more people to die than normal. Since all the data is corrupted, we can't know how many people died *from* covid-19. We must look at total deaths—what we call "all-cause mortality."

Excess mortality (or mortality displacement) is a temporary increase in the number of deaths in a specified population over a specified period of time.[40] Of course, everyone who lives, dies. The idea of excess mortality is simply that a bunch of people died earlier than usual. Their deaths were, in a sense, pulled from the future into the present. This could be for any reason—war, natural disaster, disease, and so on. In fact, this is an annual cyclical phenomenon. More people die in winter than in summer. Maybe that's because of the winter flu season, maybe weakened immune systems due to a lack of sunshine and vitamin D, maybe the emotional depression caused the lack of sunlight—nobody really knows for sure. Some years we have a bad winter flu season and quite a few people die of respiratory infections. Some years we have an easy flu season and not so many die. While the *pattern* is predictable, the actual deaths are not.

What we saw pretty much all over the world was some atypical increases in mortality during the spring of 2020. Some places, but not all, showed a late winter–early spring spike in deaths, later than the usual flu season. To my untrained eye, the graphs don't look natural. It looks like medical murder in some places but not others. The extreme geographical irregularity is not what we expect from a respiratory pandemic. But when we look at the 2020 year as a whole, there is nothing abnormal. No place in the world experienced a statistically significant increase in all-cause mortality in 2020 compared to previous years.[41] Nor was there any increase in life insurance payouts, which would occur if there was an increase in mortality. No increase in deaths equals no epidemic. Period. The only epidemic is an epidemic of fear and fraud.

The official story is such a complete and complex web of lies, all leading to the same outcomes and supported by such a massive psychological warfare campaign, that it can only be fraud. In fact, it is fifth-generation war. Only through the group psychological phenomenon of mass formation has this fraud been hidden from the majority of people. Nonetheless, Operation Covid-19 brought the simmering war against humanity into the open and kindled the fire of resistance. Yet SARS-CoV-2 wasn't the real weapon. It was only the bait for the trap. It was the feigned attack to draw the enemy into the ambush. It was part one of the multifunctional weapons system. Over ninety-nine percent of people fought off the virus without any help, and the infection fatality rate was nearly the same as the seasonal flu.[42] Part two of this weapons system was to attack everyone with a "vaccine."

What You Can Do Now

1. Stop trusting "officials." It's sad to say, but trust no one. Look for evidence, not experts. Do your own research. You're on your own. Take responsibility even though you will often be wrong. That's life.
2. Never again allow your freedoms to be usurped by lies and liars. Other frauds are sure to come. Do not comply–nonviolent noncooperation. Your best guide is your own conscience. Develop it by exercising it.

CHAPTER 15

Vaccines—Springing the Trap

"Keep the enemy in the dark about where and when our forces will attack." –MAO TSE-TUNG

It never made medical sense to vaccinate the whole world. Medical science has known for decades that you should never mass vaccinate into a pandemic. That just promotes a genetic variant of the virus that the vaccine-generated antibodies don't recognize. Mass vaccination could never be a workable response. Medical experts knew this. Also, no pandemic has ever lasted more than two years.[1] Covid-19 was so mild that if we had done nothing, humanity would hardly have noticed and would have achieved herd immunity within two years.[2] There never was any reason for a vaccine. So, the covid-19 mass vaccination could only have some other purpose. When your enemy makes an obvious blunder, assume deception.

In this chapter, we look at the how the "vaccines" work, and how they were clearly designed as a biological weapon to kill and maim millions of people. As always, we focus on evidence.

The Covid Disease

Dr. Peter McCullough (a medical doctor, professor of medicine, and heart specialist who has treated hundreds of covid patients) described the progress of the disease. It starts out like a cold, then the immune system goes crazy with clotting and thrombosis, and that's what kills you.[3] Dr. Chris

Shaw, a neuroscientist whose research includes the connections between our immune system and our central nervous system, explained that covid-19 impacts the body in four separate ways:[4]

1. Respiratory issues.
2. Cardio/blood issues (clotting, etc.).
3. Internal organ failures.
4. Central nervous system issues.

It seems that the main capsid of the coronavirus gives you a cold because it's a cold virus. Then the S-1 spike protein, the bioweapon feature, produces a blood disease. An April 2021 paper by the Salk Institute revealed two extremely important facts.[5]

1. The spike protein produces all the symptoms of the disease called covid-19. You do *not* need to have the SARS-CoV-2 virus in your body to have covid-19. You just need to have the spike protein.[6]
2. Covid-19 is a blood disease, not a respiratory infection. That is, the coronavirus itself produces a mild respiratory infection–a common cold. The spike protein causes the blood disease that kills you.

Incidentally, it has also been shown that Remdesivir causes kidney failure. Since the kidneys cannot remove waste fluids from the body, your body tries to remove these fluids by taking them to the lungs so they can be expelled as water vapor. Then your lungs fill up with fluid. So, the hospital puts you on a respirator. Then you die from multiple organ failure and drowning. Clearly, the plan of this "treatment" was to kill lots of people and blame covid.

Vaccines Provide Immunity–But Only for the Manufacturers

It is important to understand that pharmaceutical companies bear absolutely no liability if these "vaccines" injure you. They are protected by several pieces of legislation going back many decades.[7] These covid "vaccines" are being used under an emergency-use authorization (EUA) from the FDA (Food and Drug Administration). EUA legislation was first set up in the mass of new legislation after 9/11—in this case, the *Project Bioshield Act of 2004*. We have already seen that an EUA cannot be issued for a vaccine if there is an approved treatment, so the FDA had to never approve any treatment for covid-19. An EUA also relieves the manufacturer of all liability associated with their product. That liability is borne by the government, so your own government has a great incentive to deny there are any injuries—and the government runs both the system for tracking injuries and the vaccine court, where they are both the defendant and the judge. Don't expect justice here.

How the mRNA "Vaccines" Work

The mRNA "vaccines" are gene therapy treatments. A true vaccine contains a pathogen. When it is injected, your body recognizes the pathogen as a threat, attacks it, and creates antibodies specifically designed to destroy this pathogen. But mRNA "vaccines" don't work this way at all. They do not contain a pathogen. They contain genetic instructions. The mRNA "vaccine" sneaks these genetic instructions into your body inside tiny bubbles of fat—the lipid nanoparticles—which your body thinks are completely normal. Then these fat bubbles release their genetic payload directly into the cells of your body. Inside your cells, the genetic instructions cause every cell in your body to *make* the pathogen—the S-1 spike protein. Your own body produces the very disease you are trying to avoid! And there is no way to shut it off. You may be like this forever.[8]

Next, your body will realize this spike protein is foreign and will make antibodies to kill it. Your immune system sees the spike proteins on the surface of your own cells and will attack your own cells. David Martin explains the reality of these "vaccines" precisely.

> When you inject mRNA into a human being...that mRNA makes the human body produce a scheduled toxin. And by "scheduled toxin" I mean this spike protein, modeled after the coronavirus spike protein. And we need to be clear on the fact that, by all of their own admission, the spike protein that the injection manufactures is a computer simulation of a

> chimera of a spike protein of coronavirus. It is, in fact, not a coronavirus vaccine. It is a spike protein instruction to make the human body produce a toxin. And that toxin has been scheduled as a known biologic agent of concern with respect to biological weapons for the last, now, decade and a half. So...the injections are an act of bioweapons and bioterrorism. They are not a public health measure.[9]

We also now know that the "vaccines" are actually changing your DNA. This was widely thought to be impossible, but a study from Sweden showed that mRNA nanoparticles from Pfizer's covid-19 "vaccine" enter human cells and are reverse-transcribed into DNA, achieving a permanent alteration of the person's genetic code.[10] Interestingly, retroviruses like HIV and XMRV do this too.[11]

We have known all along that the "vaccines" do not prevent you from getting or transmitting covid-19.[12] There are many reasons for this. The fundamental reason is that the real covid disease, the blood disease, is produced by the spike protein that your own body is making. If you have been "vaccinated" with these products, you *have* covid-19 and you have been *transmitting* covid-19 to others. This is not how to *end* a disease. This is how to *spread* a disease.

Are The "Vaccines" Effective?

Medical doctor and microbiologist Dr. Sucharit Bhakdi explained that the infection fatality rate of covid-19 is about 0.05 percent or less.[13] That means that out of every ten thousand people who get covid-19, five will die. For any vaccine to be efficacious (to be useful at reducing deaths), it would have to reduce that five in ten thousand to something less than that. This fatality rate is so small that it is impossible to construct a clinical trial to show this, even if it were true. *It will never even be possible to show that these "vaccines" are useful!*

The vaccine trials didn't look for a mortality benefit. They only asked, "did the vaccines reduce symptoms in mild to moderate cases of covid-19?" That's not very dramatic–not even important. These trials were conducted quickly and fraudulently, and the results were presented with distorted statistics that obscured the truth about their ineffectiveness and allowed Dr. Fauci to claim they were 95 percent effective.[14] They are not effective. Pfizer seems to have admitted in court that its submission to the FDA was indeed fraudulent.[15]

Pfizer tried to have 55,000 documents on its covid vaccine research sealed for seventy-five years—until everyone now living is dead. They were finally released on a court order and Dr. Naomi Wolff has assembled a team of thousands of healthcare professionals to read and report on these documents. They show that Pfizer and the FDA knew everything. In summary,

- The vaccine didn't work. It was a failed vaccine.
- The vaccine gives you covid.
- They damaged the hearts of young people.
- The vaccines do not stay in the deltoid muscle but quickly go all over the body.
- The trials involved scientific fraud in many ways.
- The trials showed hundreds of side effects, many of them deadly.
- The trials showed up the frequent allergic reactions to the polyethylene glycol in the vaccine.
- They knew that shedding occurs through skin contact, body fluid contact (including sex and lactation), and inhalation.
- One side effect is fainting so violently you can hurt yourself.
- Pregnant women were intentionally excluded from the trials, and thus from the EUA. But 270 women became pregnant during the trials. Of these, Pfizer lost the records of 234. Of the remaining 36 who were reported, 28 lost their babies, a 78% miscarriage rate.[16]

The covid death curve follows the covid vaccination curve. Higher vaccination rates always mean more cases, hospitalizations, and deaths. In December 2021, scientist James Lyons-Weiler showed this positive relationship scientifically.[17]

Many studies have shown the vaccines have a slight positive efficacy that quickly declines and turns negative after about six months.[18] In short, these "vaccines" don't work. They do the opposite. How perverse. And this outcome was known in advance by the pharmaceutical companies, Anthony Fauci, and others at the top of this fraud.

A Multifunctionality Weapon—How the "Vaccines" Injure You

"In the field of biological weapons, there is almost no prospect of detecting a pathogen until it has been used in an attack." –BARTON GELLMAN

There is so much scientific evidence of the massive injuries caused by these "vaccines" that it is almost impossible to keep track of it all, much less deny it. A January 2022 article, *Covid Vaccine Scientific Proof Lethal*, summed it up and included hot links to over one thousand scientific papers detailing the modes of injury.[19] The subtitle reads, *Over a Thousand Scientific Study's [sic] To Prove That The Covid 19 Vaccines Are Dangerous And All Those Pushing This Agenda Are Committing The Indictable Crime Of Gross Misconduct In Public Office.*

The European vaccine injury database has recorded over forty thousand deaths from these "vaccines" (by April 2022).[20] In the United States at this time, the Vaccine Adverse Events Reporting System (VAERS) is listing over twenty-five thousand deaths. But these are incredibly understated. Accusations of fraud and meddling with the database occur constantly these days. Doctors who submit reports find they are later deleted from the database. One attempt to calculate the underreporting factor in December 2021 suggested 388,000 Americans may have already been killed by these "vaccines."[21] At the very least, these "vaccines" have killed far more people than the disease did.

Let's take a quick look at the main modes of action that are known at this time. All these had been predicted by the world's leading immunologists and vaccinologists before the vaccination program started—but they were dismissed as conspiracy theorists.

Blood Clots

The spike protein causes blood disorders such as clotting and/or bleeding. Some people experience large blood clots in the heart (causing heart attacks) and the brain (causing strokes), which kill them within days or weeks of receiving their shot. If it happens soon after the shot, you might connect the vax to the death. If the death happens weeks later, you probably won't. The knee-jerk reaction of our medical authorities is to say these deaths had nothing to do with the shots, but they never look for evidence.

Medical doctors are finding all sorts of blood disorders among their vaccinated patients, even weird things like blood oozing from the skin or from old scars. Millions of women are experiencing crazy menstrual upsets—huge menstrual flows that won't stop, even the restarting of the menstrual cycle in post-menopausal women. Pregnant women are having miscarriages. A study published in *The New England Journal of Medicine* showed that 82 percent of pregnant women vaccinated during the first two trimesters experienced miscarriages.[22]

In July 2021, a Canadian doctor reported that 62 percent of his patients had suffered micro blood clots from the vaccines.[23] In Italy, a neurosurgeon who opened the brain of an eighteen-year-old vaccinated patient to relieve the pressure caused by blood clots said, "I had never seen a brain that was affected by such an extensive and severe thrombosis."[24] Undertakers are now seeing the most incredible clotted veins and arteries in corpses that are unlike anything they have seen before.[25]

Antibody-Dependent Enhancement

There seem to be two separate processes that different doctors are applying this name to. These effects are well known and are the reason why an mRNA vaccine has never been approved for humans. In short, the vaccine weakens your immune system and makes you extremely vulnerable.

Our natural immune response is strong and covers a broad spectrum of viruses. On the other hand, the antibodies that are produced in response to a vaccine—called vaccine-generated antibodies—are very specific to the virus in the vaccine. Yet they are strong enough to sort of "push aside" our naturally generated antibodies. So, when a new variant of the covid virus comes along, our vaccine-generated antibodies don't recognize the new variant, and our natural antibodies are suppressed. We become *more* vulnerable to the disease *because* we have been vaccinated.[26]

The second process is even more deadly. It seems this can happen both if you get covid-19 and are later vaccinated, *and* if you get the vaccination and are later infected with a new variant. In simple terms, when you become infected with the SARS virus, your body produces antibodies against it–against several parts of the virus, including the spike protein. If you later get the vaccine, it does not contain the spike protein or any part of the virus. So, your immune system will not respond to the *vaccine*. But the vaccine causes every cell in your body to *produce* the spike protein. Now your immune system will go crazy. It will see this spike protein on the surface of cells all over your body and will attack your own cells. This produces what is called a cytokine storm. You can become ill and die very quickly because of the rapid over-reaction of your immune system. With so many people in the world getting vaccinated in 2021, widespread illness and massive deaths were almost guaranteed for the coming years.[27] As we will see in a moment, deaths did indeed take off partway through 2021 and show no signs of returning to normal.

Immune Escape

Viruses genetically mutate easily and constantly. When you get covid-19, you are likely infected with more than one "variant." Your immune system naturally deals with all of them. But your vaccine-generated antibodies will only deal with the variant they were designed for–the "alpha" variant. With the rest of your immune system suppressed, other variants will grow, and you will spread them. That's how new variants emerge when you mass vaccinate into a pandemic. This process is called "immune escape" or "antibody-mediated selection." This was known to be happening within three months of the vaccinations starting. Vaccinologist Geert Vander Bossche warned about this constantly during 2021, such as this statement from March 13.

> There is now a general consensus that the vaccines will, indeed, fail to generate herd immunity. In addition, they will also fail to eliminate the steadily increasing number of highly infectious strains because the vaccinal antibodies no longer match with the variant spike protein of the circulating strains whereas they're still hampering binding of natural antibodies to the virus.[28]

This effect showed up in the official statistics within a few months. Partially or fully vaccinated people were dying in higher numbers than the unvaccinated.[29] By mid-2021, we were clearly seeing an explosion in covid cases in every country with a high rate of vaccination—exactly the opposite of what was supposedly intended. Research at the Mayo Clinic showed that once a population gets to 25 percent vaccinated, the virus can still move through the population, but it forces a dominant mutant strain to emerge (the vaccine applies nonsterilizing, nonlethal pressure to the virus).[30]

A researcher at the University of Alberta came to the same conclusion in September 2021 after studying the experiences of Israel, Scotland, and England.

> People who were vaccinated in January and February of 2021 were...at 13-fold greater risk for breakthrough infection with the Delta variant compared to those previously infected.
>
> In comparing outcomes for more than 32,000 people in the database, the study also found the risk of developing symptomatic Covid was 27 times higher among vaccinated people, and the risk of hospitalization from COVID-19 was eight times higher among vaccinated people.[31]

This is exactly what vaccinology theory predicts. This outcome was predicted. The vaccination program leads to greater spread of the disease. That was obviously the real intention.

Vaccine-Induced AIDS, Cancer, Neurological Diseases, and More

The mRNA "vaccines" suppress our immune system in many ways, some of which scientists are still discovering. AIDS, or Acquired Immune Deficiency Syndrome, is simply a name for any chronic impairment of our immune system—not necessarily caused by the HIV virus. That's exactly what's happening to vaxxed people. It's being called V-AIDS (vaccine-induced AIDS) and makes you more vulnerable to every pathogen because your whole immune system doesn't work right. This change is likely permanent.

Your immune system also identifies and removes cancer cells. Weak immunity equals more cancer. Cancer is now exploding—the return of cancers in remission, higher rates of new cancer patients, and unusual and fast-moving cancers. This is part of the reason for the current increase in all-cause mortality.[32]

The lipid nanoparticles have an affinity for brain and spinal cord tissue. The Japanese biodistribution study showed that the spike protein and lipid nanoparticles end up in the brain and spinal cord. There, they affect neurons and cause age-related neurological disorders like ALS, Alzheimer's, and Parkinson's disease.[33] The same phenomenon was known at least by 2015 with aluminum nanoparticles.[34] Neuroscientist Dr. Chris Shaw notes that the spike protein from covid-19 and the "vaccines" also affects the central nervous system, as vaccine side effects such as the neurological disorder Bell's Palsy clearly show. Dr. Richard Flemming raised the same alarm in his 2021 book *Is Covid-19 a Bioweapon?*[35] He showed that the spike protein contained prion-like domains that caused neurological disease, and that Dr. Zhengli had known this since 2002 during her work with SARS-CoV-1 at the Wuhan Institute of Virology.

In fact, the slow-acting neurological damage may turn out to be one of the key stealth aspects of the vaccine bioweapon (in addition to the immune compromise feature). We have seen millions of people killed fairly quickly by the "vaccines," within a few days to a few months. But the neurological diseases will unfold over years. Dr. Shaw and other experts have predicted an explosion of what is basically early-onset Alzheimer's disease in young and middle-aged people. This will have an incredible impact on society.[36] One thirty-year-old Alzheimer's patient will require the full-time attention of at least one other person for the next forty years. This will cripple our society and collapse our health care system. Once again, this was not a blunder; it was a plan.

Reproductive Armageddon

We previously mentioned the menstrual upsets in millions of women, but the reproductive effects of these "vaccines" appear to be far greater than an annoying inconvenience. Data from VAERS shows a thousandfold increase in menstrual irregularities and a hundredfold increase in fetal abnormalities with the covid "vaccines" compared to influenza vaccines.[37] We also learned from the Japanese biodistribution study that the lipid nanoparticles concentrate in the reproductive organs—ovaries and testes—among other places.[38]

As well, the propylene glycol in the adjuvant of the "vaccines" causes the ovum to not develop within the ovaries of female fetuses. This will cause these female children to be infertile.[39] The "vaccines" also interfere with syncytin, a protein that causes the embryo to be able to implant in the uterus.[40] This seems to be the cause of the infertility and miscarriages. Evidence of this was showing up everywhere by the end of 2021. For example, in Waterloo, Ontario eighty-six cases of stillbirths were reported in six months, compared to typically five to six per year.[41] Scotland launched an investigation into the deaths of newborns in September when twenty-one newborns died within their first month of life.[42] Birth rates were falling almost everywhere in the world by late 2021. For example, Thailand reported a one-third drop in their birth rate in 2021 compared to 2020.[43] Similar reports have already come from Germany, the UK, Hungary, Taiwan, and Sweden.[44]

It seems these bioweapons will not only kill millions of people, but may also cause a reproductive collapse. With girls as young as five years old being "vaccinated," the world might lose nearly a whole generation of people.

Lipid Nanoparticles and the Transhumanism Link

The lipid nanoparticles (known to be toxic all by themselves[45]) contain genetic instructions for our body to produce the spike protein. But what else is hidden in there? It turns out they could carry all sorts of things, and some of them have been found.

All the technology discussed here is existing; some of it is quite old. Also, everything here matches the publicly stated goals of those who want to control the world. If your enemy possesses a weapon, and has stated his intention to use it, it's not a big stretch to think he *is* using it.

As much as it sounds like science fiction, the basic idea is to create a human-machine interface (or brain-computer interface) within the human body—an operating system—that can be used to constantly monitor people and direct their minds and bodies. This is the transhumanism agenda. The basic parts, and instructions for their assembly, are inserted into the human body in the lipid nanoparticles (also called hydrogels, biogels, or nanobots). Lipids are fats, a common substance in our bodies. "Nano" refers to tiny things on the scale of one molecule.

The idea of a human-machine interface is not new, as we saw in chapter 10. DARPA has been researching and implementing these types of technologies for decades; many universities and companies are involved. For example:

- Harvard has its Wyss Institute, which has developed nanorobots that can deliver a payload of anything directly to specific cells in the body—medicines, pathogens, even explosives.[46] In fact, Harvard professor and nanotechnology expert Charles Lieber has patents for self-assembling tiny computer systems capable of controlling human neurology, which is exactly what electron microscopy of the Pfizer vaccine appears to show. Lieber was recently convicted of crimes for working with the communist Chinese in Wuhan, where Pfizer runs a research and development facility.[47]
- There are many types of self-assembling nanomaterials currently in use and being developed. A recent review of those that use

external magnetic fields outlined the many types.[48] These devices also generate their own energy from body heat. A self-assembling system means that a person is injected with *instructions* that set into motion a process where a structure is assembled inside the body, using resources available in the blood (such as iron and oxygen atoms). In effect, nanotech self-assembly means that a microchip doesn't need to be injected into someone, since the circuitry can be assembled after injection.

- A company called Battelle is working with DARPA to produce an injectable, bidirectional brain-computer interface. That's exactly what we're talking about.[49]
- A company called Profusa has developed injectable body sensors that transmit and receive information to and from your cellphone.[50]
- In 2020, Microsoft was granted a patent for a cryptocurrency system using body activity data. It uses an injectable biogel (biosensor) which transmits and receives wirelessly to your smartphone, then via the 5G network to a supercomputer which makes the currency transaction.[51] This will work with any digital currency, like the ones all our central banks are developing.
- A company called INBRAIN uses the amazing material called graphene. It is just carbon, but it's a single layer of atoms arranged in a two-dimensional honeycomb lattice nanostructure. They are developing an intelligent graphene-brain interface.[52]
- Elon Musk's company, Neuralink, is developing exactly the brain-computer interface that the transhumanists want. In chapter 10, we learned this idea is already being field tested on humans.[53]

Moderna, on their website, even describes their vaccine as an operating system: "Recognizing the broad potential of mRNA science, we set out to create an mRNA technology platform that functions very much like an operating system on a computer."[54]

Moderna's operating system will allow for humans to be connected and *controlled* by an AI computer connected to the internet. Attached to the hydrogels is a DNA sequence for a drug or chemical payload. The hydrogels are *self-replicating*, and that means the alien (unidentified) DNA and RNA are being fused with your own tissue and irreversibly altering what it means to be human. This artificial substance grows inside your body using inorganic nanomaterials and microbial cells. Millions of foreign proteins are being synthesized into the bodies of vaccinated people.[55]

Nanobots and hydrogels are an "on-demand delivery system" targeting your body's cells with a DNA payload. Hydrogels are biosensors that work with external electronics, forwarding your biometric data to the AI computer. This is the ultimate intrusion of your body's cells, your personal thoughts, and your bodily autonomy, making you part synthetic.

We also know that graphene has been found in the vaccines and serves no medical purpose.[56] This fact was hotly disputed in the mainstream media but has been confirmed by many experts, including former Pfizer employee Karen Kingston.[57] Graphene oxide is highly toxic and is a key ingredient in the lipid nanoparticles. Self-assembling structures have been observed both in the vaccines and in the blood of vaccinated people. The Spanish group La Quinta Columna has been the world leader in these types of investigations.[58] Recently, a New Zealand doctor, Dr. Robin Wakeling, has confirmed these findings.[59]

Bill Gates is field testing this whole system in West Africa. Unsuspecting poor people have been injected with the covid vaccine containing these materials and instructions. The test project was conducted in Ghana starting in July 2021. "With the aim of being introduced in 'low-income, remote communities' in West Africa and later replicated worldwide; the program is the result of a public-private partnership between the GAVI vaccine alliance backed by Bill Gates, MasterCard and Trust Stamp which is an AI-powered 'identity authentication' company."[60]

The program links a vaccine passport that contains all the information about you with a complete digital ID system tied to your body and a digital money system also tied to your body and your digital ID. A similar system is being tested in the UK, the COVIPASS–a biometric

RFID-enabled coronavirus digital health passport. This is exactly the control system they plan to impose on the whole world.

Total Control: The Vaccine Link to 5G

Information is coming out about how the control system might work. It could involve many different methods and technologies. The strategic plan is to use 5G transmissions to connect every person on the planet to a central supercomputer. Then, once these metal nanoparticles and self-assembled structures are in people, they can be killed or controlled using 5G transmissions.

Dr. Dolores Cahill, a medical doctor and professor, gave one possibility in an interview with Catherine Austin Fitts.[61] The metal nanoparticles get into your cells. They can be set into vibration by the appropriate 5G frequency. Then they shake like ball bearings in a watermelon, destroying your cells. This could kill you quickly or slowly, and you would never know what happened.

We also see a clear statistical correlation between places where the 5G system is active and rates of covid-19 disease.[62] Something is going on here. There are several hypotheses, but the truth isn't yet clear.

As mentioned above, INBRAIN is using graphene oxide to build brain-computer interfaces. "The company highlights its technology as being able to 'read' a person's brain, detect specific neurological patterns, and then control that person's neurology to alter their brain function."[63]

The most advanced understanding of the graphene in the vaccines and its effects comes from the work of La Quinta Columna. Based on Dr. Ricardo Delgado's examination of the vaccines and the blood of vaccinated people, he explains the system like this.[64] The graphene oxide is self-assembling into complex structures in the blood of vaccinated people. Graphene has an affinity for electrical organs such as the heart and the brain. It causes clotting, so the graphene itself is a key part of these types of injuries (heart problems, strokes, etc.) Graphene oxide responds to 5G wireless transmissions, which is why there is higher covid illness and mortality where the 5G systems are active. The graphene is creating the brain-machine interface which will communicate with

5G transmissions. Some vaccinated people are emitting MAC addresses that can be accessed with cell phones. The body tries to clear graphene oxide by expelling it from the lungs. Some researchers are now seeing graphene in the blood of unvaccinated children of vaccinated parents, which suggests they infected their children through airborne graphene nanoparticles they exhaled in the home.

All this is no longer speculation. The physical evidence exists. Satellite and land-based 5G transmissions are being used to aggravate the covid sickness and establish wireless transhuman control over people.

As was planned, the SARS-CoV-2 virus itself was not deadly, but the vaccines are. Here's what this multifunctional bioweapon assault on humanity looks like.

The Feint–The Virus Attack

1. The SARS-CoV-2 virus itself would kill a small number of people directly.
2. Inappropriate and toxic treatments, or no treatment at all, along with the destructive and unnecessary public health policies, would kill many more.
3. The psychological warfare campaign would spread fear (which activates the limbic system and shuts down logical thinking), would facilitate the mass formation psychosis, and make people more docile–preparing the battlefield for the main assault.

The Main Assault–Vaccines

1. The vaccines would kill directly by giving people covid-19.
2. The vaccines would kill quickly through various side effects, particularly blood clots leading to heart attacks and strokes.
3. The vaccines would cause sickness and death as a result of antibody-dependent enhancement and immune escape, making people more vulnerable to the next variants and other diseases, including the HIV and XMRV viruses included in the bioweapon itself. Because of immune escape, a mild epidemic that should have been over in a

year was turned into a forever pandemic with forever "vaccine" shots and forever "emergency" powers, other sicknesses, etc.

4. People could be killed at any later time by activating the metal nanoparticles with 5G radiation, causing the destruction of cells throughout the body.
5. The vaccines would cause long-term neurological diseases and disabilities in tens of millions of people and completely collapse society.
6. Once billions of people are conditioned to get whatever vaccine they are told to get, any one of these later vaccines could contain substances to accomplish what seems to be already happening.
7. The vaccines would cause a dramatic reduction in human fertility and reproduction—a massively smaller next generation that would cause a permanent reduction in world population.
8. The graphene (and possibly other materials) in the vaccines would build a brain-machine interface in every person so they can be controlled by an AI supercomputer.

The Next Phase of the Operation

1. Several more deadly strains of the SARS-CoV virus (or other virus bioweapons) will be released (or mutate naturally), likely in an opportunistic manner.

Naturally, people who are old or sick will be more likely to die from all these tactics. This furthers the genocidal plan to rid the world of the "useless eaters." To the elites, that's most of us.

Vaccine Passports

The "vaccines" have little efficacy that quickly becomes negative so you will need repeated shots. Therefore, the vaccine passport means nothing from a scientific or medical perspective. This is not a health measure and cannot tell us who is infectious and who is not. It is a population control measure that creates two classes of citizens.[65] It also compels you to accept endless shots of whatever the government wants to inject into your body.

As was previously explained, and is demonstrated in Bill Gates's testing program in West Africa, the vaccine passport is the entry into a complete human operating system by which people will be controlled. The innocuous app on your smartphone is being used to collect every piece of information about you into a central computer database. Not only your personal identification and all your health records but every other government record about you (tax data, criminal record, work history, credit score, etc.), along with all the information on your cell phone (GPS location, internet activity, phone call history, social media interactions, etc.). This will soon be connected to your bank accounts and all your financial transactions.

Dr. Joseph Mercola wrote a great article in August 2021 explaining these very steps. He included a quote from Thales, a company involved in producing the digital ID wallets: "Thales admits vaccination passports 'will act as a precursor to the rollout of mobile digital IDs.'" He says, "It is absolutely so much more than a vaccine pass...I cannot stress enough that it has the power to turn off your life, or to turn on your life, to let you engage in society or be marginalized."[66]

Now the reason for the big push to build the 5G system becomes clear. The benefits to individuals are minor. But the Deep State absolutely must have the massive data handling capability of the 5G system to deal with all the data for the transhuman control system. Also, you may have missed the fact that for several years, when politicians spend money on "infrastructure," most of it is not for roads and bridges. It has gone into the 5G rollout. *That's* the infrastructure they're concerned about. Potholes are of no interest to them. Vaccine passports are not the road back to normal life. They are the road to slavery.

Operation Covid-19–A Great Success?

The scientific evidence has been clear since the summer of 2020. The measures taken by governments have only made things worse. There is no medical or scientific justification for what they have done. Our official political and medical response has been criminal (not just criminally negligent because they knew what they were doing, or had a fiduciary duty to know.) The response by governments was not public health measures. It was fifth-generation warfare against the whole world. They have knowingly and deliberately murdered millions of people, illegally abrogated the constitutional rights of billions, and attempted to enslave whole nations. They should all stand trial for crimes against humanity.

The "vaccination" programs started in early 2021. As previously mentioned, nowhere in the world was there an increase in all-cause mortality in 2020, during the "pandemic." But that changed in 2021. Undertakers noticed it right away. After a quiet 2020, the vaccines caused the death business to boom.[67] They also found cadavers with unbelievably clotted and rubbery veins never seen before.[68] The UK, which reports weekly, was the first to show incredible increases in mortality, particularly in young people.[69] This trend first appeared in April 2021, about four months after the vaccinations started. Soon Scotland reported the same thing,[70] then the Netherlands.[71] In December, an American insurance executive let the information out that the United States was seeing a 40 percent increase in deaths in the eighteen to sixty-four age group—that is, healthy working people.[72] The CDC confirmed it and gave the breakdown by state, which ranged as high as 65 percent in Nevada.[73] And other insurance companies reported similar experiences, such as the Dutch firm, Aegon, which saw insurance payouts skyrocket 258 percent.[74] This increase is not only statistically significant; it's statistically unbelievable! Statisticians would call this a twenty-sigma event. It never happens. It has never happened in the modern age, not even during wartime.

It looks to me like Operation Covid-19 is playing out pretty much according to plan. And it's really just getting started. This wave of deaths will keep going for years, particularly since everything is officially denied. It's not happening, and even if it is, these deaths have nothing to do with the "vaccines." That's the propaganda story. The Deep State "intellectuals" have publicly and repeatedly stated they want to get rid of billions of people. They will. World War III casualties will be counted in the billions when this is all over. And, predictably, another "wave" of covid is washing over the world as this book goes to print.

This is a forever "pandemic," and each wave will bring more draconian measures. It's all planned.

We have seen the subversion of power structures exactly as Yuri Bezmenov described it. Every single profession has been exercising a tyrannical censorship over its members during this "plandemic." This is never part of professional competence or conduct. But it is a key aspect of psychological warfare and communist control. It's just what Hitler and Mussolini did.

The psychological warfare is also succeeding in its goal of turning us against each other. Half the people believe the government propaganda and think it's their patriotic duty to coerce the other half with anger, insults, shame, and guilt. We are accused of being selfish, insensitive grandma killers. And while we are fighting among ourselves about nonissues like masks and vaccine distribution, our governments have quietly grabbed more power and turned our democracies into dictatorships. It's the old magician's trick. Your attention is drawn to his right hand while the trick happens, unnoticed, in his left hand. Their actions do not fit the pattern of a medical emergency–and the evidence for a medical emergency does not exist. It fits the pattern of a communist, totalitarian takeover. Look at the evidence. Only *evidence* reveals a fraud.

Escape to Freedom

Our whole medical system has become so corrupted by pharmaceutical firms and insurance firms that patients don't even matter anymore. All of us would be better off if we just stopped all of this and went back to paying our doctors in cash out of our pockets. We would suddenly have a huge incentive to figure out how to live healthily and never need a doctor. And millions of parasites would have to find real jobs. Your body will become ill from time to time, of course. Your body will wither away and die sometime. This is certain. But it is not to be feared. There is nothing to fear. Live in love–total love–and fear nothing.

Stop the biological weapons research. Stop it at the Pentagon, the universities, the overseas US military bases, everywhere. Cut the military budget. Many people will scream that our "enemies" will use bioweapons against us. So be it. It is also true that as long as the United States and NATO have bioweapons, everyone else thinks they need them too. You can only stop a fight when at least one person stops fighting. It is time for any adults left in the room to take away the children's toys and make them stop fighting.

What are we to do in the face of this massive fraud, this psychological warfare conducted against us by, it seems, our very own governments? I see only one way out. That way was shown to us by Mahatma Gandhi, the spiritual leader of India's independence movement: nonviolent noncooperation. As Gandhi famously said to Lord Mountbatten, the British Governor of India, "One-hundred thousand Englishmen simply cannot control 350 million Indians if those Indians refuse to cooperate." One defiant person will be eliminated; a dozen will be arrested; a hundred will be ticketed. But with a hundred thousand, all that is impossible. Tyranny collapses in the face of massive noncooperation.

Most of all, do not fear your brothers and sisters. They will not kill you. Keep your body healthy and this virus will not kill you. If you become ill, your doctor can prescribe a medicine that will restore your health. This minor illness is perfectly treatable.

My friends, my brothers, my sisters, I implore you: Live not by lies; open your hearts to love. Love one another with that unquenchable love that our divine Creator placed into our hearts. And perfect love will cast out all fear.

What You Can Do Now

1. Don't take any more "vaccines" nor give them to your children. These are biological weapons. It is impossible to trust the people behind these. Keep yourself healthy and your own immune system will work.
2. Take action to detoxify your body from the "vaccines" and "medicines" you have taken. Do your own research.
3. Whatever your profession, refuse to be bullied by your professional association. Speak the truth. Stand up to the lies, whatever the consequences. However bad they may seem, the consequences of truth are always preferable to the consequences of lies. Form a new professional association if you must. Use lawfare against your employer and your professional association.
4. If you are a lawyer, a prosecutor, or a judge, think about what you are a part of. Today, people look back at Hitler's Germany and ask, "How could the German people have allowed that to happen?" Your grandchildren will ask you the same question.
5. Dismantle the apparatus of medical dictatorship: the WHO, CDC, NIH, all of them.
6. Insist that your politicians stop all biological weapons work.
7. You have nothing to fear. Love everyone. Perfect love casts out all fear.

PART 5

Beyond Slavery to Freedom

We have looked at what I call the four big frauds—the wars on drugs, terrorism, the climate, and our health. These are all totalitarian non-issues blown into crises to grab more power for governments. Naturally, every one of these frauds involves mass formation psychosis, ideology, and psychological warfare. They are all major campaigns in this fifth-generation World War III. This is a war of the global technocratic elites against all the common people. It has been going on for many years and has many more years yet to go. It is fundamentally a spiritual war, and in chapter 19 we look at the spiritual connection more closely and end the book with a message of freedom and hope. We also look more closely at who these technocratic elites are in chapter 17. I have previously mentioned what the elites must control if they are to control the world. The keystone in this arch of control is money—as I call it, "the one ring to rule them all." That is the subject of chapter 18. But first we must turn our attention to the control of elections. Democracy is already over, and the sure sign of this is the fraudulent elections we are now seeing almost everywhere, particularly in the 2020 United States election.

CHAPTER 16

Election Fraud—The Final Frontier

"Vote early and vote often." —ATTRIBUTED TO WILLIAM LYON MACKENZIE KING, CANADA'S LONGEST-SERVING PRIME MINISTER.

Free and fair elections are both the basic requirement and the final defense of democracy. Without them, there is no democracy. In any assault on democracy, elections are the final opportunity for a free people to "throw the bastards out" without recourse to violence. In fact, that is the greatest benefit of democracy—not that it gives better government, not that it guarantees prosperity, not that it promotes equality (democracy does none of this), but simply that it permits people to change the government without violence. No other form of government ensures this.

With the 2020 election, democracy in America faced a life-and-death test. Election fraud was so deep and so obvious that, if it is allowed to stand, democracy in America is over. Not surprisingly, the mainstream media and other elites "see no evil, hear no evil, speak no evil" and infamously insist there is no evidence of election fraud.

As with uncovering every fraud, let us stick to the evidence, which, as I write this, is still being uncovered and is widely disputed. Yet it seems clear that, as with all fraud, it was carefully planned, expertly executed, and evilly intended to manipulate and control all of us.

The groundswell of opposition to this election fraud is just getting going and the great battle just beginning. Many states have now passed laws that make election fraud more difficult. The Democratic Party is, almost unbelievably, opposed to these on the ridiculous grounds that they are racially discriminatory. Millions of Americans are finally realizing that this fake "discrimination" and the "race" argument is a façade for dividing and manipulating us. It is not true, but merely part of the ideology necessary for mass formation psychosis and the imposition of totalitarianism.

However, the 2021 "voting rights" bill passed by congress guarantees that all future US elections will be rigged.[1] You can now vote from anywhere in the world without providing any identification. The battle between truth and fraud still rages, the eventual victor still unknown.

The Set Up

A couple of key facts were apparent well before the election. For years, computer experts had warned that voting machines were easy to hack. Patrick Byrne became famous as the founder of the highly successful company Overstock.com and for his outspoken criticism of Wall Street. He was intimately involved in efforts to trace the fraud in the 2020 US election and the first to publish a book about it, *The Deep Rig.*

In his book, Byrne says, "They told me to watch for counting being shut down during the election. It had happened in three other nations where sketchy elections had taken place. If it happened in our election, they warned me, it would be a sign that The Deep Rig was occurring."[2]

Several experts had warned local Department of Homeland Security (DHS) officials of what they suspected was going to happen with the election, but DHS in Washington wasn't interested.[3] That's interesting in itself.

Because of the arcane Electoral College system in the United States, it is not necessary to commit election fraud everywhere. It doesn't have to be *widespread*. It just has to be targeted. The Democrat:Republican support is nearly 50:50 and has been for several decades. Large parts of the United States reliably vote Democrat, other large sections reliably vote Republican. A small number of states typically swing back and forth between the two parties. You can change the whole election by simply controlling six cities in these swing states: Atlanta, Philadelphia, Detroit, Milwaukee, Phoenix, and Las Vegas. On election day, vote counting was shut down in precisely those six states.[4]

It should have been clear right away that something was wrong. Even the big numbers just didn't add up right.

> The U.S. Census Bureau estimates there were 153.07 million registered voters in 2020 (including dead, ghost voters, non-residents, etc–and even dogs in PA)–that's the number *registered to vote* last year. On Dec. 5th, 2020, totals were announced: Biden- 81.2 million; Trump- 74.2 million; Independents- 2.9 million; for a Total 158.2 million.[5]

There were five million more votes cast than registered voters. But it's worse: not everyone actually votes. There were really tens of millions of extra votes. Something was obviously fishy, to say the least.

The "Secret History" Boast of the Left

Many people cannot help bragging about their accomplishments. Yet it was still surprising when Time Magazine published an article on February 4, 2021, titled "The Secret History of the Shadow Campaign That Saved the 2020 Election."[6] Its Orwellian inversion of meanings would be comical if it weren't tragic.

"'Every attempt to interfere with the proper outcome of the election was defeated,' says Ian Bassin, co-founder of Protect Democracy."[7] The author, Molly Ball, either has no idea what went on or wrote a clever propaganda piece to cover up what did happen. She claims that these people "saved" the election, and now she wants everyone to know about it.

> That's why the participants want the secret history of the 2020 election told, even though it sounds like a paranoid fever dream—a well-funded cabal of powerful people, ranging across industries and ideologies, working together behind

> the scenes to influence perceptions, change rules and laws, steer media coverage and control the flow of information. They were not rigging the election; they were fortifying it.[8]

That sounds *exactly* like "rigging" to me. That's how elections worked in the Soviet Union. She describes a conspiracy (her word, not mine) of leftists and corporatists to defeat Donald Trump any way they could. She seems surprised to see labor leaders and CEOs working together. It should be clear by this point in the book that I am not surprised at all. It's been going on for decades. They are all totalitarians.

Molly Ball outlines the whole strategy and tactics that warped the democratic process.

> Their work touched every aspect of the election. They got states to change voting systems and laws and helped secure hundreds of millions in public and private funding. They fended off voter-suppression lawsuits [meaning dead people and illegal aliens could vote], recruited armies of poll workers [at least some of whom were trained to commit election fraud] and got millions of people to vote by mail for the first time [in the greatest mail-in election fraud in US history]. They successfully pressured social media companies to take a harder line against disinformation [meaning they suppressed all conservative thought] and used data-driven strategies to fight viral smears [smears from the right only, not from the left, in the most highly censored election in US history]. They executed national public-awareness campaigns that helped Americans understand how the vote count would unfold over days or weeks, preventing Trump's conspiracy theories and false claims of victory from getting more traction [meaning they prevented anyone from raising the issue of election fraud or being surprised by the hundreds of election "irregularities"]. After Election Day, they monitored every pressure point to ensure that Trump could not overturn the result [meaning they controlled the media, social

> media, the courts, the DOJ, the FBI, literally every possible avenue that might bring the fraud to light]. "The untold story of the election is the thousands of people of both parties who accomplished the triumph of American democracy at its very foundation," says Norm Eisen, a prominent lawyer and former Obama Administration official who recruited Republicans and Democrats to the board of the Voter Protection Program.[9]

The article describes the usual cabal of left-wing groups brought together by master political strategist Mike Podhorzer, senior advisor to the president of AFL-CIO. He held "back-to-back Zoom meetings for hours a day with his network of contacts across the progressive universe: the labor movement; the institutional left, like Planned Parenthood and Greenpeace; resistance groups like Indivisible and MoveOn; progressive data geeks and strategists, representatives of donors and foundations, state-level grassroots organizers, racial-justice activists and others."[10]

In a hundred ways and through dozens of channels, this group helped set up the situation where mail-in election fraud could happen, primed the public to expect delays in counting and unusual tallying swings as normal, and even researched the best wording of their messages. They also had a plan for massive demonstrations and civil disruption all over the country if Donald Trump won the election. Once you step back a bit and view this article from a broader perspective, you see that this group made the whole election fraud successful.

Voting Machines

The electronic voting machines used all over the country were easy to hack, and the whole computing industry knew it. In 2018, for example, computer scientist J. Alex Halderman published an article in the New York Times explaining how easy it is.

> All cybersecurity experts who have given electronic voting machines any thought agree. These machines have got to go... the electronic voting machines Americans got to solve the

> problem of voting integrity...turned out to be an awful idea. That's because people like me can hack them all too easily. I'm a computer scientist who has hacked a lot of electronic voting machines...Imagine what the Russians and North Koreans can do...Our highly computerized election infrastructure is vulnerable to sabotage and even to cyber-attacks.[11]

He testified before congress about this. Nobody did anything. Halderman wasn't the only one raising the alarm. Many newspaper articles appeared in the years before the 2020 election explaining how vulnerable these voting machines are. It was only *after* the 2020 election that people were labeled as idiots and conspiracy theorists for saying this.

There was even a documentary produced by HBO in 2020 that explained the problem: *Kill Chain: The Cyber War on America's Elections*. Before the election, nobody seemed to care. After the election, "making claims now such as were made 10 months ago by HBO...will today get one banned from social media, and may be illegal under the Democrats' new bill to combat 'domestic terrorism'."[12]

Of course, the government knew perfectly well these voting machines could and would be hacked. The Cybersecurity and Infrastructure Security Agency (CISA) produced a report that said exactly this in October 2020–before the election.[13] But it was kept secret for a year and a half and quietly released on June 3, 2022.

One of the basic and obvious flaws is that these voting machines were connected to the internet–a huge security hole. Anyone can get access. The voting machines use very old, obsolete software that is child's play to hack. They are programmed for fraud in many different ways. But there were other problems in addition to hacking into the machines to change votes. Patrick Byrne summarizes some of them.

- The extraordinary privileges enjoyed by precinct administrators, for example, to drag-and-drop queues of ballots waiting for adjudication.
- Evidence of packet traffic going to offshore locations during elections.

- In several foreign elections marred by allegations of election fraud, there had been windows where vote counting was shut down unexpectedly, and in those shut-down periods there had been large and controversial swings favoring one candidate.[14]

Edward Solomon demonstrated another bizarre occurrence of computer manipulation in Georgia[15] and Pennsylvania.[16]

> There were occasions where a group of precincts in a state would, in lockstep, begin counting all presidential votes 17 out of 18 for Biden, 1 out of 18 for Trump. A number of precincts, simultaneously, all did that together. Then after 90 minutes, their counting would go back to normal, but another set of precincts in the state would suddenly all flip to counting 17/18 votes for Biden, 1/18 for Trump. Precisely, for 90 minutes. Then they would flip to normal, and another set of precincts would pick up the pattern. Over and over around the state. That would never happen in nature. That fact alone demonstrates that the entire election in that state should be discounted: it is 0% trustworthy.[17]

In Antrim County, Michigan, everyone knew something was wrong. This small county always votes two-thirds Republican and one-third Democrat. When the Democrats came out on top, something was fishy. An intrepid local immediately sued the county to do an audit because he thought there was something wrong with the school board elections. He wasn't even thinking on a national level.

The Antrim County Computer Forensic Report[18] showed massive fraud. The voting machines flipped thousands of Trump votes to Biden. The voting machine results on November 3 were the following: Trump 4,509; Biden 7,769; for a total of 12,278 votes cast. The hand recount done on November 5 showed this: Trump 9,759; Biden 5,959; for a total of 15,718 votes cast. Nobody can explain where those extra 3,440 votes went on election day. The chain of custody for ballots and voting results was not followed. There were multiple opportunities for fraud.

Also, on the evening of November 4, 2020, someone accessed the voting records of this machine and deleted system files, adjudication files, and other source system files from the Dominion system in Antrim County. This is illegal.

The forensic team that examined the Dominion voting machines and did the election audit in Antrim County concluded that "the Dominion Voting System is intentionally and purposefully designed with inherent errors to create systemic fraud and influence election results."[19] People quickly started asking questions about every county in Michigan. The victorious Democrats got worried. But if the election was honest, why would anyone object to checking the ballots?

In response, the Michigan Attorney General, Dana Nessel (a Democrat), threatened lawyers with disbarment if they brought similar lawsuits challenging the election results. Later, she announced that *anyone* questioning the election results would be investigated by police and prosecuted.[20] That's not democracy. The right to challenge elections, or any other aspect of our government, is an essential feature of democracy. Dana Nessel also publicly stated that if any Michigan legislator challenged the election results, she would start an investigation against them and seek criminal charges against them. In the face of this tyrannical intimidation, no lawyer or legislator had the courage to speak up. That's exactly the intimidation that communists and other totalitarians do. This is the control of legal "structures" that Yuri Bezmenov described.

Mail-In Ballots

Anyone who has studied election integrity knows that absentee voting opens a huge door to fraud. Patrick Byrne included this famous quote in his book, "'Absentee ballots remain the largest source of potential voter fraud.'...It's the conclusion of the bipartisan 2005 report of the Commission on Federal Election Reform, chaired by former President Jimmy Carter and former Secretary of State James Baker III."[21]

When ballot counting stopped in those six states, most poll workers and observers were ushered out. Only a few key workers remained to "fix" the problems.[22] It's from this period that various videos later emerged of poll workers pulling boxes of ballots out from under tables or inside suitcases. This is when tens of thousands of "mail-in" ballots appeared on clean, straight paper that had never been folded to put into the mail-in envelopes. This is when tens of thousands of ballots were hurriedly completed that only had a vote for president, not for any of the many other candidates for other offices on the same ballot. This is when the video shows the Georgia poll worker scanning the same batch of mail-in ballots multiple times. This is when the consistent lead for President Trump instantly reversed in all six states.

There are many ways to commit fraud with mail-in ballots. Dinesh D'Sousa documented the use of "mules" in his 2022 film, *2000 Mules*.[23] Mules are people hired to deposit fraudulent mail-in ballots into ballot boxes in various places throughout a city. Using millions of bits of cellphone location data and official surveillance video, they were able to identify thousands of individuals who made multiple ballot drops.

> [They used] The cellphone IDs of more than 2,000 mules hired by left-wing organizations to do ballot trafficking in Atlanta, Phoenix, Detroit, Milwaukee, and the greater Philadelphia area. These mules alone generated approximately 400,000 illegal ballots. When you break down the fraud state by state, you see that it was more than enough fraud to tip the balance in the presidential election. Trump should have won, not Biden.[24]

The mules picked up their batches of ballots from various non-profit organizations. The film does not delve into who these are. Likely it was organizations like the ones mentioned by Molly Ball in her Time magazine article and NGOs supported by billionaires like George Soros. They play an important role in the real governance structure of the world, as we will see in chapter 17. The mail-in ballot fraud was enough to change the election outcome, but there were other frauds as well.

Foreign Interference

It is curious that in the months leading up to the 2020 election, there were many news reports about how the American security apparatus was very concerned about and had uncovered numerous attempts by foreign actors to gain access to the US voting systems. After election day, it was almost treasonous to even mention this possibility.

> So, to summarize thus far: at least some Dominion Machines are made in China, and in the 12 days before the election, the WashPost reported on, "US Agencies mount[ing] a major effort to prevent foreign (in this case, Russian) interference in the election". Meanwhile, CISA (part of DHS) and FBI co-authored a communique the three days before the election regarding other foreign (in this case, Iranian) "Advanced Persistent Threat" actors interfering in the election. It does not take reading far either into the CISA-FBI report, or the Washington Post article, to understand that our federal government was fighting an onslaught of foreign attempts to interfere in our elections, in the days before the election.[25]

Most of the voting machines in the United States are from Dominion Voting Systems (DVS). This is a Canadian company with heavy ownership and influence by Chinese nationals. In fact, shortly before the 2020 election, the Chinese Communist Party purchased a controlling interest in Dominion Voting Systems.[26] The computer experts working with Patrick Byrne found plenty of evidence of foreign interference with the election. "The cyber-specialists to whom I refer have access to such tools (and even more arcane ones), and have documented vote-flipping in the Problematic 6 states amounting to 299,567 votes, just enough in each state to flip the election. 43% of that activity came from China."[27]

Mike Lindell has also been working hard to uncover the election fraud. Here is some of the information from his video documentary *Absolute Proof: Documentary About Election 2020.*[28] In 2,995 counties in the United States, cybersecurity experts have documented unauthorized access and interference with the US election before, during, and after election day.[29] They identified a massive list of thousands of these unauthorized accesses and have all the relevant information: the IP address and the exact computer from which the attack came, time of entry into the election system, the county and state that was attacked, the exact computer in that county that was accessed, the method of access (using a credential or breaching the firewall), and what votes were changed and how many (e.g., down 2,500 for Trump, up 3,300 for Biden, etc.). These cyberattacks mostly came from China (66 percent), but also from Iran, Iraq, Ukraine, Serbia, and others.

After Voting Day

The events of election day, November 3, 2020, seemed suspicious to millions of people. Some started looking into the events right away. Some poll workers started reporting the irregularities they observed. Of course, this should have been done by federal and state election officials—the people responsible for ensuring honest and fair elections. They weren't interested. The courts, the third pillar of the democratic balance of powers, should have used the full weight of their legal authority to ensure honesty and fairness in the legislative branch. For the most part, they weren't interested. The press should have been screaming about these election irregularities. They weren't interested. The mainstream media did its best to suppress any questions about the election and to vilify anyone who did question it. As we have seen, this is the pattern of a propaganda campaign—a psychological war. This is *not* the pattern of honest people doing their duty. Also, it seems the courts, judges, and state officials have largely been "captured" either by the philosophy of socialism or the tentacles of the Deep State. One way or another, democracy in America has been severely compromised and appears to be in its death throes.

A simple citizen, Patrick Byrne, drew on his friends and connections to begin a process of documenting the election fraud. Several months later he produced the book and film *The Big Rig.* In this process, he collected signed affidavits from over fifty thousand Americans who observed irregularities and illegalities during the election. As word spread of what Byrne was doing, more and more people fed information to him.

In his book, Patrick Byrne documents many violations of federal law: ballots destroyed, voting machine records erased, local election officials refusing to cooperate with their state legislatures, election auditors threatened and shot at, and the list goes on. This is not the pattern of democracy. This is exactly the pattern of intimidation, deceit, fraud, and manipulation of communism, dictatorship, totalitarianism, or whatever you want to call it. Pattern recognition reveals what is really going on.

This election and its aftermath exactly followed the pattern set by Mussolini in 1922 when he rigged the election results to gain a majority government for his party. The US government's reaction to the January 6 incident is just what Mussolini did in rounding up opponents and imprisoning them without trial. He restricted the publishing activity of his opponents and replaced it with a heavy propaganda campaign–just like the mainstream media did after the 2020 election. Democrats calling all Trump supporters "terrorists" are vilifying their political opponents so they can be arrested. This is precisely the pattern set by Lenin, Mussolini, and Hitler. We've seen this film before, and we know how it ends. This is psychological warfare. Its purpose, as always, is to subvert the target country in order to accomplish regime change and bring in totalitarianism.

Conclusion

In all six swing states, Trump was consistently leading until counting was shut down during the night. Then, in every case, a huge injection of ballots for Biden occurred. When counting resumed, the votes for Biden consistently exceeded the votes for Trump. In this chapter, I have summarized the various fraudulent activities that created this unlikely phenomenon. These have been documented. There is evidence. This is not speculation or misinformation or conspiracy theory. There was clearly a conspiracy. It's not theory. It's history.

The 2020 US election fraud was a meticulously planned felony. It is organized crime. All the security and legal agencies that should be protecting American interests have completely dropped the ball. It would be foolish to assume this was due to incompetence. The FBI, CIA, DOJ, and other organizations have all failed, and it wasn't an accident. It was intentional. My American friends, the future of democracy in America, and democracy throughout the world, is in your hands.

What You Can Do Now

1. Everywhere in the world, voting machines have to be thrown out. Insist that your own jurisdiction returns to paper ballots, hand counting by real people, and real scrutineers. It's slow, but it's honest and can be audited.
2. If you are an American citizen, you must pressure your public officials to conduct forensic audits of the 2020 election in these six states, at the very least.
3. Any judge, politician, or election official who has resisted the legitimate calls for election audits must be removed from office. They are guilty of malfeasance in public office, at the very least. They have been clearly negligent in their prime democratic duty.
4. Pressure your state officials to pass voter integrity laws that ensure only people who are legally entitled to vote actually vote.
5. In the next election, become a scrutineer, a poll worker, or even a candidate. Only if honest people get involved and make sure that democracy is working, will democracy work.
6. Do all this without violence, anger, or hatred. Do everything with love.
7. Take a page from our opponents' playbook. Reread the article *The Secret History of the Shadow Campaign That Saved the 2020 Election.*[4] Everything they did to destroy democracy, we must do to rebuild it. Work locally. You can change your community and your town in weeks or months.

CHAPTER 17

Brave New World—The End of Democracy

"Hard times create strong men. Strong men create easy times. Easy times create weak men. Weak men create hard times. Many will not understand it, but you have to raise warriors, not parasites."
—SHEIK RASHID, FOUNDER OF DUBAI

In the 1969 film *Butch Cassidy and the Sundance Kid,*[1] an amazingly skillful posse pursues the two outlaws across the southwestern American desert. Butch and Sundance repeatedly ask each other, "Who are those guys?" They couldn't figure it out. Neither can I. Who *are* these Deep State people?

We are blaming our presidents and prime ministers, but there's clearly some force behind them in the shadows. There is something that's making all our governments march in lockstep. This has never happened before in history. We still have the *form* of independent democracies, but they are *functioning* as dictatorships, all controlled by a central power. What the hell is going on?

That's why we are left to come up with vague terms, suggesting shadowy conspiratorial figures in the backrooms of power politics. We call it the Deep State, Mr. Global, the Cabal, the Global Predators, and other such names. I often call it the billionaire oligarchs. Some of these billionaire oligarchs are out in the open, and some of their activities are fairly transparent. In this chapter, we look at how things might be connected, how the one-world government is being brought about, and what the New World Order will be like. This isn't theory. It is both history and their published plans.

Yet as I have said before, conspiracy or not, it doesn't matter. We are on a well-worn road that leads to totalitarian slavery. It doesn't matter who pushed us onto this road. We went willingly, if unknowingly. And if we choose, we can get off this road and onto a different road. That's the beauty and the horror of free will. We always choose our destiny.

What Is the Deep State?

"The Council on Foreign Relations has always opposed national sovereignty, because destroying nations is prerequisite to forming a world government." –JAMES PERLOFF

The big question today is "What is the real governance structure of the world?" Governments have a clearly defined structure. The function of each part and the relationships between the parts (such as the presidency, the senate, etc.) are spelled out in law. But governments all over the world are not really functioning the way they're supposed to. Over many decades, things changed so gradually, we didn't notice the erosion of democracy. We can get a clearer picture of what's really going on by looking at how the world is *really* functioning and see what that implies about the hidden structure.

Investigative journalist Iain Davis has developed a reasonable view of how the complex governance system is functioning.[2] I have modified his ideas with my own, which are shown graphically below. This whole system is what I have in mind when I use the term *Deep State*. Nothing here is democratic. It is a dictatorial structure and function based solely on the power of money, which suggests there might be a hidden cabal of bankers at the top. I call it the Policy Hierarchy.

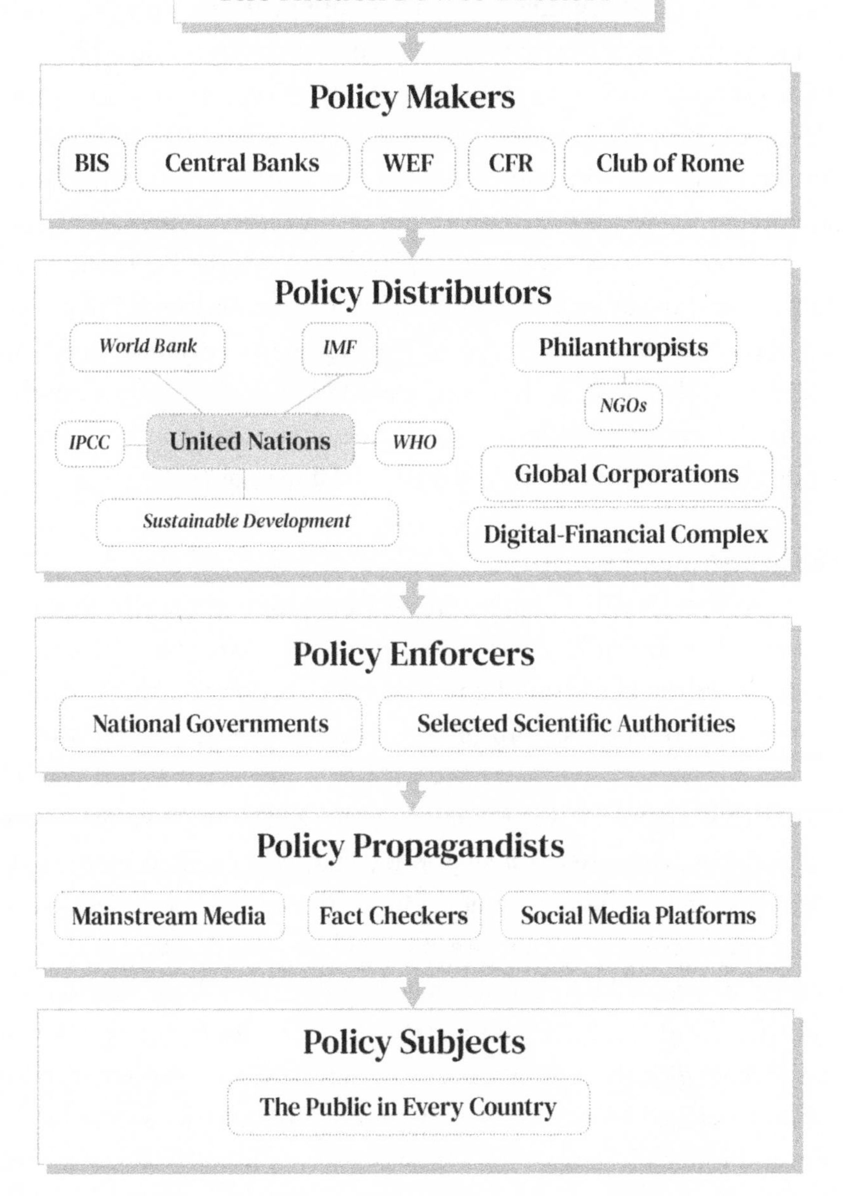
The Policy Hierarchy: How the World Is Really Governed
The Hidden Power Brokers
Policy Makers
BIS
Central Banks
WEF
CFR
Club of Rome
Policy Distributors
World Bank
IMF
Philanthropists
NGOs
IPCC
United Nations
WHO
Global Corporations
Sustainable Development
Digital-Financial Complex
Policy Enforcers
National Governments
Selected Scientific Authorities
Policy Propagandists
Mainstream Media
Fact Checkers
Social Media Platforms
Policy Subjects
The Public in Every Country

Policy Makers

We were taught in school that democratically elected legislatures set government policy and pass laws to enact that policy. This was true historically, but not anymore. Policy is now made in various think tanks and transnational organizations. These are private entities that often fly under the general banner of public-private partnerships. The *policy makers* consist of a few thousand people at the very heart of money and power–the elite of the elite–central banks, the Bank for International Settlements (BIS), the World Economic Forum (WEF), the Council on Foreign Relations (CFR), the Club of Rome, the Bilderberg Group, the Trilateral Commission, the Atlantic Council, the Rothschilds and Rockefellers, and other secret and semi-secret organizations. They decide on policies that favor–guess who–them. They make very long-term plans. In contrast, the planning horizon of elected politicians only extends to the next election. Politicians come and go, while the "policies" carry on for decades, as we have seen with the US-China policy.

Policy Distributors

Next are organizations that essentially distribute these policies. They don't really make policy, but rather pass it along through their ability to influence the behavior of governments, corporations, institutions, professions, and public opinion. For example, read an account of any honest person who has attended an IPCC conference, and you will realize that no policy was formulated there. The big, expensive conference was just to *confirm* the policy that was decided beforehand. These policy distributors include, importantly, the United Nations and all its agencies such as the International Monetary Fund (IMF), the Intergovernmental Panel on Climate Change (IPCC), the World Bank, and the World Health Organization (WHO). Other policy distributors include global corporations, billionaire philanthropists and their think tanks, and most Non-Governmental Organizations (NGOs). The Digital-Financial Complex (more on that in a minute) is also a key part of the *policy distributors*.

Policy Enforcers

National governments have been relegated to the position of *policy enforcers*. They pass the laws that enforce the policies set at higher levels. As we have seen with the various grand frauds, virtually every government in the world has moved in the directions set by the policy makers. This has been particularly obvious with the covid fraud. In first-world nations, governments are guided by key people who are part of the *policy makers* group. In third-world nations, leaders are kept in line by the CIA, as we have seen before. They do what they are told, or the CIA arranges a regime change. Second-world (communist) nations like China seem to be part of the New World Order plan. Russia appears to be bucking the system, which may explain why the *policy makers* are at war with Russia. Then again, this war might be little more than theater to distract everyone's attention from what is really going on. Or it might have other purposes that I haven't figured out yet.

The policy enforcers also include scientific organizations, professional associations, universities, and schools. They have been "captured" in the destabilization phase as previously explained. All these blindly follow instructions because they depend on the flow of money and/or legal powers granted to them from above. As well, many of the key leaders here are also part of the *policy makers* or *policy distributors* groups and personally receive money, prestige, and power because of their participation and willingness to follow orders.

Policy Propagandists

These groups put pressure on every level of the system to build the appearance of public support for the official policies and to demonize anyone who disagrees. It includes the mainstream media, social media companies, NGOs, and fact checkers (who are almost all paid by drug companies or billionaires in the *policy making* groups). The CCP's 50-cent army is part of this level, as are any similar groups we may not know about. They organize protests, demonstrations, acts of terrorism, and social media warfare campaigns to pressure the *policy enforcers* to do what they are told and to convince the public there is widespread support for these policies. Quasi-private militias like Antifa and Black Lives Matter are in this category, as are militant environmental groups like Extinction Rebellion. They are tools of subversion and terrorism used just like the Black Shirts and Brown Shirts were used by Mussolini and Hitler. They are funded by taxpayers and billionaire oligarchs. These propagandists are part of the psychological warfare and social disintegration.

Policy Subjects

At the bottom of this hierarchy are all of us—the public. We are subject to the policies but have no way of influencing them. Anyone who has tried to pressure their elected representatives or promote a different policy has likely experienced the utter futility of working through the existing political structure. It is simply nonfunctioning. To change anything, you have to understand how the system *really* works—what the hell is *really* going on.

We can also see the difference between *policy propagandists* and *policy subjects* by how their public demonstrations are treated. The BLM riots of 2020 were tolerated by governments because these were *policy propagandists*. They were fulfilling and validating policy objectives. Yet the million peaceful people who showed up at the US Capital on January 6, 2021, to protest election fraud were called insurrectionists. The police arrested hundreds of people (except their own operatives), held them illegally for over a year without trial, charges, or access to lawyers, and finally charged most of them with petty trespass—a misdemeanor. Similar events have happened everywhere.

Democracy is over. The political structure we once knew is now only a façade, an illusion, a fantasy, that puts a familiar face on a horrid structure of governance that is alien to all of us. In reality, the entire structure of governance has changed right before our very eyes, and we didn't even notice it. That's how communist subversion works. This is stage 1—undermining political structures to turn them to the communists' own purposes or make those structures ineffective. Rule or ruin.

The *policy makers* group seems large and unwieldy. Is there a smaller group above them? Quite likely. Perhaps it is the Committee of 300. Perhaps secret societies and secret quasi-religious groups like the

Illuminati have a more dominant role. Perhaps the rich banking families form the inner circle. I don't have clear evidence of such things, so I will set them aside for the moment. If you understand the basic structure outlined here, you will begin to see how the global governance system really works and what it will take to re-establish democracy.

The Digital-Financial Complex

"Men who can manage men, manage men who can manage only things, and men who can manage money, manage all." –WILL DURANT

There may be a simple way to view the world's power structure, or at least a big part of it. For thousands of years, bankers were the most powerful people in the world. Then, during the period of financial deregulation (1980s and 90s), the investment banks became dominant. After that, around the turn of the century, the hedge funds became the most powerful. Their time at the top didn't last long either, and power soon passed to the huge asset managers like BlackRock and Vanguard. As the number one and two largest institutional shareholders in almost every major company in the world, they manage assets worth $16 trillion (as of 2022–it keeps growing). This is bigger than the GDP of the EU (at $15 trillion). They can influence corporate decisions everywhere and can direct any market in the world in any direction they wish.

Typically, institutional investors are passive shareholders. If they don't like the way management is running the company, they simply sell their shares. But BlackRock is an active investor. Larry Fink, the CEO, sends regular messages to all the companies BlackRock owns, telling them to follow the ESGs, green initiatives, and all the other Deep State policies. BlackRock has no intention of selling its shares in global companies. It wants to *influence* global companies, and as the largest shareholder, it can.

BlackRock is a publicly traded company. You too can buy its shares. Vanguard has. It's BlackRock's largest shareholder. But Vanguard is a private company. It doesn't have to report anything publicly. We don't know who owns it. But we do know that Vanguard manages money for all the richest families in the world–the Rothschilds, Rockefellers, Morgans, and so on. So, following the money trail, we see it all starts from the world's richest families in Vanguard, which owns a big share of BlackRock and between them actively influence corporate policies all over the world. That's part of the financial control. Then there's data.

Data has become at least as important as money in controlling people, as we saw in chapter 10. Whoever has data has power. Lots of data equals lots of power. In the burgeoning internet of things, the vast amounts of data will bring massive power to those who control it. And people are just "things"–part of the whole system that is controlled with money and data.

The large information technology (IT) companies have used their ownership and control of data to become fabulously rich and more powerful than governments. All industries and all state institutions, including weapons manufacturers, food, pharmaceuticals, energy, media, and even the intelligence agencies, are now in the grip of the digital corporations, which have also built up their own global media power with social networks.

The financial industry has promoted this process from the start and is now involved in all leading IT groups through its most powerful representatives: BlackRock and Vanguard. It is also dependent on them at the same time. Both are merged into a kind of community of interests.

There are only seven companies at the top of the world's power and money nexus: Apple, Meta (formerly Facebook), Microsoft, Alphabet, Google, and Amazon (on the IT side), along with BlackRock and Vanguard, the big asset managers. The German economist Ernst Wolff calls these seven companies the Digital-Financial Complex. That's a good name. Most of the ideas in this section come from his work.[3]

If you put the CEOs of these seven companies in a room, they would represent more power than the heads of all the G20 nations. And the personalities involved don't even matter. If all those seven CEOs were assassinated and replaced with new CEOs, nothing would change. This concentration of power is inherently diabolical. The only solution is a massive decentralization of power.

I have placed the Digital-Financial Complex in the *policy distributors* category. They fulfill this function, but their power is so great they might also belong in the *policy makers* category. There are so many overlaps between the people in these companies and in the various policy makers' groups that it's hard to know for sure. As we will see in chapter 18, BlackRock might even be telling the central banks what to do.

United Nations—One-World Government

"The drive of the Rockefellers and their allies is to create a one-world government combining super capitalism and Communism under the same tent, all under their control." —CONGRESSMAN LARRY P. MCDONALD

The United Nations was formed right after the Second World War with the noble intention of encouraging cooperation and communication between nations so problems could be resolved peacefully without ending up in another great war. It has done some excellent work over the years. In many ways, it has lived up to its founding aspirations. Unfortunately, like any bureaucracy, it quickly took on a life of its own. Guided by the inexorable momentum of bureaucracy and by the designs of power-hungry technocrats and billionaires, it quickly morphed into a one-world "government-in-waiting." But it hasn't been waiting patiently. The UN and its many agencies have been steadily building a one-world structure of administration and control over every aspect of human life on this planet. It has slowly usurped the power and authority of national governments—something it was never intended to do.

The United Nations is not democratic. All its members are appointed, usually by heads of state. They are political patronage appointments. In most nations of the world, the appointees are friends, business associates, supporters, or family members of the head of state. They are not appointed for their knowledge, wisdom, or skill. And these are very cushy posts. In most countries, an appointment to the UN or any of its dozens of agencies and affiliated organizations brings with it a lifestyle and budget (using other people's money) that catapults the appointee into a wonderland of opulence their countrymen cannot even imagine. Most of these people have little or nothing to contribute to world governance. They will do whatever is necessary to maintain their undeserved wealth and power. They are easy targets for manipulation.

Of course, UN statements, declarations, rules, and so on ad nauseum are not binding on the member states. Those states are free to accept or reject such things as the Universal Declaration of Human Rights, the Declaration on Indigenous Peoples, the Declaration on the Rights of Children, all the "climate" agreements, and hundreds of other declarations, statements, commitments, and you-name-it. But if a nation refuses to ratify any of these, then the policy propagandists (funded by the policy makers) swing into action to vilify and discredit that government in the eyes of its own people. Standard operating procedure for totalitarians.

These propagandists and their billionaire backers have their own agendas and are accountable to no one. They influence not only national governments but also state and local governments, educational institutions, big businesses, and so forth. UN agencies and NGOs are bypassing national governments and forming coalitions with other organizations and state and city governments to enact climate scams and various "sustainable development" scams to further the UN's Agenda 2030. Again, weakening nation states, causing disunity, and undermining democracy—exactly what subversion is all about.

The policy propagandists are the new "stakeholders"—the old communist "citizen's committees" in disguise. In practice, we see these "stakeholders" turn out to be carefully selected ideologues or malleable useful idiots, all controlled by someone else with an ideological and political objective. This system is a ploy to take power and ownership away from those who legally have it and transfer it to a rabble of paid "stakeholders."

The UN is also directly taking power away from national governments in a hundred ways, such as regulating energy through the climate fraud, regulating land ownership through regional planning commissions and sustainable development guidelines, and regulating financial institutions, even central banks. They are regulating all the world's large companies through ESGs (environmental, social, and governance regulations). Now, the UN is even regulating the entire health and medical industries through the WHO, which has become focused mainly on vaccinating the whole world, as they clearly state in their Immunization Agenda 2030.[4] All of this has nothing to do with the UN's original purpose. Its only function now is to become a world government.

The UN and its many agencies are nondemocratic institutions made up of political appointees who can be (and are) bribed, persuaded, coerced, rewarded, and blackmailed by the KGB, the CCP, the CIA, NGOs, and governments. These "captured" people are then moved into positions of power to further the totalitarian objectives. On top of all that, these UN agencies and organizations are mostly funded by the taxpayers of Western democracies. (The USA alone pays for about twenty percent of the UN budget.[5]) We are paying to be subverted.

The UN Agendas: 21, 2030, What Next?

These agendas are all part of the overall UN goal to establish itself as a world totalitarian government with no borders, no nations, no sense of ethnic or national identity, and no individual rights. Dr. Vernon Coleman reviews some of the salient developments.

> In 1976, the United Nations decided that it would control the use of land around the world. And that it would also take upon itself the job of managing populations everywhere. All this was to be done for the good of the planet and mankind, of course. This was, I suppose, the beginning of communitarianism: the idea that the community's needs must be put first and individuals cannot have rights....
>
> Never before has such an innocent, honest looking, well-meaning sounding word been used to promote and sustain such a genuinely evil, Luciferian plan. The agenda 21 programme for 'sustainable development' bears an uncanny resemblance to the plans for technocracy.

> The United Nations had, in reviving the technocracy plan created in the 1930s, found the way to take power, to control us and to move towards a world government which would, of course, be controlled by the United Nations itself. Who better?...
>
> And, most terrifying of all, there was a plan to reduce the world's population – not by a few million here and a few million there, but by billions. The plan was to reduce the global population by 75% or more....
>
> Today, there are still many millions who still don't realise precisely what is happening. Everything that is happening was planned decades ago – and is only now coming to fruition.[6]

This is, indeed, technocracy. In his book *Technocracy: The Hard Road to World Order*,[7] Patrick M. Wood explains in detail the UN control mechanisms that I have only lightly sketched.

Communists and Billionaires–Strange Bedfellows?

One of the strange aspects of what we observe in the world today is the ease with which capitalist billionaires work with the communists in China. Aren't they natural enemies, on opposite ends of the political spectrum? What seems bizarre on the surface is not so once you look a little deeper.

Recall that our popular understanding of right-wing and left-wing is completely mixed up. Those who seek power over others are all left wing. On the right wing are those who seek only power over themselves and an equal freedom and responsibility for all.

Recall the support the early Bolsheviks received from prominent businessmen in the West. Communism only lost its Western corporate support with the beginning of the Cold War in 1945. Even then, a surprising amount of business cooperation continued with the Soviets. The West kept the Soviet Union alive many times. The same goes for China.

Observe the easy relationship between the Chinese Communist Party and the world's billionaires and largest companies. Power and money are natural allies. Freedom is their enemy. The Bolsheviks, Fascists, and Nazis were always happy to partner with the privileged, moneyed classes. Of course, they used the rich industrialists just like they used everyone else. It is, after all, a game of power and manipulation. The ultrarich have been perfectly willing to partner with the most tyrannical, oppressive regimes the world has ever known—as long as *they* enjoyed a privileged position. Both communists and billionaires lust for power. The billionaires also lust for wealth—communists not so much. The communists are also driven by ideology—billionaires not so much. Yet they have ample common ground on which to agree.

The billionaire oligarchs have no interest in free enterprise. They like monopoly enterprise. Monopoly and government go hand in hand. In the old days of mercantilism, governments granted royal monopolies, like the East India Company. In the modern world, monopolies often arise from crony capitalism, close contacts within governments, and military or intelligence connections. Even when monopolies develop independently from aggressive business tactics (such as John D. Rockefeller with Standard Oil at the end of the nineteenth century and Bill Gates at the end of the twentieth century), they end up in a cozy relationship with governments one way or another.

In our day, governments have devised many ways to contract their dirty work to big business. Propaganda and mind control are contracted to the media and social media companies, supervised by the CIA. Revolution and regime change are contracted to NGO "fronts" and private armies like the CIA and Blackwater. Even biological warfare is being contracted to big businesses by compelling them to enforce "vaccination" on all their employees. This is the dirty underbelly and the real reason for public-private partnerships. Private profit, public expense, and plausible deniability, all leading to greater control for the Deep State.

This is government in bed with big business. It is mercantilism, which I prefer over terms like "crony capitalism." Mercantilism can be understood as the merging of big business and big government to monopolize wealth and power in an elite class and exert control over everyone else. But we can also call it technocracy.

Sidelining Governments–The End of Democracy

Let's review some of the ways national governments have been neutered and power shifted to the Policy Hierarchy.

The massive expansion of governments over the past several decades has put bureaucrats in charge. It is impossible for elected officials to have any clear idea of what is really going on in the governments they are supposed to lead. Politicians come and go, but the bureaucracy remains for a lifetime. This is one of the main reasons why almost nothing changes in government when we elect new people. They don't actually control anything.

The United Nations and its agencies have taken much decision-making and administrative power away from nation states, which are powerless to oppose UN decisions and "recommendations."

International financial organizations, particularly the Digital-Financial Complex, essentially control international business and finance. National governments cannot control big businesses. Big Money controls policy; governments just enforce it.

NGOs have become incredibly powerful and are accountable only to their big financial sponsors. They have become fronts for billionaires, foreign communist governments, the CIA, and/or other intelligence organizations.

Public-private partnerships are a tool to sidestep democratic government decision-making and to co-opt governments into doing the bidding of private companies and private individuals who fund "nonprofit" special interest groups. It is a way for private individuals to manipulate governments with money and look good while doing it. Plus, they get government (read: taxpayers') money to achieve their private goals. For example, GAVI is really Bill Gates. Bill Gates has donated millions to GAVI, but by co-opting governments, the UN, and other philanthropists, GAVI spends over $8 billion a year.[8] Yet Bill Gates alone determines its goals and strategy.

Privatization sounds good in principle, where governments have taken roles more appropriate for individuals or companies. However, privatization has also been an excuse to contract globalist dirty work outside the sphere of government, where it cannot be seen and controlled. The CIA contracts out private wars, assassinations, drug running, chemical and biological weapons, surveillance, and torture of anyone (including of US citizens). About 70 percent of the CIA budget goes to "contractors."[9]

The "revolving door" between Wall Street and Washington ensures that the same people take turns holding the most powerful positions in the US Congress, the US administration, the bureaucracy, then in companies supposedly regulated by the bureaucracy, and in the international banker's world. It's a vast game of musical chairs where the same elites rotate through all the seats of power.

Over the past century, power has continually been taken from lower levels of governments and moved higher and higher up the power chain, to gradually coalesce at the national and supra-national levels—often even contravening national constitutions.

The welfare state has grown so large and has so many millions of beneficiaries, that it is impossible to pare it back in any meaningful way. For decades, politicians have tried to find efficiencies in these programs, but the bureaucratic and political forces against them are insurmountable. Even minor cutbacks are met with a violent and sustained reaction by socialist NGOs, various "do-gooders," and other policy propagandists.

Lobbyists have infinitely more power over government than voters. One lobbyist is worth ten thousand votes. A business investment in a good lobbyist is more profitable than an investment in a new manufacturing plant. Corruption and blackmail are everywhere. Just like we saw with prohibition, corruption is a cancer that gradually infects all of society.

Think tanks make government policy, not elected representatives, as is explained in the Policy Hierarchy. The mainstream media is not a source of truth or fact. It is a controlled part of the policy propagandists and a tool of psychological warfare.

The United States has prevented the rise of any middle powers that could jointly challenge a one-world government. The world has devolved into two main power centers: the US/EU/Japan (which is controlled by the *policy makers*) and China. Russia is not in this league. This has gathered power into few hands. Control those hands, and you control the world.

At the same time, China has been expanding its world influence and control at breakneck speed. China now controls most of sub-Saharan Africa and is well on the way to controlling most of Central Asia. It is also China's plan to prevent the emergence of independent middle power nations in its sphere of influence. China and the Western "one-world government" are hurtling headlong towards a showdown for world control.

We sit on the cusp of a new technocratic dictatorship. Democracy is over. Two centuries ago, an obscure Scotsman said that democracy was an unstable and short-lived form of government. Alexander Fraser Tytler's idea has been oft repeated and somewhat modified over the years. He said,

> A democracy cannot exist as a permanent form of government. It can only exist until the voters discover that they can vote themselves largesse from the public treasury. From that moment on, the majority always votes for the candidates promising the most benefits from the public treasury with the result that a democracy always collapses over loose fiscal policy, always followed by a dictatorship. The average age of the world's greatest civilizations has been 200 years. These nations have progressed through this sequence: From bondage to spiritual faith; From spiritual faith to great courage; From courage to liberty; From liberty to abundance; From abundance to selfishness; From selfishness to apathy; From apathy to dependence; From dependence back into bondage.[10]

The United States today, and all of Western civilization, is somewhere in a state of selfishness, apathy, and/or dependence. Our governments are doing their best to make everyone dependent, and no one seems to be objecting. Bondage is not far away. The way back to liberty requires spiritual faith and courage. That's why I chose the quote that opens this chapter. It's what we need today if we are to return to democracy and prosperity. "Many will not understand it, but you have to raise warriors, not parasites."

Do you have spiritual faith? Do you have courage? Can you develop more of both? Yes, you can. It is the only path to freedom.

The Great Reset—New World Disorder

"The history of the West, from the age of the Greek Polis down to the present-day resistance to socialism, is essentially the history of the fight for liberty against the encroachments of the officeholders." —LUDWIG VON MISES

The Great Reset and the New World Order are ideas promoted by the World Economic Forum. They have been preparing this for years. The idea has been around for ages. The Trilateral Commission called for a New World Order back in the 1970s. The Freemasons have been working toward the New World Order for centuries. (They really call it that.) It's the same people and the same plan. It has always been sophistry for a tyrannical and evil world dictatorship ruled by them.

By 2020, whoever is really behind the Great Reset was ready to launch it. They claimed the covid-19 "pandemic" was a perfect time to change the world. Of course it was. They planned it as a communist subversion crisis over a nonissue to grab more power. The New World Order is a totalitarian world ruled by a one-world government of technocrats and billionaires, manned mostly by robots, and with drastically fewer people who are divided into two distinct classes—the billionaire oligarchs and technocrats, and the "drones" or workers. The workers will all be paid by the "government." The Great Reset will be hell. Instead, we need a *Real Great Reset*—dismantling the apparatus of oppression. They want to centralize all power and control. Instead, we must decentralize everything.

Transhumanism: The New Borg

As we saw in chapter 2, transhumanism is the deliberate changing of humans into something different than what God (or evolution) made. It boils down to adding machine parts and an "operating system" into our bodies so that we can be controlled remotely by a computer. As we saw in chapter 15, the vaccines are providing the excuse to inject the operating system (or the self-assembling parts) into our bodies. The vaccine passports will become the link to the whole control system. That's where we're going.

Transhumanism is not for your benefit but for the benefit of the billionaire oligarchs who plan to rule the world. This is no longer science fiction. This is happening. This is their plan. Like the Borg of Star Trek, we will all be connected to the "one mind" computer and controlled by it.

In case you never saw the Star Trek TV series, let me explain: The Borg are alien cybernetic organisms linked in a hive mind called "the Collective." They co-opt the technology and knowledge of other species, forcibly transforming individual beings into "drones" by injecting nanoprobes into their bodies and surgically augmenting them with cybernetic body parts.

This is transhumanism in a nutshell. But it's even worse than this. By connecting humans to the AI computer in a hive mind, the computer can then quickly teach the robots how to be more human-like.[12] This hive mind won't even require very many humans to be connected. We are already at the point where the average person has trouble distinguishing between a real person and a cyborg. They are that lifelike, both in appearance and functioning. And the world's militaries are all over this. They want cyborg armies.

The billionaire elites think that by turning humans into the Borg, they will make a perfect superhuman. But they reject God, so they fail to realize we are already perfect the way God made us. They fail to understand that we are already immortal. They fail to understand that who we are is not just a physical body. "We are not human beings having a spiritual experience, we are spiritual beings having a human experience." We already *are* everything they desire and more. Transhumanism can only make us worse. Transhumanism separates us from our own souls and from our connection with God. We become *sub-human*, not *trans-human*.

Technology cannot give us deeper access to any part of ourselves. Prayer, meditation, and spiritual study can do this. Connecting to a machine cannot improve us—only connecting to God can do this. By connecting to God within, our soul, the Holy Spirit that dwells within us—we can connect to the infinite power of God, the infinite power of the universe. *This* will be the great breakthrough of the twenty-first century, not creating an army of bionic drones to be slaves in a dystopian nightmare world.

Klaus Schwab and the other billionaire oligarchs have a completely perverted view of humanity itself, of the nature of the human condition, and of our future as a species. Our future is not a dark hell of slavery. Our future is a bright, enlightened world of greater freedom, greater love, and greater connection to the Creative Force that dwells around us and within us. We must reject the slavery of the oligarchs and reclaim our freedom as divine creations of God.

The Billionaire's Big Blunder

I have said many times that the technocratic billionaire oligarchs of the Deep State are taking over the world. But I have also said that communism, and the Chinese communists in particular, are taking over the world. How can that be?

These might be one and the same, but I think the Deep State and the CCP are two separate forces. They have been working together, but it cannot last. I think the billionaire's big blunder is that they don't understand—communists share power with no one. The Chinese communists have adopted the ideas of technocracy for managing their economy—exactly the techniques the Western elites want to force on us. The billionaires have been drawn into China's web by the allure of wealth and a market of a billion people. They have been fawning over China's incredible growth in power and wealth. They envy that. But as we have seen, that growth is not really much of a miracle. Any third-world country could do the same given similar circumstances. Copying a successful business model ain't rocket science.

The Chinese communists are aiming at world domination. It's their official government policy. Their actions in recent years provide ample evidence that this is their goal. They are well on their way.

The billionaire oligarchs of the Deep State are in a similar position. Their plans and goals are public. It seems like a partnership, but communists don't have partners. They have stooges. They have useful idiots. They manipulate people. Once the useful idiots cease to be useful, they are eliminated. This pattern has been repeated a hundred times in the past century.

If we assume the plans for world domination and the enslavement of everyone actually come to fruition, then I foresee a colossal clash of titans between the Chinese communists, who will control most of Asia and Africa, and the billionaire oligarchs, who will control most of what we call Western civilization. If we have not destroyed ourselves in multiple civil wars before then, we will accomplish this in the final clash of Eastern communists and Western technocrats.

As Nietzsche understood, the philosophy that underlies all this thinking is one of power, of creating oneself into a god, of the ultimate dominance of one "strong will" over all others. In a philosophy of power, there can no more be two dominant world powers than there can be two alpha males in a pride of lions. There will be a fight to the death. It truly will be death for everything.

This is the path we are on. This is the road to enslaving everyone and to eventually destroying all life on this planet. This "Brave New World" to which we are headed should scare the crap out of you. But before we finally look at a different path to freedom, we must consider money. Money and power go together like a horse and carriage. This is the sinful duo that entices those who seek world dominion. To rule the world, they must rule the money–the one ring to rule them all. To that topic, we now turn our attention.

What You Can Do Now

1. Refuse to go along with the descent into darkness that I have described in this chapter. No one can control you without your permission. Use nonviolent noncooperation.
2. If you would have a return to democracy, you must first return to spiritual faith and courage. You must have the courage to personally oppose those who are trying to enslave you. There is a price to pay. The price of courage *may* be death—but the price of cowardice *certainly* is.
3. For democracy to work, it must be limited. Massive governments are unavoidably tyrannical. Shrink governments. Shut down those departments that take the power, freedom, and responsibility that individuals should have. Take responsibility for yourself and your family. Then elected politicians will be able to govern again.
4. Power must be removed from the Policy Hierarchy and returned to elected legislatures. Most of the organizations in the Policy Hierarchy need to be disbanded.
5. Disband the United Nations and all its agencies. Despite its past good works, it has become a mechanism for the destruction of democracy and the installation of world dictatorship. Encourage your political leaders to leave the UN. If nations start abandoning these agencies, they will collapse.
6. Stop all government grants to NGOs and any other organizations. Even athletic and artistic organizations need to return to being supported by their communities. Government grants are a source of corruption and control, and must be abolished.
7. Find ways to reduce the influence of money in politics. If money rules the world, there is no democracy.
8. Resist all the inroads of transhumanism. You are a spiritual being. Turn to God. All the greatest desires of your heart will be found there—in God.
9. Develop parallel structures; our strength is in community. Develop a "freedom group" in your own community of friends and neighbors. Be a support for each other. One who is in need is your neighbor.

CHAPTER 18

Monetary System to Control System

"Lenin was certainly right, there is no more positive, or subtler, no surer means of overturning the existing basis of society than to debauch the currency...The process engages all of the hidden forces of economic law on the side of destruction, and does it in a manner that not one man in a million is able to diagnose." –JOHN MAYNARD KEYNES

I have had an interest in monetary theory since the 1980s when I completed my economics degree. So, in recent decades I have watched, aghast, as the world's monetary authorities have continuously debased our currencies. They have accomplished exactly what Keynes describes in the opening quote.

In the simplest terms, everyone knows that we can't just print little pieces of paper, call them money, and make everyone rich. It's not the little pieces of paper that make us wealthy, it's all the real things we have—houses, cars, businesses, roads, bridges—that are produced by people actually working and building things. The paper money, in a sense, "represents" those physical assets. Yet for almost three decades, our central banks printed more and more money every time we had a minor problem. We've seen this pattern repeatedly throughout history. It doesn't end well.

As both Lenin and Keynes observed, one of the most powerful tactics of communist subversion is to destroy a nation's money. Nothing brings a country to its knees faster than this. Wealth is destroyed. Savers are wiped out. Pensions become meaningless. Debtors are released, including governments and the over-leveraged rich. Contracts become worthless. Economic decision-making becomes impossible. Investment dries up and leaves the country. The rich, who own property, are insulated. The poor, with little property, are pauperized to the point of desperation. Social order breaks down. People turn to a "savior" demagogue. Democracy gives way to totalitarianism. That's the point.

The Financial Coup D'état

> *"The currency system has been used to centralize political and economic control. If you look at this effort since the mid-1990s–the period that launched what I call the 'financial coup d'état'–the currency system has engineered a remarkable centralization of wealth. While our existing nation-states have been levered up with trillions in debt, a great deal of that credit, money, or assets has been transferred out to private hands–with liabilities retained or moved back into the nation-states. It is the greatest 'piratization' of all time."* –CATHERINE AUSTIN FITTS

The 2008–09 US financial crisis was caused by too much debt. There was fraudulent and unpayable mortgage debt in the US and that's what hurt most people. But what set off the crisis was problems in the derivatives market, the bond market, and thus the liquidity of banks and other financial institutions. The solution that our bankers and governments came up with was–wait for it–more debt. There were hundreds of criminal actions that created the crisis, but not a single criminal went to jail. It was a huge transfer of wealth from ordinary people to the super-rich bankers and elite class. The underlying financial problems were not addressed. Governments just papered over the problem with money created out of thin air and kicked the can of disaster down the road. That can of disaster showed up again in 2019 in another liquidity crisis. The bankers had prepared a *new* plan—just in time.

For almost a century, central bankers have followed the economic theories of John Maynard Keynes to manipulate the economy—attempting to avoid the business cycle by judiciously raising and lowering interest rates to adjust the supply of money. By lowering interest rates, money is created through increased borrowing. Strange as it seems, in the modern world, money is "borrowed into existence."

But after 2009, this stopped working. The economy had changed. All the textbooks became obsolete. Governments everywhere had become the largest borrowers, and their borrowing did not respond to changes in interest rates. Plus, corporations and households were already so loaded up with debt, they simply couldn't take on much more. So, lowering interest rates could not move the economy in any meaningful way. Central banks resorted to tactics never used before (that were technically illegal) under the general rubric of "quantitative easing." But by 2019, even those tactics were not working very well. They needed something more powerful.

Going Direct—The Central Banks Take Control

In a typically incestuous elite move, BlackRock hired a handful of former central bankers to develop a plan that central banks could use to manage the economy. BlackRock's plan was presented at the August 2019 annual meeting of central bankers in Jackson Hole, Wyoming. It is called the "Going Direct" plan.[1]

Normally, individuals and corporations deal with the commercial banks, which in turn deal with the central bank. You can think of it like the retail and wholesale banking systems. That's what Going Direct was about to change. Because central banks couldn't get people to borrow and spend more money by lowering interest rates, they had to figure out how to pump money directly into people's pockets. This new plan bypasses both the commercial banks and governments.

Traditional economic theory and practice say that central banks are in charge of monetary policy—that is, using interest rates to manipulate the *supply* of money. Elected governments are in charge of fiscal policy—that is, government *spending* of money and *raising* of money through taxes and borrowing. The Going Direct plan takes fiscal policy into the control of central banks—that is, out of the hands of democratically elected politicians and into the hands of the world's elite bankers. What could possibly go wrong? This usurped the financial power of governments. That's why Catherine Austin Fitts calls it a financial *coup d'état*.

To put it simply, central bankers took freshly printed money directly to consumers. But not to you and me. They gave (technically, loaned) money directly to investment funds to invest in the stock market. Naturally, the Fed (the system of federal reserve banks, which is the central bank in the United States) turned to BlackRock for investment advice and money management. BlackRock created the Going Direct plan for central banks to follow, then advised central banks on which stocks and bonds to buy, and then brokered the central bank's purchases—collecting fees at every stage. Nice work if you can get it.

In short, the central bank created money to buy stocks, driving up the stock market to make the rich richer, create a stock market bubble, and draw in the small investors so BlackRock and the ultrarich could cash out at the market top and leave the masses and the government with unpayable debts. Of course, it also gives the appearance that the economy is doing just fine.

The central bankers knew this increase in the money supply had to be permanent to be effective, and it would cause inflation. In 2021, when central bankers said the inflation was temporary, they were lying through their teeth. They planned the inflation in 2019, created the extra money in 2020, and knew it would result in permanent inflation by 2021. Also in 2021, BlackRock started buying up houses all over the United States as fast as it could, sometimes whole neighborhoods. That's a hint that inflation is not going to stop anytime soon. The "everything bubble" will continue until the elites are in a good position to crash the system and bankrupt everyone they have lured into the debt trap. To be ready, BlackRock assembled a $50 billion real estate investment pool in 2022 to buy up property after the real estate crash.[2] Most people will become debt slaves and "they" (BlackRock and the elites) will own everything.

After the engineered covid crash in March 2020 (which many insiders reported hearing about months in advance, suggesting it was orchestrated), the S&P 500 index bounced back 65 percent by the end of the year. Having been warned, the elites reduced their holdings beforehand so they could buy back in at the cheap March prices. Only the little individual investors lost money.

In 2021, the index gained another 28 percent thanks to money printing and the Going Direct plan that pumped most of that money into the stock market. Asset prices in all categories have gone ballistic. It's called the "everything bubble." Cryptocurrencies shot up like rockets in 2021. There was so much money sloshing around the financial system that people couldn't find reasonable places to put it. This boom sucked millions of little investors into the stock market, many of them for the first time. This is a classic pump and dump scam. In the fall of 2021, reports started coming out about the "smart money" cashing out. Company presidents sold their own stock at record levels.

We are being set up for a market crash of epic proportions. It will wipe out the wealth of millions of ordinary people, destroy pension funds, and possibly crash the entire global financial system. This has been orchestrated. There are several purposes: to move money from ordinary people to the elites, to create another crisis where people will call for a strong "savior" leader, and to open the way for replacing currencies and restructuring the financial system with central bankers in control of everything. The world's bankers have openly planned for this. They held a financial system collapse "war game" exercise in December 2021[3] just like Bill Gates did with "Event 201," the covid war game exercise just before the SARS "outbreak."

This may sound unbelievably fantastic, but it's been done before. The central bank of Japan pulled the same scam in the 1980s to increase its own power. The tale is beautifully told by Michael Oswald in his book and documentary *Princes of the Yen: Central Banks and the Transformation of the Economy.*[4]

The Japan bubble of the 1980s was intentionally engineered by the Bank of Japan in order to change the financial and monetary organization of the country. The structures were too secure and powerful to change without a collapse of the system, so they collapsed the system. The Bank of Japan intentionally increased the money supply during the 1980s and created an immense "everything bubble"—stocks and real estate in particular. At one point, the value of all the property in Tokyo exceeded the value of all the property in the rest of the world combined. As soon as credit growth stopped, the bubble popped. Prices of everything started to fall, loans could not be repaid, businesses failed, and homeowners lost their homes. Like every crash, there were basically no bids for stocks or property, and prices collapsed. Stocks fell 80 percent, land even more. Interest rates were dropped to zero, but the recession dragged on for decades. The Bank of Japan was trying to force changes in the structure of the economy. In the end, the previously powerful Ministry of Finance was largely dismantled and the Bank of Japan became independent. It changed the political system. That was the goal of the whole fraud. They cared nothing for the millions of lives disrupted along the way.

The best way to have a financial crisis is to have a bubble. That way, nobody stops you. Everyone is thrilled about becoming rich and thinking their own genius is doing it. Our present "everything bubble" and the inevitable crash have been orchestrated by the same forces and for the same purpose—to consolidate more power in the hands of central bankers. You likely don't know that central banks are not owned by their respective governments. Almost all central banks are privately owned, and this ownership and control lead back to a handful of immensely rich and powerful banking families that prefer to remain quietly obscure. We have been set up for a crash for the history books and a *coup d'état* of financial power like the world has never seen.

The Hidden 2019 Repo Crisis That Launched "Going Direct"

There was a financial crisis in 2019 but nobody heard about it. First, a little background. Pension funds are required by law to invest mainly in government bonds. For the past decade or so, interest rates on government bonds in Europe and Japan have been negative. From a financial standpoint, these bonds are worthless assets. Nobody will buy these bonds except their own governments and institutions that are forced to buy them. Thus, Europe and Japan have destroyed their bond markets. Pension funds cannot possibly earn the positive returns needed to actually pay their promised pensions. And European and Japanese banks simply don't have the financial assets that real banks will recognize.

Economist and forecaster Martin Armstrong claims he started noticing international capital flows changing in August,[5] but it was the bankruptcy of financial firm Thomas Cook on September 16, 2019, that set the dominoes falling. Thomas Cook had $2.7 billion in credit default swaps (a type of derivative) outstanding on its debt. Bankers worried this default would trigger a chain of defaults like the 2008 financial meltdown. Thomas Cook's bankruptcy forced the counterparties (the financial institutions holding the other side of those swaps) to pay a lot of money. So, they needed to find a lot of money in a hurry. That's called a liquidity crisis—when you need cash right now and can't get your hands on it. They turned to American banks, who refused to lend to them. The US Fed had to step in.

The very next day, September 17, the Fed put the Going Direct plan into action and started lending massive amounts of money to shaky financial institutions in Japan, Europe, and the United States. They used what are called "repo" loans (repurchase agreements with the central bank), which had not been used since the 2008 crisis. Most of these loans actually went to trading houses, not commercial banks, as their derivatives trades went sour. In the last quarter of 2019, the Fed lent a total of $4.5 *trillion* to trading houses.[6] This international liquidity crisis started before covid and was not caused by covid, but it was blamed on covid. The loans kept going into 2020 and totaled almost $12 *trillion* before the whole liquidity crisis was quietly swamped by trillions more money in "covid relief" that poured out so fast and furious that nobody knows where all that money went. Covid became the cover under which massive financial malfeasance was conducted. This is a textbook case of how money printing feeds corruption. Governments everywhere paid off their friends, underwrote mainstream media propaganda, rewarded Big Pharma, paid people to stop working, and removed the last vestiges of democracy. And they convinced *you* that it was all a wonderful thing done out of kindness, generosity, and concern for your safety.

Nomura Securities was the largest single recipient of the repo loans that all went to only six Wall Street and foreign trading houses—against the law. Nomura had almost $100 billion in derivatives liabilities.[7] This is the great repo crisis that nearly brought the financial system down again, and you likely never even heard about it. That was 2019. Nobody heeded the warning about the shaky derivatives market that could easily crash the whole financial system. Thomas Cook's derivatives book was $2.7 billion, and it shocked the system. The world derivatives market is now a hundred thousand times that much—$200 trillion![8] This financial house of cards doesn't need much of a breeze to blow it all away.

Let's pull the strands together. The international financial system is shaky and could blow up anytime. It almost did in 2019, but the Deep State wasn't ready yet. Central bankers held the financial system together with the Going Direct plan and massive money printing under the cover of covid. But the money printing is causing inflation and makes it even more obvious that all the debt in the world can never be paid back. The bankers have taken control of fiscal policy as well as monetary policy, leaving even less power in the hands of elected legislatures. What's coming is the greatest engineered communist crisis of all time, which will set things up for the greatest power grab of all time and the linchpin of total slave control—controlling all money, thereby controlling all people.

Goodbye Money System

"[Bankers] know that history is inflationary and money is the last thing a wise man will hoard." —WILL DURANT

One of the wisest and most equality-enhancing functions of any government is to ensure stable money. It prevents excesses by both individuals and governments. It provides a reliable store of value and promotes saving, which is essential for that accumulation of capital upon which economic progress depends. It allows for accurate calculation of costs, which leads to economic efficiency, good planning, and wise investment. It promotes social stability because people have something to lose through crazy, radical change. It helps tremendously to limit corruption and government waste because these are difficult to hide when real money has to be accounted for.

The alternative is constant money printing. Endless government deficits are impossible without money printing because savings are soon depleted. A population cannot be blinded to the impoverishment of wars without money printing. Massive corruption cannot be hidden without money printing. The trillions of dollars wasted on imaginary and self-destructive efforts to change the earth's climate cannot be obfuscated without money printing. When the money for these wasteful and useless activities comes directly out of people's pockets, they quickly object. Stable money is the best friend of the common man. The perversion of our currencies only benefits the wealthy and well-connected oligarchs of finance. It is the sure road to economic destruction. It is the definite plan of communist subversion. And it has been the consistent practice of our monetary authorities for the past three decades. It is not possible for this to be an accident.

Extending Government Control

I was dumbfounded when covid-19 shutdowns happened and our governments printed trillions of dollars and just gave it away. I asked an economist I know personally, "Why has not a single legitimate economist stood up publicly to say that we can't simply tell people not to work and then print money to make everything okay?"

He said, "Well...you know...almost all economists work for the government."

Then it hit me. Just like so many other professions, economists have mostly been bought off by government money. They won't criticize the hand that feeds them. Not only the majority of economists, but also scientists, teachers, professors, doctors, nurses, police, soldiers, and government employees at every level of government all depend upon money from the government. With covid-19, this picture of government control started to become clearer for me. All of these people continued to get their paychecks whether they worked or not. The same goes for everyone receiving a pension or living on welfare or social assistance. They were willing to do what the government said because they weren't being financially hurt by the shutdowns and they didn't want to challenge their source of income.

All the big businesses complied with government regulations. They will do whatever they are told, partly because they have the market power to pass the extra costs along to consumers. So, who is left to rebel? Mainly small businesses and independent tradesmen and artists. Most of these were given "special" government money. Many of them have been effectively nationalized even though they don't realize it. This is part of the plan to make everyone dependent upon the government and afraid to criticize it.

And now the silly idea of a universal basic income made sense to me. It was never about government efficiency. Governments have no interest in efficiency. It was never about helping people. That's not what governments do. It's about making *everyone* dependent upon the government in one way or another. That's exactly part of the communist subversion plan. Make everyone dependent, then everyone is too vulnerable to object, and everyone is a slave. Give everyone money to keep them quiet. But next, control all the money. The pieces were starting to fall into place in my mind.

Destroying the currencies is exactly the plan. Making it not *look* that way is also the plan. If we thought our monetary authorities were intentionally destroying the currency, we would throw the bastards out. They have to *appear* as though they are wise and capable experts responding to events outside their control. But the plan is to replace all currencies. Remember that the purpose of psychological warfare (or active measures) is to change your perception of reality to such an extent that, despite ample evidence about what is going on around you, you don't see it. Even if you do, you don't realize it's *planned*. Thus, you are unable to come to sensible conclusions in your own interests and in the interests of your nation.

On one side of the battlefield, the central banks and governments have created an "everything bubble" that will lead to an epic crash and impoverish millions of people. Governments will likely use this as an excuse to steal whatever you have left. They will likely say, "Capitalism has failed." The World Economic Forum has been chanting this tune for years. When the stock, bond, and real estate markets have collapsed, governments will likely step in, take your assets for "safekeeping," and give you government bonds in return–in perpetuity bonds that are not redeemable and pay zero interest.

On the other side of this battlefield, the central banks are destroying all currencies so they can replace them. How could you justify replacing a perfectly good currency? But a failed currency, well, replacing that is just good sense. And replacing an outmoded, obsolete, cumbersome, and (now) medically unsafe paper currency with a progressive, modern, simple, safe, digital currency for the digital age–why, what could be more obvious?

Hello Transaction System

"Who controls the food supply controls the people. Who controls the energy can control whole continents. Who controls money can control the world." –HENRY KISSINGER, 1970

The plan of the elites is to control all the money in the world. It seems ridiculous. To us normal people, it's a bizarre fantasy. But to those drunk with power, it's the next logical step. It's the lynchpin of the control system. Their plan is becoming obvious. In fact, they have even published it.

Central banks have been working on digital currencies for years. Through the "Better Than Cash Alliance," run by the UN and promoted by Bill Gates, they are connected to all the major countries and companies in the world. They will eliminate all paper money, checks, and coins. Everything will be digital. They are almost ready. It's coming. But these won't be blockchain-based decentralized currencies like Bitcoin. No, these will be completely centralized, government-controlled currencies that the central banks will have absolute control over.

At first, it will seem innocuous, just like all the other control measures. Most people have received their "paychecks" by electronic deposit for years. Most people already pay bills online and pay for retail purchases digitally with a debit or credit card. The transition will be easy. You will be enticed into this new monetary system because all government payments will be made through it. You must pay your taxes with it. If you want to receive your government pension; your government salary as a teacher, doctor, or nurse; your social security; your food stamps; your universal basic income–any payment from the government–you will only get it through the government digital money. And, of course, they will have automatic access to your bank accounts.

This will give the government complete control of all money. It won't really be a "currency" system; it will be a "transactions" system. It will likely start with different digital currencies in every country, but it's a small step from that to simply unifying them into one world currency or having an instant digital currency conversion system. Eventually, all the money on the planet will be controlled by the one-world government and the one giant quantum computer. The IMF and the BIS are working on coordinating separate national currencies into just such an international system.

Gradually, you will realize that if you have a speeding ticket, the fine will just be withdrawn from your bank account automatically. No need to appear in court. You are simply guilty when accused, just like with cancel culture. The same goes for parking tickets and library fines, automobile registration fees, fishing licenses, your income taxes, oh, and the new wealth tax and the new tax on your principal residence and the new personal carbon tax.... Get the idea? Tax evasion will be ancient history. The government will decide what you owe them and they'll just take it. And it will all be tied into your digital ID that you accepted as a "vaccine passport" because you wanted to help "stop the spread."

In fact, you will understand this system better if you don't think of it as money at all and don't think of it as *yours*. In a transaction system, there really is no money. And you don't own anything. The government owns everything in its central computer. Your "paycheck" each month is simply allowing you access to a certain quantity of transaction capacity in the central computer. Every month your transaction capacity is topped up to, say, $10,000. If you don't use it all that month, it will disappear. That way, the government ensures a steady and rapid "velocity of money." It makes central planning much easier. If you want to "save up" for a holiday or a major purchase, the government will provide a "layaway" plan for you. But you will have no ability to actually *save* anything, because personal savings would give you some independence from the government. The money is digital. It's ephemeral. It doesn't really exist. It is really just a "permission." If you misbehave or think wrong thoughts, your permission—your access to the transaction system—will be restricted or taken away.

For the elites, on the other hand, it's simple to grant themselves access to massive transactions. Loyalty is as easily rewarded as "wrong-think" is punished. This is beyond corruption. It is absolute autocracy.

All current financial assets will be converted to digital assets—your pension fund, 401K, RRSP, savings accounts, stock trading accounts, everything. Money as the world has known it for millennia will disappear. All those government debts that are unpayable will be converted into perpetual digital bonds paying zero interest. And, oh yeah, you won't be able to redeem them. That is, the government will just steal your money. This is part of how you will own nothing by 2030. Financial advisors and economists have been warning for decades that our government debts are unpayable. They cannot ever get enough money to pay all the pensions, social security, and other obligations they have promised to pay. This is their way out. The government will digitally pay your pension, welfare, salary, all wrapped into the universal basic income (UBI). It's easy. It's not money. It's just access to digital credits on a computer. And once they have you trapped, they will gradually reduce the UBI until everyone lives in poverty—except the elites.

There will be no escape from this transaction system. In the old days, if your country's currency was poorly managed, you could store some wealth in US dollars or gold coins or Bitcoin. That will no longer be possible. There will be no *real* currency. Even if you keep some, you will have no way to spend it. Stores will not be able to accept it, just like many places already won't accept *you* if you don't have your "vaccine passport."

Combine this transactions system with the coming social credit score, just like they already have in China (and is being introduced in Italy and France as I write this), and the facial recognition cameras on every corner and on every floor of every building and the GPS tracking of your location 24/7 with your own cell phone—have I missed anything? All your "smart" devices in your home and car also keep track of you. They are all connected to the cloud and the government, and they're listening to every word you say. Your home has already been turned into a digital concentration camp, and you didn't even notice. Your Fitbit—or whatever the new bio-monitoring device is going to be—is transmitting your biological and psychological condition to the AI computer 24/7. Soon it will be the bio-operating system that has been established within your own body by endless "vaccine booster shots" that will connect you with the cloud and the one-world computer. You will wave your hand in front of the scanner at the store to buy your groceries, your beer, and your dope. Just go home to your tiny apartment and get high to forget you're a slave. That's how you will be happy, because you will own nothing.

The people behind this will know absolutely everything about you—and you don't even know who they are. Asymmetrical information leads to asymmetrical power. They will have all the power, and you will have none. Remember, democracy is based on limiting the power of government. Tyranny focuses *all* power in government. You will be controlled like a machine. This is the new surveillance society. Actually, it's just the beginning of the new surveillance society.

The GPS transmissions from your cell phone know when you were jaywalking, when you strayed more than one mile from your home, and when you were speeding in your car. Actually, the onboard computer in your car already knows when you've been speeding—no need for actual police to set up speed traps. They will just access your car's records in the cloud and deduct your speeding fines from your bank "account." The government will know when you were in the bedroom of your neighbor's house when only you and the neighbor's wife were home. Through bio-monitoring, they'll even know your heart rate, body movements, and whether or not you really had an orgasm. The government will have a really nice "social credit" score for you. Better watch out, better think twice, Big Brother Santa Claus really does know if you've been naughty or nice.

Don't think so? We have been warmed up for "social credit" for years. Decades ago, several high-profile people suggested putting folks in jail if they disagreed about global warming. In the past decade we have seen thousands of people "canceled" by cancel culture for doing nothing illegal, nothing immoral, just expressing the wrong opinion. Now, millions of people support the idea of throwing their neighbors in jail for not wearing a face mask, not being injected with a biological weapon, or for visiting their grandchildren. People are publicly wishing death to their unvaccinated brothers and sisters. What have we become? There is tremendous support for governments picking "good" people and "bad" people based not on law but on mob opinion–which is manipulated by government propaganda and mind control. And if you get put on the government's "really bad" list, they will just cancel your "bank account"–your transactions system access. You cannot exist.

This is already happening. Thousands of legitimate and legal businesses have been de-monetized or completely canceled on YouTube and social media and Google. Remember, these big tech companies are effectively the "outsourced" arms of the Deep State. Even brick-and-mortar banks have simply canceled people's accounts because they disagreed with a customer's political stance or public comments. Filmmaker and author Dinesh D'Souza had his bank account and credit card with Chase Manhattan bank summarily canceled for no apparent reason except his political views.[9] They didn't like one of his recent films. Chase Bank did the same thing to General Mike Flynn.[10] It's happened in other countries as well. This is the future. Your ability to be a part of the financial system, get paid, buy anything, or to participate in society will depend on your subservience to the state and to manipulated mob opinion. This is happening in China right now. If your social credit score is too low, you can't buy airline tickets, travel outside your home province, or shop in certain stores.

Since the government controls and records every penny you earn and spend, they will only allow you to invest in "approved" investments. No buying gold without the government knowing about it. How would you buy it? There is no currency except the government digital currency. And if you get really out of hand, they'll just freeze your "bank account" as the Canadian government did in February 2022.[11] You can't leave the country. You can't get a job anywhere else. Your employment is always registered with the government. You can't work "under the table" because there is no way to pay you. The new government digital currency will give the government complete control over your life. This is *1984*.

Naturally, people won't like this idea. The big question for our totalitarian masters has been "How do we put this system in place without people realizing what we're doing?" That's part of where the virus crisis comes in. All the fake crises have been designed to create more and more fear in people, make people willing to give more power to governments, and collect power into fewer and fewer hands. With "contact tracing," you've accepted the government's constantly tracking your movements and your biological status. With the vaccine passport, you have accepted your connection to the whole digital-biological control system. They have almost all the power they need to make things irreversible.

We are very close to all of this. China field tested its digital currency in 2020–21 and plans to launch it in 2022.[12] The Chinese people realize this is happening, but there is not much they can do about it. Some are trying to buy small gold wafers. Other countries are following quickly. Sweden officially launched its digital Krona in early 2022. France and Switzerland tested their central bank digital currency (CBDC) exchange system in late 2021. The Bank for International Settlements (BIS) announced in early 2022 they had developed two international CBDC exchange systems. This is coming to you. As we've seen with all the covid control measures, whatever happens *somewhere* in the world, soon happens *everywhere* in the world. That's the plan. That's how the Policy Hierarchy works.

One-World Money for One-World Government

"One ring to rule them all." –J.R.R. TOLKIEN,
THE FELLOWSHIP OF THE RING

The complete control of all money through central bank digital currency really is the "one ring to rule them all." It ties together all the other control systems. Money is power. Both will reside in the central computer. National tax departments will be unnecessary. Tax laws will gradually become unified around the world to prevent companies and individuals from moving to a different place to avoid taxes. The annual budget debate circus that goes on in every country will end. Government spending decisions will also be made by the central computer and/or the central technocrats. National governments will simply be administrative, not legislative. No governance will actually happen there, just like no real policy is decided there right now. We will still "elect" people in the same way that "elections" happen in communist countries. But, as they have often already become, the main job of our elected representatives will be to explain the central decisions to their local people–not to impress our wishes upon the central authority.

Putting Together All the Pieces

Through multiple and massive frauds, the Deep State has quietly slipped a dozen nooses around our necks. They will soon have total control over all of us slaves. All the powerful segments of our society have their role to play.

- Through the (mal)nutrition and medical business model, you are kept unhealthy with maladjusted metabolic, endocrine, and immune systems, subject to chronic diseases and fraudulent diagnoses, all of which require lifetime medical treatment, so you cannot live outside the "medical mind/body control system."
- Through baseless fears about terrorism, the whole world has been turned into a police state where the function of the police is increasingly to manage people who disagree with our leaders,

not to deal with crime. Also, to "stop terrorism," you have been convinced to give up all financial privacy and personal privacy—for your "protection." It's a protection racket.

- The media is controlling the propaganda, the mind control, and the mass hypnosis operation.
- Big pharma is developing the "vaccines" that will massacre billions of people, change everyone's DNA, and create that biological "operating system" that Bill Gates has developed. People will be changed from human to transhuman. With this bio-operating system, they won't need your smartphone or other smart devices. In the internet of things, *humans* are just things. Your body becomes the smart device—constantly transmitting and receiving with the central computer. You are the Borg.
- The military is putting up the satellites and 5G towers that will complete the communication and control system over all the transhuman people and robots in the world. Elon Musk's company, SpaceX, has launched thousands of satellites in the past few years for this purpose. Another of his companies, Neuralink, is building the brain-computer interface systems.
- Big Tech is building the cloud information storage system, quantum computers, and software for the control system of the transhuman people. They are also intimately involved in controlling the propaganda and disinformation on social media platforms and the internet.
- The intelligence agencies have politically destabilized much of the world so there are no "middle powers" left, and they keep their own respective populations under constant surveillance. They are specifically targeting selected people with directed energy weapons and likely already have the ability to do this to everyone.
- The weaponized mass migrations have nearly destroyed the national character and social cohesiveness of most countries in the Western world. The entire concept of the nation-state is weaker every day.
- The UN, through its many agencies, has established itself as the

world government. The WHO will control the "health" (that is, the body) of every person in the world. The IPCC and the climate apparatus will control everyone's energy use through personal carbon budgets that will gradually reduce everyone to poverty. The sustainable development scheme has built an alternative governance structure almost everywhere in the world that bypasses national governments and controls almost all the land.

- Also, the UN and its agencies are tightening their control over all food and are engineering a collapse of the world food supply. The Deep State is promoting factory-grown insects as food, which will likely be contaminated with whatever "vaccine" they want to get into your body. When real food runs out, you will have to choose between starvation and poisoning.
- The central bankers are developing the digital currency that will control all money, all economic activity, and every person in the world. It is the capstone on the arch of control.

The Deep State is trying to keep all these systems separate so we don't see the connections. They don't want us to see the trap being built around us. Transparency can blow this whole game wide open. Whether by accident or design (but design is far more likely), we are in World War III—a fifth-generation war never before seen by humanity. You must pick a side; neutrality is impossible. You will choose freedom or slavery, truth or lies, spiritual independence or cult control. We are unwittingly building our own slavery system, and we have the power to stop. Catherine Austin Fitts gives some ideas on how to stop this.

- Understand where this system is going.
- Bring transparency to it.
- Stop building it.
- Avoid centralization. Create new decentralized structures everywhere.
- Stop doing business with the slave owners: Amazon, Facebook, military suppliers, etc.
- Don't watch mainstream media or buy their TV shows or movies.

- Don't help the military build or install 5G towers.
- Don't help big pharma make or distribute vaccines that will kill us.
- Do not accept a digital ID or a digital currency.

In short, stop cooperating with the enemy. We can end tyranny with nonviolent noncooperation. If we don't stop it, we will come under the most complete slave system ever imagined. Our world has come to the brink of total government, total war, total mind control, total money control, total body control, and total slavery.

Possible Next Phases in the War

"Study the past if you want to define the future." –CONFUCIUS

I cannot predict the future. I don't know how this fifth-generation World War III will unfold. But if we keep in mind the obvious goals, strategies, and tactics that I have pointed out in this book, we will be able to see the patterns in events. All the frauds and crises in this book are nonissues that transcend national borders, weaken nation states, and transfer power to a one-world government. Look for more of the same.

I have explained throughout this book how we have experienced not just one communist crisis, but a rolling series of crises each with its own objectives of increased control. For example, the drug crisis provided a constant stream of money to the Deep State to fund all its activities and frauds and to demoralize society. The terrorism crisis provided the excuse to build a police state and put everyone under surveillance. The climate crisis provided money to bribe and corrupt whoever needed it, to build the UN control institutions, and to gradually control all energy. Now that nitrogen is being demonized as an environmental killer, the climate fraud is also being used to destroy food production. The virus crisis provided the excuse to bring in social isolation, ramp up the propaganda network, identify and shut down dissidents, bring in the digital ID, hide the 5G rollout, start the societal collapse, extend the financial fraud and dependence of everyone, and insert the brain-computer interface into everyone. Each new fraud brings its own new crisis and achieves discrete parts of the long-term plan. This is the pattern. More frauds and crises will come until world totalitarianism is complete and you are either dead or a slave.

The Deep State may launch another bioweapon attack with a more deadly virus like Marburg, which has been weaponized since 1990. I have heard rumors about this, but nothing has yet emerged as this book goes to press. Most people have not yet figured out that covid is a fraud, so they are vulnerable to repeated "virus" attacks. As this book goes to press, the Monkeypox attack is building (also weaponized by the Soviets in 1990), despite it being almost a carbon copy of the covid attack. Monkeypox is a rare disease, difficult to spread, and limited mostly to Africa. Its sudden appearance all over the world indicates a bioweapon attack. Or it might not be Monkeypox at all but simply "vaccine" injuries mislabeled.

The propaganda campaign is rolling out cover stories to hide the vaccine injuries. The term *Sudden Adult Death Syndrome* (SAD) has emerged.[13] "Golly gee, we can't figure out why healthy, young 'vaccinated' people are suddenly dropping dead." The new AIDS story sprung up, V-AIDS, or vaccine-induced AIDS, because the "vaccine" has destroyed your immune system. The Deep State may once again use the AIDS fraud to murder people with AZT or some equally toxic "medicine." The rolling disaster of vaccine injuries will continue to unfold for years, maybe decades. It seems unlikely we will find a way to stop it because people refuse to see it for what it is. However, there are protocols for removing the spike protein and other toxins from your body.

The orchestrated collapse of supply chains continues to develop. This is part of the overall planned breakdown of the world economy and societal collapse. It is not the "failure of capitalism." It is a tactic of unrestricted warfare. The goal of societal collapse is to get people to cry out for a "savior" demagogue—hence, dictatorship. The goal of destroying the world's food supply is a siege warfare tactic to reduce the population through starvation and to make us dependent on artificial, DNA-altering factory food.

The buildout of the 5G system of towers and satellites continues apace. The public has not yet realized this is a weapons system—directed at you. Chemtrails are still widely regarded as a conspiracy theory, so they continue to be used to spread pathogens that infect everyone and metal nanoparticles that make both the atmosphere and your body better conductors. This increases the effectiveness of 5G weapons and control systems. The metal nanoparticles in your body are toxic in themselves and provide aluminum for the self-assembling structures that create a brain-computer interface within your body. You cannot escape them. You breathe them in. They penetrate your skin. They are in your food and water. However, there *are* ways to help detox aluminum and other metals from your body.

A cyberwar may be coming. The WEF has been warning about cyberattacks for several years. This is predictive programming. They war gamed the cyberattack operation in a simulation called "Cyber Polygon" in early 2021. The cyberattacks will likely come from the CIA or NSA and be made to look like they came from Russia—since Russia is the current scapegoat. This attack might be the pretense to take down the whole internet and bring it back up with embedded censorship or some other type of control measures. Or it might be the pretense to destroy cryptocurrencies. Or it might simply be another way to bring about economic destruction and further the societal collapse. Many things are possible. I have no crystal ball. Keep your eyes and minds open.

All the long-term programs that have been creating a one-world government continue. Even after the covid panic, governments continue to pass legislation for vaccine passports to give permanence to the "temporary" powers they grabbed. Sustainable Development initiatives continue their cancerous growth throughout the world. Ever more ludicrous "green energy" initiatives waste money and resources, inhibit real progress in energy technology, cripple industry and individuals, and collect more control of energy into the Deep State organs of power.

As ridiculous as it may seem, the Deep State may even be planning a false "alien" invasion of earth. After decades of official denials about UFOs and space aliens, the US government has recently started releasing information and talking more openly about official knowledge of aliens. In 2022, the Department of Defense renamed the former *Airborne Object Identification and Management Group.*[14] It is now the *All-Domain Anomaly Resolution Office* and has expanded powers to deal with "anomalies." Its mandate seems very broad. Their only clarification of "anomalies" is given by, "This includes anomalous, unidentified space, airborne, submerged and transmedium objects." (That is, objects from other dimensions of reality.) It's hard to know if this is really true or just predictive programming for a coming false flag "attack" by imaginary space aliens. This potential fraud would require a united world military response to "save humanity" and the establishment of a one-world military, superseding all national militaries.

As this book goes to press, China has locked down Shanghai and other cities for no medical reason. It's not clear why. There may be internal political objectives. The shutdown is certainly to further disrupt world trade since Shanghai is the world's busiest port. Just as Chinese lockdowns in 2020 were a harbinger of events in the rest of the world, we can expect the same in 2022.

As well, a third-generation kinetic war is raging between Russia and Ukraine. It was fomented by the United States, which has engaged in criminal behavior in Ukraine through the CIA and the State Department. They rigged the 2014 and 2019 elections and funded and operated biological weapons labs in Ukraine. The Pentagon finally admitted in June 2022 they had forty-six biolabs there, but we still don't know what really went on in all those labs.[15] I will leave it to future historians to uncover the truth behind the propaganda, but it's clear that the mainstream media reporting on this war exactly fits the pattern of an information influence operation to prepare the minds of people for an expansion into a kinetic World War III. Every world leader is talking about war. No one is talking about peace. Why? This makes no sense. It guarantees an expansion of war.

There is no strategic benefit for the North Atlantic Treaty Organization (NATO) to fight a proxy war with Russia. What could we possibly gain? Yet the potential risk is thermonuclear war that destroys the whole planet.

The risk-reward setup is wildly asymmetrical. This is exactly why ordinary people look at their political leaders and say, "These people are idiots." But as I have tried to convince you, they are not idiots. They are liars. There must be hidden reasons for this war. NATO is marshaling hundreds of thousands of troops and military equipment in Poland. For what reason? This can only be in preparation for a NATO invasion of Russia or Ukraine. NATO is not accountable to any government. Who controls it? That's not clear. Perfect. Every NATO country has lost control of its own foreign policy and even its own military, which has silently slipped into the control of the Policy Hierarchy. Our elites seem to be planning further escalations of an already unnecessary and nonsensical war. We should expect war to escalate into 2023 and possibly 2024. War is the classic tactic of a government desperate to distract its people from domestic problems.

In the twenty-first century, Russia's actions and statements suggest it has no aggressive intentions in the world. Russia today is also a second-tier power. It does not present an existential threat to the United States. Only China does. But Russia's actions seem to be re-establishing the importance of the *state*, whereas the Deep State's goal is to eliminate *states* and establish a one-world totalitarian government. This brings Russia and the Western elites into an existential conflict.

The only way this war in Ukraine brings any benefit to the *real* world powers is in the context of the *real* World War III. The Deep State's goal is societal collapse so they can justify the complete restructuring of the world into a technocratic dictatorship with the enslavement of humanity. Here are the obvious benefits of the Ukraine war.

- The war distracted everyone from the emerging failure of the covid operation and the growing push-back against it. The psychological warfare apparatus has shifted completely to Russia over what is really a minor, regional, short-term conflict with a simple solution–if the United States and NATO would stay out of it.
- It provided another scapegoat to blame for everything and another reason to spread fear.

- It provided the cover to advance the destruction of the world's financial and currency systems, and to disrupt trade flows and production (especially of food). Governments everywhere are illegally seizing the financial and real assets of Russian companies and citizens. It seems they will sequentially demonize every possible group in society until they have stolen everyone's money. Disrupting food, energy, and fertilizer production adds to their now two-year campaign to starve millions of people to death and control all food.
- It is providing an excuse to form an EU army, part of the slow process of moving to a world government. First, move to regional, multination governments. Europe is the most advanced in this regard. First came the European Economic Community, a trade arrangement. Then came the European Union, a supranational government that made national governments mere policy enforcers. Then came the Euro, a supranational currency that took the control of money out of the hands of national legislatures. Next, they want a supranational army that will leave every European nation individually defenseless.

One might ask what the UN is doing in all this world conflict; it has been mysteriously silent. The UN's purpose was to prevent and help solve wars like this. The UN is not dysfunctional. Its function has changed. The UN is a tool in the hands of the policy makers. The war in Ukraine is a carefully planned and orchestrated operation that serves the interests of the Deep State policy makers. The UN will do nothing to reduce tensions or resolve this conflict. It may suddenly appear at the end of the war to bestow its blessing on whatever outcome the Deep State wants to achieve, or perhaps to emerge as the world's savior. Since every nation and leader in the Western World is pushing for more war, the UN may be set up to override every nation and bring peace by forcing its power over every nation.

The WHO has already made its next move. In February 2022 it announced its intention to take control of the health care systems in every country of the world. There is no medical reason for this; it's entirely about controlling people. The WHO will become the Ministry of Sickness and Human Control in the New World Order. The IPCC will become the Ministry of Energy and Activity Control. Sustainable Development will become the Ministry of Land (and all objects) Control. The BIS will become the Ministry of Transaction Control. The CIA-military-industrial complex will become the Ministry of Violence and Oppression. The mainstream media and the big tech companies will become the Ministry of Disinformation and Mind Control. National governments will continue their descent into mere policy enforcers. Welcome to Paradise.

As you watch World War III unfold, be alert to every event that brings us closer to this reality, to every event that is used to generate more fear, to every event that turns humans against their neighbors. Before 2020, it was blacks against whites, gays against straights, woke against unwoke. With covid, it was vaxxed against unvaxxed, rebels against complacent true believers. With the war in Ukraine, it's everyone against Russians, and Russian vodka, and Russian sopranos at the Metropolitan Opera, and the private property of Russian citizens. You are not safe. Whoever you are, your turn for demonization and stealing your assets will come. This is the pattern of totalitarian sociopaths. Hitler did exactly the same thing, pithily recorded in this famous poem by Martin Niemoller.[15]

First they came for the Jews
and I did not speak out
because I was not a Jew.
Then they came for the Communists
and I did not speak out
because I was not a Communist.
Then they came for the trade unionists
and I did not speak out
because I was not a trade unionist.
Then they came for me
and there was no one left
to speak out for me.

We either stand together as simple humans, or we will all fall, one at a time. This is the final battle. We shiver in fear like the remnant army of Men before the Gates of Mordor. Yet a small flicker of hope remains. Read on, you who still retain in your heart the courage to fight for liberty and justice and to hope for the return of the King.

What You Can Do Now

1. Keep some cash where the government can't get it. The only way to avoid slavery is through some sort of black market, and some sort of "cash" will be needed: old paper currency, coins, small-denomination gold or silver wafers, coins, etc.
2. Hang on to any real property, real goods. Owning a bit of land anywhere will be a help.
3. Object to this evil plan to replace our currencies. Object to the ongoing debasement of our currencies. Object to unrestrained government spending that *causes* the debasement of the currency and corruption and wars and omnipotent government that takes away our rights and freedoms.
4. Explain what is going on to everyone who will listen. Elect political leaders at all levels of government who have their eyes open to this subversion and will work against it.
5. Use cash for as many purchases as you can. If people keep using cash, the digital currency plans will fail.
6. Get out of debt as much as you can. They will find ways to turn your debts against you–taking everything you own and turning you into a debt slave.
7. We have to dismantle the central banks. They are not needed for a smoothly functioning modern economy. I don't know what kind of financial system we will end up with when this war is over, but what we have now is so thoroughly corrupt and unstable that a financial collapse is inevitable.
8. Almost all assets are going to drop in value. Take steps to protect yourself. Avoid all leveraged investments.

9. Societal collapse on some scale has been planned, is being orchestrated, and is now unavoidable. In response, decentralize everything; go local; take care of your own health, food (grow some), energy, etc. through local connections in your freedom group.
10. Create parallel structures:
    a. Find or start a support group to help each other and push back against the tyranny.
    b. Find people in your community who will continue to use cash or other forms of payment. We must develop an alternative economy so we can operate outside the control system that is quickly enveloping us.
    c. Avoid financial assets as much as possible. These will be taken from you, digitalized, and/or their value will be manipulated to steal any wealth you have.
    d. It may be possible to use local credit unions that are small enough to operate outside the large financial control network. Move your bank accounts out of the major financial institutions and into a purely local one. It might not work, but it might.
    e. Stop working for the enemy. Don't worry about being fired. It's happening to millions of people. It means we are free to set up parallel structures, a new society, and a new way of life.

CHAPTER 19

Solutions—The Escape to Freedom

"Liberty is not the right to do as we please but the opportunity to do what is right."
–REVEREND PETER MARSHALL

A New Level of Thinking

"A new type of thinking is essential if mankind is to survive and move toward higher levels." –ALBERT EINSTEIN

If we accept that nuclear weapons can be used in war and that war can be used to solve problems, then sooner or later we will arrive at the destruction of all life on this planet. In fact, we have come very close to this on at least three occasions during my lifetime. Since no one considers this a desirable outcome, we must find a different way of thinking—a different way of solving problems. As a general rule for both individuals and nations, we must find solutions that do not involve killing people. We are better than that. We *have* to be better than that.

Communism is a philosophy of power. Einstein correctly observed that we cannot solve our problems of power on the level that created those problems. We cannot allow ourselves to take the path of violence. Totalitarianism concentrates power into few hands. As the founding fathers understood, freedom can only exist when power is dispersed—when it is in the hands of everyone. We've had our warning. We need a new paradigm—a new way of thinking. Let me illustrate what I mean with an example from history.

Up to medieval times, cities had protective walls. If anyone had suggested tearing them down and living differently, they would have been rejected as a fool. Yet today no cities have defensive walls. What happened? Artillery happened. Artillery made city walls useless, and people had to think differently. Today, we must once again rethink our "walls." But these are not physical walls.

There is a new iron curtain going up everywhere in the world, but it does not separate geography. World War III is unlike any war in history. In this fifth-generation war, the enemy is invisible. The weapons are electronic, psychological, chemical, and biological. The new iron curtain is tearing apart every family, every community, every nation. We are at war with ourselves. Walls are going up between brothers and sisters, husbands and wives, parents and children. The True Believers who are hypnotized are on one side, the Rebels who perceive what's going on are on the other side. As I have said many times, this is fundamentally a spiritual war and our defense must be spiritual—fought with love, not with force. We must reach across these walls with love and extend a loving hand to anyone who is willing to open their eyes and hearts. The new iron curtain also tries to separate us from God. Seek Him within. He is as close as your breathing.

Just as the lie of Marxism and its physically destructive results stems from a spiritual lie—the denial of God—humanity's physical salvation lies in a spiritual truth. Almost paradoxically, to solve the problems of the world, we must go beyond the world. To solve the problems of philosophy, we must go beyond philosophy. To solve the problems of man, we must turn to God.

The human race has a choice between rebirth and catastrophe. Either we move beyond our present way of thinking, or we will descend into a living hell of violence and oppression. There is no longer a middle path. Fear holds us in the egoic, animal state of consciousness. Love moves us into the divine state of consciousness. The walls we have to tear down are the walls that stop us from loving our neighbors—all our neighbors.

We Have Forgotten God—The Spiritual War

"The most profound analysts of the totalitarian societies of the 20th-century...come to the same conclusion. The totalitarian states would not have been possible without the moral corruption of the individuals within that society." –JORDAN PETERSON

Journalist Jean Chen related the following story in a recent article.

> In 1983, at the Templeton Prize award ceremony in London, Alexander Solzhenitsyn, a survivor of the Soviet Gulag concentration camp, began his remarks with the following memorable words:
>
> "More than half a century ago, while I was still a child, I recall hearing a number of older people offer the following explanation for the great disasters that had befallen Russia: Men have forgotten God; that's why all this has happened.
>
> "Since then I have spent well-nigh fifty years working on the history of our Revolution...But if I were asked today to formulate as concisely as possible the main cause of the ruinous Revolution that swallowed up some sixty million of our people, I could not put it more accurately than to repeat: Men have forgotten God; that's why all this has happened."[1]

We must turn to God. If we succeed in this spiritual war, our victory will be a spiritual victory. And every spiritual war is fought within. Our descent into technocratic totalitarianism is fundamentally caused by the denial of God, which is the denial of love; the worship of power and wealth; the practice of violence, greed, envy, and oppression. It is the choice of death instead of life.

The human disaster that the Deep State oligarchs are heading toward springs from the materialist philosophy of Karl Marx–from a worldview that denies God and attempts to destroy God. We need a higher level of thinking. Humans are not electro-chemical machines to be compared with robots in a simple measure of efficiency. Our purpose for being in this world is not simply a selfish, hedonistic enjoyment of material comforts. And reality itself is not just material reality. Things are not as they seem.

It should come as no surprise that a philosophy that denies the soul, sees human existence only through the narrow lens of eternal class conflict, and exalts power as the supreme human virtue, results in a hell on earth, bereft of peace and love and joy, and most notable for its pulverization of the human person. If you accept the existence of God in any way, then you should be able to understand this cause-consequence relationship. As individuals, and as a society, we either move toward God or away from God. As we move toward God, we will increasingly experience the presence of God: love, peace, joy, compassion, honesty, justice, equality. As we move away from God, especially if we try to attack God, we will increasingly experience the opposite: fear, hatred, anger, violence, destruction, envy, greed, pride, selfishness.

In Truth, there is a greater reality—a spiritual reality—of which the material world is merely a projection, a reflection, an avatar. We are spiritual beings having a human experience. We are created in the image and likeness of God. God is Light and Love. So are we. We are eternal beings of Light and Love. Our purpose in this world is to love, to *be* love, to manifest in physical form the love that we truly are, to be portals through which the Love that is God shines forth into materiality.

This is the higher level of thinking that will lead us out of the darkness that is closing in around us. When we begin to incorporate this thinking into our actions, there will be no need to fight against racism or sexism or any other "ism." There will be no need to fight anything. Love does not fight. Love is what you *are*. The only difficult question becomes "What does love look like in this particular situation?" For Love is not always gentle—sometimes it is firm. Love does not always say "yes"—sometimes it says "no." Love is the beginning for some things—but the ending for other things. Love always forgives—but Love does not remove consequences. Love does not wish for pain—neither does it avoid pain. There is a time for everything under the sun, and the time has come for some things to end. The time has come for lies to end, for fraud to end, for corruption to end, for excessive state and quasi-state power to end. The time has come for a new rebirth of freedom.

The Deep State seeks power over others. But the greatest power is God. The power we seek will not be found in AI but in God—in uniting ourselves with God so completely that His power works through us. Our future lies in realizing that we are One in spirit, not in government. Our unity lies in our humanity and in our spiritual kinship, not in any one-world government.

The Deep State's oppression is sparking a reaction—a reaction of Love. People everywhere, perhaps faced with the common enemy of communism and billionaire oligarchs, are awakening to our common essence. Our uprising in love will lead not only to our emancipation from world tyranny but also to a unity of peace, respect, and understanding that has been the eternal vision of reformers. But the reformation must be in our own hearts. The time has come for all of us to embrace our oneness as members of the human family. To realize there are no strangers, only friends we haven't met yet. It is the unity of good that will abolish the tyranny of evil.

There is no utopia. Perfection is not a characteristic of this universe. Human existence is always full of problems and difficulties. We constantly encounter other people who are selfish, hateful, egotistic, prideful, violent, and fearful. And we constantly encounter these evils within our own hearts. Part of our purpose in this life is to learn to deal with all this and to transcend it through love. If there were no problems, then we would have no opportunity to *choose* love. The choice to improve the world is always the choice to improve ourselves, never to coerce others.

Whatever sin or evil you think you see in another, it is within you—since we are all one. You can never correct the evil by condemning your brother. You must replace it with love *in your own heart.* These beautiful words of Edgar Cayce are perhaps even more appropriate today than when he first spoke them almost a century ago in the depths of the Second World War. They summarize the attitude and actions we must adopt today, in the depths of the Third World War.

> Men may not have the same idea, but man, all men may have the same ideal.
>
> As the spirit of God moved to bring peace and harmony out of chaos, so must the Spirit now move over the earth and magnify itself in the hearts and minds and souls of men that they may dwell together in peace, harmony and understanding; for peace and harmony may only come from having the one ideal as set by Him who gave: "Thou shalt love the Lord thy God with all thine heart, thine neighbor as thyself." This is the whole law, this the answer to the world's troubles today. This ideal in the heart and soul of each will bring peace and plenty out of chaos.
>
> How shall this be brought about? As each, in his respective sphere, puts into action that which he knows to be the fulfilling of that ideal, that law of love, so will the little leaven the whole lump.
>
> Man's answer to everything has been POWER–power of money, power of position, power of this, that or the other. This has never been God's way. Rather, little by little, line upon line, here a little, there a little. When individuals have taken thought of others, they have kept the world intact. Where there were ten just persons, even, many a city, many a nation, has been saved from destruction. We may feel or think the lesson given Abraham as he viewed the cities of the plain and plead for them is an allegorical story, a beautiful tale to be told children that it might bring fear into their hearts, but may it not warm our hearts today? Will you make your own heart right and answer for your brother and neighbor? Who is your neighbor? he that lives next door, or he that lives on the other side of the world? Rather, he who has faltered, he who has fallen by the way; he is your neighbor, and you must answer for him.[2]

What we need most today is not AI or 5G. There is no real need to be served by robots or to have our cars drive themselves or to have our refrigerators tell us when the cottage cheese is moldy or to download video games in three seconds to our cell phones or to pay for our beer by waving our hand at a scanner or for our phone to tell us our blood pressure. We have no need to idle away our lives playing video games in a fantasy metaverse.

But there *is* a need for every soul on earth to find the true meaning of their life through creative service to their brothers and sisters. There *is* a need for every one of us to help those around us to become all they can be. Perhaps ironically, it is in this way that we become all that *we* can be. As Maslow finally realized, self-actualization is achieved *through* self-transcendence.

Your mission, should you choose to accept it, is to manifest this reality in your own life. The *Real* Great Reset needs to be dismantling the apparatus of oppression and setting free your brothers and sisters. We are fighting a battle against darkness, and the weapon of darkness is fear. Love disarms fear. The way you look at the world is the way the world looks back at you. Look with eyes of love. We are warriors of love. We are leaving the consciousness of fear and moving into the consciousness of love. This is the new level of thinking that will save all of us from disaster.

Justice, Forgiveness, and Healing

"The weak can never forgive. Forgiveness is the attribute of the strong." –GANDHI

Many of you are ready to leave behind power struggles, strife, and hatred. Many are not. We need enough loving and forgiving people in our world that those who foment hatred and war no longer have the power to get others to follow them. Healing past injustices only comes through forgiveness–for ALL healing comes through forgiveness. Forgive yourself and forgive others. Replace your guilt and blame with love. The path of love does not travel through justice but through forgiveness. Desire for justice quickly transmutes into the desire for revenge.

But what of justice? We cannot simply forgive everything and allow ourselves to be enslaved by liars, thieves, murderers, and communists. Nor can we allow ourselves to descend into the same murderous rage that we decry in others. How are we to balance forgiveness on the one hand with justice on the other hand? This is always difficult.

The balance between forgiveness and justice was beautifully captured in the famous words of Jesus to the woman who was caught in adultery. The law of that time and place was clear. She was to be stoned to death. Jesus's final words to her were, "Neither do I condemn thee: go, and sin no more" (John 8:11). In short, "I'm not going to kill you, but you must stop doing those things." The unspoken implication being that if she doesn't stop committing adultery, sooner or later, she will be killed.

So it is with the liars, thieves, murderers, and communists who are running our world. We must remove them from their positions where they have been abusing their power. They should stand trial where there is clear evidence of criminality. But just as there is no justice and no peace in throwing stones at sin, we cannot simply grab our guns and start shooting people. That will turn *us* into murderers, drag our nations into endless violence, and hasten the advent of totalitarianism and world destruction. The balance between justice and forgiveness is to be found in nonviolent noncooperation.

Nonviolent Noncooperation

"One hundred thousand Englishman cannot control three hundred million Indians if the Indians simply refuse to cooperate." —GANDHI

As I have said before, we must follow the example of Mahatma Gandhi. In this spiritual war, our strategy is love, our tactic is forgiveness, our weapon is nonviolent noncooperation. If the majority of people refuse to cooperate with the dictatorial decrees of their government, that government will fall.

Millions of us all over the free world have been abdicating our responsibility to democracy. We have been "going along" with encroaching totalitarianism. Every one of us must find the courage to stand up and say "No." We must say "no" to social media cancel smears. We must say "No, we don't fire people from our company based on social media smear campaigns and trolls. We have a fair process in our company for resolving disagreements between people and healing relationships. If you have a complaint against our employee, you can come to our office and discuss it. Otherwise, go away."

We must have the courage to stop financing totalitarian NGOs, and even political parties who don't stand up for liberty and honesty. We must stop funding fraudulent science that is ideologically motivated. We must stop wearing useless face masks and allowing the government to inject unknown substances and biological weapons into our bodies. We must stop allowing our uniformed neighbors and friends to chastise us for visiting our children, playing sports, or singing.

We must stop the 5G system, which is fundamentally a weapons system. It is electromagnetic pollution that is destroying our minds and bodies. We must remove ourselves from the UN completely and all its many fraudulent control arms. We must re-establish sovereignty—of individuals, communities, and nation states. We must re-create our lost democracy. We must not allow the digitalization of everything. Especially, refuse to participate in the digital ID and digital currency systems.

Stop listening to music that appeals to your lowest animal nature and leads you to violence and hatred. Listen instead to music that uplifts, inspires, and leads to transcendence. Reject the Culture of Death, the Philosophy of Death, in all its many manifestations and turn again to God—in whatever way and along whatever path seems true to you and leads to love.

Stop watching television. It is through your screens that the government is controlling your mind. You must be a watchful gatekeeper of your mind and your consciousness. Over 90 percent of what you see there is not real. It is fiction. Media is narrative, and we are in a war of narratives.

Even the news is theater. It is carefully constructed so you will love the protagonist and hate the antagonist. The producers have already picked these roles for you. You are not making these judgments for yourself. You are simply absorbing the value judgments that someone else is intentionally foisting upon you to manipulate you. And Netflix is no better than the news. As bizarre as this sounds, it is all a giant web of mind control. Shut it all off. Be free.

The Rule of Law

"Liberty lies in the hearts of men and women; when it dies there, no constitution, no law, no court can save it; no constitution, no law, no court can even do much to help it." –JUDGE BILLINGS LEARNED HAND

Everyone must insist on the rule of law, not the rule of quasi-dictators or the rule *by* law. Stand up for law and justice, particularly if you are part of the justice system—police, lawyers, prosecutors, judges, prison guards, soldiers. Remember that your allegiance is first to God, to justice, and to your constitution. International law at the Nuremberg trials affirmed that following orders is not a legal defense for any crime. You are called to maintain peace and order and to protect the weak from the abuses of the powerful. That is the noble task entrusted to you. Have courage. You signed on to be strong. *Be strong.* You have the duty to suppress violence, not stand idly by while rioters destroy property and assault peaceful citizens. You can refuse to enforce decrees that violate the constitution. You can refuse to issue tickets to people who simply choose to go to work, to open their businesses, to go for a walk in the park, or to attend their church. The freedoms to do these things are guaranteed in your constitution and in Natural Law.

You must have to courage to say "No" to your superiors when they give you orders that contravene divine law or constitutional law. You will face consequences. There are consequences for every action. However scary it might seem at the time, acting with love and justice brings the most favorable consequences possible. However bitter the pill of honesty may seem, the sickness of lies is worse.

Politicians, scientists, doctors, journalists, judges, lawyers—you have a fiduciary duty you are ignoring while you perpetrate fraud on the whole world. You *will* be brought to justice. You cannot escape the consequences of your present fraud. You are complicit unless you stand up for truth. It's time for all of you to come clean, tell the truth, and give up the lies and fraud and subversion that you have been perpetrating on the rest of us. The time has come to re-establish the rule of law, not the rule of men.

The End of Geopolitics

"You never change things by fighting the existing reality. To change something, build a new model that makes the existing model obsolete." —BUCKMINSTER FULLER

Geopolitics is the study and practice of power. It is the grand game of global despots. People and nations are but pawns in this game of world domination. It's time to put away the game and start behaving like adults. No one can control the whole world. Any attempt to do so will kill us all.

Once you let go of your fear of your fellow human, your desire to control him vanishes. There is no need to fear a strong Iran, or a strong Turkey, or a strong Egypt, or a strong Iraq. There is no possibility that any of these countries could attack the United States, or Britain, or Germany. Nor do the people who live there have any desire to do so. We are being destroyed by our own fear. Let go of fear. Embrace the love that you are. Leave behind the adolescent game of geopolitical power—the giant game of *Risk* that our childish leaders fret and strut about. This has put all of us at risk. It's time to just stop.

The game of geopolitics is enabled by the political structures that have allowed power to be concentrated in so few hands. In almost every country, the national government is supreme and the provincial and local governments are, in a sense, creations of the national government. This is a "top-down" structure of power. We need to reverse this. We need to recognize that the basic unit of *sovereignty* is the individual, then the family, then the community, then the province, then the nation. Each higher level must be firmly restricted in its legal ability to impinge on the sovereignty of the lower levels. Power and responsibility need to be pushed down as far as possible. There is no need for federal power over education or health. These are concerns for the individual, the family, and the community.

The basic unit of *government* is the community or municipality. Various municipalities can voluntarily join together into leagues or provinces, somewhat akin to the Hanseatic League in Medieval Europe, or the cantons of Switzerland. Municipalities can join or leave at will and can define for themselves the benefits and responsibilities of membership. Such a league need not even be amongst geographically contiguous communities. Finally, leagues may join into nation states or leave them if they so choose. Thus, the power and responsibilities of governments are pushed down to the lowest possible level, and the potential for despotism is minimized because communities can simply leave. Under such a distribution of power, we would find little need for large standing armies or for "intelligence" organizations. Those individuals, communities, and leagues that are best able to foster cooperation, peace, and productivity will attract people and wealth to themselves. Those who try to build empires will find themselves isolated and powerless. This is the new level of thinking we need to save our world.

The Butterfly Will Emerge

"The end result, we know, is a butterfly, but the truly astonishing thing is that there is no structural similarity at all between a caterpillar and a butterfly." –ROB EVANS

The world, and all the people in it, are going through an almost unbelievable and historically unprecedented metamorphosis. We are in the chrysalis. The caterpillar calls this the end of the world. Wisdom calls it a butterfly.

We are witnessing incredible destruction all around us. It is not just the human deaths. We are seeing the destruction of society, of the arts, of sports, of long-held beliefs, of whole professions, of industries, of our social structure, of respect for people and professions, and the list goes on. It is a form of societal collapse. This societal collapse is the final communist crisis and the excuse to impose totalitarian tyranny over the whole world. We know it's planned because we know every step leading up to it has been planned, because these events perfectly match the pattern of communist subversion, and because this societal collapse cannot possibly occur naturally.

This darkness is already upon us. There is no escaping the consequences we have already set in motion. The 2020s will be the most tumultuous decade of our lives. Already, we are seeing brother turn against brother. Social behavior is breaking down. Formerly good-willed people are wishing death upon their neighbors. In public, people treat each other with previously unheard-of cruelty while thinking themselves virtuous. Every family is torn apart by "vaxxed" vs. "unvaxxed." Politics is being turned on its head. Leftists and rightists are aligning against tyranny. The older ideological divisions are giving way. Every traditional political party is captured by this tyranny and is self-destructing. What was inconceivable yesterday is happening today.

Economic disruption is everywhere. All the "shutdowns" were planned and unnecessary. All the "supply chain disruptions" were orchestrated for economic collapse. The "everything bubble" will soon pop, and billions of people will lose their life's savings. "By 2030 you will own nothing" was never a prediction. It was the plan. We cannot possibly have economic growth when so many resources are wasted. Just think about how many people, both within governments and without, are spending time and money dealing with nonexistent or engineered problems: fighting drugs, fighting terrorism, fighting the climate, fighting a virus. Think of all the government regulations, the work to comply with these regulations, the taxes, the weapons built then destroyed, the property destroyed, the lives snuffed out, the businesses disrupted, the money misspent. Think about how much richer everyone would be if all of us spent our time and effort actually solving real problems instead of misspending our time, talents, money, and creative energy on destructive and useless activities.

Many will struggle in the coming economic tribulation. We will need to help each other–our brothers and sisters. Do not turn to our corrupt and unreliable governments. Do it yourself. It is darkest just before the dawn. We are entering a great darkness before the light of spiritual love shines through. You can bring darkness, or you can bring light. The choice is yours.

No one is coming to save you. Too many Christians think that Jesus will come on the clouds with a flaming sword to kill all the "bad guys" and save the "good guys." That's not how it works. God gave *you* free will. He put the tools of salvation into *your* hands. *You* must choose. Others think the secret "white hats" will emerge in the final scene to destroy the "black hats" and save the world. You've got the wrong film. Your life, your fortune, and your sacred honor are in your hands alone.[3] *You* must choose. *You* must act.

Remember that totalitarianism is always based on mass formation which is always based on an ideology–it's not "bad guys" but ideology, faulty thinking, distorted perception. You can never simply kill the "bad guys" to end totalitarianism. Other despots will take their place as long as people adhere to the ideology and the mass formation psychosis. You must break the ideology, the lies, the constricted *perception*. As I have said many times, only by *perceiving differently* can you see the truth and avoid totalitarianism.

Those selfish people who seek to impose a modern "divine right of kings" must be swept away with a new "magna carta." Our new "magna carta" must be not simply a power of barons to balance the power of kings but a new constitution that *prevents* the accumulation of power that could enslave others. It must recognize the rights and responsibilities of each person for their own lives. The founding documents of the United States attempted to do this. We must try again.

Many people will resist this. Many will fear it. Responsibility is scary. You might fail. That's the chance you take with freedom. But without freedom, you have no chance at all. Many will ask, "How will people find work without the Department of Labor? How will people be healthy without the Department of Health? How will our children learn without the Department of Education? How will business prosper without the Department of Commerce? How will we avoid drugs without the DEA? How can we be safe without the CIA, the FBI, the DHS, and a dozen other acronyms?"

I hope you are beginning to realize that our oft-lauded government institutions do not help people solve their problems in life. Most often, they do exactly the opposite. We need to learn again that it is not charity to do for a man what he could and should do for himself. That is enslavement. Throughout the world, we have allowed ourselves to become enslaved by the promise of something for nothing. There is no such reality.

The butterfly must fight its own way out of its chrysalis. If you assist it, it dies. So it is with man–with our present metamorphosis. This is true for us as individuals and as a collective. Each of us must struggle against the forces of oppression and coercion that we face in our daily lives. You might be fired from your job if you speak the truth to power. So be it. You might be decertified by your professional association if you call out the lies within it. So be it. You might be insulted and ostracized by your friends and neighbors if you try to show them how they have been deceived. So be it. Your business might be bankrupted by a boycott organized by a collection of communist zealots. So be it. You might be assaulted by police for peacefully protesting against the tyranny of our oppressors. So be it.

You must find the courage within your own heart to do what you believe is right. This is Liberty. As the opening quote to this chapter says, Liberty is not the right to do as we please but the opportunity to do what is right. You *have* the courage to do what is right. It is within you because the Spirit of God is within you and it knows no fear, only love. To fly free like the butterfly you truly are, you must accept the death of the caterpillar and struggle through the chrysalis of fear–on your own. But you are never truly on your own. God is always with you. God is within you. If you are willing to accept it, God is you. If you are Christian, then you know that the Holy Spirit dwells within you. You *are* God expressing through you in your manifestation as a particular human being at a particular moment in time. You are already "one with God." You simply need to recognize this reality.

For those of you with no spiritual understanding, at least know that you have within you the ability to solve every problem that life throws at you. You already have the intelligence, the courage, and the love you need for your life. Just like the Wizard of Oz told the scarecrow, the lion, and the tin man, you already have what you seek. You only need the recognition that it is there. I am not a wizard, but take my word for it. You have all you need. You *can* do it!

Escape to Freedom

"Live not by lies." –ALEKSANDR SOLZHENITSYN

Remember Aleksandr Solzhenitsyn and *Live Not By Lies*. Do not tolerate lies. Insist on honesty. Insist on the truth. Lies bring slavery. "The truth will set you free," (Jn 8:32). Every thought, true or false, is contagious. Your thoughts affect the collective consciousness of the whole planet. When you turn your mind from falsehoods to true thoughts, you help to bring freedom to everyone. Like the hundredth monkey phenomenon, when enough people insist on the truth, all the lies will crumble.

But understand also that freedom lives on the same coin as responsibility. Therefore, accept responsibility, welcome it, embrace it–as if your life depended on it. It does. Your freedom has not been taken from you. You have given it away with your responsibility. Take it back. To shirk your responsibility is a form of corruption. This may be hard for you to accept–that you too have become corrupt. It's much more comforting to blame others for this. You were corrupted by the siren call of ease, by the promise of something for nothing, to trade your sacred freedom for a bowl of porridge. It is a lie. Live not by lies. There is no reality of something for nothing. The little "something" you received you paid for with your responsibility, and your freedom slipped out the door in responsibility's embrace.

Tell your politicians that you do not want handouts or benefits from the government. You want the government to leave you alone—to live your life in peace and to solve your own problems. Do not ask for a government pension, for social security, for welfare, for food stamps, for free medicine, for jobs, or for protection from terrorists or the weather or sickness. You do not need the government to do for you what you can and should do for yourself.

Many will be shocked by this. Some will be offended, some bewildered. If you ever want to see the dawn of a new day of freedom, you must struggle through the dark night of responsibility. Such is the diurnal cycle of life. You cannot have day without night. You cannot have accomplishment without struggle. You cannot have freedom without responsibility. You will never win if you shrink from the fight. You will never find truth if you believe everything you are told. You will never again entertain freedom if you do not also welcome responsibility. This is what it means to truly "grow up."

The escape to freedom is the escape from fear. As the Master Teacher said, there is nothing to fear. Fear is the opposite of love. God is Love. In God there is no fear, for "perfect love casts out all fear," (1 Jn 4:18). Do not fear a virus nor terrorists nor the climate. Do not fear your neighbors—and everyone is your neighbor. In truth, they are your brothers and sisters. They wish you no harm. Those who wish to enslave us have taught us to fear our own brothers and sisters. It is a lie. Live not by lies.

You already have within you all you need, for God is with you. God is your Father, your Creator, your Animator, your Protector, your Refuge, your Confidant, your Guide, your Beginning, and your Ending. It is in God that you live and move and have your Being. You are an eternal being of Light and Love. For you, dear butterfly, there is no death, only transformation. For you, there is no loneliness; God is always with you.

For you, there is no despair; the Joy of God dwells within you. For you, there is no hatred; the Love of God is who you are. For you there is no failure; there is always another opportunity. For you, with God, all things are possible.

The End

Endnotes

Chapter Quotes

Introduction

"I would rather have questions ..."

Richard Feynman (@ProfFeynman), "I would rather have questions that can't be answered than answers that can't be questioned," Twitter, May 12, 2018.

Chapter 1

"Telling the truth ...."

Nirmala. *Nothing Personal: Seeing Beyond the Illusion of a Separate Self.* CreateSpace Publishing, March 2014.

"But know that mercy and truth and justice ...."

Cayce, Edgar. Reading 2995-1. Edgar Cayce Readings. © 1971, 1993-2007 The Edgar Cayce Foundation. All Rights Reserved.

Chapter 2

"The world had never before known ..."

Solzhenitsyn, Aleksandr I. "'Men Have Forgotten God': Aleksandr Solzhenitsyn's 1983 Templeton Address." *National Review.* December 11, 2018.

"The majority believes that everything hard to comprehend ..."
Viktor Schauberger, *Living Energies* (Рипол Классик Publishing, n.d.), 31.

"The only real revolution is ..."
Durant, Will. *The Lessons of History*, 72. Simon & Schuster, 1968.

Chapter 3

"Socialism is a philosophy of failure ...."
Sir Winston Churchill in his speech to the Scottish Unionist Conference at Perth, Scotland on May 28, 1948.

Chapter 4

"The most profound analysts of the totalitarian societies of the twentieth century ..."
Peterson, Jordan. Hoaxed. Documentary film. Random Media & Cerno Films, 2021.

"One death is a tragedy..."
This quote has been attributed to Joseph Stalin since 1947, but it's not clear whether or not he actually said this.

"Thanks to ideology ...."
Solzhenitsyn, Aleksandr. *The Gulag Archipelago: 1918–1956*. 1973.

"Nazism conquered Germany ...."
Von Mises, Ludwig. *Omnipotent Government: The Rise of Total State and Total War.* Yale University Press, 1944.

"The solemn pledge..."
Solzhenitsyn, Aleksandr I. *The Gulag Archipelago: 1918–1956*. 1973.

Chapter 5

"Remember, though, that fraud..."
Cashill, Jack. *Hoodwinked: How Intellectual Hucksters Have Hijacked American Culture*, 215. Thomas Nelson, 2009.

"The urge to save humanity..."
Mencken, Henry Louis. "Minority report: H. L. Mencken's Notebooks," Entry 369, Page 247. Alfred A. Knopf, New York, fourth printing, January 1967.

"The only thing we have to fear...."
Roosevelt, Franklin D. "First Inaugural Address." 1933. Franklin D. Roosevelt Presidential Library & Museum.

"For, the warnings have been given again and again ..."
Cayce, Edgar. "Edgar Cayce Reading 257-228." Edgar Cayce Readings. The Edgar Cayce Foundation, 1971.

Chapter 6

"For some time, I have been disturbed by the way the CIA ..."
Truman, Harry. *The Washington Post*. December 22, 1963.

"The war in Southeast Asia that encompassed Vietnam, ..."
Guyatt, David. "The Octopus: The Criminal Cabal of Guns and Drugs." *SPY Magazine*. November 12, 2001.

Chapter 7

"Empirical evidence is the truth that theory must mimic, not the other way around."
Wood, Judy. "Where Did The Towers Go?" *Jerm Warfare*. Podcast interview. Friday, September 17, 2021

"Another way to cover up the truth ...."
Wood, Judy. "Where Did The Towers Go?" *Jerm Warfare*. Podcast interview. Friday, September 17, 2021.

"The 'human-caused global warming' ..."
Robinson, Arthur B.; Robinson, Noah E.; and Soon, Willie. "Environmental Effects of Increased Atmospheric Carbon Dioxide." *Journal of American Physicians and Surgeons* (2007) 12, 79-90.

"There is no energy crisis, only a crisis of ignorance."
R. Buckminster Fuller in SocialSynergistics, Curricula for Evolving Organizations, "R. Buckminster Fuller," accessed August 8, 2022,

"We know that no one ever seizes ..."
Orwell, George. *1984*. Secker & Warburg, 1949.

"A dictatorship means muzzles all round and consequently stultification."
Einstein, Albert. "Science and Dictatorship." *Dictatorship on Its Trial, by Eminent Leaders of Modern Thought*. Otto Forst de Battaglia, ed., Huntley Paterson, trans., introduction by Winston Churchill. George G. Harrap & Co., 1930. Reprinted 1977, Beaufort Books Inc. Original text of this "nineteen word essay" appears under the German title "Wissenschaft und Diktatur" in *Prozess der Diktatur* (1930), Otto Forst de Battaglia, ed., Amalthea-Verlag.

Chapter 8

"Don't make a fuss about a world war. ..."
Mao Zedong in Jung Chang and Jon Halliday, *Mao: The Unknown Story* (Jonathan Cape, 2005), 458.

"War is everything. Everything is war."
Lee, Donald.

Chapter 9

"The most dangerous of all sciences ..."
Mundy, Talbot. Quoted in Jones, Marie D. and Flaxman, Larry. *Mind Wars: Who's Been Watching You From the Shadows?*, 21. New Page Books, 2015.

"The ultimate tyranny in a society ...."
Marciniak, Barbara. *Bringers of the Dawn*. Bear & Co., 1992.

"The basic tool for the manipulation of ..."
Dick, Philip K. Quoted in Jones, Marie D. and Flaxman, Larry. *Mind Wars: Who's Been Watching You From the Shadows?*, 71. New Page Books, 2015.

"The mind is everything. What you think, you become."
Buddha.

Chapter 10

"The rise of the internet ..."
Epstein, Robert. "Google's Triple Threat: To Democracy, Our Children, and Our Minds," 3. January 20, 2022

"The NSA has built an infrastructure that allows it to intercept almost everything."
Edward Snowden, interview by Ewan MacAskill, *The Guardian,* accessed August 8, 2022,

"The media's the most powerful entity on earth. ..."
Malcolm X, in Nick Friar, "Kyrie Irving Shares Malcolm X Quote on Instagram: "Media's the most Powerful Entity on Earth," *USA Today.com,* September 2, 2020,

Chapter 11

"Most terrorists are false flag terrorists..."
David Steele, in Shoshi Hershu, *Mass Awakening* (Bloomington, IN: Balboa Press, 2018), chapter 5.

"We will know our disinformation program is complete ..."
William Casey, in Tony Heller, Real Climate Science, April 13, 2022,

Chapter 12

"Let us not forget that violence ...."
Solzhenitsyn, Aleksandr. *The Oak and the Calf.* 1975.

"Another way to cover up the truth ...."
Wood, Judy. "Where Did The Towers Go?" *Jerm Warfare.* Podcast interview. Friday, September 17, 2021

"When people who are honestly ...!" –Anonymous

Chapter 13

"In times of universal deceit..."
–Wrongly attributed to George Orwell, source unknown.

"Never do anything against conscience even if the state demands it."
Einstein, Albert. Quoted in Henshaw, Virgil. *Albert Einstein: Philosopher Scientist*. Schilpp, Paul A., ed. 1949.

"No enterprise is more likely to succeed ..."
Machiavelli, Niccolo. *The Art of War, Book 7*, trans. Christopher Lynch. (University of Chicago Press. 2005).

Chapter 14

"Truth is the first casualty of war. With ...."
Lee, Donald.

"We therefore define SARS-CoV-2 as an Unrestricted Bioweapon and the current pandemic a result of Unrestricted Biowarfare."
Yan, Li-Meng; Kang, Shu; and Hu, Shanchang. "SARS-CoV-2 Is an Unrestricted Bioweapon: A Truth Revealed through Uncovering a Large-Scale, Organized Scientific Fraud." *Zenodo*. October 8, 2020.

Chapter 15

"Keep the enemy in the dark about where and when our forces will attack."
Mao Zedong, in Shu Guang Zhang, China and the Korean War, 1950–1953 (Lawrence, KS: University Press of Kansas, 1995), 22.

"In the field of biological weapons, there is almost no prospect of detecting a pathogen until it has been used in an attack."
Barton Gellman, "U.S., Terrorism's Peril Undiminished," *Washington Post*, December 24, 2002,

Chapter 16

"Vote early and vote often."

Often attributed to William Lyon MacKenzie King, Canada's longest-serving prime minister, 1921–1930 and 1935–1948.

Chapter 17

"Hard times create strong men. ..."

This quote is found in Rob Scott, *Resonance* (Lulu.com, 2022) and is attributed to a sheik. Some report it may have been Sheik Rashid, founder of Dubai.

"The Council on Foreign Relations has always opposed national sovereignty, ..."

Perloff, James. *Truth is a Lonely Warrior: Unmasking the Forces Behind Global Destruction*, 88. Refuge Books. Kindle Edition. 2013.

"Men who can manage men, ..."

Durant, Will and Durant, Ariel. *The Lessons of History*, 54. Simon & Schuster, New York. 1968.

"The drive of the Rockefellers and their ...."

This quote is widely attributed to Congressman Larry P. McDonald, 1976, killed on the Korean Airlines 747 flight.

"The history of the West, from the age of the Greek Polis down to the present-day resistance to socialism, is essentially the history of the fight for liberty against the encroachments of the officeholders."

Von Mises, Ludwig. *The Ultimate Foundation of Economic Science: An Essay on Method, 98.* Princeton, NJ: D. Van Nostrand. 1962.

Chapter 18

"Lenin was certainly right, there is no more positive, ..."

Keynes, John Maynard. *The Economic Consequences of the Peace: With a New Introduction by Michael Cox.* Cox, Michael ed. Palgrave Macmillan Cham. 2019.

"The currency system has been used to ..."
Fitts, Catherine Austin. "The State of Our Currencies: The End of Currencies, 2nd Quarter Wrapup." *The Solari Report* 2019, no. 4 (April 2020): 20.

"[Bankers] know that history is inflationary, and money is the last thing a wise man will hoard."
Durant, Will and Durant, Ariel. *The Lessons of History*, 54. Simon & Schuster, New York. 1968.

"Who controls the food supply controls the people. ..."
–Apparently misattributed to Henry Kissinger. Attribution unknown.

"One ring to rule them all."
Tolkien, J.R.R. *The Fellowship of the Ring.* HarperCollins, 1999.

"Study the past if you want to define the future."
Confucious

Chapter 19

"Liberty is not the right to do as we please but the opportunity to do what is right."
Marshall, Reverend Peter. Quoted in Wogan, Gen. John B. "Rights And Duties Of Citizens" Quote Page B4, Column 6. *Asheville Citizen-Times.* Asheville, North Carolina. April 10, 1949.

"A new type of thinking is essential if mankind is to survive and move toward higher levels."
Einstein, Albert. Quoted in "Atomic Education Urged By Einstein: Scientist in Plea for $200,000 to Promote New Type of Essential Thinking." *New York Times.* May 25, 1946.

"The most profound analysts of the totalitarian ..."
Peterson, Jordan. Hoaxed. Documentary film. Random Media & Cerno Films, 2021.

"The weak can never forgive. Forgiveness is the attribute of the strong."
Gandhi, Mahatma. Quoted in *Young India.* April 2, 1931.

"One hundred thousand Englishman cannot ..."
Gandhi. Film, 1982. Sony Pictures. Richard Attenborough, director.

"Liberty lies in the hearts of men and women..."
Billings Learned Hand, "We Seek Liberty: If It Dies in Men's Hearts, No Court Can Save It," *Life*, June 3, 1944, 20.

"You never change things by fighting the existing reality...."
Fuller, Buckminster. Quoted in Quinn, Daniel. *Beyond Civilization: Humanity's Next Great Adventure*, 137. 1999.

"The end result, we know, is a butterfly, but ..."
Evans, Rob. "The Story of Imaginal Cells." *Imaginal Labs.* Accessed June 23, 2022.

"Live not by lies."
Alexander Solzhenitsyn, *Between Two Milestones, Book 1: Sketches of Exile, 1974–1978* (Indiana: Notre Dame Press, 2018).

Chapter Notes

Introduction

1. Juliana Kaplan, "American Billionaires Added $1.1 Trillion in Wealth During the Pandemic," *Business Insider Australia*, January 26, 2021.

Chapter 1

1. "Alexander Solzhenitsyn: Live Not by Lies," *Sign of the Times*,

2. John J. Couglin, "Pope John Paul II and the Dignity of the Human Being," *NDL Scholarship* 27 no. 1 (2003): 65. The description seems to stem from this comment, quoted from a 1968 letter to Henri de Lubac: *"The evil of our times consists in the first place in a kind of degradation,* ***indeed in a pulverization, of the fundamental uniqueness of each human person.*** *This evil is even more of the metaphysical order than of the moral order. To this disintegration planned at times by atheistic ideologies we must oppose, rather than sterile polemics, a kind of 'recapitulation' of the inviolable mystery of the person."*

3. Elena Gorokhova, *A Mountain of Crumbs* (Simon and Schuster, 2011).

4. *The New Jerusalem Bible* (Doubleday, 1985).

5. *The New Jerusalem Bible* (Doubleday, 1985).

6. Pierre Teilhard De Chardin, *The Phenomenon of Man* (1955).

7. Saul McLeod, "Simply Psychology: Maslow's Hierarchy of Needs," May 21, 2018.

8. *The New Jerusalem Bible* (Doubleday, 1985).

9. Susan Shumsky, *The Big Book of Chakras and Chakra Healing: How to Unlock Your Seven Energy Centers for Healing, Happiness, and Transformation* (Weiser Books, 2019).

Chapter 2

1. Murray Rothbard, "The American Revolution and Classical Liberalism," *Mises Institute*, July 3, 2021.

2. Chris Calton, "How the Progressives Conquered Corporate America," *Mises Institute*, February 5, 2021.

3. Karl Marx and Fredrich Engels, "The Communist Manifesto," London, 1948.

4. Ludwig von Mises, *Theory and History: An Interpretation of Social and Economic History,* (The Ludwig von Mises Institute, 1957). 190.

5. Friedrich Nietzsche, *The Gay Science*, trans. Thomas Common. (Dover Publ. 2006). 90-91

6. Jean Paul Sartre, *Being and Nothingness (Washington Square Press, 1993).* The quote comes originally from Dostoyevsky's novel *The Brothers Karamazov,* in which a character suggests that if God does not exist, then everything would be permitted. Sartre adopted this fictional character's thought as his own, saying, since there is no god, then everything is permitted.

7. Paul Kengor, *The Devil and Karl Marx: Communism's Long March of Death, Deception, and Infiltration*, Kindle edition (Tan Books, 2020): 345.

8. Helen Pluckrose and James Lindsay, "Postmodernism: A Revolution in Knowledge and Power" in *Cynical Theories: How Activist Scholarship Made Everything about Race, Gender, and Identity□and Why This Harms Everybody,* Audiobook (Pitchstone Publishing, 2020): 21–44.

9. Paul Kengor, *The Devil and Karl Marx: Communism's Long March of Death, Deception, and Infiltration*, Kindle edition (Tan Books, 2020): 392–393.

10. Dr. Ed Prida, "Subversion Against America," PDF slide presentation, *Academia.edu*, accessed March 29, 2021.

11. Patrick M. Wood, *Technocracy: The Hard Road to World Order*, Audiobook version (Coherent Publishing, 2018).

12. Hannah Arendt, *The Origins of Totalitarianism* (Andesite Press, August 2017).

13. Dr. Peter Breggin and Ginger R. Breggin, *Covid-19 and the Global Predators: We Are the Prey*, Kindle edition (Lake Edge Press, 2021). 420

14. Arthur C. Clarke, *Profiles of the Future: An Inquiry Into the Limits of the Possible* (Henry Holt & Company, 1984).

15. *New International Version Bible* (Zondervan, 2018).

Chapter 3

1. Tomas D. Schuman [Yuri Bezmenov], "The Four Stages of Subversion of a Country" in *Love Letter to America* (W.I.N. Almanac Panorama, Los Angeles, 1984).

2. Sun Tzu, "Laying Plans" in *The Art of War*, verse 18.

3. Yuri Bezmenov, "Subversion of the Free-World Press: A Conversation with Yuri Bezmenov," interview by G. Edward Griffin, *All West Media*, retrieved July 8, 2020.

4. Schuman, 17–18.

5. Schuman, 21.

6. Schuman, 27.

7. Schuman, 33.

8. Vaclav Havel, *The Power of the Powerless*, Vintage Classics, trans. Paul Wilson (Penguin Random House, London, 2018).

Chapter 4

1. Jean Chen, "Opinion: A Mom's Research (Part 4): Why Are Many Elites Leftists?," *The Epoch Times* (April 26, 2021).

2. Jesse Greenspan, "9 Things You May Not Know About Mussolini," History.com, accessed Feb. 22, 2021.

3. Greenspan.

4. Benito Mussolini, "The Political and Social Doctrine of Fascism," trans. Jane Soames, *Day to Day Pamphlets #18* (The Hogarth Press, London, 1933).

5. Mussolini, 20.

6. Mussolini, 21.

7. F.L. Carsten, *The Rise of Fascism*, 2nd ed. (University of California Press, 1982): 62.

8. María Andrea Gomez Torrealba, "Joseph Goebbels' Principles of Nazi Propaganda applied to Digital Marketing," *Visionar* (September 6, 2017).

9. Ludwig von Mises, "The Weimar Republic" in *Omnipotent Government: The Rise of Total State and Total War* (Yale University Press, 1944): 222.

10. Dr. Daniel Amen, "Col. Oliver North Interviews Dr. Daniel Amen on the 'Global Amygdala Hijacking'," *Amen Clinics* (May 29, 2020).

11. This section is based on the work of Mattias Desmet, expressed in many interviews and in his book: Mattias Desmet, *The Psychology of Totalitarianism* (Chelsea Green Publishing, June 2022). Also see his podcast interview: Mattias Desmet, "The Covid Narrative is Mass Hypnosis," interview on *Jerm Warfare* podcast, September 4, 2021.

12. Helen Schucman, *A Course in Miracles: Combined Volume,* 3rd ed. (Foundation for Inner Peace, 2007): W-p1.161.7.1-5

Chapter 5

1. Jason Fernando, "Bre-X Minerals Ltd.," *Investopedia* (October 12, 2020).

2. "U.S. Life Expectancy 1950–2022," *Macrotrends*, accessed March 18, 2022.

3. Josh Sigurdson, "Hidden Vaccines In Your Food?," *The White Rose*, October 12, 2021.

4. "What Is Codex? The Origins of Codex," *National Health Freedom*, January 2, 2016.

5. Denise Minger, *Death by Food Pyramid: How Shoddy Science, Sketchy Politics and Shady Special Interests Have Ruined Our Health* (Primal Nutrition, Inc., 2014): 148.

6. Nina Teicholz, *The Big Fat Surprise: Why Butter, Meat and Cheese Belong in a Healthy Diet* (Simon & Schuster, 2014): 115.

7. Mark Sisson, *Mark's Daily Apple*.

8. Mark Sisson, "Updating the Primal Stance on Vegetable Oils: High-Oleic Varieties," *Mark's Daily Apple*.

9. Jordan Gill, "Almost Half of Canadians Will Get Cancer: Meet One Island Survivor," *CBC News*, June 20, 2017.

10. Torsten Engelbrecht and Claus Köhnlein, *Virus Mania: Corona/COVID-19, Measles, Swine Flu, Cervical Cancer, Avian Flu, SARS, BSE, Hepatitis C, AIDS, Polio, Spanish Flu. How the Medical Industry Continually Invents Epidemics, Making Billion-Dollar Profits At Our Expense* (Books On Demand, 2021): 10.

11. "US Healthcare Industry in 2022: Analysis of the Health Sector, Healthcare Trends, & Future of Digital Health," *Insider Intelligence*, January 11, 2022.

12. There are many examples of these prosecutions, such as the following: Christine Niles, "Colorado Catholic Hospital Sued for Disallowing Euthanasia," *Church Militant News*, September 10, 2019.

13. Health Canada, "Medical Assistance in Dying," *Government of Canada*, accessed March 18, 2022..

14. Right to Life Michigan, "Doctors and Hospitals are Placing Secret DNR Orders in Patient's Files," *Life News*, November 16, 2017.

Chapter 6

1. University of Toronto, "Archaeologists find earliest evidence of winemaking: Discovery of 8,000-year-old wine production in ancient Middle East," *ScienceDaily*, November 13, 2017.

2. Mike Lofgren, "Essay: Anatomy of the Deep State," *Bill Moyers*, blog post, February 19, 2014.

3. "Opium Trade," in *Encyclopædia Britannica* (2008), retrieved March 18, 2022.

4. Emily Bell, "This 75 Billion Dollar Business Was Built Selling Whiskey During Prohibition...Legally," *VinePair*, November 16, 2015.

5. "What were some positive effects of prohibition?" *Treehozz*, June 2, 2020.

6. History.com Editors, "Prohibition," *A&E Television Networks*, January 27, 2020.

7. Joel van der Reijden, CIA Drug Trafficking Timeline: 1940s–21st Century in "A History of CIA Drug Trafficking: How Drug Cartels and Drug-Dealing Death Squads Have Been the CIA's Best Friends for Many Decades," *Institute for the Study of Globalization and Convert Politics*, August 19, 2020. https://isgp-studies.com/cia-heroin-and-cocaine-drug-trafficking.

8. Van der Reijden.

9. Fred Burks, "Military Smuggling Drugs Heroin Smuggled in Body Bags of GIs reported by Military Eye Witness," *WanttoKnow.info*, accessed March 18, 2022.

10. Alfred W. McCoy, *The Politics of Heroin in Southeast Asia* (HarperCollins, 1972): 8.

11. David Guyatt, "The Octopus: The Criminal Cabal of Guns and Drugs," *SPY Magazine*, November 12, 2001.

12. Van der Reijden.

13. The Epoch Times, "The Cultural Revolution of the West" in *How The Specter of Communism is Ruling Our World* (2020), 114.

14. Epoch Times, 115.

15. Epoch Times, 164.

16. Alexander Cockburn and Jeffrey St. Claire, *Whiteout: The CIA, Drugs, And the Press* (Verso, 1999): 180.

17. Cockburn and St. Claire, 181.

18. "A Complete History of Crack Cocaine," *Lighthouse Treatment Center*, March 28, 2018.

19. PBS, "Interview: Peter Bourne," *Frontline*, 2020.

20. Van der Reijden, Globalization and Convert Politics, endnote 14.

21. Cheri Seymour [Carol Marshall], "Chapter 8" in *The Last Circle: Danny Casolaro's Investigation into the Octopus and the PROMIS Software Scandal* (2010).

22. Loretta Napoleoni, *Modern Jihad: Tracing the Dollars Behind the Terror Networks* (Pluto Press, 2003). See also Chris Petit, *Smart Money* (The Guardian, December 13, 2003).

23. Van der Reijden, Globalization and Convert Politics, endnote 44. See also Jeremy Hammond, "The CIA's Suitcases of Cash to Afghan Drug Lords," Jeremyrhamon.com, April 30, 2013. See also Reality Check Team, "Afghanistan: How much opium is produced and what's the Taliban's record?," *BBC News*, August 25, 2021.

24. Daniel Lizt [The Dark Journalist], "Secret Space Program Conference Roundtable with Catherine Austin Fitts, Linda Moulton Howe, & Dr. Joseph Farrell," *The Secret Space Program Conference*, 2015, 1 hour and 30 minutes into the video.

25. Adrianna Belmonte, "How China flooded the U.S. with lethal fentanyl, fueling the opioid crisis," *Yahoo Finance*, February 20, 2020.

26. Gordon Chang, "Gordon Chang on Chinese Drug Warfare, Military Buildup on the China-India Border, and Crackdown on Didi," *The Epoch Times*, documentary, July 13, 2021.

27. NIH, "Overdose Death Rates," *National Institute on Drug Abuse*, updated January 20, 2022.

28. Canadian Press, "B.C. Records Deadliest February yet for Illicit Drug Overdose Deaths," *The Epoch Times*, March 25, 2021.

29. Charlotte Cuthbertson, "Fentanyl Flowing Into United States at Record Volume," *The Epoch Times*, March 14, 2021.

30. Peter Skurkiss, "Wuhan's Fingerprints Are Also All Over the Opiod Epidemic," *American Thinker*, May 26, 2020.

31. Commission on Combating Synthetic Opioid Trafficking, "Final Report," *Rand.org*, February 2022, page 9.

32. "Facing Fentanyl: How Americans are Facing the Facts, Overcoming Stigma, and Saving Lives Today. Life and Times," Youtube video, April 7, 2021.

33. Captain Rodney Stich, *Drugging America: A Trojan Horse*, 2nd ed. (Silverpeak Publishers, 2008).

34. Stich, 4160–4180.

35. Michael Levine, *The Big White Lie: The Deep Cover Operation That Exposed the CIA Sabotage of the Drug War* (Laura Cavangh-Levine, 2012).

Chapter 7

1. Arthur B. Robinson, Noah E. Robinson, and Willie Soon, "Environmental Effects of Increased Atmospheric Carbon Dioxide," *Global Warming Petition Project. Journal of American Physicians and Surgeons* (2007) 12, 79-90

2. Robinson, Robinson, and Soon, 5.

3. C.B. Thorington, "CO_2 Levels In Air Dangerously Low for Life," *A Divided World*, May 13, 2017.

4. Robinson, Robinson, and Soon, 6.

5. CO_2 Coalition, "Carbon Dioxide Benefits the Earth: See for Yourself," *CO_2 Coalition.*

6. Chi Chen et al., "China and India Lead in Greening of the World Through Land-Use Management," *Nature Sustainability* 2 (2019): 122–129.

7. Paul Cooper, "These 4 Ancient Apocalypses Changed the Course of Civilization," *Discover Magazine*, July 26, 2019.

8. David Lappi, "65 Million Years of Cooling," *JoNova*, February 18, 2010.

9. Dr. Tim Ball, *Human Caused Global Warming: The Biggest Deception in History* (Tellwell Talent, 2016): 34.

10. Ball, 35

11. Francis Menton, "More Confirmation Of The Infeasibility Of A Fully Wind/Solar/Storage Electricity System," *Manhattan Contrarian*, March 21, 2022.

12. Nina Chestney, "Global Carbon Markets Value Surged to Record $851 Bln Last Year-Refinitiv," *Reuters*, January 31, 2022.

13. Donella H. Meadows, Jorgen Randers, Dennis L. Meadows, and William W. Behrens, *Limits to Growth: A report for the Club of Rome's Project on the Predicament of Mankind* (Universe Book, 1972).

14. Paul R. Ehrlich, *The Population Bomb* (MacMillan, 1968).

15. Alexander King, *The First Global Revolution: A Report by the Council of the Club of Rome* (Pantheon, 1991).

16. Ball, 80–81.

17. Dr. Patrick Moore, *Ecosense.*

18. Ball, 79.

19. Jordan Hayne, "Marine Scientist Peter Ridd Gets Chance to Fight James Cook University Dismissal in High Court," *ABC News*, February 11, 2021.

20. Michael Haverluck, "Former NOAA Scientist from Climate-Change Alarmist to 'Denier'," *One News Now*, August 3, 2019.

21. Ball, 42.

22. J. Hansen, R. Ruedy, J. Glascoe, and M. Sato, "GISS Analysis of Surface Temperature Change," *NASA Goddard Institute for Space Studies, New York* (1999): 37, figure 6.

23. "U.S. Temperature," *NASA.*

24. Bjorn Lomborg, *False Alarm: How Climate Change Panic Costs Us Trillions, Hurts the Poor, and Fails to Fix the Planet* (Basic Books, NY, 2020): 4.

25. Elana Freeland, *Geoengineered Transhumanism: How the Environment Has Been Weaponized by Chemicals, Electromagnetism & Nanotechnology for Synthetic Biology* (self-pub, Amazon Digital Services, October 2021): 45. Kindle.

26. Fred Burks, "HAARP: Weather Control Is the HAARP Project a Weather Control Weapon?," *WantToKnow.info*.

27. Susan Duclos, "Air Force Bombshell: Admits They Can Control Weather–HAARP," *Wake Up America*, May 15, 2014.

28. Bernard Potter, "IPCC Official: 'Climate Policy is Redistributing The World's Wealth,'" interview with Ottmar Edenhofer, *Neue Zurcher Zeitung*, November 14, 2010.

Chapter 8

1. Patrick M. Wood, "12 Days of Technocracy: Day 7: China Is A Technocracy," *Technocracy News*, December 27, 2021.

2. Cathy He, "'Fighting Us on a Daily Basis': Expert Sounds Alarm on CCP's Political Warfare Against the West," *The Epoch Times*, March 27, 2021.

3. Kathy He, "'3 Warfares' Doctrine Underpins CCP's Sprawling Campaign to Infiltrate the West: Report," *The Epoch Times*, September 29, 2021.

4. Mimi Nguyen Li, "Harvard Professor Charles Lieber Convicted of Lying About China Ties," *The Epoch Times*, December 22, 2021.

5. Michael Phillsbury, *The Hundred-Year Marathon, China's Secret Strategy to Replace America as the Global Superpower* (St. Martin's Griffin, 2016).

6. James Dale Davidson, "China Builds 27 Empty New York Cities," *The Epoch Times*, January 23, 2022.

7. Davidson.

8. "Murder in Malta, money trail leads to China...," *China In Focus*, April 6, 2021.

9. Michael Birnbaum, "Montenegro Mortgaged Itself to China. Now It Wants Europe's Help to Cut It Free," Washington Post, April 18, 2021.

10. Bradley S. Van Gosen, Philip L. Verplanck, Robert R. Seal II, Keith R. Long, and Joseph Gambogi, "Rare-Earth Elements, Chapter O of Critical Mineral Resources of the United States–Economic and Environmental Geology and Prospects for Future Supply," Klaus J. Schulz, John H. DeYoung, Jr., Robert R. Seal II, and Dwight C. Bradley ed., *Professional Paper 1802–O, U.S. Department of the Interior U.S. Geological Survey, U.S. Geological Survey, Reston, Virginia* (2017).

11. Frank Fang, "China Has Fully Militarized 3 South China Sea Islands: US Indo-Pacific Commander," *The Epoch Times*, March 21, 2022.

12. Michael Pillsbury, "The Hundred-Year Marathon: China's Secret Strategy to Replace America as the Global Superpower," *The Hundred-Year* Marathon.

13. Jim Garamone, "Esper: Air Force, Space Force Leading Charge to New Technologies," *Department of Defense News*, September 16, 2020.

14. Jeff Brown, "China Is Building a Solar Power Plant in Space," *Brownstone Research*, newsletter, July 7, 2021.

15. Gordon Chang, "Gordon Chang on Chinese Drug Warfare, Military Buildup on the China-India Border, and Crackdown on Didi," *The Epoch Times*, documentary, July 13, 2021.

16. Peter Falkenburg Brown, "America: The Last Best Hope of Earth," *CD Media*, March 16, 2022. /. The whole translated speech is reproduced here: "The Secret Speech of General Chi Haotian," *J.R. Nyquist Blog*, September 11, 2019.

17. Qiao Liang and Wang Xiangsui, "Unrestricted Warfare (1999)," *Beijing: PLA Literature and Arts Publishing House*, February 1999.

18. "Fifth Generation Warfare–How We Have Already Entered an Ambiguous WWIII," *Superesse*, April 15, 2021.

19. Jeffrey Prather, "Socom Secret Shawdonet Stolen," *Prather Point*, March 31, 2022.

20. Nicole Hao, "CCP at 100 Years: A Century of Killing and Deceit," *The Epoch Times*, July 2, 2021.

21. Eva Fu, "Stay Away From the CCP, It's 'Like Poison': Chinese Torture Survivor Tells the World," *The Epoch Times*, July 14, 2021.

22. Fu.

Chapter 9

1. Marie D. Jones and& Larry Flaxman, *Mind Wars: A History of Mind Control, Surveillance, and Social Engineering by the Government, Media, and Secret Societies* (New Page Books, 2015): 33.

2. Jones and Flaxman, 45.

3. George K. Simon, *In Sheep's Clothing: Understanding and Dealing With Manipulative People* (Parkhurst Bros., Chicago, Illinois, 1996).

4. Jones and Flaxman, 73–74.

5. Jones and Flaxman, 73–74.

6. Dr. Margaret Singer, "Coercive Mind Control Tactics," *F.A.C.T.Net.org.*

7. J.R.R. Tolkien, *The Hobbit* (Harper Collins, 2011).

8. George Orwell, *1984* (Praetorian Books, 2021).

9. Jones and Flaxman, 162.

10. Stefan Molyneux, "Cancel Culture Is a Dress Rehearsal for Mass Murder," Youtube video, accessed Feb. 23, 2021.

11. Quoted in Paul Kengor, *The Devil and Karl Marx: Communism's Long March of Death, Deception, and Infiltration* (Tan Books, 2020): 363.

12. Dr. Daniel Amen, "The Devastation of Mobbing," *Amen Clinics Newsletter*, March 15, 2021.

13. Sharyl Attkisson, *Slanted: How the News Media Taught Us to Love Censorship and Hate Journalism* (Harper, 2020).

14. Bari Weiss, "Letter of Resignation," *BariWeiss.com.*

15. Kipp Jones, "Top-Rated News Anchor Resigns, Destroys Establishment Media Bias in Video," *The Western Journal*, March 2, 2021.

16. Udo Ulfkotte, *Presstitutes: Imbedded in the Pay of the CIA–A Confession from the Profession*, trans. Andrew Schlademan (Progressive Press, 2019).

17. Catherine Austin Fitts, Chapter IV: Space, the National Security State, Secrecy, and Privatization in "The State of Our Currencies: The End of Currencies, 2nd Quarter Wrapup," *The Solari Report* 2019, no. 4 (April 2020).

18. Dick Russell, "Part 1: CIA's Extraordinary Role Influencing Liberal Media Outlets Daily Kos, The Daily Beast, Rolling Stone," *The Defender*, December 12, 2021.

19. Jones and Flaxman, 138.

20. Jones and Flaxman,135.

21. Jones and Flaxman, 141.

22. Jones and Flaxman, 141.

23. Jerry Mander, *Four Arguments for the Elimination of Television* (William Morrow Paperbacks, 1978).

24. Alex Ansary, "Mass Mind Control Through Network Television: Are Your Thoughts Your Own?," *Rense.com*, December 29, 2005.

25. Scott Z. Burns, *Contagion*, 2011, film, directed by Steven Soderbergh.

26. Jones and Flaxman, 138–9.

27. Colonel Paul E. Valley and Lieutenant Colonel Michael A. Aquino, "From PSYOP to MindWar: The Psychology of Victory," *US PSYOP Research & Analysis Team Leader* (1980): 2.

28. Valley and Aquino, 9.

29. Valley and Aquino, 9–10.

30. Jones and Flaxman, 166.

31. Jones and Flaxman, 167.

32. Jones and Flaxman, 177.

33. Gloria Naylor, *1996* (Chicago, Illinois: Third World Press, 2007).

34. John Hall, *Guinea Pigs: Technologies of Control* (Strategic Book Publishing, 2015). E-book.

35. John Hall, *A New Breed: Satellite Terrorism in America* (Lightning Source Inc., 2009).

36. N.I. Anisimov, *Psychotronic Golgotha* (1999).

37. Shobhit Seth, "The World's Top Media Companies," *Investopedia*, October 7, 2020.

38. Larry Sanger, *Essays on Free Knowledge: The Origins of Wikipedia and the New Politics of Knowledge* (Sanger Press, September 2020).

Chapter 10

1. Yasha Levine, *Surveillance Valley: The Secret Military History of the Internet* (PublicAffairs/Hachette, New York, 2018): 186. E-book.

2. Levine, 189.

3. Levine, 192.

4. Ryan Gallagher and Glen Greenwald, "How the NSA Plans to Infect "Millions" of Computers with Malware," *The Intercept*, March 12, 2014.

5. Levine, 121.

6. Levine, 200–250.

7. Levine, 261–262.

8. Levine, 61–62.

9. Levine, 87–90.

10. John Hall, *Guinea Pigs: Technologies of Control* (Strategic Book Publishing, 2015): 91.

11. Dr. Robert Epstein, "Google's Triple Threat: To Democracy, Our Children, and Our Minds," January 20, 2022.

12. Epstein, 16.

13. Dustin Broadbery, "How the West Was Won: Counterinsurgency, PSYOPS and the Military Origins of the Internet, Part 1," *The Cogent*, March 4, 2022.

14. Broadberry.

15. Levine, 231–33.

16. Levine, 249.

17. Levine, 251.

18. Hall, 76.

19. Jane Wakefield, "Elon Musk's Neuralink 'shows monkey playing Pong with mind,'" *BBC News*, April 9, 2021. Also see "Monkey MindPong," *NeuraLink*.

20. Jack El-Hai, "The Man Who Fought a Bull With Mind Control," *Discover Magazine*, March 21. 2016.

21. Sarah Westall and Dave Hodges, "COVID & Mind Control, How They Did It–Sarah Westall on the Dave Hodges Show," *Business Game Changers*. See also: Ash, "Darpa, Nano, Mind Control, Dreadds, Chemogenetics, Hive Mind," UGETube, December 24, 2020.

22. Hall, 92.

23. Hall, 24.

24. Hall, 25.

Chapter 11

1. Dwight D. Eisenhower, "Military-Industrial Complex Speech," *Lilian Goldman Law Library, The Avalon Project*, 1961.

2. Robert F. Kennedy. Jr. *American Values: Lessons I Learned From My Family* (Harper, 2018).

3. John Perkins, *The Secret History of the American Empire: The Truth About Economic Hitmen, Jackals, and How to Change the World* (Plume, 2008).

4. Perkins, 6.

5. Brian Shilhavy, "Ron Paul Interview: Robert F Kennedy Jr Admits CIA Killed Father and Uncle," *Before It's News*, August 16, 2020.

6. Joe Quinn, "Syria's Fake Color Revolution," in *ISIS Is Us: The Shocking Truth Behind the Army of Terror*, Washington's Blog, Wayne Madsen, SyrianGirlPartisan, and John-Paul Leonard (Progressive Press, 2016): 24.

7. *Charlie Wilson's War*, film, 2007, Universal Pictures, directed by Mike Nichols.

8. Thierry Meyssan, *Before Our Very Eyes: Fake Wars and Big Lies from 9/11 to Donald Trump* (Progressive Press, 2019): 87–88. E-book.

9. Meyssan, 87–88.

10. Meyssan, 93.

11. Michael Springmann, *Visas for Al Qaeda* (Daena Publications, 2015).

12. Meyssan, 94–95.

13. Meyssan, 101–102.

14. Michael Springmann, *MichaelSpringmann.com*, accessed March 2021.

15. Brandon Tubeville, "'7 Countries In 5 Years': 2007 Wesley Clark Interview Reveals US Plan to Go to War with Iraq, Iran, Syria, Libya, Lebanon, Somalia, and Sudan," interview with General Wesley Clark, *Light on Conspiracies*, May 24, 2018.

16. Christopher Bollyn, *Solving 9-11: The Deception That Changed the World* (2009).

17. Bollyn, 32.

18. Ted Gunderson, *Corruption: The Satanic Drug Cult Network and Missing Children*. See also Ted Gunderson, "Finders: Child Kidnapping in America–The CIA Connection (2000).

19. Darren Beattie, "They've Done This Before: Five Past Cases of FBI Incitement," *Revolver News*, June 21, 2021.

20. Ken Silva, "2 Acquitted, Mistrial Declared for 2 Others in Michigan Gov. Whitmer Kidnap Plot," *The Epoch Times*, April 8, 2022.

21. Alexandra Bruce, "Was 1/6 an FBI Operation?," *Forbidden Knowledge*, July 14, 2021. See also Darren Beattie, "Revolver's Jan. 6th Reporting Changed the Game: Read Our Top Jan. 6 Investigative Stories Here," *Revolver News*, June 18, 2021.

Chapter 12

1. Thierry Meyssan, *Before Our Very Eyes: Fake Wars and Big Lies from 9/11 to Donald Trump* (Progressive Press, 2019): 104. E-book.

2. Consensus9/11, "9/11: Was There Foreknowledge by Officials that the Pentagon would be Attacked?" *GlobalResearch.ca*, September 9, 2015.

3. Meyssan, 136.

4. Meyssan, 138.

5. Christopher Bollyn, *Solving 9-11: The Deception That Changed The World* (2009): 95.

6. Captain Eric H. May, quoted in Bollyn, 86.

7. Consensus9/11.

8. Meyssan,141.

9. Bollyn, 32.

10. "Loose Change–The Final Cut," Youtube video, *Louder Than Words*, produced by Kory Rowe, executive producer Alex Jones, 2007.

11. Dr. Judy Wood, "Where Did The Towers Go?," *The New Investigation*, 2010. wheredidthetowersgo.com.

12. "What Happened to the Bodies of 9/11 Victims That Are Missing to This Day?," *Altered Dimensions*, August 19, 2016.

13. Wood, xxviii.

14. Wood, 485.

15. Andrew Johnson, "9/11 Holding the Truth," *CheckttheEvidence.com* (2017): 1.

16. Meyssan, 104–5.

17. Jason Goodman, "Abel Danger's Field McConnell on Las Vegas, Paddock, Pedogate, 9/11 and JFK," *CrowdSourcetheTruth*, podcast. This interview has been taken down from Youtube.

18. Don Brown, "Fallen Angel, Call Sign: Extortion 17," *RPM Films and Triple Horse Studios*, August 2, 2021. Based on the book by Don Brown.

19. Meyssan, 144.

20. Kyle Fitzgerald, "How much US military gear remains in Afghanistan?" *The National News*, August 27, 2021. Fitzgerald estimates over $85 billion worth of military equipment.

21. Alfred W. McCoy, "How the Heroin Trade Explains US-UK Failure in Afghanistan," *The Guardian*, January 9, 2018.

22. Meyssan, 175–6.

23. Meyssan, 176.

24. Meyssan, 176.

25. Meyssan, 181.

26. Meyssan, 183.

27. Kelly M. Greenhill, "Strategic Engineered Migration As A Weapon of War," *Internet Archive*, 2008.

28. Meyssan, 213–214.

29. Dr. Katherine Horton, "The Joint Investigation," *JointInvestigation.org.*

30. Office of the Director of National Intelligence, *DNI.gov*, website, accessed June 9, 2022.

31. John Perkins, *The Secret History of the American Empire: The Truth About Economic Hitmen, Jackals, and How to Change the World* (Plume, 2008).

Chapter 13

1. Dr. John, "Danielle Smith & Dr. John," *Western Standard*, March 8, 2021. See also Angell M, *New York Review of Books*, January 19, 2009. See also Noel Thomas, "Why We Can't Trust Clinical Guidelines," *BMJ*, July 5, 2013.

2. Dr. John. Dr. John quotes Richard Horton, editor of *The Lancet*.

3. Sarah Boseley and Melissa Davey, "Covid-19: Lancet Retracts Paper That Halted Hydroxychloroquine Trials," *The Guardian*, June 4, 2020. See also Leo Goldstein, "Anti-HCQ Paper in The Lancet Uses Fake Data," *Science for Freedom and Humans Institute*, May 23, 2020.

4. Vernon Coleman, *Endgame: The Hidden Agenda 21* (March 2021): 207–8. Kindle.

5. Dr. Joseph Mercola, "How Bill Gates Premeditated COVID Vaccine Injury Censorship," *GreenMedInfo*, March 30, 2021.

6. Laura Schumm, "What Was Operation Paperclip?," *History Stories*, The History Channel, March 4, 2020.

7. Michael C. Carroll, *Lab 257: The Disturbing Story of the Government's Secret Germ Laboratory* (HarperCollins, 2009). E-book.

8. Ken Alibek with Stephen Handelman, *Biohazard: The Chilling True Story of the Largest Covert Biological Weapons Program in the World–Told from the Inside By the Man Who Ran It* (Delta/Random House, 1999), 8–9.

9. Alibek and Handelman. 329, 166.

10. Alibek and Handelman, 157-159.

11. "Introduction to Biological Weapons," in "Weapons of Mass Destruction," *Global Security*, accessed April 15, 2021.

12. Dr. David E. Martin, "The Fauci/COVID-19 Dossier," *Creative Commons License CCBY-NC-SA*, February, 2021.

13. Martin, "The Fauci/COVID-19 Dossier," 2.

14. Martin, "The Fauci/COVID-19 Dossier," 2. See also Dr. David E. Martin, "David Martin & Judy Mikovits," *Plandemic Documentary Series*, Bitchute video, June 5, 2021, 9 minutes. Dr. Martin talks about the beginning of the Fauci/Baric coronavirus work.

15. Dr. David Martin, "David Martin on the Vaccine Choice Canada Livestream," video interview on Facebook, August, 2021, 12 minutes.

16. Martin, "The Fauci/COVID-19 Dossier," 5.

17. Martin, "The Fauci/COVID-19 Dossier," 7.

18. Martin, "Vaccine Choice." See 11 minutes into the interview.

19. Paul Craig Roberts, "The Vaccine Is as Deadly as the Virus," *Free West Media*, June 16, 2021.

20. Dr. Judy Mikovits, "'Doctors & Scientists' Episode 24: From Robert Gallo to Anthony Fauci–Judy Mikovits' Crusade for Truth," Dr. Brian Hooker host, *CHD.TV*, April 14, 2022. 46 minutes.

21. Spiro Skouras, "Creator of US BioWeapons Act Says Coronavirus Is a Biological Warfare Weapon," Youtube video, February 8, 2020.

22. Brad Rothman, "Letter to Friends and Family," *Corner Stone Codes*, February 18, 2020.

23. Li-Meng Yan, Shu Kang, and Shanchang Hu. "SARS-CoV-2 Is an Unrestricted Bioweapon: A Truth Revealed through Uncovering a Large-Scale, Organized Scientific Fraud." *Zenodo*. October 8, 2020.

24. Nicole Hao, "Evidence Reveals That Military Team Collaborated With Lab Where COVID-19 Pandemic Originated," *The Epoch Times*, May 3, 2021.

25. Barry Cooper and Marco Navarro-Genie, "'It All Began in China'– Book Excerpt From 'COVID-19: The Politics of a Pandemic Moral Panic,'" *The Epoch Times*, April 9, 2021.

26. Andrew Kerr, "US Grant to Wuhan Lab to Enhance Bat-Based Coronaviruses Was Never Scrutinized by HHS Review Board: NIH," *The Epoch Times*, April 6, 2021.

27. Riah Matthews, "Leaked Chinese Document Reveals a Sinister Plan to 'Unleash' Coronaviruses," *news.com.au*, May 8, 2021.

28. Jack Roberts, "Laboratory Viruses Pose 'Existential Threat', Biosecurity Expert Warns," *Vision Times*, March 24, 2021.

29. Hao.

30. Michael Houston, "More Athletes Claim They Contracted COVID-19 at Military World Games in Wuhan," *Inside the Games*, May 17, 2020.

31. Dr. Larry Romanoff, "Covid-19 Un-Explained," *The Unz Review*, December 14, 2020.

32. "Trusted News Initiative Degrades Into 'Shadowy' Media Spin Factory Representing Power & Money Interests," *TrialSite News*, August 14, 2021.

33. Scott White, "How China Used the Media to Spread Its COVID Narrative–and Win Friends Around the World," *The Conversation*, May 12, 2021.

Chapter 14

1. Julius Ruechel, "Washington's Inoculation Gamble: Calculating the Vegas Odds of Virus vs Vax Risks, and the Goal of Herd Immunity," *Julius Ruechel*, June 16, 2021.

2. Abdelilah Majdoubi et. al., "A Majority of Uninfected Adults Show Preexisting Antibody Reactivity Against SARS-CoV-2," *JCI Insight*, March 15, 2021.

3. Beda M. Stadler, "Coronavirus: Why Everyone Was Wrong. It is Not a 'New Virus'. 'The Fairy Tale of No Immunity,'" *Global Research*, December 19, 2020.

4. "9 in 10 Adults Have COVID-19 Antibodies, According to New Survey," *Open Access Government*, July 8, 2021.

5. The case fatality rate is calculated by dividing the number of people who actually die from COVID-19 by the number of people who are actually sick with covid-19. Since the data is completely corrupted, both these numbers are impossible to know for sure.

6. Dr. Peter McCullough, "Dr. Peter McCullough Speaks on the Beginnings of covid-19, Vaccine Danger and Treatment Options," Bitchute video, May 30, 2021. See also Dr. Peter McCullough, "COVID Vaccine Breakthrough Info by Dr. Peter McCullough MD, MPH," *The Dr. Peter Breggin Hour, Progressive Radio Network*, September 8, 2021.

7. Keyaerts E., Vijgen L., Maes P., Neyts J., and Van Ranst M. "In Vitro Inhibition of Severe Acute Respiratory Syndrome Coronavirus by Chloroquine," *Biochem Biophys Res Commun* 323, no.1 (October 8, 2004): 264–8. doi: 10.1016/j.bbrc.2004.08.085.

8. Torsten Engelbrecht and Claus Köhnlein, *Virus Mania: Corona/COVID-19, Measles, Swine Flu, Cervical Cancer, Avian Flu, SARS, BSE, Hepatitis C, AIDS, Polio, Spanish Flu. How the Medical Industry Continually Invents Epidemics, Making Billion-Dollar Profits At Our Expense* (Books On Demand, 2021). The explanation of the SOLIDARITY Study begins on page 509.

9. Engelbrecht and Köhnlein, 511.

10. Engelbrecht and Köhnlein, 512–515. These pages offer a complete discussion of these trials, the toxic dosages of HCQ, and the apparent ignorance of the doctors.

11. Engelbrecht and Köhnlein, 510.

12. Engelbrecht and Köhnlein, 515.

13. Dr. Joseph Mercola, "How a False Hydroxychloroquine Narrative Was Created," *Citizen's Journal*, July 17, 2020.

14. Hal Turner, "Japan Drops Vax Rollout, Goes To Ivermectin, ENDS COVID Almost Overnight," *Truth, Freedom, and Health*, October 27, 2021.

15. "First International Ivermectin for Covid Conference," *BIRD*, April 24–25, 2021.

16. Tucker Carlson, "Tucker Carlson Interviews Dr. Peter Mccullough on Covid Worldwide Conspiracy," *Tucker Carlson Today, Health Impact News*, May 13, 2021.

17. Andrew Chen, "Professor Explains Flaw in Many Models Used for COVID-19 Lockdown Policies," *The Epoch Times*, May 10, 2021.

18. Thierry Meyssan, "Two Strategic Errors in Facing Covid-19," *VoltaireNet.org*, February 4, 2021.

19. Vernon Coleman, *Endgame: The Hidden Agenda 21* (March 2021): 56. Kindle.

20. Shiyi Cao et. al., "Post-Lockdown SARS-CoV-2 Nucleic Acid Screening in Nearly Ten Million Residents of Wuhan, China," *Nature Communication*, November 20, 2020.

21. David Leonhardt, "A Misleading C.D.C. Number," *New York Times*, May 11, 2021.

22. Julius Reuchel, "The Lies Exposed by the Numbers: Fear, Misdirection, & Institutional Deaths (An Investigative Report)," *JueliusRuechel.com*, May 28, 2021.

23. Kary Mullis, "Kary Mullis Explains the PCR Test," Youtube video, accessed April 16, 2022.

24. Jaafar, R. et. al., "Correlation Between 3790 qPCR Positives Samples and Positive Cell Cultures Including 1941 SARS-CoV-2 Isolates," *Clin Infect Dis* (Sept 28, 2020).

25. Chris Shaw, *Dispatches from the Vaccine Wars–Fighting for Human Freedom During the Great Reset* (Skyhorse Publishing, 2021): 418.

26."Manitoba Chief Microbiologist and Laboratory Specialist: 56% of Positive "Cases" Are Not Infections." *Justice Centre for Constitutional Freedoms*, May 11, 2021.

27. Toby Young, "Lockdown Skeptics: Pepsi Max Tests Positive for Covid-19," *Patrick Herbert*, April 21, 2021.

28. Dr. Paul Elias Alexander, "More Than 400 Studies on the Failure of Compulsory Covid Interventions," *The Brownstone Institute*, November 30, 2021.

29. Meyssan.

30. Julius Reuchel, "The False God of Central Planning: The Mysterious Reappearance of the Flu, Natural vs Vaccine-Induced Immunity, the Inability of the Vaccines to Control the Virus, and Other Extraordinary Lessons About the End of the Pandemic (Investigative Report)," *JuliusReuchel.com*, January 5, 2022.

31. McCullough, COVID Vaccine Breakthrough Info.

32. Maxford Nelson, "Washington Health Officials: Gunshot Victims Counted As Covid-19 Deaths," *Freedom Foundation*, May 21, 2020.

33. Henry Ealy et. al., "COVID-19 Data Collection, Comorbidity & Federal Law: A Historical Retrospective," *Science, Public Health Policy, and The Law* 2, no.4-22 (October 12, 2020): 1–25.

34. Lance D. Johnson, "Italy's Suspected Covid Death Tally Corrected from 132,161 to 3,783... This Is Where Covid Hysteria Began, and It Was 97% FICTION," *Natural News*, November 3, 2021.

35. Martin Armstrong, "Has Fauci Lied Under Oath...," *Armstrong Economics*, January 11, 2022.

36. Brian Shilhavey, "Operation Omicron: The Globalists Are Preparing for Mass Murder in the Weeks Ahead," *Health Impact News*, December 17, 2021. See also *Jacqui Deevoy*, "Euthanasia–Good Death?," *The White Rose*, June 4, 2022. See also *A Good Death?*, documentary. This film documents the medical murder in Britain using morphine and Midazolam.

37. Dr. Ryan Cole, "Talk About Covid-19, mRNA Bioweapon, Ivermectin, & the Importance of Vitamin D," *99 Percent*, Bitchute.

38. Joe Vaughan, "Highest COVID-19 Death Rates Seen in Countries with Most Overweight Populations: Report," *The Post Millennial*, April 8, 2021.

39. Kyle Allred with Professor Roger Seheult, "Vitamin D and COVID 19: The Evidence for Prevention and Treatment of Coronavirus (SARS COV2)," *MedCram*.

40. Dr. Sam Bailey, "You Cannot Deny Excess Mortality–Or Can You?, SARS-CoV2: Exploring Behind Singular Narrative," *Rumble*, January 17, 2021.

41. Dr. Vernon Coleman, "Proof There Never Was a Pandemic in 2020," *The White Rose*, January 26, 2022.

42. "2 Years On–In Conversation, Professor Jay Bhattacharya and Professor John Ioannidis," Youtube video, *Collateral Global*, March 9, 2022.

Chapter 15

1. Geert Vanden Bosshe, "The Science Behind the Catastrophic Consequences of Thoughtless Human Interventon in the Covid-19 Pandemic," March 13, 2021.

2. Vanden Bosshe.

3. Tucker Carlson, "Tucker Carlson Interviews Dr. Peter Mccullough on Covid Worldwide Conspiracy," *Tucker Carlson Today, Health Impact News*, May 13, 2021.

4. Chris Shaw, *Dispatches from the Vaccine Wars–Fighting for Human Freedom During the Great Reset* (Skyhorse Publishing, 2021).

5. Salk Institute, "The Novel Coronavirus's Spike Protein Plays Additional Key Role in Illness," *Salk News*, April 30, 2021.

6. Dr. Larry Palevsky, "Follow-up to the 5 Doctors Discussion of the COVID Shots as Bioweapons," *Brighteon*.

7. The most recent legislation was in 2005. See Torsten Engelbrecht and Claus Köhnlein, Virus Mania: Corona/COVID-19, Measles, Swine Flu, Cervical Cancer, Avian Flu, SARS, BSE, Hepatitis C, AIDS, Polio, Spanish Flu. How the Medical Industry Continually Invents Epidemics, Making Billion-Dollar Profits At Our Expense (Books On Demand, 2021): 295–96.

8. World Council for Health, "Spike Protein Detox Guide," *World Council for Health*, November 30, 2021, updated March 9, 2022.

9. Greg Hunter, "700 Million Worldwide Will Die From CV19 Vaxx By 2028–Dr. David Martin," Forbidden Knowledge TV. July 1, 2022.

10. Meiling Lee, "Pfizer's COVID-19 Vaccine Goes Into Liver Cells and Is Converted to DNA: Study," *The Epoch Times*, March 2, 2022.

11. Peter Breggin, "Genetic Menace of Covid Vaccines Disclosed," podcast interview with Stephanie Seneff, *The Dr. Peter Breggin Hour*, March 16, 2022.

12. Vanden Bosshe.

13. Alex Newman, "Dr. Sucharit Bhakdi Warns Covid Shots Will Decimate World Population," *Yellowgenius*, podcast on Bitchute, April 16, 2021.

14. Alex Jones, "Emergency Saturday Broadcast! Pentagon A.I. Confirms Covid Shots Triggering Deadly ADE In The Vaccinated," *InfoWars*, October 3, 2021.

15. Steve Kirsch, "Pfizer Admits to Fraud in Court," *Rumble*, June 15, 2022.

16. Dr. Naomi Wolff, "Dear Friends, Sorry to Announce a Genocide," *Daily Clout*, May 29, 2022.

17. James Lyons-Weiler, "In the United States, Vaccination Rates Are Associated with Increased Rate of Spread of SARS-CoV-2, But Not How They Should Be, Popular Rationalism," December 9, 2021.

18. Staff, "THE UK HAS FALLEN–85% of Covid-19 Deaths Are Among the Vaccinated, Child Deaths Have Risen by 83% Since They Were Offered the Jab, the Covid-19 Vaccines Have Negative Effectiveness as Low as -132%," *The Expose*, November 4, 2021.

19. "Covid Vaccine Scientific Proof Lethal," *Save Us Now*, January 5, 2022.

20. Brian Shilhavy, "65,615 Deaths Now Reported in Europe and the USA Following Covid-19 Vaccines–Corporate Media Refuses to Publish This Data," *Health Impact News*, March 5, 2022.

21. WayneTheDBA, "Using CMS Whistleblower Data to Approximate the Under-Reporting Factor for VAERS," *VAERS Analysis*, December 13, 2021.

22. Tom T Shimabukuro et. al., "Preliminary Findings of mRNA Covid-19 Vaccine Safety in Pregnant Persons," *New England Journal of Medicine* 384, no. 23 (June 17, 2021): 2273–2282. doi: 10.1056/NEJMoa2104983.

23. Brian Shilhavey, "Canadian Doctor: 62% of Patients Vaccinated for COVID Have Permanent Heart Damage," *Health Impact News*, July 14, 2021.

24. Free West Media Staff, "Surgeon Who Operated on Young Italian Vaccine Victim: 'You Have Never Seen Anything Like This,'" *Free West Media*, July 8, 2021.

25. Nolan Barton, "Funeral Director Finds Bizarre, Rubbery Blood Clots in Bodies of the Vaccinated," *Natural News*, January 29, 2022.

26. Vanden Bosshe, 2.

27. John O'Sullivan, "Professor Dolores Cahill: People Will Start Dying After COVID Vaccine," *Principia Scientific*, January 5, 2021.

28. Vanden Bosshe.

29. "Whilst You've Been Distracted by Hancock's Affair, PHE Released a Report Revealing 62% of Alleged Covid Deaths Are People Who've Been Vaccinated," *The Expose*, June 26, 2021.

30. Dr. Peter McCullough, "COVID Vaccine Breakthrough Info by Dr. Peter McCullough MD, MPH," *The Dr. Peter Breggin Hour, Progressive Radio Network*, September 8, 2021.

31. Dave Naylor, "EXCLUSIVE: U of A Health Professor Says the Vaccinated Are More Likely to Contract Delta Variant," *The Western Standard*, September 29, 2021.

32. "Scotland's Excess Deaths at Highest Level Since January," *BBC News*, October 13, 2021.

33. Dr. Chris Shaw, *Dispatches from the Vaccine Wars–Fighting for Human Freedom During the Great Reset* (Skyhorse Publishing, 2021): 442.

34. Shaw, 198. Dr. Shaw references page 541 of the Gherardi 2015 paper.

35. Dr. Richard M. Fleming, *Is COVID-19 a Bioweapon?: A Scientific and Forensic investigation* (Skyhorse Publishing, September 2021): 110-111. Kindle.

36. Dr. Chris Shaw, "The Coming Wave of Neurological Vaccine Damage," *Brand New Tube*, August 23, 2021.

37. Enrico Trigoso, "COVID Vaccines Increase Menstrual Irregularities Thousandfold, Fetal Abnormalities Hundredfold: Doctors' VAERS Analysis," *The Epoch Times*, July 1, 2022.

38. "The Dangers of Booster Shots and COVID-19 'Vaccines': Boosting Blood Clots and Leaky Vessels," *Doctors for Covid Ethics*, September 17, 2021.

39. Dr. Bryan Ardis, "Are people dying misdiagnosed? dr. bryan ardis, dr. reiner fuellmich and dr. wolfgang wodarg, Angel Realm," Brand New Tube, August 1, 2021.

40. Mi, S., Lee, X., Li, Xp. *et al.* Syncytin is a captive retroviral envelope protein involved in human placental morphogenesis. *Nature* 403, 785–789 (2000). https://doi.org/10.1038/35001608

41. Mark Docherty, "Explosive Rise in Ontario Stillbirths Triggers Parliamentary Questions," *Non Veni Pacem*, December 10, 2021.

42. Helen McArdle, "Investigation launched into abnormal spike in newborn baby deaths in Scotland," *The Herald* (Scotland) November 18, 2021.

43. Amy Sukwan, "There's Been a Stunning 1/3 Drop in Births Between 2020 and 2021 in Thailand," *Amy's Newsletter*, January 17, 2022.

44. Dr. Joseph Mercola, "COVID Jabs Impact Both Male and Female Fertility," *The Epoch Times*, July 25, 2022.

45. Justus R. Hope, "Lipid Nanoparticles kill 80 percent of mice in PubMed Study," *The Desert Review*, January 16, 2022.

46. "DNA Nanorobot: Cell-Targeted, Payload-Delivering," *Harvard Wyss Institute*.

47. Mimi Nguyen Li, "Harvard Professor Charles Lieber Convicted of Lying About China Ties," *The Epoch Times*, December 22, 2021.

48. Shuren Wang et. al., "Self-Assembled Magnetic Nanomaterials: Versatile Theranostics Nanoplatforms for Cancer," *Wiley Online Library*, January 19, 2021.

49. Katy Delaney, "Battelle-Led Team Wins DARPA Award to Develop Injectable, Bi-Directional Brain Computer Interface," *Businesswire*, May 20, 2019.

50. Profusa, "Injectable Body Sensors Take Personal Chemistry to a Cell Phone Closer to Reality," *Profusa*, March 2018.

51. "Covid Shots, DNA & Transhumanism with Dr. Madej," *The New American*, April 29, 2021. See 35 minutes in.

52. "INBRAIN Neuroelectronics Secures $17 Million in Series A Funding for First AI-Powered Graphene-Brain Interface," *Businesswire*, March 30, 2021.

53. Isodbel Asher Hamilton, "Elon Musk's Neuralink Wants to Embed Microchips in People's Skulls and Get Robots to Perform Brain Surgery," *Business Insider*, February 16, 2022.

54. Moderna, "mRNA Platform: Enabling Drug Discovery & Development," *Moderna*, accessed September 27, 2021.

55. Dr. Ariyana Love, "Slovakia Report: Covid "Tests" Contaminated With Nanotech Hydrogels And Lithium," *Ambassador Love*, May 21, 2021.

56. Ricardo Delgado, "La Quinta Columna: '98% to 99% of the Vaccination Vial Is Graphene Oxide,'" *Orwell City*, July 3, 2021.

57. Stew Peters, "Former Pfizer Employee Confirms Poison Graphene Oxide in Vaccine," interview with Karen Kingston, *StewPeters.TV*, July 29, 2021.

58. Ricardo Delgado, "5G Is a Target Acquiring Weapon System—This Is Not for Control but an Extermination Technology," *Brighteon*, December 26, 2021.

59. Alexandra Bruce, "New Zealand Scientist, Dr Robin Wakeling Has Reproduced the Microscopy Findings of the Spanish Research Group, La Quinta Columna of What Appears to Be Self-Assembling Nanocircuitry in the Vaxx Recorded in Samples of Comirnaty®," *Forbidden Knowledge*, June 15, 2022.

60. James Fetzer, "Trust Stamp—Bill Gates Funded Program That Will Create Your Digital Identity Based on Your Vaccination History," *James Fetzer: Exposing Falsehoods and Revealing Truths*, January 24, 2021.

61. Dolores Cahill, "What Is the Real Cost of Vaccines? Part 1," *The Solari Report*, February 10, 2021, 30.

62. Mike Adams, "Study: 5G Exposure a "Significant Factor" in Higher Covid Cases, Deaths," *Natural News*, December 13, 2021.

63. David John Sorensen and Dr. Vladimir Zelenko, MD, "The Vaccine Death Report, Version 1.0," September 2021.

64. Delgado.

65. Shaw, *Dispatches from the Vaccine Wars*, 428.

66. Dr. Joseph Mercola, "Vaccine Passports: Your Ticket to a New Social Control System?," *The Defender*, August 31, 2021.

67. A.J. Roberts, "Undertaker John O'Looney: People Need to Wake Up—Children Will Die from the Covid Jab," *The AJ Roberts Show*,

68. Dr. Jane Ruby, "Worldwide Exclusive: Embalmers Find Veins & Arteries Filled with Never Before Seen Rubbery Clots," *The Dr. Jane Ruby Show*, January 26, 2022.

69. Alex Berenson, "Vaccinated English Adults Under 60 Are Dying at Twice the Rate of Unvaccinated People the Same Age," *Unreported Truths*, November 20, 2021.

70. "Scotland's Excess Deaths."

71. "Last Week of November: 1100 More Dutch Citizens Died than on Average," *Free West Media*, December 5, 2021.

72. Margaret Menge, "Indiana Life Insurance CEO Says Deaths Are Up 40% Among People Ages 18–64," *The Center Square*, January 1, 2022.

73. Petr Svab, "EXCLUSIVE: States Investigating Surge in Mortality Rate Among 18–49-Year-Olds, Majority Unrelated to COVID-19," *The Epoch Times*, January 14, 2022.

74. Mike Adams, "THE DIE-OFF IS HERE: Life Insurance Payouts Skyrocket 258% as Post-Vaccine Deaths Rapidly Accelerate," *Natural News*, February 1, 2022.

Chapter 16

1. Martin Armstrong, "The Voting Rights Bill Amounts to Treason," *Armstrong Economics*, January 14, 2022.

2. Patrick Byrne, *The Deep Rig: How Election Fraud Cost Donald J. Trump the White House, by a Man Who Did Not Vote for Him* (Deep Capture LLC, March 2021): 22.

3. Byrne, 22–23.

4. Byrne, 24–25.

5. Howell Woltz, "Mike Lindell Wins Big Against Dominion," *The Richardson Post*, July 2, 2021.

6. Molly Ball, "The Secret History of the Shadow Campaign That Saved the 2020 Election," *Time Magazine*, February 4, 2021.

7. Ball.

8. Ball.

9. Ball.

10. Ball.

11. J. Alex Halderman, "I Hacked an Election. So Can the Russians," *New York Times*, April 5, 2018.

12. Byrne, 19.

13. CISA, "ICS Advisory (ICSA-22-154-01): Vulnerabilities Affecting Dominion Voting Systems ImageCast X," *Cybersecurity and Infrastructure Security Agency*, June 3, 2022.

14. Byrne, 50–75.

15. Edward Solomon, "Geometric Proof for Georgia," video February 7, 2021.

16. Edward Soloman, "PA Edward Solomon Has Found Disturbing Signs of Statistically Impossible Patterns."

17. Byrne, 32.

18. Patrick Byrne, "BOMBSHELL: Antrim County Computer Forensic Report," *Deep Capture*, December 14, 2020.

19. Byrne, "BOMBSHELL," 1.

20. Zachary Stieber, "Michigan Attorney General, Police to Probe People Who Made Election Fraud Claims," *The Epoch Times*, July 9, 2021.

21. Byrne, *The Deep Rig*, 217–218.

22. Byrne, *The Deep Rig*, 25–29.

23. Dinesh D'Sousa, *2000 Mules*, documentary, produced by Dinesh D'Sousa, May 2022.

24. Dinesh D'Sousa, "Of Mules and Donkeys," *The Epoch Times*, May 2, 2022.

25. Byrne, *The Deep Rig*, 51.

26. Howell Woltz, "Mike Lindell Wins Big Against Dominion," *The Richardson Post*, July 2, 2021.

27. Byrne, *The Deep Rig*, 73.

28. Mike Lindell, "Absolute Proof: Documentary About Election 2020," February 2021,

29. Lindell, 36 minutes in.

Chapter 17

1. *Butch Cassidy and the Sundance Kid*, William Goldman, directed by George Roy Hill. (1969).

2. Iain Davis, "What Is the Global Public-Private Partnership?," *In This Together: The Disillusioned Blogger*, October 6, 2021.

3. Ernst Wolff, "The Deep State and the Digital-Financial Complex," *Forbidden Knowledge*, contributed by Alexandra Bruce, January 9, 2022.

4. *Immunization agenda 2030: A Global Strategy to Leave No One Behind*. (World Health Organization, April 2020).

5. "Funding the United Nations: How Much Does the US Pay?," Council on Foreign Relations, April 4, 2022.

6. Vernon Coleman, *Endgame: The Hidden Agenda 21* (March 2021): 30. Kindle.

7. Patrick M. Wood, *Technocracy: The Hard Road to World Order* (Coherent Publishing, 2018). Audiobook.

8. "GAVI, the Vaccine Alliance, Annual Financial Report 2021," www.gavi.org.

9. Robert Levinson and Cameron Leuthy, "Intelligence Contractors Vying for Slimmer Spy Budget in FY 2021," *Bloomberg Government*, October 23, 2020.

10. Loren Collins, "The Truth About Tytler," *LorenCollins.net*, January 25, 2009. Others share Collins's claim that this famous quotation does not belong to Alexander Tytler and we're not sure who first said these words.

Chapter 18

1. John Titus, Larry and Carstens' Excellent Pandemic," *The Titus Report/Red Pill Channel*, August 14, 2021. This video provides a more detailed explanation of how central banks operate, what the Going Direct Plan is, and where this is all leading.

2. Tyler Durden, "Blackstone Prepares A Record $50 Billion To Snap Up Real Estate During The Coming Crash," *The Durden Dispatch*, July 22, 2022.

3. Michael Nevradakis, "International Finance Leaders Hold 'War Game' Exercise Simulating Global Financial Collapse. Should We Be Worried?," *The Defender*, January 7, 2022.

4. Richard Werner, *Princes of the Yen: Central Banks and the Transformation of the Economy* (Routledge, 2003).

5. Martin Armstrong, "Gold–Repo Crisis–Green New World Order," *Armstrong Economics*, September 11, 2020.

6. Pam Martens and Russ Martens, "The Fed is About to Reveal Which Wall Street Banks Needed $4.5 Trillion in Repo Loans in Q4 2019," *Wall Street on Parade*, December 29, 2021.

7. Pam Martens and Russ Martens, "A Nomura Document May Shed Light on the Repo Blowup and Fed Bailout of the Gang of Six in 2019," *Wall Street on Parade*, January 19, 2022.

8. Pam Martens and Russ Martens, "U.S. Banking System Has a $168 Trillion Nightmare Looming. It Was Ignored in Written Testimony for Today's Senate Banking Hearing," *Wall Street On Parade*, August 3, 2021.

9. Dinesh D'Sousa, "My Experience With 'Woke' Corporations," *The Epoch Times*, March 29, 2021.

10. Tyler Durden, "Chase Bank Cancels General Mike Flynn's Credit Cards," *Zero Hedge*, August 31, 2021.

11. John Paul Tasker, "Banks are moving to freeze accounts linked to convoy protests. Here's what you need to know," *CBC News*, February 16, 2022.

12. Jeff Brown, "China Begins Testing Digital Yuan in Other Nations," *The Bleeding Edge Newsletter*, April 5, 2021.

13. Roman Balmakov, "Over 5000 Cases of Sudden Adult Death Syndrome (SADS): Doctors Trying to Figure Out Why Young People Are Suddenly Dying," *The Epoch Times*, July 25, 2022.

14. Dean Ryan, "The Big Event is Looming," *Real Deal Media*, July 22, 2022.

15. Ethan Huff, "After repeatedly denying the existence of Ukrainian biolabs, Pentagon finally admits to running 46 of them," *Natural News*, June 13, 2022.

16. Martin Niemoller, "First They Came for the Socialists," *Holocaust Museum*, accessed May 6, 2022.

Chapter 19: Escape to Freedom

1. Jean Chen, "Opinion: A Mom's Research (Part 4): Why Are Many Elites Leftists?," *The Epoch Times*, April 26, 2021.

2. Edgar, Cayce, "Edgar Cayce Reading 3976-11," in Edgar Cayce Readings (The Edgar Cayce Foundation, 1971).

3. A reference to the American Declaration of Independence (see "Declaration of Independence: A Transcription," *National Archives*. The last eight words in the Declaration of Independence, a document that forever changed the world in which we live, were bold and courageous: "Our Lives, our Fortunes and our sacred Honor."

About the Author

The eclectic Donald Lee is a musician, teacher, band director, economist, power engineer, marketer, businessman, athlete, public speaker, and author. He holds degrees in economics and education. Donald is an Albertan, growing and raising his family in Fort Saskatchewan. He has always been active in his community in many ways: founder of the Fort Saskatchewan Community Band, of a children's choir, a performer in many local bands, orchestras and choirs, as well as coaching minor sports.

Donald spent two decades in the fertilizer industry in many roles: labourer, chemical process operator, marketer, and new product developer with the research group.

He made a mid-life career change and returned to his first love - music—then spent two decades as a teacher and band director in various schools in Alberta, Kuwait, and Pakistan. Primarily a band director, Donald has also taught choir, musical theatre, jazz band, English, math, drama, social studies, even art and carpentry.

He has often been active in the political process and has run for provincial party nominations twice. Donald has also been an active member of Toastmasters, advancing to the World Championship of Public Speaking in 1995.

Donald remains an avid sportsman and athlete - skiing, swimming, running, hiking, canoeing, fishing, and hunting in the great Alberta outdoors. In his 50's he took up triathlon, competing in local and national events including the 2013 ITU World Finals as part of the Canadian Team.

As a band director and a religion teacher, Donald melds the two genres to bring the "life of the spirit" truly to life in stories. Inspired by his teaching experience, Donald turned classroom episodes into modern-day parables in his book, *The Band Director's Lessons About Life.*

Added to his own convoluted, life-long spiritual quest, Donald draws on his many years of teaching religion classes–everything from A to Z, the Apostle's Creed to Zen Buddhism. Following humbly in the footsteps of Jesus, Donald picks up the pedagogy of the parable to instruct through story. His spiritual work aims to bring spirit into materiality, to help people be *in* the world but not *of* the world, to guide people along their individual spiritual journey back to God. And in the process, to live our physical life to the fullest.

Visit his website at, www.cominghomespirit.com

CPSIA information can be obtained
at www.ICGtesting.com
Printed in the USA
BVHW040246080223
658118BV00004B/29

9 781990 893001